HUMANITY BEFORE
GOD

"Humanity before God *is a wonderfully ecumenical exploration of the foundations of the three great theistic religions — foundations that can form the foundation of irenic coexistence and cooperation.*"

— Judge John T. Noonan Jr.
United States Circuit Court
San Francisco

HUMANITY BEFORE
GOD

CONTEMPORARY FACES OF
JEWISH, CHRISTIAN, AND ISLAMIC ETHICS

EDITED BY WILLIAM SCHWEIKER,
MICHAEL A. JOHNSON, AND KEVIN JUNG

FORTRESS PRESS   MINNEAPOLIS

HUMANITY BEFORE GOD
Contemporary Faces of Jewish, Christian, and Islamic Ethics

Cover art: Pat Eide, Berland Printing © University of Chicago Divinity School
Cover design: Diana Running
Book design: John Eagleson

Library of Congress Cataloging-in-Publication Data
Humanity before God : contemporary faces of Jewish, Christian, and Islamic ethics / edited by William Schweiker, Michael A. Johnson, Kevin Jung.
    p. cm.
  ISBN 0-8006-3822-0 (alk. paper)
  1. Religious ethics—Comparative studies. 2. Religions—Comparative studies.
I. Schweiker, William. II. Johnson, Michael A., 1963- III. Jung, Kevin, 1970-
BJ1188.H84 2006
205—dc22
                                        2005036735

Manufactured in the U.S.A.

10   09   08   07   06   1   2   3   4   5   6   7   8   9   10

*Many people make the work of scholars possible.
In gratitude, the editors would like to dedicate
this volume to the following individuals*

*— Michael A. Johnson —
to my brother, Mark A. Johnson,
and to my parents, Waldo and Nordis Johnson*

*— Kevin Jung —
to my wife, Karen Ryu*

*— William Schweiker —
to my sisters, Kathryn Barnhill and Claire S. Hanson*

CONTENTS

Part Two
HUMANITY IN CREATION

Contributors

Azizah Y. al-Hibri
Professor of Law, University of Richmond Law School

Lisa Sowle Cahill
Monan Professor of Theology, Boston College

Michael Fishbane
Nathan Cummings Professor of Jewish Studies, University of Chicago

Tikva Frymer-Kensky
Professor of Hebrew Bible and the History of Judaism, University of Chicago

Michael A. Johnson
Ph.D. candidate, University of Chicago

Kevin Jung
Visiting Professor of Religious Studies, College of William and Mary

John Kelsay
Richard L. Rubenstein Professor of Religion, Florida State University

David Little
T. J. Dermot Dunphy Professor of the Practice in Religion, Ethnicity, and International Conflict, Harvard Divinity School

Paul Mendes-Flohr
Professor of Modern Jewish Thought, University of Chicago

Seyyed Hossein Nasr
University Professor of Islamic Studies, George Washington University

Hilary Putnam
Cogan University Professor Emeritus, Harvard University

Abdulaziz Sachedina
Professor of Religious Studies, University of Virginia

William Schweiker
Professor of Theological Ethics, University of Chicago

Lawrence Vogel
Associate Professor of Philosophy, Connecticut College

Introduction
Michael A. Johnson, Kevin Jung,
and William Schweiker

This book is the consequence of a remarkable event. In the autumn of 2003, the University of Chicago Divinity School and the Disciples Divinity House of the University of Chicago hosted a group of renowned Jewish, Christian, and Islamic scholars, including philosophers, theologians, ethicists, historians, and legal thinkers, for the 2003 D. R. Sharpe/Hoover Lectures entitled "Humanity before God: Contemporary Faces of Jewish, Christian, and Islamic Ethics." The D. R. Sharpe Lectureship, in the words of its benefactor, provides "the opportunity for the best and most creative minds to explore society's social needs and present an ethical standard for modern life." More importantly, Sharpe wrote that the "modern problem is whether there are ethical principles sensitive to the religious and cultural heritages and enlightened by contemporary knowledge adequate for the evolving needs of society in its search for purposeful life on this planet." The purpose of the conference from which this book originated was precisely to examine anew the shared ways in which the three monotheistic faiths in the Abrahamic tradition conceive the idea of humanity before God and how each contributes to contemporary understandings of fundamental claims about the inalienable worth of human life. Rarely before had representatives of these three great traditions met, not to discuss their differences or their interactions but, rather, to specify unique perspectives on a shared moral and religious concern. This event signals emerging directions for religious thinking through careful and engaged reflection on the human project

---

Translations of Qur'an passages in this essay are from *The Holy Qur'an: Text, Translation, and Commentary* (Brentwood, Md.: Amana Press, 1992).

1

from within the resources of these world religions. This introduction will orient the reader to the purpose and scope of the book.

Religious Forces in a Global Context

Throughout history, religions have been powerful forces of both healing and destruction. The same is true today. At the beginning of the twenty-first century, theorists of globalization point to an increasing interconnection between nations and cultures. This new reality of global interdependence brings to the forefront the role of religions as forces of conflict and cooperation. A quick glance at the front-page headlines of the major newspapers on any given day confirms this assessment of the situation. In a time defined by the 2001 attacks on the World Trade Center and Pentagon and the ensuing "war on terrorism" and invasion of Iraq, not to mention religious and cultural violence around the world, journalists and other commentators on religion are paying renewed attention to how the visions of humanity within the Abrahamic faiths of Judaism, Christianity, and Islam shape contemporary debates about human rights and responsibilities.

Far too often debates about the role religious traditions play in conflicts between peoples and cultures become trapped by a picture of religions as monolithic entities. Political scientist Samuel P. Huntington's hotly debated thesis of a "clash of civilizations," for example, predicts that future geopolitical conflict will take place at fault lines emerging between blocs of nations aligned by culture and values (for example, religions) rather than through past allegiances to the Cold War superpowers (for example, ideology).[1] This kind of cultural analysis certainly makes the job of political scientists easier, but it vastly oversimplifies the real relations of cultures and religions "on the ground." Still, this kind of analysis does contain a kernel of insight regarding the relation of religious traditions and culture. While not monolithic entities, religions may be viewed as constructing moral and social spaces based upon different visions for the flourishing of human life. The religious imagination

---

1. See Samuel P. Huntington, *The Clash of Civilizations and the Remaking of World Order* (New York: Simon and Schuster, 1996); Samuel P. Huntington, "The Clash of Civilizations," *Foreign Affairs* 72, no. 3 (Summer 1993): 22–49.

defines a dynamic domain of life that shapes perceptions of the goods of life, obligations, and the reasons and motives for the ends pursued by our actions and practices. Not just ideology and economic forces alone, but also culture and religion, motivate peoples and drive history.

Contemporary media sources often depict religious outlooks as otherworldly, denying the integrity and worth of finite, temporal life. Not surprisingly, this occurs most often when people from one culture speak about religions of other cultures — especially about the kind labeled "fundamentalist." Faced with the need to diagnose the spread of a new geopolitical reality called "global terrorism," religious fundamentalism is often identified as one of the root causes that abets and nurtures terrorism. This rhetoric continues, even though social scientists consistently point out that religious fundamentalism results from political and economic disenfranchisement of peoples from basic human rights. Too often, politicians, pundits, and preachers blithely ignore the fact that acts of terrorism and suicide bombings often are correlated with foreign occupations of countries and instead try to explain religious violence purely in terms of religious belief and practice. Although Western governments always take pains to distinguish Al-Qaeda from Islam in their rhetoric of the "war on terrorism," they also, in seeking support for their policies, more often than not fail to disavow publicly political support emanating from portions of the electorate not concerned with making such fine distinctions.

On the morning of 9/11, the consciousness of the world fused into one for a single moment of time, focusing its attention on an event of horrible destruction that seemed to defy all rational explanation. In response to such inexplicable acts of violence and destruction and a heightened awareness of the fragility of human life, many people turned inward toward the sustenance of religious meaning and practice. In American politics we witnessed a deeper melding of the political right and religious conservatism beyond what had been seen in previous decades. While religion has always played a complicated role in American politics, this kind of open and strategic alliance between a political party and religious groups is striking, given the long tradition of the separation of church and state in the United States. These shifting political alignments may not be totally unrelated to the turn to religion as a means to deal with the unsettling realities of temporal life. Indeed, religious commentators nowadays speak of a new "Great Awakening." Major news magazines such as *Time* and *Newsweek* now regularly devote cover stories to the resurgence of religion and spirituality in American life. Articles frequently appear that explain the unexpected popularity of films such as *The Passion of the Christ* or fictional books like the Left Behind series as due to this reawakening of faith.

In this context, attention seems due to the task of religious scholarship in face of proliferating violence and the dynamic power of religion in contemporary life. The present volume is an effort to advance a fruitful dialogue among scholars and thinkers from the three Abrahamic traditions. Our hope is to clarify and understand their shared roots in history and also the moral responsibilities of believers in a time in which the destructive potentials of these religions have come to dominate world events. This book, then, is a collaborative enterprise of thinking about how each tradition figures and conceives the idea of humanity before God. These conceptions help to inform contemporary understandings of fundamental claims about the inalienable worth of human life in a global context.

An Emerging Perspective
on the Religions of the Book

The great monotheistic traditions are forces driving "civilizations." However, if we persist in thinking of such religious traditions as monolithic entities in competition for territory and influence, the result can only be social and political conflict. In reality, these traditions are vastly complex sociocultural realities that contain great internal diversity and bear multifaceted interactions both with each other and with diverse other cultures and traditions. In this time of globalization, an intensified awareness of the proximity of peoples' traditions results from vast improvements in communication technologies and accompanying exchange of information.

Despite this increasing awareness of the "other," however, the underlying fact of interaction between cultural self-understandings among the monotheistic traditions is not something new. To the contrary, the scope and range of interactions among the Abrahamic traditions — cultural, economic, and social — has been immense across different historical epochs. To different degrees at various stages of their development, Christianity, Islam, and Judaism have drawn upon the images, meanings, and concepts of traditions of other cultures and faiths living alongside them. This was especially true during the astonishing intellectual exchanges, often polemical and usually apologetic, among thinkers of these traditions during the so-called Middle Ages in the West.[2] History notwithstanding, the editors of this book believe that the growing consciousness of global interdependence opens up a space out of which a new perspective for critical and comparative reflection can be seen emerging.

The fact that the monotheistic traditions are complex in both their internal and external interactions means they remain open to new and vital understandings of the human. In fact, the dialogical encounter in a time of globalization creates a new cultural space in which each tradition can reinterpret its own resources reflexively, that is, in light of the practices and discourses of the other traditions. The perspective of the present volume is that the current situation of global cultural interdependence and conflict brings this ever-present dimension of interaction and feedback among the traditions increasingly to the forefront. When we construe religions themselves as forms of culture with transnational power and planetary reach, the question of how the religions define "the human" reflexively — that is, in internalizing and thus transforming parallel definitions by other religions — takes on new importance and greater urgency. This book manifests reflexive interactions among thinkers representative of these traditions.

Seen from the perspective of past and present interactions among these religious traditions, a new possibility for religious life itself becomes apparent. Infusing the various chapters of the book is the orienting power of what may be called "religious humanism" as a much-needed outlook in a pluralistic world. Critically engaging the resources of the monotheistic religions, the contributors to this volume share the view

2. See Richard E. Rubenstein, *Aristotle's Children: How Christians, Muslims, and Jews Rediscovered Ancient Wisdom and Illuminated the Dark Ages* (New York: Harcourt, Inc., 2003).

that these religions still offer critical resources that could and should be used to protect, respect, and enhance the flourishing of human life in mutual coexistence and moral responsibility. With this shared concern for humanity, the authors of the book address the challenges faced by the religions and consider the distinctive ways in which they can contribute to human well-being. Instead of seeing religious traditions as otherworldly and life denying, the authors unite to interpret their own traditions in ways that counteract anti-humanistic readings of the Abrahamic faiths.

This is not to say that all the authors would wish to adopt the label of "religious humanism." For some, the term *humanism* may seem to carry with it connotations of an improper elevation of the human in relation to the Divine and the sacred — or even the denial of the Divine. Still others may regard their contributions as being more philosophical (or historical) than "religious" in their point of view. Be that as it may, what we wish to emphasize is not the term but the general orientation held in common among the various authors in how they approach their own traditions — a shared concern for the forces and meanings that respect the worth of human persons and enhance the flourishing of human life.

The various contributors are joined in the belief that human persons experience similar problems and sufferings across different cultures. Nevertheless, the task undertaken by the authors is not to isolate some watered-down, "lowest-common-denominator" ethic that everybody can agree upon. Without minimizing differences among the religions, the authors tackle issues from within their own religions in order to render such resources available for both assessment and dialogue. These writers are deeply sensitive to the unique histories and characteristics that distinguish their traditions from others as well as of the moral problems that they share with people of other faiths.

Resources from the Traditions

Then God said, "Let us make humankind [*adam*] in our own image, according to our likeness; and let them have dominion over the fish of the sea, and over the birds of the air, and over the cattle, and over all the wild animals of the earth, and over every creeping thing that creeps upon the earth." So God created humankind in his image, in the image of God he created them; male and female he created them. (Gen. 1:26–27)

With [the tongue] we bless the Lord and Father, and with it we curse those who are made in the likeness of God. From the same mouth come blessing and curse. My brothers and sisters, this ought not to be so. (James 3:9–10)

He is the image of the invisible God, the firstborn of all creation; for in him all things in heaven and on earth were created, things visible and invisible. (Col. 1:15)

Behold thy Lord said to the angels: "I will create a vicegerent on earth." They said: "Wilt thou place therein one who will make mischief therein and shed blood? — whilst we do celebrate Thy praises and glorify Thy holy name?" He said, "I know what you know not." (Qur'an 2:30)

In light of current developments around the world just noted, the importance of finding and exploring common grounds among these great religions can hardly be doubted.[3] Thankfully, in the latter decades of the twentieth century there took place an unprecedented but welcome shift in Jewish and Christian relations. The catastrophic events of the Holocaust compelled many Christians to look inside their own tradition and examine the often distorted picture of Judaism within historical Christian theology. In turn, conscientious Jews responded by reflecting on what the Jewish faith can say constructively about Christianity.[4] From each perspective, the two communities of faith have begun to articulate understandings of what it means to worship God and seek authority from shared texts.

Central to this renewed dialogue among Christians and Jews is the common acceptance of the core moral principles of the Torah. At the heart of Torah one finds the recognition of the inalienable worth of

3. On this see Max Stackhouse, et al., eds., *God and Globalization,* 4 vols. (Trinity Press International, 2000–2004). Also see William Schweiker, *Theological Ethics and Global Dynamics: In the Time of Many Worlds* (Oxford: Blackwell, 2004).
    4. For a recent example, see Tikva Frymer-Kensky, et al., eds., *Christianity in Jewish Terms* (Boulder, Co.: Westview, 2002).

every human being. According to this shared tradition, the worth of persons is grounded in the reality that each human person is created in the image of God. A similar kind of dialogue now needs to be encouraged between representatives of these two traditions and Islamic scholars. The Qur'anic story of the creation of humanity expresses a similar belief about the worth of the human person as found among Jews and Christians. Yet the Qur'an conceives human worth through a different but perhaps related figure: The human person is the "vicegerent of God," entrusted to a position in creation higher than the angels and other beings, and possessing a special relation to God.

Each of the monotheistic traditions has then within its sacred texts as well as ritual practices and legacy of saints and moral exemplars profound and complex resources for thinking about the status and worth of human beings. These resources appeal in each tradition to accounts of creation and also to the decisive revelation of a religion. This point of commonality forms the focal point for this book. Not unsurprisingly, the thinkers represented herein draw upon the deep wellsprings of their traditions to think about human life in our times. A brief review of some of the traditional ideas about humanity before God is thereby in order.[5]

In the Torah, specifically the Genesis creation story, one finds a depiction of human persons as created in the "image of God" (in Hebrew, *tselem 'Elohim*; in Greek, *imago Dei*). The terms *image* or *likeness* in the Torah passages, according to some exegetical scholars, refer not simply to a static similitude between God and the human person but signify also the institution of a special set of dynamic relations between God, humanity, and creation. In the direction of the Divine, humanity is created for fellowship with God. Toward creation, humankind is commissioned to manifest God's rule on earth, to be stewards or caretakers of this good gift. Toward other human beings, men and women are to be participants in the creativity of God, to bring forth life, and also, with others, to form societies characterized by justice and peace. In a word, humans have the grand responsibility to walk in God's way and to imitate the living God.

---

5. For background on each of these traditions as well as their development and current trajectories see William Schweiker, ed., *The Blackwell Companion to Religious Ethics*, Blackwell Companions to Religion (Oxford: Blackwell, 2005).

Within the classical Christian tradition these same distinctions are also used to specify the condition of human beings before and after the "fall" into sin and in redemption. The "image" denotes what is retained while the "likeness" is what is lost through sin, and the fullness of humanity (image *and* likeness) is restored by redemption in Christ. Indeed, as the passage from Paul's letter to the Colossians cited above notes, Christ is the true image of God. In this way, the ideas of "image" and "likeness" denote not only the relations within which human beings exist (before God, for creation, with others), but also spiritual conditions: created, fallen, and redeemed. They have also provided many Christians a way to understand the meaning and significance of Jesus as the Christ. Throughout the centuries, Jewish and Christian thinkers have pondered the resources of the creation story in order to specify the distinctive worth, moral responsibility, and spiritual condition of human beings.

The Qur'an employs a different but related figure of thought: humankind as the "vicegerent" (*khalīfa*) of Allah. The human being is authorized to represent God on earth as the caretaker of creation. Insofar as Allah, the One God, is without and beyond "image," then even the human being, although being God's vicegerent on earth, cannot properly be said to be made in the image of God. Nevertheless, being created as God's vicegerent means that human beings possess intrinsic worth and also, in submission to God, have the calling to live in justice. In this respect, Islam is understood to be the one, original religion that stipulates the unique purpose of human existence. The revelation of the Qur'an to the Prophet Muhammad, as the final and decisive revelation for Muslims, specifies human status and responsibility in order that justice may reign over the created world. A Muslim thereby relies on the Qur'an as setting forth God's relation to humanity in order to understand both God and also God's purposes for human beings and human communities. In ways analogous to Jews and Christians, Islamic claims about creation are linked to the decisive revelation of God's will. But, of course, this is an analogical relation among traditions. The decisive revelation differs among them (the Tanakh, the Christian Bible, and the Qur'an), even as the created status of human beings is conceptualized in different ways.

The rich resources of these traditions about humanity before God specify a set of ideas marked by similarity insofar as Jews, Christians, and

Muslims all insist on the unique value and moral responsibility of human beings. Amidst similarities, significant differences exist among the ways in which these figures or ideas function within the overall trajectories of the three traditions. These differences, as intimated, arise from how the human being as a creature of God is and ought to relate to the Divine, to creation, and to other human beings. Embedded in the discourse of image/likeness and vicegerent are divergent resources for articulating the specific worth and standing of human beings, their temptation to usurp the Divine, and also the moral calling of human life.

The goal of this book is to further reflexive engagement among a diversity of viewpoints about human existence arising with the similarities and differences of the Religions of the Book. It aims to further nothing less than a vibrant interchange among thinkers and believers in our global era that at best has rough historical precedent. Points of divergence — as well as convergence — may likely emerge between the views presented. Indeed, even within the traditions themselves, interpreters acknowledge an internal plurality of readings of these textual figures or themes. Christians, for instance, hold divergent ideas about the human as "image" and "likeness" of God and what these ideas mean for understanding the spiritual condition of humanity. In fact, the central sacred text of each tradition and their long histories of commentary attest to the reality of differentiated horizons of memory and expectation. Mindful of the real differences as well as similarities within and among these traditions, the authors of this book nevertheless probe the resources of their own traditions in order to determine whether there is common ground to be found in the idea of humanity before God. An initial answer to this question is seemingly made possible by the linguistic richness of each tradition in thinking about the human as the image or vicegerent of God on earth.

Themes

As the authors of this book seek to articulate what it means for human beings to be or to stand before God, exploring constructively ways in which the rich resources of their traditions may be utilized to clarify, revise, or change how these religions relate to the world, readers will find several important themes developed and sometimes shared by many authors. While the resources, approaches, and reflections that each Abrahamic religion brings forth are profoundly rich and unique, it is important to note that there are points of convergence among the authors.

First, there is a strong affirmation of the sanctity of human life understood in the religious and moral contexts of the human-Divine relationship. Various contributors note the deep theological anthropology found within each tradition in which the meaning and the value of human life are intricately related to the divine purpose of creation. The authors focus on narratives of the creation of human beings bearing parallel provenances within the Torah, the Christian Bible, or the Qur'an. Various authors provide subtle and profound meditations on how to understand the idea that humans are created in the image of God or as God's vicegerent on earth. The theological anthropology derived or developed from these narratives then informs our understandings not only of the ontological status of human beings vis-à-vis God but also of our moral status, that is, the value of the human person *qua* being. In other words, these creation narratives deeply embed axiology, a theory of value, in layers of ontology, a theory about being itself. We return to this point in more detail below.

A second prominent theme, closely related to that of the sanctity of human life, is the notion of moral responsibility. Different authors argue that, like the idea of human worth, the proper meaning of moral responsibility becomes fully intelligible only within our relationship with the Divine. If the human-Divine relationship sheds light on the basic and inalienable rights of human beings, the same relationship also illumines human responsibilities toward the Divine, fellow human beings, and other forms of creaturely life. On this view, our rights and our responsibilities are two sides of the same coin, so to speak. To emphasize one without the other distorts the whole picture. Yet, across many disciplines in the contemporary academy, there abounds a pervasive skepticism about the epistemological and anthropological grounding of such moral notions as rights and responsibilities. The idea of universal moral values has been attacked on many philosophical fronts — for instance, naturalism, materialism, historicism, and postmodernism. Can religious ethics, especially those drawing on the Abrahamic monotheistic religions, claim universal relevance, while still retaining their unique religious and moral outlooks? For many authors of this book, this is not impossible because these religions contain plentiful resources that, if appropriated properly, attest to commonalities both in general human experience and in the values we have in common. The question, then, is not *if* but *how* we can or should appropriate our religious traditions for the betterment of human life in common.

This leads to the third theme, more subtle but not to be overlooked, shared explicitly or implicitly by many of our authors. It lies not in any particular concepts but in a distinctive methodology, that is, how one thinks about religious narratives, symbols, and practices. These authors do not simply refer to the moral values buried under the meanings of some religious text or the history of a tradition, as if they could just point a camera and take a snapshot of those values that may be useful for us today. Rather, they all acknowledge the arduous task of critical interpretation, or *hermeneutics,* in striving to understand the moral fabric of the world depicted in religious texts and tradition and the world we inhabit now. They rearticulate boldly and constructively traditional religious concepts, practices, and narratives in innovative ways. That is to say, these authors are not concerned only with whether axiology can be based on ontology (the fact-value problem of modern moral philosophy), nor are they interested just in advocating particular prescriptions or remedies to fix current problems. What these thinkers actually are doing penetrates to a much deeper level. On the one hand, they decode the meanings of those religious, cultural, and social practices that support or belie other beliefs or insights held by their own traditions. On the other hand, they reconstrue ontology or fundamental religious concepts through a reimagination of the moral spaces inhabited by both members of these traditions and others as well. Addressing issues ranging from the moral standing of nature and body in bioethics and feminist ethics to the question of human rights in religions and war, from the reflections on the biblical "image of God" and "vicegerency" to concepts of justice and love, the authors undertake the difficult task of going back into resources of text and tradition, always reemerging to say what these mean for human life in the present world. In this way, they undertake the arduous task of religious thinking in our present situation.

Structure of the Book

Human life before God has many dimensions. In approaching these dimensions, the strategy of this book is to focus on shared or overlapping narrative figurations of the Divine-human relation as the point of departure and which will serve as the basis of comparison. With this in mind, the book is divided into two main parts corresponding to two main dimensions of the complex idea of "humanity before God." The essays in the respective parts are designed to foreground complementary dimensions implied in that phrase. Each part consists of seven essays written by scholars who in some way represent one of the three Abrahamic traditions.

In using this metaphor of dimensions, we want to avoid any suggestion that one way of thinking about human life has any necessary priority over the others — epistemological, ontological, or axiological. Instead, we envision the phenomenon of human life more like a multifaceted prism that can be viewed from different perspectives. So the essays in both parts of the book provide accounts of the same concrete phenomenon of the living, human person, but they do so from different angles of vision.

In part one, the authors attempt to address the moral worth of the *human person* as *distinctive* in relation to the rest of creation, specifically in connection to the image of God motif in Genesis or the theme of vicegerency in the Qur'an. In the first part, the essays inquire, from both philosophical and theological perspectives, how the idea of human life before God informs reflection on various questions of fundamental anthropology and value. What is distinctive about human being? What is the fundamental nature of personhood? What are the sources of human value? What are the resources within the religious traditions that answer to these questions?

In part two, the book moves from a focus on fundamental anthropology to practical, temporal issues of human life that all three religions must answer. The essays in the second part pay special attention to the fact that human beings are *living* persons *inseparable* from their embodied, gendered, and social existence in the natural world. Human persons bear a distinctive relation to God and the rest of creation, but they are also *creatures* and a part of the rest of creation, nature, and society. Thus, the topics addressed in part two serve to counterbalance the emphases of the essays in part one. How have past ways of construing embodied life in the image of God, for example, been distorted by patriarchal images? How do we apply the idea of the worth of persons to practical problems in various areas of human activity, such as biomedical or environmental ethics?

Part two places the human being in the created world, making explicit the *natural* and *intersubjective* dimensions of human life before God. Essays in this part address contemporary moral questions that probe the ideas of humanity in the natural and social world. They explore how the ideas of humanity before God inform or shape our natural, social, and political obligations. Topics here range from normative questions of bioethics, justice, human rights, and political theory, on the one hand, to issues of literature and culture, on the other hand.

Conclusion

At the heart of the Abrahamic religions stands the central reality of the oneness of God. In all three faiths the revelation of the oneness of God — to Abraham and the Hebrew prophets, in the teachings and person of Christ, to Muhammad, the Messenger of God in Islam — occupies the center of belief and practice. In close association with this central revelation, however, the creation narratives of all three religions portray human responsibility as flowing forth from the further revelation that human beings are created to be God's representatives on earth. As an essential aspect of this role, in the creation narratives both of Genesis and in the Qur'an, God endows human beings with the power of naming the other creatures of creation. In culture-making activities, human beings continue and participate in the creative activity initiated by God.[6] The mandate of dominion over nature ought not to be reduced simplistically to one of exploitation or stewardship of nature or competition for territory and limited resources. To humanity, God bestows the capacity and responsibility not only to distinguish pluralistic systems and orders

---

6. On this see Michael Welker, *Creation and Reality*, trans. John F. Hoffmeyer (Minneapolis: Fortress Press, 1999).

of life, each evaluated as having its own goodness and integrity, but also to relate these orders in new and vibrant ways that promote the flourishing of life. The creation narratives depict God as placing a deep trust in human beings. The divine purpose in creating life on earth continues in part when human beings carry out this trust in ethical ways. A deep vision of religious humanism lies untapped at the center of the creation narratives of the Abrahamic religious traditions. Human beings exist before God and are called to manifest God's justice on earth.

A truly extraordinary vision informs this book in both attitude and subject matter. In attitude, the contributors share a deep concern to promote the flourishing of life, including nonhuman life, before God. In subject matter, the examination of the place of the human in the creation narratives taps a deep reservoir of ethical meaning and insight that promotes rather than denigrates human life. Indeed, the reflections of the authors from the various traditions strive to enact in practice the very capacity for responsible culture-making figured in the narratives themselves. Contributions from each of the traditions realize this coincidence of attitude, focus of reflection, and practice in a distinctive and creative way. The hope is that by placing such reflections in proximity an enlivened understanding of human life before God refracting across the ethical visions of the three great faiths will become evident.

Acknowledgments

The editors wish to express their deep gratitude to all those who have contributed their energies and resources in making this collaborative vision become a reality. The conference whose focus became the subject of this book was sponsored by the Divinity School of the University of Chicago in conjunction with the Martin Marty Center and made possible by the D. R. Sharpe Lectureship Fund. Richard Rosengarten, dean of the Divinity School, and Clark Gilpin, director of the Marty Center, encouraged and supported this project from inception to completion. Their guidance was critical. The conference was also made possible through the generous support of the following persons and institutions associated with the University of Chicago: Kristine Culp, dean of Disciples Divinity House, and the Hoover Lectureship at the Disciples Divinity House; the

Franke Institute for the Humanities; and the Norman Wait Harris Fund
at the Center of International Studies. Conference organization requires
the help of many individuals on numerous levels. Preparation for the
conference would have been impossible without the precise guidance and
tireless logistical support of Sandra Peppers and Jenny Quijano Sax at
the Divinity School. Sandy Crane, Peder Jothen, and Santiago Piñón all
assisted the organizers at various points in the conference. Sandy Crane
aided preparation of the manuscript, Elizabeth M. Bucar helped greatly
with the final editing of the text, and Anne Knafl provided speedy and
accurate editorial assistance in a moment of great need. Pat Eide of University of Chicago Printing provided us with a beautiful poster design
for the conference. Thanks are also due to Scott Alexander at Catholic
Theological Union, W. David Hall at Centre College, Kristine Culp, and
Clark Gilpin for their roles in serving as conference panel moderators.
Finally, we would like to convey our gratitude to all the contributors of
this volume who not only participated in the conference enthusiastically
but also prepared their essays for this publication with great care. Without their effort and insight throughout the project, this book would not
have been possible.

Part One

The Distinctiveness of Human Being

Chapter 1

MONOTHEISM AND HUMANISM
Hilary Putnam

"The Dignity of Difference"

Among writers speaking from within the Jewish tradition (which is also my tradition) in recent years, few, if any, have expressed more powerfully than Jonathan Sacks, in his book *The Dignity of Difference*,[1] the need for a "covenantal relation," a relation of love and responsibility, between persons and persons and between persons and God. Even more importantly for our time, Sacks calls for people of all faiths to recognize that God speaks to humanity through different religions and, thus, that no religion has the right to claim to be humanity's only path to salvation or one and only link to God. Sacks's beautiful and passionate plea for religious tolerance impresses me deeply, and I shall begin by entering into a dialogue with this text.

If all religious leaders spoke at all times in the same tone and with the same depth of feeling as does Sacks, then we could simply compare the different ways in which our different traditions call for peace, mutual respect, tolerance, and so on. Unhappily, that is not the situation.[2]

In the prologue to *The Dignity of Difference*, Sacks relates that, in January 2002, representatives of the world's faiths, including Sacks himself, stood together at Ground Zero, the site of the destruction of the World

---

1. Jonathan Sacks, *The Dignity of Difference: How to Avoid the Clash of Civilizations* (London and New York: Continuum, 2002, 2003). Sacks is the chief rabbi of the United Hebrew Congregations of the British Commonwealth.

2. As Dr. Sacks points out, traditional Jewish theology holds that "the righteous of the nations have a place in the world to come." See my article, "Jewish Ethics?" in William Schweiker, ed., *The Blackwell Companion to Religious Ethics,* Blackwell Companions to Religion (Oxford: Blackwell, 2005), 159–65.

19

Trade Center. They were brought together by their joint participation in the World Economic Forum, which had moved from Davos, Switzerland, to New York as a symbol of solidarity with the people of New York and with the victims of 9/11. He writes, "the Archbishop of Canterbury said a prayer; so did a Muslim imam. A Hindu guru from India recited a meditation and sprinkled rose petals on the site together with holy water from the Ganges. The Chief Rabbi of Israel read a reflection he had written for the occasion. Another Rabbi said Kaddish, the traditional Jewish prayer for the dead. It was a rare moment of togetherness in the face of mankind's awesome powers of destruction. I found myself wondering at the contrast between the religious fervor of the hijackers and the no less intense longing for peace among the religious leaders who were there."[3] A few pages later, however, Sacks reflects somewhat somberly on what was lacking at this impressive and certainly sincere moment of shared longing for peace. He writes, "No one should underestimate the difficulties of peace. There are times, as at the United Nations, when it seemed so simple. Every one of the religious leaders there could find words within his or her religious tradition that spoke of peace in the world or within the soul as a great and noble ideal. Yet even then an outsider could understand why religion is as often a cause of conflict as it is of conciliation. The peace spoken of was too often 'peace on our terms.' The argument was this: 'our faith speaks of peace; our holy texts praise peace; therefore if only the world shared our faith and our texts there would be peace.' Tragically, that path does not lead to peace. In this not-yet-fully-redeemed world, peace means living with those who have a different faith and other texts. There is a fundamental difference between the end-of-days peace of religious unity and the historic peace of compromise and coexistence. The attempt to force the former can sometimes be the most formidable enemy of the latter."[4]

Sacks's purpose in writing this book, however, was not simply to compose a plea (what the French call a *pladoyer*) for tolerance and peace. He suggests something that he himself knows to be quite radical, namely, a change or addition — one might call it a "constitutional amendment" —

3. Sacks, *The Dignity of Difference*, 1.
4. Ibid., 9–10.

to the theologies of *all* the monotheistic religions. (Sacks makes it clear that he is willing to count Hinduism, Buddhism, Taoism, and Confucianism as monotheistic religions, by the way.) The "amendment" (as I am calling it), in Sacks's words, is that "The one God, creator of diversity, commands us to honor his creation by respecting diversity. God, the parent of mankind, loves us as a parent loves — each child for what he or she uniquely is. The idea that one God entails one faith, one truth, one covenant is countered by the story of Babel. The story is preceded by the covenant with Noah and thus with all mankind — the moral basis of a shared humanity, and thus ultimately of universal human rights."[5]

Here Sacks formulates his proposal in the language of the Jewish faith, but he is aware that each faith must find its own way to formulate it — "As Jews, we believe that God has made a covenant with a singular people, but that does not exclude the possibility of other peoples, cultures, and faiths finding their own relationship with God within the shared frame of the Noahide laws.... *God is the god of all of humanity, but between Babel and the end of days no single faith is the faith of all humanity.*"[6]

Many of Sacks's critics fastened on the version of this quote that appeared in the first edition of the book, which stated, "God has spoken to mankind in many languages: through Judaism to Jews, Christianity to Christians, through Islam to Muslims,"[7] as one of several passages that could be understood in ways incompatible with Jewish belief. According to some of these critics, to say that God speaks to Christians and Muslims is to deny what they regard as a fundamental tenet of the Jewish faith, namely, that "the Revelation at Sinai was a unique event never to be repeated in history. Thus any prophet who attempts to abrogate or alter any part of the Torah reveals himself as a false prophet, no matter what signs and wonders he may amass."[8] (On the other hand, others,

---

5. Ibid., 200.

6. The seven Noahide commandments as traditionally enumerated are the prohibition of idolatry, blasphemy, bloodshed, sexual sins, theft, and eating from a living animal, as well as the injunction to establish a legal system (TB [Babylonian Talmud], Tractate *Sanhedrin* 56a). They are derived from divine commands addressed to Adam (Gen. 2:16) and Noah (TB *Sanhedrin* 59b), the ancestors of all mankind. Ibid, 55.

7. Ibid., p. vii.

8. The quotation is from Jonathan Rosenblum, "Blurring of Differences," *Hamodia*, October 25, 2002. This essay is posted online, with the permission of the author, on the Web site http://www.tzemachdovid.org/amechad/blurring.shtml.

including some representatives of the liberal wing of British Orthodoxy, criticized Sacks for what they saw as backing down in the face of this fundamentalist reaction in his second edition revision.)

Such a response within Sacks's own immediate community, the British orthodox Jewish community, indicates that amending the theology of any traditional faith is enormously difficult. And yet, if these faiths cannot amend their theologies in the direction Sacks has proposed, it may be extremely difficult for the "Abrahamic religions" to claim the role that D. R. Sharpe wanted them to claim, namely to serve as social and ethical guides to "modern life and social policy."

It is enormously significant to say that God speaks *to* Christians and Muslims (and, let us add, Buddhists, Hindus, Taoists, Confucians, Druse, and so forth), where that can (and I think *should*) be taken to mean that the voice of God can be *heard* in their great religious texts. Sacks is perhaps right to think that the Abrahamic religions (and the other religions as well) can accept the radical (his own description) idea that *God values diversity* while "circumnavigating" the debate over the claim made by certain traditionalists in each religion that their scripture *and their scripture alone* was, as it were, "dictated" by God. It seems to me, however, that to hold on to such an idea that one scripture *alone* is literally the voice of the living God inevitably constitutes triumphalism and supercessionism. Sacks himself tells us that *"If religion is not part of a solution, it will certainly be part of the problem."*[9] But isn't it the case that if any one of the major faiths holds on to its triumphalist and supercessionist claims, then indeed religion is part of the problem, and not part of the solution? Sacks is quite right that the monotheistic religions have to revise (or at least add to) their theologies explicitly, that there has to be, to use a very American metaphor, an "amendment to the constitution" of each of the major religions, particularly, for our purposes, to those of the three "Abrahamic" faiths. If we keep to the language of the first edition of *The Dignity of Difference,* that amendment has to be to the effect that each religion recognizes that God "speaks to" the other two. I hail Sacks for raising this suggestion, even if he himself is ambivalent about exactly how to formulate it. Even if the suggestion does not

9. Sacks, *The Dignity of Difference,* 9.

bear fruit in our time, I hope it may at least provoke a much-needed discussion within and between each of the faiths.

For sure, at least some people within the spacious mansions of each of the three Abrahamic faiths will be willing to support such an "amendment," but, unfortunately, not in the foreseeable future will all, or perhaps even a majority, of the leaders of these faiths be willing to be so accepting. I think Sacks's revision indicates that there is a "next best thing" to the acceptance of the idea that God "speaks to" Jews and Christians and Muslims (and to other faith communities as well) by the Abrahamic religions — namely, that each of the religions can and should simply find resources within its own texts to support the idea that "God values diversity." Perhaps this is more realistic. But in order to help, it needs to amount to a real granting of dignity to the *forms* that such diversity takes, as I am sure Sacks is aware.

The "Authority" of Religion

If the great faiths (or at least their more orthodox forms) are unable to abandon their claims to what epistemologists call "privileged access" to the truth, then why should those of us who are not willing to concede privileged access to the truth to *any* human institution, and who regard the religions, however divinely inspired, as still *human* institutions, listen to them? To use philosophical jargon, Why should we concede epistemic authority to any religion?

The social and ethical principles set out by the Christian and Jewish religious communities — particularly the way such are elaborated in canon law, in Jewish halakha, and so on — includes much that present-day thinkers have called into question. That the traditional forms of certain faiths do not allow women full religious and social equality is certainly a prime example. Even if we confine ourselves to the sayings attributed to "the prophets of Judah and Israel and of Jesus of Nazareth" (as specified in the content description of the Sharpe Lectures), it is hard to find any unequivocal statement against male chauvinism, or, indeed, any unequivocal statement against the institution of slavery. And yet, as I recite these familiar reasons for refusing to regard any religious tradition or institution as infallible, I am reminded that, ever since the Enlighten-ment, exactly the same question has been raised repeatedly concerning the authority of my own discipline of philosophy. In his great essay, "The Moral Philosopher and the Moral Life," William James wrote,

> [The philosopher's] books upon ethics, therefore, so far as they truly touch the moral life, must more and more ally themselves with a literature which is confessedly tentative and suggestive rather than dogmatic — I mean with novels and dramas of the deeper sort, with sermons, with books on statecraft and philanthropy and social and economical reform. Treated in this way ethical treatises may be voluminous and luminous as well; but they can never be *final*, except in their abstractest and vaguest features; and they must more and more abandon the old-fashioned, clear-cut, and would-be "scientific" form.[10]

More recently, but in very much the same spirit, philosopher and legal scholar Michelle Moody-Adams has written,

> An effective response to . . . skepticism about the relevance of moral theory to moral life must begin by relinquishing the vain insistence upon the authoritative status of philosophical moral inquiry — along with the implausible notion that moral philosophy produces moral expertise. There is a middle way between the skeptical anti-theorist view on which moral philosophy should be *replaced* by some other discipline — such as cultural anthropology, or experi-mental psychology, or literature, or some combination thereof — and the unsupportable view that moral philosophy is the final court of appeal on questions of moral justification. That middle way involves thinking of moral philosophy as a valuable and distinctive participant in the ongoing process of moral inquiry.[11]

---

10. William James, "The Moral Philosopher and the Moral Life," in *The Will to Believe and Other Essays, The Works of William James*, ed. F. H. Burkhardt and F. Bowers (Cam-bridge: Harvard University Press, 1979), 158–59. The opening sentence of the essay (p. 141) is, "The main purpose of this paper is to show that there is no such thing possible as an ethical philosophy dogmatically made up in advance. We all help to determine the content of ethical philosophy so far as we contribute to the race's moral life."

11. Michelle Moody-Adams, *Fieldwork in Familiar Places: Morality, Culture, and Philos-ophy* (Cambridge: Harvard University Press, 1997), 176.

I believe that James's and Moody-Adams's remarks apply just as well to the authority of religions in general, and of the Abrahamic religions in particular. Echoing Moody-Adams, I want to say that there is a middle way between the skeptical anti-religious view on which religion should be *replaced* by some other source of enlightenment — such as sociobiology, or moral philosophy, or cognitive science, or literature, or some combination thereof — and the unsupportable view that religion is the final court of appeal on questions of moral justification. That middle way involves thinking of religion as a valuable and distinctive participant in the ongoing process of moral inquiry.

That *all* the great religions (not only the Abrahamic ones) have distinctive contributions to make to the discussion of the political and moral issues of our time is something I do not doubt. Each of the religions, and each of the many communities of faith within each of the great religions, has its own distinctive insights as well as distinctive shortcomings. But I would like now to focus on two insights that I see as *common* to the world's great religions.

The first of these insights is that, next to but inseparable from love of God, compassion is *the* all-important moral virtue. In the Jewish Bible, this is encapsulated in the two great injunctions to "love your neighbor as yourself" and to "love the stranger." But, when one says that one should love one's neighbor as oneself and that one should love the stranger, it is necessary to stress that compassion must *override* such values as "manly honor," or the defense of the honor and glory of a class or a nation or a sovereign. Unfortunately, many people, including too many "religious" people, agree that one should love one's neighbor as oneself and that one should love the stranger, but show by their actions, or by the other ideas that they advocate, that they regard certain values as *more important* than loving one's neighbor and loving the stranger. I am not talking about mere selfishness or weakness of will, but of what people regard as important — even *morally* important — "when the chips are down."

The persistence of the institution of dueling in Europe until at least the end of the nineteenth century recently struck me as a remarkable example of the manner in which the value of manly honor was able to "trump" the commandment "thou shalt not kill," even among people who thought of themselves as good Christians. The glorification of warfare and *machismo* is certainly much older in the history of human cultures than the idea that one has an obligation to alleviate suffering regardless of the nationality or class or race or gender of the sufferer, but it is this latter idea that finds its deep roots in the great religious traditions of the world — not in only the religious traditions of the West, but in Islam, Confucianism, Hinduism, and Buddhism as well. The specific contribution that the great religions made to human ethical consciousness, starting perhaps in the so-called axial age or axial millennium beginning in 2000 B.C.E., was to put compassion, love of one's neighbor, ahead of *machismo* and other such "values." And the struggle is still not over.

When I describe the prioritization of compassion as a contribution of the great *religions,* I do not mean for one moment to suggest that one cannot be a compassionate person, or an ethical person, or, indeed, a wonderful person, while being an atheist. But I do think that it is a historic fact that the idea that compassion trumps the poisonous values I just listed (though, unfortunately, not patriarchy and hierarchy) came into the world through the teachings and the personal examples of great religious figures.

Following the Enlightenment, the idea of universal compassion was also preached by two great secular philosophies: utilitarianism and Kantianism, this attempt to provide a *philosophical* foundation for compassionate ethics seems to me to have serious shortcomings, however. Kantianism, for example, founds compassion on an idea that goes back to Plato and Aristotle, the idea that what is uniquely valuable about human beings is what is (supposedly) totally unique about them, namely Reason. But an ethics that identifies the ideal ethical commonwealth — "the Kingdom of Ends" as Kant called it — with the totality of all rational beings, where a "rational being" is a being capable of "giving itself the moral law," has obvious weaknesses. Not only does it fail to do justice to the ethical demands of animals or retarded humans, but it always leaves open the possibility that some will say, as did the Nazis, for example, that some group of humans possessed of normal human "rationality" only *appear* to be capable of giving themselves the moral law, that the hated group consists of "parasites" in human form. As Emmanuel Lévinas tried to teach us, any attempt to say that one should be concerned with the other's suffering *because* the other has some property in common with us, because of a *sameness* between oneself and the other, opens the door to persecution and genocide.[12]

As for utilitarianism, there is a huge philosophical literature criticizing this moral theory, and I won't review the arguments against it here; I shall only say that this doctrine, like Kantianism, and like the philosophy of David Hume, which really inspired the fathers of utilitarianism, likewise seeks to found ethics on the idea of human *sameness*. I find Emmanuel Lévinas's refusal to base ethics on *any* sort of "sameness," empirical or metaphysical, far more profound. What Lévinas asked of us was not that we should *ignore* the respects in which human beings are similar — it is a common misunderstanding of Lévinas to think that he was simply asking us to pay more attention to *empirical* differences between human beings — rather, Lévinas asked us to be aware (as his mentor Heidegger famously was) of the gulf between oneself, one's own fate, one's own death, and the existence, the fate, the death, of any other human being, however "similar" — the way in which each of us is *irreducibly* alone in this world — while turning that awareness of "otherness" in a wholly different direction from Heidegger. For Heidegger, the uniqueness of my own *Dasein,* my own being-in-the-world, meant that I should be preoccupied with my own existence and my own death; for Lévinas the moment of preoccupation with my own death and my own fate should be just that, a "moment" in both the ordinary language sense and the Hegelian sense — a moment that one has to go beyond in order to attain full humanity. That is, one has to come to see the suffering of the other — both the obvious suffering and the suffering that it requires sensitivity and insight to perceive — as something about which I am "commanded" to do something. One is not commanded by a theology, or even by God — although the command in question *is,* in Lévinas's view, divine — but commanded *by the other himself or herself,* and by the very fact of that suffering. Lévinas does not give us a *reason* why we should see the suffering of the other as something to which we are

---

12. See my article, "Lévinas and Judaism," in Simon Critchley and Robert Bernasconi, eds., *The Cambridge Companion to Lévinas,* Cambridge Companions to Theology (Cambridge, UK: Cambridge University Press, 2002), 33–62, for a discussion of this and other aspects of Lévinas's thought.

commanded to respond; rather, he sees the very demand for a "reason" as an obscenity.

It is not that Lévinas thinks there is no place for reasoning in difficult ethical situations: that is another way of misunderstanding him. But ethics cannot be *founded* on reasons that come from metaphysics or the empirical sciences, or, indeed, on any reasons more fundamental than the recognition that we are commanded to help the other. That command "trumps" all others. And one is to obey it because one recognizes that to do so is to experience what Lévinas calls "the glory of the Infinite."

The Finiteness of Our Responsibility

So far I have emphasized one great contribution that I believe the great religions made to human moral consciousness: the idea that, in the end, compassion "trumps" ethical concerns. Of course, they were not wholly consistent in this. The great religions teach us that one cannot love God without loving one's fellow human beings, but, sadly, the love of God and the love of one's fellow beings have at times been treated as if they could be in conflict, and as if the love of God *trumps* the value of compassion, as if it were a value that requires one to exterminate one's fellow man, to burn him at the stake, to torture him into submission, and so forth. Such a story has often been told, but it is important to recognize that, however inconsistent any human institution may be in its ideology and in its working, the thematization of universal compassion is a value that represents a tremendously important contribution of the great religions to ethics.

But ethics is not enough for human life. In addition to the centrality of compassion, a second distinctive theme of the great religions is summarized for me in the words of Rabbi Tarfon, reported in the Mishnaic tractate *Pirke Avot* ("The Chapters of the Fathers"): "It is not up to you to finish the work, but neither are you free not to take it up."[13]

All the great religions teach us to see the value in "taking up the task," even though one may not be able to finish it, and even though the task may never be finished. I am not trying here to convert anyone

---

13. Mishna, *Pirke Avot* 2.21. Translation is my own.

to "religion," or to criticize purely secular ways of living. But I know from portions of my own life that for purely secular outlooks — I don't say "philosophies," because the outlooks of which I speak are much less conceptual than philosophies — the temptations of groundless optimism and total pessimism are ever present. Rabbi Tarfon pointed out the only viable alternative to these temptations.

Wilfred Cantwell Smith frequently pointed out that religion can make people behave either better or worse (although it does, he said, make one take the question "how to live" seriously).[14] Similarly, one might say that religious faith can make people either more or less sane (it seems to drive some people crazy). But it *can* make one saner. And when it does make one saner, I think that one of the ways in which it does so is precisely by giving one not only the sense, but also the peace of mind that comes with the sense that "it is not up to one to finish the task, but neither is one free not to take it up."

Religious Humanism

It is clear, I trust, why the word *monotheism* appears in the title of this essay, but what about the word *humanism?* Today the term *humanism* is widely misused by those who attack what they call "secular humanism," by which they simply seem to mean any nontheistic ethical philosophy at all. But this is not the bogeyman I had in mind when I used the term as part of my title. Rather, I was thinking of the phenomenon called "Renaissance Humanism." Scholars have argued that in many ways the Renaissance Humanists set the stage for the French *philosophes* and for the Enlightenment as a whole.[15] Renaissance Humanism was a many-sided movement, which began in the enthusiastic Platonism of Pico della Mirandola, but came to include more skeptical figures, such as Erasmus and Montaigne. What is, I think, heartening about the Humanists, start-ing with Mirandola's "Oration on the Dignity of Man," is that, while

14. See, for example, Smith's overview article on religion in the fifteenth edition of the Encyclopedia Britannica.

15. See, for example, Gary Remer, *Humanism and the Rhetoric of Toleration* (University Park: Pennsylvania State University Press, 1996); and George Huppert, *The Style of Paris: Renaissance Origins of the French Enlightenment* (Bloomington: Indiana University Press, 1999).

they retained an allegiance to their (Christian) faith, they insisted on several things.

First, Mirandola's insistence that the great teachings of the Christian religion are fundamentally reconcilable with the teachings of Greek philosophy (in particular, with Plato) was early generalized to the idea, radical at the time, that the different Christian denominations really agree on "essentials," and still later generalized to the idea that there are fundamental commonalties in the teaching of Christianity, Judaism, and Islam. The idea of toleration was at least nascent in Renaissance Humanism, and, indeed, as I just mentioned, scholars have recently traced the idea of toleration in Christian Europe back to that movement.

Second, in the process of teaching at least a nascent form of toleration, Renaissance Humanism refused to accept the doctrine that this life is divinely meant to be no more than a testing ground — a period of suffering that we have to go through in order to achieve happiness in an afterlife. Whatever one may believe about an afterlife — and the Renaissance Humanists did believe in the immortality of the soul — the Humanists held that *this* life has its own value, that this world *can* be improved, that human autonomous reason is needed to improve the world, and that human autonomous reason and religious faith need not be set in opposition to one another.

What I have tried to do here is to say some words that are in the *spirit* of the Humanist movement. If the great religions are to fulfill their divinely appointed tasks, then they must give rise, not to an anti-humanism, but to a true *religious* humanism.

Chapter 2

HUMAN VICEGERENCY:
A BLESSING OR A CURSE?

The Challenge to Be God's Caliph in the Qur'an

Abdulaziz Sachedina

"See, I am creating a mortal of a clay. When I have shaped him, and breathed My spirit in him, fall you down, prostrate before him!"
(Qur'an 38:72)

And when your Lord said to angels, "Behold I am about to place a vicegerent in the earth!" They said, "What, would You place therein one who will spread corruption and shed blood, while we proclaim Your praise and call You Holy?" He said, "Assuredly I know what you do not know." (Qur'an 2:30)

I place at the beginning of my reflections two citations drawn from some of the most thought-provoking sections of the Qur'an. These passages concern the story of Adam's creation. In Muslim tradition Adam is the father of humankind (*abū al-bashar*). The Qur'anic account about Adam's creation is short and precise. It relates one of the most memorable moments in the history of humankind — its first encounter with its Creator. There could not have been a more momentous event, which lays down in most clear terms the future direction of humanity: "Behold, I am about to place a vicegerent in the earth!" By God's fiat humanity is going to be endowed with a destiny to lead the creation as its caretaker. This is the beginning of the challenge to represent God's will and purposes

---

Translations of Qur'an passages in this essay are the author's.

31

on earth. The destiny is to lead as God's vicegerent. In order to make sure that humanity realizes its constructive potentials, after fashioning it God endows it with the innate nature (*fiṭra*), capable of realizing good and avoiding evil. Then God provides humanity with further guidance through the revelation He sends through His prophets to overcome the temptation to become self-centered and self-serving at the expense of the common good. The creation of human being is the culmination of God's plan and, accordingly, it comes toward the end, following the creation of all that is on earth and in the heavens.

Adam is no ordinary creature. God has breathed God's own spirit in him. He is human and yet he carries within himself the divine attributes that are predicated only to God as the Creator. This significance is under-scored by God's announcement to place human beings on earth as God's representative. And, as the designation process shows, the only prepara-tion that is deemed necessary by God for making humanity responsible to exercise God's authority over the entire creation is the knowledge of "the names":

> He taught Adam the names, all of them; then He presented them before the angels and said, "Now tell me the names of these, if you speak truly." (Qur'an 2:31)

> They said, "Glory be to You! We know not save what You have taught us. Surely You are the All-knowing, the All-wise." (2:32)

> He said, "Adam, tell them their names." And when he had told them their names He said, "Did I not tell you I know the unseen things of the heavens and earth? And I know what things you reveal, and what you hide." (2:33)

The superiority of humanity over the angels is established in an academic fashion in the form of a test based on "Let us see how much you know!" The angels are given the opportunity first and are asked to give the names of the entities presented to them. After all, they had an argument against God's plan to place Adam as God's vicegerent. The angels fail the test and confess with much humility: "We know not save what You have taught us." The examination reaches the climax when Adam is asked the same question that was put to the angels. Adam reveals his knowledge of "the names" to the gathered assembly of the heavenly beings. The concluding statement seals the future destiny of humankind known to God alone. God is omniscient. God alone knows "the unseen things of the heavens and the earth." God is now asking the angels to show utmost respect to the very creature about whose qualifications to become God's vicegerent they had doubts:

> And when We said to the angels, "Prostrate yourselves before Adam"; so they prostrated themselves, except Iblīs; he refused, and waxed proud, and so he became among the rejecters of faith. (2:34)

A new character is introduced in the creation narrative at this stage: Iblīs, the Devil, the tempter, who succeeds in bringing about the fall of Adam. And then Adam's female companion is mentioned without any details as to how or when she was created:

> And We said, "Adam, dwell you, and your wife, in the Garden, and eat thereof easefully where you desire; but do not approach this tree, for then you would be among the wrongdoers." (2:35)

> Then Satan caused them to slip from the garden and brought them out of that they were in; and We said, "Get you all down, each of you an enemy of each; in the earth a sojourn shall be yours, and enjoyment for a time." (2:36)

It is indeed a very sad moment for Adam. He has disobeyed God's command by approaching the tree and eating its fruit. Alas, Satan caused him and his wife to slip. He lost his dwelling place in the garden for which, according to a tradition preserved in the commentaries, he wept for many years. "Get you all down!" conveys God's displeasure at what had happened in the blissful garden. Adam was despairing when God intervened to save the situation. Adam realized his need to restore himself in God's presence. The omniscient and compassionate God knows Adam's remorseful condition and, hence, teaches him how to turn toward God in difficult moments of despair. With a promise of continued guidance from God the first act of the drama comes to an end:

> Thereafter Adam received certain words from his Lord, and He turned toward him; truly He turns, and is All-compassionate. (2:37)

We said, "Get you down out of it, all together; yet there shall come to you guidance from Me, and whoever follows My guidance, no fear shall be on them, neither shall they sorrow." (2:38)

"As for those who have rejected faith, who cry lies to Our signs, those shall be the inhabitants of the Fire, therein dwelling forever." (2:39)

Further Reflection on the Muslim Version of Genesis

Each set of creation verses carries a mythic moment that can be captured only in imagination. The presence of the angels and God's address to them provide an extraordinary opening scene of the cosmic drama that will culminate in God's breathing the divine spirit in the first human, and God's declaration to appoint Adam as God's caliph in the earth. There is no mention of human being created in God's image in the Qur'an. The ḥadīth-literature has preserved a tradition that speaks about it, however.[1] The Qur'an seems to lay enormous emphasis on Adam's appointment as God's vicegerent. In fact, the sole purpose of narrating the story of creation appears to recount God's covenant with Adam, Adam's special status as God's representative on earth, and the threat Satan poses to human success in carrying out God's purposes for human society. And yet, references to human origins underscore the purpose of creation and its cosmic significance for the future of humanity as God's vicegerent, before it is called on the Day of Judgment to account for its performance.

Adam, it is worth keeping in mind, is a generic name for human being created with a specific mission to become God's vicegerent. The Qur'an repeats this short narrative at least three times — every time with an added facet to draw attention to God's special relation with humanity. The cosmic drama of creation unfolds in the presence of the inhabitants of the heavens. The phrase "And [recall] when" implies that this is not the first time that the narrative has been recounted. Apparently, the edifying element of the drama is so important that it has been

1. Muḥammad Al-Bukhārī, *Ṣaḥīḥ Bukhārī*, *Kitāb al-Isti'dhān*.

narrated before. The audience is not surprised at the command to prostrate before Adam. They all obey the order, except the Satan, who in
his haughtiness regarded himself to be superior to Adam. What the
angels have a problem with is God's decision to place Adam as God's
representative.

If this is just the beginning of human history, however, what is the
basis for the angels' negative evaluation of human performance on earth?
Is it not the first time that Adam is being brought to the world as
human being and as God's vicegerent? What do the angels know when
they assert that human beings will shed blood and spread corruption
on earth? To be sure, the suspicion about human ability to withstand
the responsibilities of vicegerency could not be based on some previous
observations about human life on earth when there was no such existence in the first place. Muslim commentators have tried to explain this
dilemma in the moral evaluation of human performance prior to their
creation by pointing out that before human beings it was the *jinn*, the
human counterpart in the world of "invisible existence," who inhabited the earth and spread corruption in it, shed blood and killed one
another. The angels, also part of this invisible realm, were privileged to
witness the mischief caused by the *jinn*. Hence, when the angels made a
reference to negative human tendencies it was based on the corruption
that was spread by the *jinn*, who like human beings, were endowed with
free will.[2]

Be that as it may, the objection by the angels creates a complex theological and moral picture of the encounter between Divine and human
that actually continues to confound humanity even today. It is also
important to note that to the objection raised by the angels, instead
of affirming or denying the negative evaluation about humanity, God
simply declares: "Assuredly I know what you do not know." Does it
mean that regardless of the capacity to do evil in human beings, ultimately it is only God who knows that God's plan to appoint humankind
to represent and exercise God's power on earth is part of God's overall
benevolent plan for the creation?

2. Muhammad b. Jarir al-Tabari, *Jamī' al-Bayan 'an Ta'wīl al-Quran* (Cairo: Dār
al-Ma'arīf, 1954), vol. 1, pp. 449–50.

Theological-Ethical Implications of Adam's Creation

The theological-ethical implications of this narrative can be fully elaborated when attention is paid to another cosmic event in the Qur'an. Apparently, this event is also part of the creation story. It deals with the offering of the Trust (*amāna*) and its acceptance by humankind:

> We offered the trust to the heavens and the earth and the mountains, but they refused to carry it and were afraid of it; and human being carried it. Surely he is unjust, ignorant. (33:73)

Scholars of the Qur'an have speculated on two related issues in this passage. First, what exactly was the nature of the Trust that the awesome heavens and the earth and the mountains refused to carry and were afraid of it? Second, if human being, who in comparison to the tremendous heavens and the earth is so insignificant, demonstrated courage and daring to accept the Trust, why was he being criticized as being unjust and ignorant? Did he not deserve to be praised for his willingness and daring instead? After all, it was God offering the Trust, which humanity accepted. Knowing everything that the omniscient God knows about humanity, why should God even offer them the Trust?

Here, based on some classical exegetical elaboration, one can link God's decision to commission humankind to rule on earth to humankind's boldness in assuming the Trust. As God's representative, humankind is commissioned to assume authority and exact obedience in practice. Human vicegerency is intrinsically related to the moral vision of the Qur'anic revelation. The Qur'an regards public life as an inevitable projection of personal response to the moral challenge of creating a divinely ordained public order on earth. Personal devotion to God implies responsibility of furthering the realization of a just society, embodying all the manifestations of religious faith in the material as well as spiritual life of humankind.

This responsibility of striving for one's own welfare and that of the society in which one lives derives from the fact that humankind has boldly assumed the Trust that God offered. The Trust has been variously interpreted. But, in light of the creation narrative and Adam's appointment as God's caliph, the Trust, which must be ultimately returned to its owner intact, must have something to do with the exercise of divine authority. To be sure, the criticism leveled at humanity as being "unjust" and "ignorant" has an inherent connection with the ethics of political power. How else can we understand the nature of the Trust if not in terms of its ethical implications for human life on earth? Consequently, of all the interpretations given by Muslim exegetes about the Trust, from its being affirmation of God's unity (*tawḥīd*) to adherence to God's laws in the *Sharīʿa*, there is evidence to suggest that the Trust deals with human ability to exercise God's authority as God's representative with justice and knowledge on earth. The fact that only human beings assumed the Trust indicates that it is only human beings who possess the potential to attain perfection as the caretaker of the creation. More importantly, only human beings are not afraid to bear the burden of this Trust, and to accept the consequences of being a tyrant and ignorant, because they alone can acquire the opposite attributes — namely, those of being "just" and "knowledgeable." In fact, both tyranny and ignorance are the primary counterpoise of human responsibility in accepting the vicegerency, especially as it concerns God's providential purpose in allowing imperfect humanity to accept responsibility. It is indeed through the acceptance of this Trust of God's rule on earth that human beings acquire both the responsibility for their actions as well as superiority over all other creatures in the world. God's vicegerency enables them to put society into order in accordance with their unique comprehension of "the names."

What were these names, which God taught to Adam? There is much speculation about it in the exegetical literature. Some commentators maintain that God taught Adam the names of things animate and inanimate. Others have speculated that Adam was taught the names of all things and essences. The verses leave little doubt that God displayed before the doubting angels the essences of things named with the challenge: "Inform me of the names of these if you speak the truth!" In other words, attainment of higher station of vicegerency came from the acquisition of knowledge. Acquired knowledge necessitating higher attainments belongs especially to the human community. This is what the angels do not know. The divine mystery of God's love and knowledge, which God deposited in human being, is what God has safeguarded in God's knowledge.

However, God's vicegerency is given to humankind with a clear warning that it will have to rise above "tyranny" and "ignorance" by heeding the call of divine guidance. Human beings, according to the Qur'an, have been endowed with the cognition needed to further their comprehension of the purpose for which they are created, and the volition to realize it by using their knowledge. It is through divine guidance that human beings are expected to develop the ability to judge their actions and choose what will lead them to prosperity. But this is not an easy task. It involves spiritual and moral development, something that is most challenging in the face of the basic human weakness indicated by the Qur'an:

> Surely human being was created fretful, when evil visits him, impatient, when good visits him, grudging. (70:19–20)

Human beings need to be constantly reminded of their origins. This is the central function of the Qur'an. The Qur'an is essentially the Reminder (*dhikr*). Hence, the story of creation, which is crucial for human ethical and spiritual progression, is repeated for moral edification and to inspire religious commitment. The following two selections from Qur'an 7:19–23 and 20:115–19 add some remarkable facets:

> "O Adam, inherit, you and your wife, the Garden, and eat of where you will, but come not close to this tree, lest you be of the evildoers." (7:19)
>
> The Satan whispered to them [both], to reveal to them that which was hidden from them of their nakedness. He said: "Your Lord has only prohibited from this tree lest you become angels, or lest you become immortals." (20) And he swore to them [both], "Truly, I am for you [both] a sincere adviser." (21)
>
> So he led them [both] on by delusion; and when they [both] tasted the tree, their nakedness revealed to them, so they took to stitching upon themselves leaves of the Garden. And their Lord called to them, "Did I not prohibit you [both] from this tree, and say to you, 'Verily Satan is for you a manifest foe'?" (22)
>
> They said, "Lord, we have wronged ourselves, and if You do not forgive us, and have mercy upon us, we shall surely be among the lost." (23)

In yet another place the challenge to Adam posed by the Satan is repeated with a warning to all humans that it is worth remembering what our parents suffered in the hands of the accursed devil:

> And We made covenant with Adam before, but he forgot, and We found in him no firm resolve whatsoever. (20:115) And when We said to the angels, "Bow yourselves to Adam"; so they bowed themselves, save Iblīs; he refused. (116)
>
> Then We said, "Adam surely this is an enemy to you and your wife. So let him not expel you both from the Garden, so that you are unprosperous. (117) It is assuredly given to you neither to hunger therein, nor to go naked, (118) neither to thirst therein, nor to suffer the sun." (119)

There is a common thread in the earlier and these two instances of the creation narrative: Adam's creation; the command to the angels to bow to him and the refusal of Iblīs to do so; Adam's dwelling in the Garden with his wife; their being tempted by the Satan and the subsequent expulsion of all of them. A number of interesting questions arise from this cryptic description of Adam's mission as God's vicegerent. What concerns us here, however, is God's choice to deputize humanity to represent God in exercising power and authority to build up the earth and inhabit it. Retrospectively, we can ask: Is God's vicegerency a source of blessing or a curse for humanity?

There is a tension in the narrative as the angels question God's decision. A further element of tension enters with the appearance of Satan — the one who has caused humanity to slip. The Qur'anic purpose in relating parts of the genesis story seems to underscore two contradictory characteristics in Adam: on the one hand, the Qur'an demonstrates Adam's cognitive ability and asserts his superiority over the angels who proclaim God's praise and sanctity; and, on the other, it reveals Adam's vulnerability to the satanic temptations and ensuing misguidance that could be detrimental for the development of an ethical society on the earth. To be sure, it is the temptation followed by eating the forbidden fruit that caused the first human couple to slip from the Garden. What is most revealing in the second set of verses is that "when they both tasted the tree, their nakedness revealed to them, so they took to stitching upon themselves leaves of the Garden" (7:22). Until that time their nakedness was not an issue. In fact, the Garden offered them more than that. It offered them a place in which Adam did not have to toil. As the third set of the verses states: "It is assuredly given to you neither to hunger therein, nor to go naked, neither to thirst therein, nor to suffer the sun" (20:119). In other words, the Garden was the state of nature, the state of innocence in which Adam and his wife could live forever without having to worry about making any ethical decisions or toil for their livelihood with all its challenges. Everything was perfect and provided. And, yet, Adam and Eve allowed themselves to be led astray by the Satan and face the grim consequence of "each of you an enemy to each."

At this juncture it is important to clarify that in the Qur'anic story of genesis the blame of being tempted is not put squarely on Eve's shoulder. Actually, according to the carefully used dual verbal and pronominal forms of Arabic, the Qur'an puts the blame on "both" Adam and Eve. The Satan whispered to both of them, to reveal to them that which was hidden from them of their nakedness. In other words, he led them both on by delusion; and when they both tasted the fruit, their nakedness revealed to them, so they took to stitching upon themselves leaves of the Garden. In the words of the Qur'an, it was only then that "the two of them ate of it, and their nakedness revealed to them." Nevertheless, although both Adam and Eve became deluded, the Qur'an puts the blame of disobedience squarely on Adam, God's vicegerent, who erred. Hence, we read: "And Adam disobeyed his Lord, and so he erred."

Remarkably, Eve is not mentioned by name in any of these passages that speak about human creation. She is, as the Qur'an says, Adam's companion. The details about Eve's role in "Adam's fall" are in the commentaries of the Qur'an, where the main source for this exegetical information is the *Isrā'īliyyāt*, that is, Jewish and Christian traditions.[3] A number of traditions are related that elaborate the role Eve played in Adam's fall. And, yet, it is important to keep in mind that the Qur'an incriminates both, and lays the blame on Adam. Contrary to the passages from the Qur'an, however, if one were to follow the logic of these traditions, then God-human encounter would appear to have been

3. Ibid., 525–26.

predetermined by some kind of divine decree. The questioning of God's purpose of appointing human being as God's vicegerent by the angels is in the form of protest, indicating that they knew something about negative human tendencies. God could have responded very directly to the angels and pointed out that despite such contradictions that might hurt God's purpose for humanity, God is willing to take a chance by making Adam God's *khalīfa*. Instead, God asks Adam to inform the angels the names of the beings, who are displayed for everyone to look. Adam does so and God retorts at the angels, saying: "Did I not tell you that I know what is concealed in the heavens and the earth, and I know what you disclose and what you hide." In other words, don't question My wisdom and My knowledge about My servant. What God knows about Adam is mentioned in terms of a potential in humanity to follow God's guidance and become prosperous, or to reject and become unprosperous. God's guidance, then, is the key to undo the damage that can be caused by the loss of innocence ensuing from eating the forbidden fruit. The narrative takes its readers to acknowledge the necessity of religious guidance in reaching the goal and undoing the damage caused by the act of disobedience.

The important consequences of Adam's disobedience and expulsion from the Garden are underscored by the emphasis laid on the lessons that his future progeny could ill afford to forget. Symbolically, the Qur'an speaks about the loss of innocence in terms of its impact on human relationship and what it entails in terms of mutual responsibilities. The life in the Garden was "given to you neither to hunger therein, nor to go naked, neither to thirst therein, nor to suffer the sun." But now human beings will have to work for all these comforts, keeping the ethical framework provided in human nature, the *fiṭra*, as a universal standard of moral conduct:

> We have honored (*karrāmna;* related to *karam,* "noble nature") the children of Adam and carried them on land and sea, and provided them with good things, and preferred them greatly over many of those We created. (17:70)

The Qur'an views this "noble nature" as endowed with ethical cognition and the capacity to reason morally in order to know right from wrong. The Garden narrative evidently points to this when it relates the effect of tasting the fruit: "they [both] tasted the tree, their nakedness revealed to them, so they took to stitching upon themselves leaves of the Garden." Why would the couple feel the embarrassment of the nakedness being revealed to them if there was no naturally endowed ability to know the right from the wrong? However, this apparently universal reaction to the knowledge about nakedness points to the concrete and historical context of the Semitic moral sensibilities. This relative dimension of the Qur'anic ethics suggests an important caveat in the search for universal ethics. If a paradigm for universal ethics has to emerge as a principle of human interaction in society it has to acknowledge communitarian boundaries of application within variable cultural and historical experience of the communities. In other words, there will always remain a tension between a particular revelation with its specific appeal to the community of the faithful, and a universal ethics that will require the community to relate itself beyond its communal affiliation to the larger world community.

This tension is inevitable, because in Islam Adam is not only God's vicegerent; he is also God's prophet with specific guidance at a certain point in history. This historical relativity of God's guidance to human beings at a particular time leads to the problem in searching for a moral language in the Qur'an that can allow for a universal ethics to serve as an important source for organizing human community on earth. Does the Qur'an address this problem?

Human Dignity and Religious Particularity

The Qur'an is concerned about the tension between universal and communitarian ethics; therefore, it undertakes to address the issue on several occasions. The strategy employed by the Qur'an to connect humanity as a single community, even when it recognizes the plurality of scriptural guidance given through various prophets, is to relate them through the "innate nature" that is capable of recognizing a moral good (*al-khayr, al-ma'rūf*). This "innate nature" is the source of the very first qualities in virtue of which someone becomes human:

So set your purpose for religion, a human by nature upright —
God's original [nature] upon which He created humankind. There
is no altering [the laws of] God's creation. (30:30)

In addition, God also honors humanity with the "noble nature" (*karam*).
As part of their noble nature, all humans are endowed with an innate
scale with which they can weigh rightness and wrongness. This innate
scale is connected with universal ethical cognition as stated in another
reference to human creation:

By the soul and That which shaped it and inspired it [with conscience of] what is wrong for it and [what is] right for it. Prosperous
is he who purifies it, and failed has he who seduces it. (91:7–10)

Hence, "human by nature upright" or created in "original nature" (*fitrat
Allāh* = "God's nature") is endowed with a morality that cannot be
arbitrary. Ethical knowledge is "inspired by God" that does not require
any justification independent of the naturally endowed innate scale. The
Qur'an leads humankind with "upright nature" to achieve a balance
between the known (the convictions determined through the process of
reflection) and the unknown moral judgments by placing the known in
history and culture at the same time. Consequently, the Qur'an anchors
moral convictions in the reflective process and invites human beings to
ponder the consequences of their actions and learn to avoid such perilous
actions. Moreover, it appeals to the human capacity for learning from
past destructiveness in order to avoid it in future. The assumption in the
Qur'an is that there is something concrete about human conditions that
cannot be denied by any reasonable persons endowed with "hearts to
understand" (22:46).

Accordingly, the concept of a known prerevelatory moral language in
the Qur'an does not fail to acknowledge the concrete historical and social
conditioning of moral concepts. But it insists that different cultures must
seek to elicit the universal ideal out of the diversity of concrete human
conditions — a common foundation upon which to construct an ethical
language that can be shared cross-culturally in the project of creating a
just society:

O humankind, We have created you male and female, and appointed you races and tribes, that you may know one another. Surely, the noblest among you in the sight of God is most morally [and spiritually] aware among you. God is All-knowing, All-aware. (49:13)

Both the known and the unknown moral principles in the Qur'an point to concrete ways of life constructed in different cultural idioms ("races and tribes") that must be understood in order to elicit the universals and to apply them in similar context. The moral and spiritual awareness (*taqwā*) that ennobles human existence and leads it to carry out duties to God and other humans functions as a torch of the divinely created innate human nature, enabling it to discover the universals that can build bridges of understanding across cultures.

Universal Accessible through Particular-Communitarian

In search for universals the moderns have tended to devalue the role the particular, that is, the religious, plays in preparing humanity to undertake the challenge of treating the other as equal in dignity, regardless of differences in creed, race, and gender. The modern's prescription to create world citizenship has been to secularize the public sphere in its entirety by restricting the particular derived from the religious to the private domain. Today, many commentators view religion as a major threat to the world peace. There is much evidence in religious histories to suggest that God-human encounter in the form of specific revelation given to a community, at one time or other, has been distorted to accommodate the political ambitions of that community. Such accommodation between the core spiritual message of the particular tradition and political power has actually led to the disestablishment of the universal ethical foundations of various religious traditions.

Nevertheless, the Qur'an regards God-human encounter as an important source for the universal ethical code founded upon human relations. God created the first human couple from a single soul — the very foundation of human relations to one another, so that people would be aware of their duties to one another and realize the greatest good of establishing interpersonal justice in their relations (4:1–2). This teaching of the Qur'an about human creation, in addition to the emphasis on the "noble nature," promotes human sociability and positive bonds between peoples because they share a common ethical responsibility toward one another. Recognition of universal parentage fosters mutual expectations and relationship in human society.

At the same time, the Qur'an lays importance on the community that can foster in its membership concern for the common good. To this end, the communal order promotes religious-moral institutions through which the community's ethical aspirations are fulfilled. The doctrine of the noble nature is properly anchored in the history of human struggle toward discovering what it is to be properly human. The greatest challenge facing the community of the faithful is its claim about the transcending quality and the unique relation it has to truth. The conflicting and even incommensurable theological positions held by different communities on their exclusive claim to religious truth has led to oppressive use of force to ensure adherence to a single comprehensive religious doctrine. The ensuing intolerance has manifested itself in inter- and intra-faith relations. Yet, the spirit of accommodation and tolerance certainly demands that a common ground should be sought for implementing the common good in society. Working for the common good without insisting on imposing the beliefs and desires each holds most dear can result in a legitimate public space for diverse human religious experience. Can this public space be realized without interfering with the ability of each person to work out his or her own individual salvation?

The debate has its origin in ideas about the highest ends of human existence on the earth. Can they be accomplished through communal cooperation for the collective good or for widely different and even irreconcilable individual interests? How can a particular religious community remain neutral and noninterventionist on ethical issues that, from the individual's point of view, might run counter to one's sense of the highest ends in life? As members of a democratic society, individuals are free to endorse various religious views or none at all. Religious pluralism is a prerequisite for a peaceful accommodation of the differences in the individual and the communal sense of the highest good.

The secular prescription seems to suggest that religious toleration can be achieved only when the idea of freedom of conscience is institutionalized in the form of a basic individual right to worship freely, to propagate one's religion, or even to renounce religion altogether. In other words, the principle of toleration is equated with the idea of individual freedom of conscience. Moreover, it delimits the role of conscience to the domain of private faith, which is clearly demarcated from the public realm — the separation of church from state. Whereas one has freedom to choose between competing doctrines and pursue one's belief in private religious institutions, one is linked in common citizenry in public state institutions. This is the secularist foundation of a public order in which, in pursuit of freedom of conscience, all considerations drawn from belief in God or other sacred authority in one's private life are excluded from the administration of public life.

Here, it is important to consider a nonsecularist model of religious tolerance offered by a public sphere founded on religious considerations, a society founded upon belief that God alone provides the center of gravity for developing a sense of loyalty to a comprehensive political life.

The belief in God as the principle of unity presupposes a link between this world and the next world in such a way that faith becomes the essential medium for the comprehension of the norm that guides collective life of socially responsible individuals. The Qur'an propounds a set of beliefs and practices, embodies a public dimension in which the integration of the private and public spheres is grounded in the contract between two parties. It constructs the community on the principle of equality among believers who, through their personal commitment to Islamic faith, undertook to realize interpersonal justice.

> Say [Muhammad]: "My Lord has commanded justice. Set your faces in every place of worship and call on Him [when you pray], making your religion sincerely His. As He originated you so you will return." (7:30)

In other words, God's religion is the command to act with justice and equity in such a way that justice is at the heart of everything one does. The emphasis is on the individual to obey the command of God. In the absence of a mediating religious institution like a church to represent

God's claims, the community felt justified in insisting upon individual responsibility in constructing and maintaining an ethical order founded upon justice and equity as a collective response to the Prophet's call of obedience.

Abrahamic traditions are characteristically founded upon the scriptures that favor the creation of a just community on earth. Accordingly, instead of merely favoring the future appearance of a restorer or redresser of mutilated justice or a purely esoteric stress on disciplining a believer on the mystical path of realizing the true calling of human beings, they emphasize the Divine-human covenant that locates justice in history through community. The indispensable connection between the religious and ethical dimensions of personal life inevitably introduces religious precepts into the public arena. In other words, church and state are closely linked, requiring the involvement of the religious community in taking the responsibility for law and order. All human beings are called on to support the community, the norms of which — defined as exclusive, comprehensive, universal, and uncompromising — form the boundaries of an individual's spiritual life. There is one true faith represented by the religious body, and all else is false. Hence, the tendency for people to be divided among the confessional religious bodies, belonging exclusively and decisively to one or other of them, is strong. Hence, the organization of the entire population of the region into many mutually exclusive rival communities defined more by religious identity than by territorial claims. For an individual, it is as socially unthinkable to be associated with two or more such communities as it would be to be associated with none.

The questions of individual autonomy and human agency presuppose a shared foundation of morality and binding sentiments that unite autonomous individuals who are unable to negotiate their own spiritual space. When it came to interacting and associating with other human beings in public space, however, diverse groups fell back on their religious resources to derive and articulate the rules affecting public life:

Say [Muhammad]: "My Lord has forbidden only those deeds which are shameful, be they done in public or in private, and [my Lord has forbidden] acts of oppression and transgression against the rights of others." (7:24)

The recognition and implementation of the religious values of sharing and mutuality created a civil religion that encouraged coexistence with those who, even when they did not share the dominant group's particular vision of salvation, could share in a concern for living in peace with justice. There is nothing modern or liberal about such an acknowledgment of individual autonomous dignity and the human need for moral and spiritual nourishment — such yearnings are evident throughout history. The existence of similar human conditions in other cultures and the universally recognizable laws of nature that regulate interaction between religion and history, faith and power, ideology and politics, suggests the common moral and spiritual terrain that human beings treat in their perennial search for solutions to the problem of injustice, oppression, and poverty.

Reminder to the Children of Adam

Children of Adam! Let not Satan tempt you as he brought your parents out of the Garden, stripping them of their garments to show them their nakedness. Surely Satan sees you, he and his tribe, from where you see them not. We have made the Satans the friends of those who have rejected faith. (7:26)

The capacity to be tempted and to accept or reject faith with its grave consequences on the moral conduct presupposes the existence of an innate ability that can guide a person to a desired goal. This innate capability is part of the human nature — the *fitra* — with which God shapes humanity. The innate capability encompasses the faculty of moral reasoning. Satanic forces are intent to strip human beings of this moral sensibility, which the Qur'an regards as impending if humanity does not heed to the warning in the above-cited verse. The innate capacity is endowed with the ethical awareness whose ability to shape laws of conduct is hampered when human beings fall victim to the whisperings of Satan. But is this unavoidable, especially when God has allowed Satan to engage in his trickery and deception? The conversation following Satan's refusal to prostrate before Adam seems to suggest that it is God's decision to allow Satan to tempt and misguide humanity:

Said God: "Get you [Satan] down out of the garden; It is not for you to wax proud here. So get out, you are surely among the humbled." Satan said: "Respite me till the day they shall be raised [up from the grave]." God said: "[Your request has been granted.] You are among the ones who have respite." Satan said: "Now, because You have [thrown me out] and I have lost the way, I shall surely sit in ambush for them on Your straight path; then I shall come on them before them and from behind them, from their right hands and their left hands; You will not find most of them thankful." God said: "Go forth from here in disgrace and banished. Those of them that follow you — I shall assuredly fill the Hell with all of you." (7:14–19)

Do human beings have a choice in the matter of being misguided by Satan? To be sure, the verse plainly limits Satan's ability to misguide only "those of them that follow" him, and only these will be punished with the Hell. Thus, God assures humankind that Satan "has no hold over those who believe and trust in their Lord. His hold is over those who take him for their friend and ascribe associates to God" (16:100). In other words, one needs faith in God and trust in God to withstand Satanic attacks on one's moral sense. This is the role of revelatory guidance that becomes accessible through declaration of faith.

In this sense morality needs religion to become a dependable force in the human spiritual and ethical development. Adam, as God's vicegerent, is the founder of universal ethical life, fortified with the particular revelation received from God as God's envoy. It is indeed God's decree that humanity will always need both religion and morality to lead it to create an ethical order on earth. One without the other will be an easy prey to Satanic temptations. The Qur'an demonstrates, time and again, that when Satan enters the ethical realm he destroys the human ability to distinguish right from wrong, exposing the human "nakedness" as a ploy for further corruption and wickedness; and, when he enters the religious sphere he destroys sincerity and humility, replacing these with arrogance and self-righteousness. Hence, it behooves humanity to thank God for entrusting it with the knowledge to defeat ignorance and immorality, and charging it with justice to uproot injustices and inequities.

At the same time, Satan's entry in human life right from the genesis shows that had it not been for Satan the first human couple would
have continued to live in the Garden, rendering life on earth hardly a
challenge for the posterity. Nevertheless, it seems that as a vicegerent of
God, human being had to inhabit the world outside the garden in order
to exercise divinely invested authority among God's creation. As such,
for Adam to remain in the Garden forever was inconceivable. His terrestrial connection is part of the divine plan. The life on earth provides
him with an opportunity to work hard to earn his lasting reward back
in the Garden in the Hereafter. Is this what God meant in replying to the
angels' objection to put Adam as God's vicegerent on earth: "Assuredly
I know what you do not know"?

This unfolding of the drama of creation with Adam playing the main
role renders God's vicegerency a blessing for humanity. It also explains
the divine Trust — the *amāna,* which the heavens and mountains shirked
from accepting, and which God let human being accept, despite knowing
his ignorance and tyranny. The Qur'an reminds its readers that God
is Omniscient Creator and God certainly knows where to put God's
message as a trust (6:124). The angels did not know this. They were
veiled from the knowledge about the future of humanity that only God
possessed. It was through the creation of humanity and endowing it with
vicegerency that the divine sovereignty could be manifested on earth. In
turn, human exercise of the divinely endowed authority could create
the ideal public order that would reflect the divine justice. Through the
creation of such an order will human beings deserve to earn their final
reward with God.

The last mystery in God-human encounter that still awaits a vindica-
tion is the spreading of corruption and bloodshed by humanity. When
the angels pointed out the human tendency to shed blood and spread
corruption, God did not reject it as a false accusation against humanity,
but simply retorted by declaring that what God knew the angels did not.
The Qur'an vividly draws the images of violent confrontations in human
society. It regards humans as capable of the kind of wrongdoing that is
best addressed by punitive measures designed to combat threats to the
social fabric. However, God's solution to this reality of human tendencies
to resort to violence is to teach Adam to "turn unto your Lord":

Thereafter Adam received certain words from his Lord, and He turned toward him; truly He turns, and is All-compassionate. (2:37)

These words inspired Adam to repent. The overarching message of the Qur'an is God's forgiving power to compensate for human shortcomings, whether in dealing with oneself or others. God's forgiveness leads to restoration of self-respect, which can lead to better human relationships. There is a deep moral insight in the following verse of the Qur'an:

Your Lord has made bestowal of Mercy incumbent upon Himself; if any of you commits an evil in ignorance, and then repents and mends his ways, [he will be certainly forgiven]. Be sure that He is All-forgiving and All-merciful. (6:55)

On the one hand, humankind is assured of God's forgiving nature; on the other, humans are required to demonstrate their predisposition to moral humility in reforming and restoring membership in society. In order to earn divine forgiveness, human beings must act responsibly toward one another. They must take the responsibility for wrongdoing in a personal and social way. Acknowledgment of harm or injury caused to others or to oneself is the first and key step in seeking forgiveness. "Turning to God" is turning in repentance to earn divine mercy and forgiveness. It is a withdrawal from behavior injurious to oneself and to others. "Turning to God in repentance" (39:53) serves as the most important means by which a wrongdoer can distance oneself from one's wrongdoing. Those who are looking to establish peace within themselves and with others in society must engage in the ritual of apology by sincerely humbling themselves to repair their self-respect. According to the Qur'an, it is unthinkable to regain the confidence of other humans without first working toward the restoration of one's vitiated sense of security and integrity.

Providing an inner sense of security and integrity is the function of faith. Faith bestows safety and peace. The most important Qur'anic teaching concerning faith and its external projection in action undergirds the notion of *īmān* (faith) in the meaning of "to be at peace," "to be safe." In order to gain security and tap their vast potential for creating an ideal public order, human beings can and ought to avoid moral and physical peril, individually and collectively. The destiny of every society depends on how faith shapes the quality of individual and collective behavior. Genuine faith in God sharpens the human ability to know that wrongs done to others are more profoundly wrongs done to oneself.

The fundamental problem faced by humanity today is lack of firm resolve in matters of divine guidance made accessible through revelation. Words harkening to God's warnings about the perils of disobedience are repeated throughout the Qur'an. The paradigm case of this situation occurs in the context of Adam's disobedience despite God's warning about the consequences of eating the forbidden fruit. Individuals and societies cannot ignore the potential of disobedience, as reminded in the creation narrative. These acts lead to fragmentation and destruction. Disbelief in God's guidance leads to self-deception, narrow-mindedness, rejection of truth, and a total privation of moral energy. The crucial human defense against such self-abasement is vigilance against the self-deception that arises from all myopic interests, whether individual or collective. Although the Qur'an frequently emphasizes God's mercy, pardon, and forgiveness, it requires human beings to respond to their divinely ordained inner disposition that gives humans the ability to extricate the self from self-deception. Interpersonal human justice depends on one's ability to realize a moral injury done to others and to work toward wiping the slate clean. Divine mercy and pardon await those who care deeply about others and their relationships with those who seek their forgiveness. The humility expressed through genuine repentance and surrender to God restores our self-respect in the community.

What stops human beings from self-reform, from turning toward God, seeking divine forgiveness, and working toward the betterment of society? Two grievous sins highlighted in the Qur'an are arrogance and jealousy. Religious arrogance has been one of the major causes of antagonism across cultures. Powerful political and religious institutions in some parts of the world have ironically worked hand in hand to institutionalize hatred in the name of God and to suffocate any attempt to pave the way for better understanding among different religious communities. Arrogance leads to the trampling of the rights of others and thus often engenders violent conflicts.

Jealousy is also a source of arrogant behavior. Jealousy leads to aggressive behavior, inflicting physical, psychological, or social harm on others. Since jealousy is self-cultivated vice, it is remediable. The antidote to jealousy is social interaction, which fosters a sense of interdependence, thereby reducing violence caused by jealousy among individuals. Furthermore, recognition of interdependence requires people to realize that intentional wrongdoing prompted by resentment degrades others and causes moral and spiritual injury. Hence, when jealousy occurs, an essential and effective remedy for it is an act of sincere repentance and public apology for the wrongdoing. Such an acknowledgment in public can serve as a religious prelude to the just resolution of the conflict caused by the injury inflicted upon those whose well-being should be the concern of the entire community.

As God's vicegerent Adam is entrusted with the responsibility of exercising God's authority with justice. Since authority engenders arrogance Adam needs to constantly remind himself that when God's caliph begins to wrong people he then becomes God's adversary. In return for this behavior God renders null and void the argument of whoever contends with God. It is in this specific meaning that the fall of God's vicegerent is conceivable in Islam. The source of the angels' objection to Adam's appointment as God's vicegerent is the human capacity to do evil and shed blood. According to the Qur'an, the source of this socially depraved conduct is the worship of Satan, who was the first being to utter the statement that has become the source of all human conflicts: "I am better than he!" (38:76). The Qur'an warns all humanity against succumbing to this Satanic claim of superiority:

> "Children of Adam! Did I not make a covenant with you that you should not serve Satan? [Did I not tell you that] he is your sworn enemy? And that you should serve Me, for this is a straight path." (36:61–62).

"Serving Satan" (literally, worshiping Satan) is actually following Satan's path of arrogance and zest for conflict, which were demonstrated at the time of creation when, as discussed above, Satan swore that he would entrap human beings and drag them to perdition (17:63) by instigating them to rebel against God's order. "Serving Me," that is, God, restores the original state of creation through the *fitra*, that natural inclination toward obedience and doing good, the straight path.

In final analysis, the question this essay's title raises — namely, whether God's vicegerency is a blessing or a curse for humanity — is logically inconsistent with God's overall plan, which is clearly stated in the Qur'an as the establishment of a divinely ordained system that institutes good and prevents evil. Why would God place someone on earth who, as the angels thought, would spread corruption and shed blood? It is unthinkable that God, being most merciful and most compassionate, would place someone prone to do evil as God's representative and caretaker on earth. Despite an explicit recognition of human weaknesses that can be manipulated by Satan to undo God's work, the very fact that God entrusted humanity with the exercise of God's authority over the creation says a great deal about God's confidence in God's appointment. Hence, while it is true that people harm one another, their inherent social nature demands their commitment to interpersonal justice. In order to achieve the ideal of justice they need to act responsibly toward one another. This is the challenge of being God's vicegerent. God has not repealed God's decision in this matter as yet. Hence, we can assume that the authority is invested in humanity until the End of History. In the meantime, human beings are faced with a constant struggle to find ways of defeating tyranny and ignorance, the two deadliest enemies of humankind, and to prove to the angels that, despite the horrors of human destruction from time to time in history, God's decision to make Adam God's vicegerent and entrust him as the caretaker of God's creation was wise.

Chapter 3

EMBODYING GOD'S IMAGE
Created, Broken, and Redeemed
Lisa Sowle Cahill

I begin with a statement of theological conviction, a confession of biblical faith:

> The book of Genesis proclaims the unity of the human race as God's good creation. Humanity's destiny is to represent God on earth through fellowship enacted in God's image. Sinfulness mars this human vocation, bringing violence among humans, and between humans and the rest of creation. Yet God's redeeming action in history will continue and heal the dynamic of creation. God brings all that is created into consummate union with the divine reality itself. Wherever justice and compassion heal suffering and create inclusive communities, there divine presence is discovered and the image of God restored.
>
> Moreover, the realm of "natural embodied life" refers to everything human and especially to all moral relationships, not just to sex, gender, and procreation. Family, work, education, political cooperation, and religious practice all constitute our concrete "place" on earth and within creation, inhabited through the body. Our embodied existence is the forum within which reconciliation and salvation come to us.

In essence, this is a statement of classic Christian faith; yet I have framed it in terms designed to have ecumenical appeal, hoping that Jews and Muslims would agree to sign on. Its key elements are that the image of God in humanity resides in embodied relationships, not in unique attributes; that the realm of "natural embodied life" includes every dimension of morality; that God's image in us is restored through just and compassionate relationships; and that human relationships that image God engage the whole creation and are responsible for it.

One cannot, however, move quickly on to fine-tune the details of a faith statement such as this. Why not? My faith statement is, upon consideration, quite problematic. It is limited. It is provincial. Worst of all, it may not be true. And even if the interpretation I recommend is true to Genesis, Genesis may not be true to human existence as we find it, nor true to an authentic experience of the divine. My teacher at the University of Chicago was James Gustafson. While Gustafson grants that his theology may have transgressed the limits of orthodox Christianity,[1] Gustafson insists in his later writings that religious believers confront history and the hard edges of their own experience, as well as the frightening reality of cosmic forces that bear down upon and destroy human beings as well as bear them up. Human aspirations to universal compassion and justice may go against the design of creation, or fly in the face of the fact that there is no "design" at all. In a 2003 book, aptly and characteristically titled *An Examined Faith: The Grace of Self-Doubt*,[2] Gustafson challenges us with a favorite point:

> Does *any* historical and other human evidence count against our teaching and preaching about a providential Deity who provides redemption and hope to those in despair, to the people of nations devastated by decades of strife in Asia, Africa, or Central America? If God is gracious, is God also impotent to actualize those gracious purposes in natural and human-generated catastrophes?
>
> ...Can I, who have suffered with the destitute vicariously more than actually, not wonder if God's preference for the poor and the oppressed is only some kind of generous wish, and not a divine intention actualized in human events and actions?
>
> ...The Almighty has his own purposes.[3]

---

1. James M. Gustafson, *Ethics from a Theocentric Perspective, Volume One: Theology and Ethics* (Chicago: University of Chicago Press, 1981), 278–79.
2. James M. Gustafson, *An Examined Faith: The Grace of Self-Doubt* (Minneapolis: Fortress Press, 2003).
3. Ibid., 100–101, 105–6.

The statement with which I began, and which I truly believe, represents a point of view — one not shared by Gustafson, for example. I am a Christian, Catholic, feminist theologian, a social ethicist, a white woman, a member of a North Atlantic, so-called democratic, and also capitalist society, a society with liberal political traditions. I am living at the beginning of the third millennium, I am a wife and mother, and a member of the academic establishment and socioeconomic upper class. None of my close relations has been killed in war, raped, or tortured; my children are safe, well fed, and educated. I can more easily than some others, perhaps, have confidence that justice and compassion, uniting all human beings and the entire creation, are stronger than hatred, violence, and death; they are available to us in trust and hope through the creative and reclaiming power of a transcendent, merciful God.

Let me point out some of the aspects of my opening statement about the image of God that reflect these particular circumstances. First of all, the very fact that I left any mention of Jesus Christ out of it reflects the ability of a twenty-first century North American Christian theologian to enter into ecumenical situations with Jews and Muslims. In a new millennium departure from our historic traditions, we are discussing the original and contemporary meanings, and the political impact, of "scripture" in a calm and dialogical way, seeking common understanding. In particular, as a Catholic Christian, I believe that God is found in all the world's major religious traditions, and is discovered not only in explicitly religious endeavors, but wherever just communities are established. (Despite its flat-footed, tactless, and untimely assertion that Christianity is the superior religion, the essential message of the 2000 Vatican document, *Dominus Iesus,* was that *all* genuine religions mediate salvation from God.)

Moreover, as a modern-day heir of the Thomistic natural-law tradition, I believe that human *moral* experiences are shared in some fundamental way, that the contours of basic human flourishing can be discussed reasonably by cultures together, and can result in values to inform just societies. For that matter, with the modern papal social encyclicals, I believe that societies can *become* more just. Indeed, justice can, on the whole, increase for the peoples of the world if we come together in good will and good faith to discuss what justice demands of us. Although that seems to be the essential premise on which this book is centered, it is in fact one of the most vulnerable assumptions for social reformers of any stripe today. Today's newspaper headlines offer plenty of reasons to think that genocidal violence, economic exploitation, racism, crimes against children, the manipulation of religion for political ends, and degradation of the environment are in undiminished evidence among us.

As far as the image of God in humanity is concerned, I do not need to belabor the point that religious traditions supposedly adhering to this doctrine have been just as industrious as any others in disproving its force. Gustavo Gutiérrez quotes a sixteenth-century conqueror, Juan Ginés de Sepúlveda, who had this to say in defense of the enslavement of the native peoples of the Americas:

> ... in prudence, invention, and every manner of virtue and human sentiment, they are as inferior to the Spaniards as children to adults, women to men, the cruel and inhumane to the gentle, those intemperate beyond all bounds to the continent and moderate ... [and] finally, I might almost say, as monkeys to human beings.[4]

We Christians kept up this tradition well when we brought Africans here in bondage and exterminated six million "subhumans" during the Shoah. The Catholic feminist Margaret Farley, in commenting on the Christian tradition of women's subordination, refers to "the devastating refusal by Christian theology to attribute the fullness of the *imago Dei* to women,"[5] since major thinkers like Augustine and Aquinas hold women inferior to and subordinate to men in both body and soul. Mary Catherine Hilkert, another feminist theologian, has asked whether the symbol "image of God" has a future at all, pointing to "the history of

---

4. Gustavo Gutiérrez, *Las Casas: In Search of the Poor of Jesus Christ* (Maryknoll, N.Y.: Orbis Books, 1993), 293.

5. Margaret A. Farley, "Sources of Sexual Inequality in the History of Christian Thought," *Journal of Religion* 56, no. 2 (1976): 166. See also Nonna Verna Harrison, "Women, Human Identity, and the Image of God: Antiochene Interpretations," *Journal of Early Christian Studies* 9, no. 2 (2001): 205–49; Kari Elisabeth Børreson, *Subordination and Equivalence: The Nature and Role of Woman in Augustine and Thomas Aquinas*, trans. Charles H. Talbot (Washington, D.C.: University Press of America, 1981); and Kari Elisabeth Børreson, ed., *The Image of God: Gender Models in Judaeo-Christian Tradition* (Minneapolis: Fortress Press, 1995).

human domination it has served to foster."[6] Historically, this metaphor has licensed humanity to exploit the rest of the natural world, and justified the oppression of huge categories of people who are judged to be less in God's image than the dominating class — most universally, men over women.

And yet: Christians, Jews, and Muslims find continuing power in the metaphor of humanity as "God's image." It speaks to our hope for a less violent future, it draws out other themes in our respective traditions having to do with real experiences of grace and redemption, and, perhaps most importantly, it does resonate with "the real" as we experience it morally. That is to say, there is a commonality across cultures of forms of human need, vulnerability, opportunity, sustenance, and accomplishment. Hence, William Schweiker calls for a renewal of Christian humanism.[7] Identifying one of the main theological tasks today as the negotiation of the space between the local and the global, Robert Schreiter notes that "denial of difference can lead to the colonization of a culture and its imagination," but "denial of similarities promotes an anomic situation where no dialogue appears possible and only power will prevail."[8]

The biblical symbol "image of God" reflects actual fellowship, healing, and redemption experienced on occasions when we do meet in understanding, overcome old hatreds, and begin to work together for shared goals. There a transcendent power is discovered that convinces us we are at last manifesting in our relationships God's creative power. These experiences are fragmentary, fragile, and elusive. But they evoke the connection between the human and the divine that the biblical symbol captures. The full power of "image of God" lies in its judgment upon the broken connection, the violence toward humanity's divine origin, which constitutes defection from the created fellowship for which we are meant. Judgment in light of the original vocation to be God's

6. Mary Catherine Hilkert,, "*Imago Dei:* Does the Symbol Have a Future?," Santa Clara Lectures 8/3 (Santa Clara, Calif.: Bannan Institute, Santa Clara University, 2002): 2.

7. William Schweiker, *Theological Ethics and Global Dynamics: In the Time of Many Worlds* (Oxford: Blackwell, 2004); "A Preface to Ethics," *Journal of Religious Ethics* 32 (2004): 13–37.

8. Robert J. Schreiter, *The New Catholicity: Theology between the Global and the Local* (Maryknoll, N.Y.: Orbis Books, 1997), 43.

image thus names sin and enables convinced action toward a lost but still perceptible ideal.

Those who suffer most from the personal and systemic violence that sin wreaks on the human body and spirit seem *not* to be those most in despair of using religious symbols like image of God to urge the restoration of just relationships. The African theologian Mercy Amba Oduyoye (from Ghana) writes of the suffering of African women, mentioning lack of education, unemployment, sickness, ecological threats, natural disasters, female circumcision, patriarchal marriage, and widowhood rites. She depicts Africa today as a "hostile world" that "debases one's very humanity by the intention of race and racism," that "places the onus of human survival on women but slights them," that "exploits the weak to enrich the strong," and that "seems to know nothing of what it means to share community with God, the Beginner."[9] Yet Oduyoye still champions a "spirituality of resistance" and hopes for renewed community that can make "a concerted effort towards building up an empowering society that upholds and promotes the full humanity of every individual."[10]

She concludes her essay with the following:

In the search for liberating hermeneutics, many women have claimed the biblical affirmation of our being created "in the image of God" both for the promotion of women's self-worth and self-esteem and to protest dehumanization by others. Granted, this seems to be wearing thin, but without it the whole edifice of human relations seems to crumble and fall. If one is in the image of God, then one is expected to practice the hospitality, compassion, and justice that characterize God. The Akan say, "All human beings are the children of God." What this calls for is mutuality in our relationships, seeking "one earth community," one household of the God of life.[11]

Reversing the usual order of things, I have given you my conclusions first. Next I will expand and interpret the biblical evidence in favor of my

---

9. Mercy Amba Oduyoye, "Spirituality of Resistance and Reconstruction," in Mary John Mananzan, et al., eds., *Women Resisting Violence: Spirituality for Life* (Maryknoll N.Y.: Orbis Books, 1996), 162. I found this essay cited by Mary Catherine Hilkert (see n. 6 above).

10. Ibid., 169.

11. Ibid., 170.

statement of theological conviction, then turn to the grounds for its truth and realism. Ultimately, evidence of the truth of all that "image of God" symbolizes consists in collaborative action, in which the experiences of God in human life, and of human life in God's image, are expanded and reconfirmed. Such collaboration must bring together intercultural, inter-religious, interracial, and interclass "communities," created and built up by "transversal" work among people whose starting points are different religious and moral traditions.[12]

"Image of God" in Genesis

The Image as Created

In both Genesis and the Qur'an, God creates the first human body from "the slime of the earth," and breathes into it the human spirit, quickly following with the creation of a companion. Body, spirit, and companionship are all essential to being human. In interpretations of Genesis 1:27, there has been a tendency for theologians and ethicists to seek substantive and unique human attributes with which to associate the divine image in "man." Intellect and free will, or the soul in general, have been favorites. Some commentators distinguish theologians who hang the image on certain attributes from another set who are said to have a more relational view of the image[13] — especially Karl Barth, for whom the image consists primarily in our being called to "fellow-humanity," to "freedom in fellowship."[14] According to Barth, "God created man in His own image in the fact that He did not create him alone but in this connexion and fellowship," for God, like humanity, "is not solitary," but properly "in connexion and fellowship."[15]

---

12. On the concept of "transversal" (rather than universal) moral values, see Hilary Charlesworth and Christine Chinkin, *The Boundaries of International Law: A Feminist Analysis* (Manchester, UK: Manchester University Press, 2000), 51, citing Nira Yuval-Davis, "Women, Ethnicity and Empowerment," in A. Oakley and J. Mitchell, eds., *Who's Afraid of Feminism? Seeing Through the Backlash* (New York: The New Press, 1997), 77, 95–97.

13. Douglas John Hall, *Imaging God: Dominion as Stewardship* (Grand Rapids, Mich.: Eerdmans; New York: Friendship, 1986); Paul A. Brink, "Selves in Relation: Theories of Community and the Imago Dei Doctrine," in Thomas W. Heilke and Ashley Woodiwiss, eds., *The Re-Enchantment of Political Science: Christian Scholars Engage Their Discipline* (Lanham, Md., and Boulder, Co.: Lexington Books, 2001).

14. Karl Barth, *Church Dogmatics* III/4 (Edinburgh: T. & T. Clark, 1961), 117.

15. Karl Barth, *Church Dogmatics* III/2 (Edinburgh: T. & T. Clark, 1960), 324.

In a work on "stewardship" commissioned by the National Council of Churches, Douglas John Hall contrasts a "substantialist" and a "relational" strand of historical interpretations of the image of God. In his view, whenever "ratiocination" is given a privileged place in conceptions of the image, and thus made "the chief good and end in life," the inevitable result is that "every being — nonhuman and human — not manifesting this capacity, or manifesting it insufficiently, must be relegated to a lower category of existence and value."[16] Moreover, the substantialist strand, focused as it usually is on rationality, tends to overlook the implication of human reason in sin and evil. It also ignores the fact that human existence, and hence the image of God, involves the human body and human physicality as much as spirituality and reason. As he puts it, mentioning the Manhattan project and all that has followed from it, faith in "untrammeled reason — answerable to no gods, no holy writ, no moral law — [has] built a *civitas terrena* poised on the edge of oblivion."[17]

An alternative, more biblical, conception, in Hall's view, links the image with relationality, especially humanity's created capacity for love (*agapē, khesed*).[18] God intends humanity as a "being-in-relationship." Humanity's essential nature is not found in the abstract or in an isolated specimen defined by certain capacities, but "by considering human beings in the context of their many-dimensioned relationships."[19] The distinctive "endowments" of human beings exist only for the purpose of entering into relationships with others and with God.[20]

In Christian tradition, rationality and will have certainly been stressed as components of the image of God in "man." But even if we consider premodern authors, we can see that the social and relational dimensions of the image of God in humanity are hardly absent. Augustine looks for the image in "the rational or intellectual soul of man," but stresses that image refers to the soul's power to understand and behold God (not to its innate characteristics as such), and that this power consists

16. Hall, *Imaging God*, 109.
17. Ibid., 111.
18. Ibid., 113.
19. Ibid., 115.
20. Ibid., 116.

in a trinity of memory, understanding, and will.[21] Thus, the intrinsic relationality of God and of humanity are brought together in analogy, and it is in this mutual analogous relationship that the image of God in humans is realized. Similarly, Aquinas attributes the image of God to "man," "by reason of his intellectual nature." However, Aquinas clarifies that humans' distinctive intellect images God because it is the basis of relationship; he holds that the primary meaning of the divine image, as "common to men," is "a natural aptitude for understanding and loving God."[22] Again, John Calvin asserts that the image of God is in the human soul and its powers, and extends to everything in respect of which humans surpass animals. But humans are not truly a "mirror of the divine glory" unless they possess "knowledge" of God's will, "true righteousness and holiness." Unless the intellect is enlightened and the heart righteous in relation to God, the image of God in the human soul is vitiated.[23]

In the last thirty years, biblical scholars, preeminently Claus Westermann among Christian scholars,[24] have confirmed this hunch of theologians that the image of God in humanity must be sought in forms and directions of relationship. They have developed the point that humans' relationships to one another as well as to God are part of God's image in humanity. According to Westermann, the image of God has an inherently social meaning: "man in the Creation narrative is a collective. Creation in the image of God is not concerned with an individual, but with mankind, the species, man."[25] By now it is well known that the precise original meaning of the term translated "image" is unclear, but that it probably connotes a representative or representation of an authoritative figure such as a king. An overview article in the *Anchor Bible Dictionary* is

21. Augustine, "The Trinity," in John Burnaby, ed., *Augustine: Later Works* (Philadelphia: Westminster, 1955), 103, 105–6; Book IV.6, 8.

22. Thomas Aquinas, *Summa Theologica*, trans. Fathers of the English Dominican Province (New York: Benziger Brothers, 1948), 471.

23. John Calvin, *Institutes of the Christian Religion*, ed. John T. McNeill; trans. Ford Lewis Battles, vol. 1 (Louisville: Westminster John Knox, 1960), 186–90.

24. Claus Westermann, *Creation*, trans. John J. Scullion, S.J. (Philadelphia: Fortress Press, 1974); *Genesis 1–11*, *Genesis 12–36*, and *Genesis 37–50*, Continental Commentaries, trans. John Scullion (Minneapolis: Augsburg, 1984, 1985, and 1986, respectively); *Genesis*, trans. David E. Green (Edinburgh: T. & T. Clark, 1995; originally published in the U.S. by Wm. B. Eerdmans, 1987).

25. Westermann, *Creation*, 56.

typical. The author sensibly suggests (in the light of Gen. 5:1–2, in which Adam's son is said to be according to his image) that the image of God implies that humans are created with the capacity for relationship with God, but also as able to function analogously to God and on behalf of God within created relationships. In fact, their relation to God is realized and tested in and through their relations with others, and in the collective or social forms these relations take. Hence, it is the whole person who is ultimately the image, rather than a distinct aspect, and the image is fulfilled in community with God and others, not in the being of an individual as such.[26]

The points that I especially want to develop are that the image of God in humans is communal, and that community and all human relations are embodied. The norm of human community established by the biblical symbol image of God is a social unity-in-difference. This is revealed by the declaration of the first human being in recognizing his counterpart: "This at last is bone of my bones, and flesh of my flesh" (Gen. 2:23).

The paradoxical paradigm of humanity's "different sameness" is the creation of woman and man as "helpers" and partners for one another. I here place the emphasis not on gender duality or sex, in their own right or as somehow most definitive of what it is to be human, but on the essential fact of human differences in general, differences that are part of our being human. Human beings are always and everywhere differentiated (symbolized aptly in Genesis by sex differences, since this is the most universally occurring difference in human embodiment). Yet humans, as constitutively different are also constitutively destined for fellowship or union, and so are human collectivities or societies.

I want to emphasize, as a Christian ethicist, that the sociality of human beings, through which they image God, is made possible by and expressed through human embodiment. In Genesis 2, it is specifically their embodiment that distinguishes the woman and man as "different" partners in relationship, and it is their embodiment that allows mutual recognition (granting that the Yahwist tells the story from the man's

---

26. Edward M. Curtis, "Image of God (OT)," *Anchor Bible Dictionary,* ed. David Noel Freedman (New York: Doubleday, 1992), 3:390.

point of view!). The human body establishes the most basic needs that society serves for everyone in every culture: food, shelter, labor that provides these; reproduction of the species and the institutions that organize and socialize reproduction, that is, marriage and family. The human body makes it possible for us to communicate and to express our spiritual capacities in art and religious practices. Above all, the human body makes it possible to recognize and acknowledge other human beings as like ourselves, with the same essential needs and vulnerabilities, and as persons with whom we can enter into relationship. The exclamation of the first man, when presented with the first human "other," represents the capacity for fellowship of all human beings, inherent in our embodied connectedness and communicative capacity: "This at last is bone of my bones, flesh of my flesh" (2:23). This declaration shows us a human being recognizing, not just a woman, but a human counterpart, much better than any other "living creature" that had been brought to him as a remedy for his loneliness (2:18–20).

The imaginative device of depicting the woman as taken from the rib of the man, while obviously counterfactual to the literal processes of human reproduction, sex, or marriage, underscores the unity of two differentiated creatures in a single embodied nature. It tells us that the bond of woman and man can be just as strong as the bond of parent and child, or kin and kin, and indicates that sexual unions that establish new households create bonds as strong or stronger than that of the original kin groups of the partners (2:24). The embodied differences of the first two, symbolized by nakedness, are not yet cause for suffering or strife (2:25). The first instance and experience of human difference tell us instead that human difference is always destined and called to union. "Bone of my bones, flesh of my flesh" fellowship is the moral ideal or criterion that should structure all human relationships in the image of God. From the beginning of their existence, God is in beneficent relation to humans; so to be in God's image, humans are to be in similar fellowship with each other. In Genesis, the two most fundamental of all embodied social endeavors are family and work. Each is connected to the creation of the human body in God's image, because each constitutes a basic form of relationship, in which bodily needs and capacities bring people together cooperatively, in joint projects.

In Genesis, creation itself has a forward momentum, manifested in the command to "subdue the earth" and in the blessing of fertility (1:28), as well as in the idea that the humans are not only to "keep" and preserve the garden, but also to "till" or cultivate it (2:15). Humans are not placed in creation as a completed paradise made for their passive enjoyment. Work, as endowing human life with purpose and fulfillment, and as an activity that images God's own creative work, is a fundamental aspect of human existence.[27] Throughout the book of Genesis, work on the land, tilling the land, and reaping the bounty of the land are part of God's promises. Humans are also to create and nurture the next generation, contributing "pro-creatively" to the open-ended future of all for which God is providing. Procreation establishes the family and kin groups that carry God's promises forward, in Abraham, Isaac, and Jacob. The embodied work of procreation, parenthood, and contribution to the ongoing life of extended families blesses humans with their most fundamental and universal experiences of love, whose possibilities are also suggested by the polyvalent "one flesh" unity of the first couple (2:24).

The book of Genesis is, of course, a composite of many different oral and written traditions, accomplished by many editors over generations. The natures of God, of ideal humanity, and of faithful or heroic individual and community behavior, are presented in different ways. We see this already in the contrast of "the majestic deity of chapter 1, who creates by issuing executive decrees, with the earthy God of chapter 2, who sits in the mud and plays with clay."[28] Nevertheless, biblical scholar Thomas Mann identifies two literary devices in the book of Genesis that serve to link originally diverse sources: the "generations" formula, which occurs eleven times in Genesis; and the divine "promises" of blessing, beginning immediately after the creation of male and female in God's image (1:28), and eventually extended to "all the families of the earth" through Abraham (12:3).[29] The generations and promises themes work to extend the relation and calling of two first *individuals* into *communal* vocations.

27. Westermann, *Creation*, 80–82.
28. Thomas W. Mann, " 'All the Families of the Earth': The Theological Unity of Genesis," *Interpretation* 45, no. 4 (1991): 342.
29. Ibid., 343.

The promises include children, land, and nationhood, but above all and beyond these, as their meaning and fulfillment, is relation in community to God. These devices of generational connection and faithful divine promise link the creation of humanity, man and woman, with a family history and a community under God.

To recapitulate, the image of God consists in human bonds and communal relations, which the biblical book of Genesis places in the midst of the whole creation, and focuses through the universal, embodied, and social experiences of family and work. Human relations that image God carry forward the dynamic of creation, uniting differences through fellowship, and fulfilling God's promise of a human future in which the human relation to God is embodied in family, social cooperation, and work, and productive stewardship of the environment.

The Image Broken by Sin

It is in humanity's whole history, through generations, that the image of God should be fulfilled in relationship to God, but in which the curse of sin is instead experienced. "Human beings are created 'in the image of God' to be vice-regents of the world (1:28), but they quickly and repeatedly attempt to be more than that, to 'become like God' by overcoming their limitations (3:5), to be superhuman rather than human, supernatural rather than natural, autonomous ('by one's own law') rather than responsible."[30] They consequently violate the unity that structures their very existence by turning on one another as the first two humans do in Genesis 3. The same spheres of relationship in which God's image is manifest also present human beings with their opportunity to use deception, domination, and violence to cause great harm. Sin and redemption both work within the frame of historical action — focused on work and family — projected by the book of Genesis.[31]

Sin is more than spiritual pride or intellectual arrogance. The full "human nature" of sin is displayed mythically in Genesis 2 and 3. As we have seen, the first man's and woman's shared humanity is signified in their bodily sharing of the first human's rib (2:21–22). They

---

30. Ibid., 347.
31. Terence E. Fretheim, "The Reclamation of Creation: Redemption and Law in Exodus," *Interpretation* 45, no.4 (1991): 358–59.

create community as "one flesh" (2:23), and inhabit a lush garden in harmony with other creatures. On the downside, they enact disobedience by mutual physical accompaniment in the eating of fruit (3:6), in unison become ashamed and even afraid of their differentiated embodiment (symbolically their "nakedness," 3:7, 10), and hide from the view of the Lord (3:8).

The result of their crime is the breaking of relationships with God, one another, and even their physical environment. The earth now exacts toil before it feeds them (3:19). Even their own bodies mediate suffering, making pain part of human embodied being. Just as creation and image apply to humanity existing in community, so does sin. Not alone but together do human beings sin, and their sin affects their entire life in community,[32] as well as their embodiment. Their own bodies mediate suffering, making pain intrinsic to human physicality; physical "labor" will henceforth be painful, for woman and for man alike, in productive and reproductive work, symbolized by agriculture and by childbirth (3:16; 3:9). Sin brings conflict with one's own body, and with life borne within it, for the woman (representing not all women, but all human beings); and sin brings conflict between human bodily needs and capacities and the physical environment on which human sustenance is dependent, for the man (representing not all men, but all human beings) (Genesis 3).

Furthermore, bodily sexual differentiation becomes an excuse for domination of man over woman, prefiguring the exploitation of human physical differences to justify all kinds of oppression. In Genesis, Cain and Abel present the almost immediate and ultimate destruction of God-imaging relationship. In a corruption of the embodied "generations" trajectory of creation, which ought to be the basis and school of fellowship, Adam's and Eve's own children pull their parents' embodied sexual and familial unity into the future in horrific ways. The brothers divide in conflict over the value and rights of their physical work on the land, and its social and religious significance. Their fraternal and human "one flesh" unity ends in fratricidal violence, causing further alienation from the earth itself, and exile from kindred and community (4:1–14). The

32. Westermann, *Creation,* 73.

later bestowal of blessing on Noah and his sons in Genesis 9, with its companion outlawing of murder, confirms that human life in the image of God especially excludes the killing of other human beings (9:6).

Fundamentally, sin consists in wanting to be like God, knowing good and evil, and also having control over the results of this knowledge. Humans and their communities sin when they, like Cain, make themselves and their particular projects the center of religion and morality, perversely validating their limited and particular goals with idolatrous rhetoric about their own transcendent worth and the ultimacy of their work.

The corruption of sin in and through our natural embodied existence is especially evident in the fact that human groups invariably define and stigmatize other groups by identifying physically different characteristics — real, imagined, or exaggerated. Sex differences provide the most basic and universal instance of this phenomenon in Genesis when, after the fall, the man rules over the woman. Racism, ethnic chauvinism, and nationalism likewise exaggerate and reify variations in physical appearance or distinctions of geographical residence or history, in order to give a material basis to spurious claims of supremacy and privilege. Oppression by means of sex differences begins the fateful process of defacing God's image, breaking the created connection between human differentiation and unity. Racism and other forms of violence against stigmatized populations deface the image as destined to be fulfilled through God's blessing on all the families of the earth.

Family is another key biblical framework for indicating the human capacity for and call to a "one flesh" unity-in-difference. "Family" designates biologically connected, intergenerational groups that are forward moving and have porous boundaries. Sex and procreation constitute both the embodied continuity of families and their inherent openness and amenability to change. Socially institutionalized and culturally ritualized procreative cooperation ("marriage") brings families together to create new configurations and unities. Families are the primal human experience of social cooperation, and should serve as schools in which the virtues of compassion and altruism are nurtured.

Races, ethnic groups, peoples, and nations derive their identities from embodied similarities of physicality and place, on analogy to extended family groupings. Racism, ethnocentrism, and nationalism violate the capacity of humans to image God by closing the boundaries of these groups, denying their adaptability, and severing their linkages to neighboring human families. The conjunction of racism, sexism, and ethnocentrism produces some of the most violent perversions of God's image imaginable; for example, the rape, torture, and killing of women in war, of women refugees, of women under colonization, of enslaved women, and of women in the sex trade. Commenting on the need to define rape as a form of genocide, the legal theorists Hilary Charlesworth and Christine Chinkin illustrate the nexus of embodiment, group identity, and social sin with the following examples:

> In reviewing the indictments against the Bosnian Serbs, Radovan Karadzic and Ratko Mladic, a Trial Chamber of the ICTY invited the prosecution to broaden the scope of its characterization of genocide, suggesting that: "The systematic rape of women ... is in some cases intended to transmit a new ethnic identity to the child. In other cases humiliation and terror serve to dismember the group." This characterization is further supported by the phenomenon of forced detention of women, first for impregnation and subsequently to prevent abortion.
>
> So too in Rwanda, it has been contended that rape and sexual brutality in Rwanda was not incidental to the genocide but was an integral part of the aim to eradicate the Tutsi.[33]

It should be noted that neither the "embodied" distinctions between Serbs and Croats, nor between Tutsi and Hutu, are hard and fast demarcations or barriers. What we have are constellations of biological, geographical, historical, and cultural factors that together constitute an embodied "ethnic" identity that is manipulated to further the domination of one ethnic group by another.

Historically, the most pervasive form of sin is war, an institutionalization of murder, in which sin is wreaked in and through the human body, the bodies of other creatures, and the "body" of creation. Killing,

---

33. Charlesworth and Chinkin, *The Boundaries of International Law,* 318, quoting Trial Chamber I, *Review of Indictment pursuant to Rule 61, Karaadzic and Mladic cases,* 11 July 1996, IT-95–5–R61, IT-95–18–R61, paras. 94 and 95.

maiming, torture, rape — whatever its theoretical justifications, war is inevitably an occasion on which all these are perpetrated, usually for the sake of laying exclusionary claims to territory and goods for which human "tribes" are in competition. Finally, we must not forget the types of "benign" violence that have equally lethal if less sensational effects, and that accompany colonization, neocolonization through economic globalization, and any imbalance of social power in which the resources of the many are conscripted by the few.

Genesis attributes suffering in human life primarily to human perversity. We suffer because we sin, rejecting through our bodies and on the bodies of fellow humanity the kinds of relationships that mirror God. Yet undeniably, Genesis also presents the intransigent ambiguity of human life as embodied and as "in place" in the physical universe, an ambiguity that seems to beset human decision making from the beginning. The trees of the garden presumably come from God, but also are the occasion of temptation (2:9; 3:22, 24); the serpent appears abruptly and suggests transgressive possibilities for no apparent reason (3:1–5). The absurdity of evil and an inexplicable pressure on humans to capitulate are vividly rendered in such details. Yet the ultimate effect of the contrast between sin and creation, image and brokenness, blessing and suffering, is to further the judgment of "what is" in light of "what should be." Genesis ascribes responsibility to humans for the brokenness of their own situation. This assignment of responsibility is necessary if we are to be able to affirm a counterpart responsibility for transformation that also falls to humans. All is placed under God's sovereignty and made contingent on God's call, both the original imaging of God and the restoration of the image to broken humanity.

The Image Redeemed

Sin distorts the relations among human beings (bodies and souls), to God (here and hereafter), and to the rest of creation (both in what it yields to us and in what we wreak on it). Yet the book of Genesis as a whole displays God's faithfulness to humanity, even if its family history, the feats of its heroes, and their forward movement into blessing remain fractured and fragmentary. The working out of sin and salvation through a family history and a promise of children and land inscribes creaturely embodiment, material connection, and interdependence with transcendent meaning. The relationships in which humans either image God or deface God's image are concrete and physical, specific to time and place, full of possibility, but still contingent in origin and limited in scope. The book of Genesis grounds salvation in the action of God within a historical process, calling human beings, especially faith communities, forward to a time when "*shalom* [and] 'wholeness' will be a reality among 'all the families of the earth.' "[34] What this implies concretely is recognition of human needs and capacities, the sharing of goods, respect for all persons irrespective of bodily and geographic differences (such as race, gender, ethnicity, and nationality), and commitment to the well-being of all in concrete communities of belonging (structured by work and family).

Pope John Paul II believed that a crucial precondition of social justice is the reawakening among peoples of the sort of religious consciousness that finds in human interdependence a mandate for compassion and cooperation:

> Solidarity helps us to see the "other" — whether a person, people, or nation — not just as some kind of instrument, with a work capacity and physical strength to be exploited at low cost and then discarded when no longer useful, but as our "neighbor," a "helper" (cf. Gen. 2:18–20), to be made a sharer, on a par with ourselves, in the banquet of life to which all are equally invited by God.[35]

Redemption unfurling within history, at least in the perspective of Genesis, is a dynamic process, not a return to a prelapsarian time. This trajectory has a strong future orientation, and even a universalizing one. Paul Santmire, a biblical scholar who has long been concerned about human degradation of the natural environment,[36] asserts that there are practical and ethical reasons that require our traditions to move the dynamic of the divine image in our humanity forward. "In this global age when the universal questions of justice and ecology ring from every

34. Fretheim, "The Reclamation of Creation," 353.
35. John Paul II, *Sollicitudo Rei Socialis*, no. 39, in David J. O'Brien and Thomas A. Shannon, eds., *Catholic Social Thought: The Documentary Heritage* (Maryknoll, N.Y.: Orbis Books, 1998), 422.
36. H. Paul Santmire, *The Travail of Nature: The Ambiguous Ecological Promise of Christian Theology* (Philadelphia: Fortress Press, 1985).

mountain and wetland, from every tumultuous city and sequestered village, our churches can no longer afford to stay at home with the particularistic theology of yesterday."[37] Thomas Mann is even more specific in naming the need for a forward-moving dynamic of redemption. It is alarming that he made the following comment in 1991, not 2003 (or for many years thereafter):

> [Recently] a ... coalition, dominated by the United States, completed a war against Iraq, making all too evident the irresolution of the promise of the blessing to "all the families of the earth," and especially to those "families" in the Middle East so closely connected to the families of the Book of Genesis. This relatively recent situation reminds us ... why the poignant resolutions within the family of Abraham are presented by the biblical authors as pointing beyond themselves ultimately to an international horizon.[38]

The image of God in humanity takes its meaning from a theology of deliverance and restored relationship within which the image symbolizes humanity's end point as well as its origin. The image of God is about the coexistence of creatures under God in a corporate as well as corporeal world. Even in speaking about redemption it is important to recognize that we are placed in a world that is contingent and finite. Conflict in and through the body, in respect of bodily needs, vulnerabilities, and capacities is not only a part of the historical record but inevitable, since our space, resources, and capacity for relationship are abundant but not endless.

According to Santmire, humans are divinely called "to care for the earth," as well as "to find sustenance for their bodies and establish a rich and just communal life." Yet this implies limits. "Since humans are earth-creatures, not gods, they must live with, and indeed can only flourish within, limits of knowledge, capacity, and place (niche). Hence

---

37. H. Paul Santmire, "The Genesis Creation Narratives Revisited: Themes for a Global Age," *Interpretation* 45, no. 4 (1991): 367. Ecological theology and ethics is a major concern of feminist theologians. See, for example, Rosemary Radford Ruether, *Gaia and God: An Ecofeminist Theology of Earth Healing* (New York: HarperCollins, 1992).

38. Mann, " 'All the Families ...,' " 352.

humility and restraint before all the creatures of the earth are virtues willed by God."[39]

Right relationship as God's image in humanity is one way to define "justice." Justice is the norm and goal of all human relations and societies, and essential to the earthly beginning of redemption. In our present condition of finitude and sin, humans require a conversion to the compassionate attitudes necessary to motivate beneficent action toward others, as well as restraint of our own self-interest. Without a fundamental renewal of our bonds of fellowship-in-difference, the historical juggernaut of violence and sin will be impossible to reverse. While mutual recognition and the pull to unity were "natural" to Adam and Eve, it is our obligation in our sinful condition to restore and cultivate these responses. Compassion is the ability to feel with and for other human beings, and to adopt their sufferings and aspirations as our own. According to the philosopher Martha Nussbaum, compassion is the ability to consider the suffering of another as significant to our own goals and happiness, so that we make ourselves vulnerable in the person of the other.[40] Another philosopher, Paul Ricoeur, sets compassion at the foundation of morality when he envisions the ability to see "oneself as another" as key to the "ethical intention" as *aiming at the 'good life' with and for others, in just institutions.*"[41]

Religious symbols and identity have a crucial moral role. They can enhance compassion as a personal and social virtue, by immersing believers in narratives and practices that hold it up as an ideal, and particularly by idealizing empathy and sacrifice for those to whom we feel no "natural" attraction or bond. Compassion for and mercy on those in broken situations, even when they are blameworthy, can be assimilated to the divine image, becoming a model for humans. Consider God's action toward the hiding and naked guilty parties, whom God was poised to throw out of their paradise: "The Lord God made garments of skins for the man and for his wife and clothed them" (3:21).

---

39. Santmire, "Genesis Creation Narratives," 378.
40. Martha C. Nussbaum, *Upheavals of Thought: The Intelligence of Emotions* (New York: Cambridge University Press, 2001), 319.
41. Paul Ricoeur, *Oneself as Another,* trans. Kathleen Blamey (Chicago: University of Chicago Press, 1992), 172 (italics in original).

Religious ethicist Diana Fritz Cates, following Thomas Aquinas, describes humans' proper relation to God as one of friendship, a vocation to which we are called by God's grace. Compassion for others is a way of including them in our friendship with God. "When the friend of God perceives a particular person in pain, he 'sees' that the other is like him in important respects — the other has been befriended by God, just as the self has."[42] One of Cates's main points is that compassion is not something we just *happen* to feel or are *fortunate* to feel, but that we *choose* to feel and can *educate* ourselves to feel. We can place ourselves in communities where narratives, symbols, and practices of compassion are more likely to habituate our responses and agency. In fact, as religious persons, we have an obligation to accentuate and develop these aspects of our traditions. To experience compassion for others, we must confront our own uncertainty, vulnerability, and powerlessness so that we may forgive the desperate but futile attempts of others to escape the constraints of their own finitude by exerting control over others. To connect the redemptive theme of "friendship with God" with creation, we can say that it restores the "image of God" in humans. When one acting in God's image perceives another in pain, he or she "sees" that the other is like oneself — the other has been created and called by God, just as the self has.

Interreligious Dialogue, Community, and Action

Cates notes that compassion requires some sense of the particularity of others,[43] which is of course enhanced by actual association, and especially by collaborative undertakings. Sociologist Nira Yuval-Davis explains that dialogue — not the simple fact of having been oppressed — is the basis of knowledge about what justice is and how it can be achieved. She explains that the term *transversalism* originated with an Italian feminist project to bring together members of conflicting national groups, "like the Serbs and Croats, but especially Palestinian

---

42. Diana Fritz Cates, *Choosing to Feel: Virtue, Friendship, and Compassion for Friends* (Notre Dame, Ind.: University of Notre Dame Press, 1997), 227.

43. Ibid., 233.

and Israeli Jewish women."[44] Charlesworth and Chinkin use the term *transversalism* to refer to a variety of feminist approaches that come together in a similar interest in international, intercultural, and inter-religious dialogue to enable moral judgment and shared action around values, but without "homogenization," arrogance, or moral imperial-ism.[45] Transversalism is a good model for our dialogue about the ethical ramifications of our shared religious symbol, the image of God.

Ethical collaboration can be a starting point for religious coopera-tion around shared religious meaning, such as we are seeking now in the image of God. Ethical collaboration can enhance and even vali-date fundamental experiences of God and God's will. In the beginning, I introduced as a serious question James Gustafson's doubt that an hon-est reading of humanity's real experience of the powers that encompass us would bear up an optimistic, hopeful account of God's reconciling action in history, working for our good, to restore God's broken image. The challenge for interreligious dialogue and ethics is to embody, not merely to talk about, a different reading of divine power. A more hopeful reading must be verified as authentic by bearing fruit in mutual under-standing and collaboration, in "one flesh" fellowship, and in a mutually strengthened trust in divine blessing.

Paul Knitter proposes that interreligious truths are disclosed in what he calls "basic interreligious communities."[46] These communities begin with the practical, not with the theologically abstract, nor even with the scripturally authoritative. Real interreligious community begins, accord-ing to Knitter, at the most practical level: with *compassion*, with shared feelings of "sorrow, horror, and consternation" at situations of suffering, scarring humanity and the earth. These feelings lead to *conversion*, as simply "a call to do something." The surprising, miraculous result can be that unanticipated bridges over difference materialize or are suddenly recognized for what they always were. *Collaboration* or actual praxis confronting problems brings "new bondings," and can even succeed in creating "religious brothers and sisters among those who may know

---

44. Yuval-Davis, "Women, Ethnicity, and Empowerment," 95.
45. Charlesworth and Chinkin, *The Boundaries of International Law,* 51–52.
46. Paul F. Knitter, "A Common Creation Story? Interreligious Dialogue and Ecology," *Journal of Ecumenical Studies* 16 (2000): 13.

little about each other's religions." Then the time is ripe for genuine *communication*, as dialogue partners and collaborators witness to each other about how their own religious traditions "nourish" and guide their ethical practices. *Communion*, in Knitter's terms, is the consummate interreligious outcome. Communion is an experience of clarity about the shared experience of the transcendent that was already present in the first steps of compassion, in the original recognition of suffering that became a call to action for everyone.[47]

Conclusion

Conversion to live peaceably in a global society can only occur in "global" — that is, intercultural and interreligious — contexts.[48] We must rediscover the embodied fellowship for which we were created. Redemption of our created yet broken corporate existence can be symbolized as the restoration of God's image in human relationships. The image has always had a future orientation. The future to which humans are called is God's corporate and corporeal blessing: human fecundity and family relationship, the generosity of the land, cooperative work to meet human needs and create cultures, and the flourishing of all through peaceful negotiation of shares in the earth's abundant but finite resources. Let "image of God" be for us a sign of compassion, on the way to conversion, collaboration, and communion. Let us hope that our work together, bridging differences, can authenticate the truth and faithfulness of God's blessing.

47. Ibid., 13–17.
48. On this prospect in general, see Schreiter, *The New Catholicity*, especially 14–27 on "global theological flows," and 108–15, on the present tasks of theology.

Chapter 4

THE IMAGE OF GOD
AND THE HUMAN IDEAL

Reflections from the Varieties of Judaism

Michael Fishbane

As heirs of the great and complex traditions of Judaism, Christianity, and Islam, we have inherited numerous images of the human being as a creature of God — images that have been of foundational importance, both for the theological anthropology they describe, as well as for the spiritual ideals they project for human perfection or fulfillment. In some instances, these images have been of very great religious and moral consequence in cultivating certain aspects of the distinctiveness of human beings; but in other cases, certain formulations have variously limited or constrained a certain sense of human flourishing. Times change, and so do the values and hierarchies of moral worth. Thus the challenge to reflect upon our inherited images of personhood, and to reformulate them anew, is a task given to each generation as it comes to understand its theological and ethical tasks within the framework of its received traditions. Our time is no different; and for this reason see my present concern as penetrating the resources of the Jewish tradition for models of moral and theological worth as we grope forward in this age. Accordingly, I shall be less interested here in cataloging or summarizing the vast range of teachings on the distinctive nature of the human being as a creature of God in Jewish philosophy and religious thought, as in attempting to use the texts of the vast rabbinic tradition as an armature for contemporary reflection. In the process I shall try to be faithful to historical Judaism and its range of creative expressions, but seek to

78

do so in my own voice and in accordance with my own theological perspective.

In order to speak within a broad hermeneutical framework shared variously by Judaism, Christianity, and Islam, I shall choose topics for phenomenological reflection that are either indicated directly in the initial chapters of the book of Genesis, or are features entailed in their theological and literary presentation. Four topics impose themselves for consideration. I shall mention them summarily at the outset, and discuss each one separately and at greater length, even adding matters drawn from rabbinic tradition. In this way, the issues I first raise from the perspective of a philosophical anthropology regarding distinctive aspects of human life are subsequently given a certain Jewish resonance and theological character.

The major topics I now wish to present, guided by issues and concerns found in Genesis 1–2, are the following:

1. that human life is one expression of a vast and varied phenomenon of life that is not grounded in itself, but is rather the product of a source transcendent to itself and designated as God, and that, within this framework, the human species is marked as the most distinctive realization of the divine source of life, and is marked as such through the designation of it being in the "image of God";

2. that this human species alone has a task of value or responsibility, which marks it off as different from the other life-forms, and that this distinctive task is denominated as having a particular sovereignty or dominion over those other life-forms — a task further denominated by the duty "to cultivate and protect" the habitat of the world in which such life develops and proliferates;

3. that the life-forms are variously marked as "good" by the divine source of life, and that this designation of value spans the entire spectrum of the creation (also called, altogether, "very good") — albeit the human life-form is of a particularly lordly and Divine-like status; and

4. that all this information is formulated in a highly stylized literary accounts, these marking creative human expressions or renditions

of the nature of the natural world and of its supernatural source in God — hence the image of the world we inhabit is not simply given, as some necessary epistemic *a priori,* but is rather a particular product of the distinctive human imagination and the values that may or may not guide it.

Let me now develop these matters with more extended reflection. I believe that, in different ways, they each address or sponsor vital dimensions of the distinctiveness of the human self, and may thus contribute to an emergent theology and social ethics for our time — both grounded in Scripture and in tune with an independent philosophical anthropology. To appreciate this last point, let me turn first to the anthropological aspects of these features, independent of Scripture. Only thereafter, in the course of reflection, shall I make reference to our Genesis text; and then I shall further develop my reflections through certain texts drawn from the rabbinic tradition. In this way we shall work upwards from the ground of natural and anthropological reflections to their biblical adumbration, and thence to rabbinic materials that variously elaborate certain considerations and bring the inquiry forward to a cultural hermeneutics of a particular theological character. In my case, this theological dimension is thoroughly Jewish, though my formulation of it vibrates with all the books I have read from outside the particular Jewish orbit of ideas and values. This done, I shall return in the end to Genesis 1–2 in order to give these reflections an entirely personal character, while also refocusing my insights around a passage from Scripture — this text being a common core, quite apart from the vast differences of exegetical and canonical extension that distinguish Judaism, Christianity, and Islam. This final hermeneutical turn will be the most overtly theological of the successive levels of reflection in which I here engage.

The Will to Life

I turn first to the topic of the phenomenon of life as the natural ground of our subject. A broad spectrum of life-forms fills our world, as the simplest observation attests; but despite their diversity and bounty, one impulse pervades them all: the impulse to life or vitality. This impulse characterizes all living things, each according to its kind, and is variously expressed by modalities of proliferation, self-preservation, and tropisms (reflecting different orientations, depending on what best supports the specific life-form).[1] To speak of this drive to life or vitality as an impulse is to attempt to be as neutral as possible; but it is the fact that, as the various species and kinds differentiate and become more complex, this impulse is not just some blind force or directionality, but is linked to "will" of some sort. We thus see, increasingly, something of the order of a "will to life" among the life-forms in the natural world — though this is of different degrees of magnitude, and certainly never cut off from various autonomic impulses. At the highest end of these forms is the human species, whose "will to life" is the most distinctive — not solely by virtue of the very nature of human nature, but by virtue of a certain reflexivity that is aware of the will to life in itself and throughout the realm of nature. This reflexivity is marked by a sense of value and responsibility for the diverse phenomenon of life per se, which includes both the specific life-forms themselves as well as the sacred center of all life: the inhering core of vitality that is both the transcendent mystery of all life as well as the many manifestations or images of its imageless reality. As the highest manifestation of this source of life on earth, and with a sense of care for the life world, noted in Scripture by the phrase *le-'ovedah ule-shamerah* ("to cultivate and protect"), the human being is the fullest earthly expression of the transnatural or divine "will for life" with responsibilities for the sustenance of the natural realm. It is in this sense, I would say, that the human person is distinctly designated in Scripture as being in the "divine image."

The sense of duty to cultivate and protect the life-forms of the world is the natural ground of ethics, and takes on different tasks of innovation or restraint in accordance with the different life-forms themselves, at different times and places. One may even say that this sense of duty is the ground of culture itself, and is manifest in law and value — most particularly in the cultural expressions of that highest of all legal and social

---

1. These thoughts are related to the thinking of Hans Jonas, and his consideration of the ongoing "metabolic" intensity and identity of organism; see, for example, the concise consideration in his *Mortality and Morality: A Search for the Good after Auschwitz*, ed. Lawrence Vogel (Evanston, Ill.: Northwestern University Press, 1996), chapter 1, "Evolution and Freedom: On the Continuity among Life-Forms."

values: the duty to protect and honor the human species as a whole. I
have suggested that this notion is grounded in Scripture, or is at least
adumbrated in its language; and this factor gives my first reflection a
certain scriptural adumbration, however inchoate or allusive. Withal, I
now wish to exemplify from a uniquely Jewish point of view my argument that a distinctive task devolving upon the human species as the
most reflective and powerful of life-forms on earth, and also as the most
aware of the fragility of these forms and its capacity to impact them for
good or ill, is the task to safeguard the earthly habitat of vital forms —
and human life and culture most especially.

The text I wish to adduce is formulated in an ancient *Mishna* found
in the tractate of *Sanhedrin,* a document dealing with certain features of
ancient Jewish law and legal process. More specifically, this text, deriving from the oldest strata of classical rabbinic legal culture in the first
centuries of our era, treats the admonition of witnesses before they are to
give testimony before a court of judges duly constituted to try a capital
case. For rabbinic law, there is no graver social responsibility than the
duty to testify with absolute care and honesty to what one has seen or
heard directly — for on this testimony a human life, that of the accused,
hangs in the balance. Accordingly, justice is never abstract, but always
deals with persons, and thus the admonition of witnesses in capital cases
centers on inculcating a consciousness of the value of life in those whose
words will shape the court's decision. I now quote from chapter 4 of
the tractate, the fifth *Mishna.* After warning the witness to consider
the nature of their evidence, and to make sure that it is not based on
presumption, or inference, or on any second-hand accounts, the judges
sharpen their language, and say:

> Know ye that criminal cases are not like capital cases [*diney
> nefashot*]; for in criminal cases [if a person gives false testimony]
> he gives money [for restitution] and it [namely, his crime] is thereby
> atoned for, whereas in capital cases the blood [of the person killed
> because of the testimony], and the blood of all that person's [sub-
> sequent] progeny devolve upon the witness [as his responsibility]
> until the end of the world. Just such a situation is specified with
> respect to Cain, who killed his brother; as it says [in Scripture],

"your brother's bloods [*demey akhika*] cry out" (Gen. 4:10). Note that Scripture does not say "your brother's blood" [*dam akhika*] but "your brother's bloods" — which is to indicate both his blood and the blood of [all] his progeny.... Therefore [moreover] the first person [Adam] was created alone, in order to teach you that whoever causes the death of any person, Scripture regards him as if he destroyed an entire world; and whoever sustains the life of any person, is regarded as one who maintains an entire world.[2]

Certainly, this is a remarkable admonition delivered by the court, and indicates something of the high seriousness attributed in classical rabbinic law to the value of human life and the task of culture to cultivate and protect it by every possible means. The fact that the admonition leans on the biblical text for support, and derives that support through an exegetical construction in each of the cases, suggests that the sages did not wish simply to assert the importance of life as a natural fact, but wished to link their words to the authority of Scripture. In this way, we may say, the unique distinction of the human person to think about the world and its sustenance is deepened by the fact that the culture-bearing responsibility of the person is not just to assert values but also to provide reasons and justifications for them in the realm of reason and discourse. Hence, what I earlier referred to as the "will to life" is not just a blind drive, but one that involves (in the human instance, at least) the cultivation of reflective thoughtfulness, and one that must be transmitted and even inculcated in one's fellow person in order for the duty to cultivate and protect life to be a common human enterprise. The remarkable assertion that each person must be regarded as a stream of life extending throughout the time of the world, and that extinguishing a life is to destroy a virtual life-world, aligns the human project of care for human life with one's care for the world and its survival; the more religious justification given, that links this imperative to the fact that Adam was created "alone," means that care for persons is care for the divine

2. For the phrase "entire world" and its variants as the preferred reading, see the evidence adduced by Ephraim E. Urbach, "'Kol Ha-meqayyem Nefesh Ahat...'; Gilgulav shel Nusah, Tahapuhot Tzenzurah ve-'Isqei Madpisim," in *Me-'Olamam shel Hakhamim* (Jerusalem: Magnes Press, 1988), 561–77. Cf. also the comment of Rashi on Babylonian Talmud, *Sanhedrin* 37a, s.v. "*lefikhakh.*"

image in the world — even care for its flourishing and survival. From this perspective, judicial ethics is a special mode of theological attentiveness, one uniquely and distinctively given to human beings.

The Will to Good

But human care for the world is not only expressed through a commitment to human life and its protection; it is also expressed through an attentive regard for the cultivation and protection of all the life-forms of nature in the earthly habitat — a commitment to their particularity, each according to its kind, and to the peculiar goodness that each bears in its nature and contributes to the natural whole of which it is a part. Another distinctive feature of the human being, therefore, is the capacity to reflect upon the variety of life-forms as an ensemble of parts, both in relationship to the character of human life and apart from it. This extends the "will to life" that is distinctively a feature of the human being to a readiness and willingness to "will the good" of each and every element as a matter of principle, and to try and serve that principle to the best of one's ability. In my view, a commitment to the "good" of each life-form includes a commitment to an order that extends beyond human beings and may or may not specifically benefit their self-interest — this being, in other terms, a commitment to an ethics of the whole, as expressions of the life-source that informs it. It is this multiple and diverse reality of earthly life that is affirmed in Genesis 1 when it speaks of God seeing that this or that element of the creation is "good," and it is this very same reality which we humans may acknowledge and serve. To acknowledge the good of each creation, and thus the totality as a complex of goods, is to acknowledge the thick biosphere and ecosphere within which human life is cultivated and protected, and to will its good is to accept the principle that all life and action is not centered around human beings and human society — although this latter sphere is a distinctive realm for "willing the good," even as the capacity or readiness to will the good of both part and whole is a distinctive human capacity. This does not mean that one may know the universal good in truth, or that one's intention to will the good will always be right and just, or even pure and selfless; it only means that the human cultivation and protection of life involves a unique attentiveness to and responsibility for the value of all forms of existence — even if and when priorities have to be made under the low ceiling of human knowledge. Human regency in the world should therefore be guided by a "will to empower," precisely because of the human capacity for power that changes the balance of each life-form in relationship to itself and to the whole.

Different aspects of the Jewish tradition help set this philosophical anthropology into a wider theological matrix. Particularly important to me in this regard are some thoughts of Rabbi Moses Cordovero, one of the greatest exponents of Jewish mysticism and mystical ethics, who lived in the Galilee in the city of Safed in the sixteenth century. Among his many writings is the remarkable handbook of ethics and spirituality known as the *Tomer Devorah* (or *Palm Tree of Deborah*). It sets the tasks of human will and ethics within a cosmic framework, one that actually imagines the flow of creative life and energy as a Cosmic Anthropos. Indeed, this anthropoidal structure of all being provides the model for the true flow of life and energy at all levels of reality.

What this means from a theological perspective is that the creative charge of life is imagined to erupt as a spark of will, and that it is empowered by a ceaseless and gratuitous will for the good of all things — even if and when this flow of life is diverted or perverted in the course of its earthly realization, whether because of some ill-will among persons or some corruption in the overall chain of being. God, Cordovero says, does not cease to emanate God's creative energy or cease to will the good under such circumstances — and just that is God's great goodness and humility. The human being, who is in the image of this gracious Being, is called upon to imitate and replicate this ceaseless and gracious will for the good, no matter how incomplete or even perverted this will may be bent in the world of nature and society. For Cordovero, this act of will is the deep ground of ethics, and is in fact grounded in an *imitatio Dei* — God being imagined as nothing less than a Power that emanates the powers and potentials of all life in a maximal and ceaseless will for the reality and realization of the whole. This is the ultimate care for being, for the cultivation of the all; and its gesture of maximal gratuity is the ultimate humility, for it gives without any prior or subsequent consideration of personal benefit. Such an ideal of perfection would mean the ultimate identification of the human being with Divine Being — in the sense that the human will for the good would be a perfected channel for the realization of the divine will for the good of all life, each element according to its kind.

Surely this is a luminous ideal, distinctly given to the human being created in the divine image. To give you a flavor of it, consider the following words of Cordovero, which express the teaching that I have just adumbrated. It comes near the beginning of chapter 1 of the tract, and is formulated as a comment on the opening clause of Micah 7:18–20.

> *Who is a God like unto You (bearing iniquity)?* This refers to the fact that the Holy One, blessed be He, is an injured King, who bears injury [insult] in a many beyond Human understanding. For indeed, without doubt, there is nothing hidden from His providence. Moreover, there is no moment when man is not nourished and sustained by the great power that flows down upon him. And surely it follows that no person ever sins against God without the divine affluence flowing down upon him, enabling his existence and the movement of his limbs; and despite the fact that the individual uses that power for sin, it is not withheld from him in any way. But rather the Holy One, blessed be He, bears this injury, such that He continues to empower the person to move his limbs even while he uses that power in that moment for sin and perversity. . . . Nor must you say, heaven forbid, that God cannot withhold that good [from the person], for it lies within His power, in the moment it takes to say it, to wither the sinner's hand or foot. . . . [But] He does not, on this account, withhold His goodness from man, but bears the injury [or insult]. . . . And this is the meaning of the prophet's words, *Who is a God like You (bearing iniquity)?* . . . [And] indeed, this is a virtue [or quality] that [each] person should make their own; namely, to be patient and allow himself to be injured [or insulted] even to this extent, yet not refuse to bestow his goodness to the recipients.

Thus taught our master and teacher Rabbi Moses Cordovero.

The Will to Imagine

Let me now turn to a final matter entailed in the narrative of Genesis 1, and seek to understand it first as a feature of philosophical anthropology, that is, as a constitutive feature of the human being per se, and then to put it into a wider theological framework by means of a text from the Jewish tradition that treats the same subject. This is the way that we have proceeded with respect to the "will to life" and the "will to the good"; and this is the way we shall now proceed with respect to the fact that our accounts of the world and of life within it are narrative constructs, derived from tradition and from the individual imagination. We are always accounting for our place in the world and the nature of things through such creative constructs, and allowing these to guide us, give us orientation, and to provide a framework of value — at least until some crisis introduces a dissonance that requires a revision or reinterpretation or reconfiguration of the implicit or explicit narrative account we have of things. Surely the text of Genesis 1, by virtue of its structure and emphases, is such a tendentious cultural accounting, serving implied and explicit theological and pedagogical purposes. Indeed, just this perception was stressed by two of the great French Jewish commentators of the high Middle Ages, Rashi (Rabbi Shelomo Yitzhaki) and his grandson Rashbam (Rabbi Shemuel ben Meir), for they variously stressed that Genesis 1 can hardly be regarded as a complete or literal account of the origins of things, insofar as it deletes certain details and emphasizes others in a highly stylized manner, all in order to provide a pedagogical focus for the account (for Rashbam this was the Sabbath and its observance).[3]

Theological narratives thus construct images of the world, from the fabric of traditional wisdom and the creative imagination, in order to further tradition and to adapt it to its purposes. The human being is thus constituted by a creative impulse or "will to imagine," and this quality is certainly a distinctive feature of this species and distinctive among the species of life. The world is thus not a *de facto* given, but an

---

3. Cf. the discussion of Sarah Kamin, *Beyn Yehudim le-Notzrim Be-Farshanut Ha-Miqra'* (Jerusalem: Magnes Press, 1991), ("Rashbam's conception of the Creation in the Light of the Intellectual Currents of his Time"), in the English section, with separate pagination, *27–*68.

image of what is imagined and imaginable. To share these constructions, and to benefit from the world-images imagined by others, opens a wider horizon of possibilities for the self. To deny this pluralism of perspectives is to constrain oneself to a particular angle of cultural vision. Similarly, the possibility of imagining new structures within one's cultural tradition is the potency of that specific application of the "will to imagine" that we know of as cultural and textual hermeneutics. Exegesis may thus imagine new images of the world and of value beyond the original formulations and meanings of the received canonical texts — if not also in and through the formulations themselves.

The power and possibility of hermeneutics or creative interpretation to construct new worlds of meaning is given a very striking and explicit articulation in a passage found in the book of *Zohar,* that singularly great compendium of Jewish mystical exegesis of Scripture that appeared in Castile in the latter half of the thirteenth century. And if this passage puts the power of interpretation into a cosmic setting far beyond our own epistemological reach and capacity for cognitive assent, one can hardly deny that it gives bold expression to the sense that, through creative interpretation, one can transform one's cultural canon and even construct new epistemic worlds for habitation and value. Commenting on the eschatological passage in Isaiah 51:15, in which God says to the prophet, "I have put my word in your mouth...to plant heavens and to establish [the] earth," Rabbi Simeon bar Yochai states: "One should expend great effort in studying Torah day and night, because the Holy One, blessed be He, listens to the voice of those who study Torah, and every new interpretation of the Torah that is originated by someone who studies Torah makes a firmament" (I.4b-5a). The teacher goes on to portray in dramatic fashion how each particular "[i]nterpretation moves, ascends and descends, and becomes a firmament."

This formulation should not be dismissed as a mere trope or metaphor for the mystagogue; it is, rather, a strong ontological assertion and belief that human interpretation of Torah is of a creative and world-building nature. And if we are to understand the teaching correctly, and even find some meaning of it for ourselves, it is necessary to observe that Rabbi Simeon's theological comment is in fact a sermonic response to Genesis 1:1, the sponsoring Pentateuchal passage in the *Zohar*. What this means,

I would suggest, is that the sage presents the human acts of creative interpretation, or theological exegesis, as a continuation of God's initial act of creation and revelation; and that just as the primordial Torah is the blueprint for our world, so is the interpretation of the historical Torah the matrix for its renewal and remaking. Similarly, the divine act of creation is extended and vitalized by humans created in God's image — such that the distinctive *imitatio Dei* is presented as the creative act of constructing worlds through speech and interpretation. To be sure, this is an inner-cultural act of a specific type; but its reach goes beyond this sphere; for by sharing interpretative possibilities with other persons, beyond our immediate social setting, we engage in an inter-cultural act whereby new ways of being human may be shared, with consequences for the enrichment and transformation of our own cultural sphere.[4] By linking our "will to imagine" to our creative potential, and also imagining this as related to God's own creativity, Rabbi Simeon thus opens us to an unexpected theological horizon wherein the human imagination is our distinctive capacity as creatures in the image of God; and further, as I would now propose, that it is this very imagination which forms the core of our capacity to "will the good" and to "cultivate and protect" the streams of life in our world. Truly, this is our distinctive human way of being before and with God.

Conclusion

I wish to conclude these various reflections by making a theological statement that builds on my attempt to think through the notion of humanity before God from the ground up: starting with reflections of a distinctive anthropological nature, and giving this a Jewish dimension through insights from its textual tradition, both biblical and rabbinic — all with the goal of constructing a model that allows for a vibrant religious and epistemological pluralism, simultaneously alive to the human and non-human other while assertive of one's particular values and perspectives.

4. Elsewhere, I have used this text to inaugurate a more wide-ranging discussion about exegesis and textuality; see my discussion on "Canonical Text, Covenantal Communities, and the Patterns of Exegetical Culture: Reflections on the Past Century," in *Covenant and Context: Essays in Honour of E. W. Nicholson,* ed. A. D. H. Mayes and R. B. Salters (Oxford: Oxford University Press, 2003), 135–61.

Since the core issues of my discussion were inspired by features of the opening chapters of the book of Genesis, I now wish to return to that source as a foundation for the following brief statement. It is a personal formulation of where I now stand on the matters about which I have been brooding here.

As I understand it, Genesis 1–2 may provide the theological model of a world filled with the power and variety of life, which finds its source in the vitality of the Divine Being. This vitality fills our world and proliferates into the diversity of earthly life. All life-forms manifest this image of God, and the human being most distinctively — and particularly in the human capacity to reflect on the deep will to life that pulses in our world, and to develop values that seek to enhance and serve the good of all beings, as well as to imagine new images of the possible — thereby replicating the divine nature and its ceaseless creative vitality. Finding images of the Divine in all things, the human may find a divine imperative in the task of cultivating and protecting these images through appropriate acts of innovation and restraint. And by recognizing the distinctive divine image in all other humans, each person may imitate God's own purpose — so that each human life be seen as a good in its own right. Only this comprehensive regard for all beings, of every order and variety, each according to its kind, is the blessing that we now, at this most perilous hour, may give the created order, and thus serve the divine bounty that throbs in the veins of nature.

Chapter 5

DISTINCTIVE LOVE

Gratitude for Life and Theological Humanism

William Schweiker

Upheaval after upheaval has reminded us that modern man is traveling along a road called hate. Far from being the pious injunction of a Utopian dreamer, the command to love one's enemy is an absolute necessity for our survival.

— Martin Luther King Jr.[1]

Love encumbers us with life. Love binds up the sorrowful and cradles those lost, making them present anew in the bonds of memory. Love ignites hope and grasps for what we can never reach but ennobles our fleeting days. Lovers crave each other's touch, the embrace of one life with another. We are even told that love can triumph over estrangement, the hostility of enemies that severs the bonds of life. It is said that while faith, hope, and love abide, love is the greatest of these (1 Cor. 13:13). If one subtracts love from a human life while adding as much power or knowledge as one likes, is that life worth living? Only the most ardent Stoic bent on escaping the entanglements of life to enjoy self-sufficiency would seek to exile love and its passions from human existence. As John Wesley noted, "For, how far is love, even with many wrong opinions,

I want to thank Michael A. Johnson and Kevin Jung for the organization of the D. R. Sharpe Lectures of 2003 conference and also for helpful comments on the argument of this essay.

1. Martin Luther King Jr., "Love Your Enemies," in *Strength to Love* (Philadelphia: Fortress Press, 1981), 47.

91

to be preferred before truth itself without love. We may die without the knowledge of many truths, and yet be carried to Abraham's bosom. But, if we die without love, what will knowledge avail?"[2]

The craving, aspiration, and hope that infuse love are testimonies to what is most worthy of devotion. Granted that love is important in the turns and twists of human life, does it have a legitimate place in thinking about ethics, commitments to virtue, goodness, and the demands of justice? The moral life seems to require the reasonable conduct of human affairs, and, therefore, some have insisted that love, rooted in fickle and chaotic passions or the whims of God's commands, cannot and ought not to subvert dedication to justice, benevolence, and virtue. Yet Christianity has often been called a religion of love, specifically, the love of God and the love of neighbor as oneself. Little wonder, then, that the question about the place of love in the moral life has long been pondered within the many sides of the Christian tradition.

Love Commands and Christian Imagination

My focus here is on the various love commands within Christian faith (love of God, neighbor, self, and even enemy) that are important for any viable contemporary expression of Christian faith and life. True human love, for Christians, is rooted in divine love, the confession that God so loved the world through Christ's life, death, and resurrection as to redeem existence. The unmerited and extravagant love of God has usually, and rightly, been seen as the ground and goal of Christian living, properly understood. However, it is important in a Christian context to see that commandments must be understood in two distinct but related ways.[3] A command is, most obviously, a directive for action. It specifies what to do and what kind of person and community to be. Yet a command is just as importantly the means of sense-making through

---

2. John Wesley, *Sermons on Several Occasions,* preface, first series (London: Epworth, 1975), p. vii.

3. This point was often made by the classical Protestant theologians by noting that every command is also a promise. I am extending this insight in order to unfold the moral ontology articulated in Christian claims about love. On the idea of a moral ontology and also the viability of ideas about divine commands in theological ethics, see William Schweiker, *Power, Value, and Conviction: Theological Ethics in the Postmodern Age* (Cleveland: Pilgrim, 1998).

an insight into the moral depths of reality. It displays the conditions for action, and, thereby, also the goods that human action is to respect and enhance. It is the connection between a command as action-guide and command as sense-making by disclosing reality, indeed revealing the being of God, which comes to focus in pondering a Christian conception of love. On my account, the love commands (God; self/neighbor; enemy), more than being just directives for action, present in compressed form a Christian hermeneutics of moral reality, a way of apprehending and understanding the meaning and purpose of human existence.

Matters are not as simple as they seem, however, even with the distinction in hand between commands as action-guides and commands as reality disclosing. Christian faith also inscribes a paradox at its very core.[4] The great love commands are apprehended most pointedly in what seems their negations. The love of God is seen in the cross of Christ. The love of neighbor as self is extended to the love of enemy so that "you may be children of your Father in heaven" (Matt. 5:45a). The command to love the enemy is, shockingly, bound back to the first command, to love God. The Christian imagination works through negation of commonsense perception in order to enable an apprehension of truth not knowable otherwise. In doing so, the all-too-popular contention that moral norms are rooted in sentiment or preference is likewise overturned. An action-guide, say, a command, is grounded in reality, the reality of God.[5] But

---

4. The claim here is not unlike Martin Luther's insistence that God is known under God's opposite, namely, that God's mercy is known under judgment; faith, then, is the apprehension of God's promise of mercy in spite of the fact of judgment. See Martin Luther, *Commentary on Galatians*, in *Luther's Works*, vol. 27, ed. Jaroslav J. Pelikan, trans. Richard Jungkuntz (St. Louis: Concordia, 1963). It may be the case with all religions that the meaning of central convictions is often grasped in what appears to be their negation. Consider some examples: a Buddhist holds that enlightenment is extinguishing the fire of desire, the insight of no-self, which, accordingly, can and cannot be sought. How can one seek enlightenment if in truth there is no-self with which to seek? The faithful Jew knows that the election of Israel requires testimony to the living God and service to the nations. Yet "election" might also include suffering and, as history too readily attests, even persecution.

5. There is, of course, an immense body of scholarship on the love commands and also their connection, if any, to the so-called Golden Rule ("Do unto others as you would have done unto you," Matt. 7:12a) and its connection to what is sometimes called the "silver rule" articulated by Hillel ("What is hateful to yourself do not do to anyone else. This is the whole law.") and in Tobit 4:15. I cannot pursue these historical questions here, much less the massive subject of the validity of any kind of divine-command ethics. For some recent work on these topics, see Jeffrey Wattles, *The Golden Rule* (New York: Oxford University Press, 1996); Keith D. Stanglin, "The Historical Connection between the Golden Rule and the Second Greatest Love Command," in *Journal of Religious Ethics* 33, no. 2 (2005): 357–71; and Edmund N. Santurri

the "reality condition" for the action-guide is not something one can just point to or pick out like some natural object. It is knowable by a detour of interpretation of the symbols, narratives, and commands central to Christian life. What these forms do is to open a vision of the meaning of what is real beyond our all-too-human knowledge of the world and life. Religion has been called a "cult of the invisible." Christian faith itself has been defined as "evidence of things unseen" (Heb. 11:1). Faith's moral vision is not just a matter of mystical insight; it is an understanding of the moral space of existence made possible by the paradoxical formulation of the love commands that upends usual moral and religious ideas.

Many theologians interested in ethics explore the action-guiding character of the love commands and thereby forgo inquiry into the reality claims implied in Christian love. The intent of this essay is to articulate the vision of reality disclosed by the love commands. Christian love, I contend, is a "yes-saying" to life in spite of the madness, sorrow, and violence that too often drains existence of worth and breeds hatred of life and the God of life. This "yes-saying" to life flows from gratitude for the givenness of life in creation and new creation. Paradoxically, the insight into the moral depths of reality comes through the command to love the enemy and its specific connection to the other great love commands. In the face of threats and enemies, the Christian is given neither to fateful resignation nor world-denial, nor is she or he to think and to live only within the logic of hatred, retribution, and retaliation. Christian existence is about real joy in new life. Christian love is thereby a means to end "traveling along a road called hate," as Martin Luther King Jr. put it.

In what follows, I am trying to explain how Christian claims about love enable one to articulate the deepest challenge and also highest possibility of our lives as moral and mortal creatures. The perspective is obviously Christian, but the object of my reflection is human moral existence.[6] If successful If successful I will have presented a kind of theological humanism developed from Christian sources. Human bounds will

---

and William Werpehowski, eds., *The Love Commandments: Essays in Christian Ethics and Moral Philosophy* (Washington, D.C.: Georgetown University Press, 1992).

6. What follows is an exercise in Christian moral philosophy. On this see H. Richard Niebuhr, *The Responsible Self: An Essay in Christian Moral Philosophy* (Louisville: Westminster John Knox, 1998); and also William Schweiker, *Responsibility and Christian Ethics* (Cambridge: Cambridge University Press, 1995).

be respected and enhanced against forces of hatred and animosity that threaten our survival. This version of humanism reclaims and revises ancient humanistic insights that have historical analogues in other religious and cultural traditions. However, this renewed vision is needed, we will see, in order to respond to problems in previous accounts of Christian love.

Sustaining these admittedly far-reaching claims requires several steps of argument, an acknowledgment, and also a caveat. The acknowledgment is about the failure of Christians to live by love. Exploring a hermeneutics of love in no way suggests that every Christian or every Christian community acts in love! Centuries of war, hatred, crusades, persecutions, racism, anti-Semitism, witch hunts, and genocide waged under the high-flying banner of the cross of Christ are too well known. Christians, like other religious people, rarely live truthfully their deepest convictions. The idea that Christianity is a religion of love cannot be primarily an empirical claim about Christian believers. It is, rather, about where to place the accent in Christian piety and in a Christian outlook on the world. That accent demands repentance on the part of Christians and also the struggle to live with greater faithfulness.

A caveat is also absolutely essential to my argument. I do not believe that any ethics can be developed around just one idea or concept. Many theologians have tried mightily to develop what is called "love monism" in Christian ethics. By that term is meant an account of Christian ethics where love and love alone is the norm for all moral and political decisions. On my reasoning, a distinctly Christian account of love is not meant to cover all the ethical bases, as it were. A good deal of mischief is done in ethics when we try to press one concept (such as love, virtue, narrative, or command) to cover all moral matters. I hope to avoid such mischief.

With respect to the steps in the argument, I will turn next to explore a specific twentieth-century Protestant account of Christian love, or *agapē*, to glean its insights and oversights. With that discussion in hand, I will briefly explore an epitome of Jesus' Torah teaching in order to advance a different account of the love commands and their place in the Christian life. Having thought in and through systematic and scriptural forms, I conclude with thoughts about a Christian understanding of love and the moral life.

Agapē and Forms of Love

Accounts of Christian love have changed throughout the ages as thinkers and communities respond to different realities and place different accents in faith. Given the wide range of interpretations of Christian love, I intend to focus my analysis on a typically modern, twentieth-century Protestant account of love. I am exploring a conceptual "type," mindful that all typological analysis must be enriched by further details in the specifics of a thinker's work.[7] My reason for taking this tactic is that these Protestants developed a penetrating account of Christian love that entailed a novel conception of the being of God as the reality that grounds and sustains the love commands as action-guides. Eventually, their thought had an impact on the whole scope of Christian theology that continues even today.

The Standard Account

Twentieth-century Protestant theology and ethics were dominated by a certain conception of Christian love supposedly modeled on the actions of Christ. The account was developed through the semantics of love in ancient Greek texts, distinctions between *erōs, agapē,* and *philia.* Importantly, this varied semantic field, the polysemy of love, was taken to designate not just a complex way of talking about human love, but, in fact, different loves. Semantic distinctions were wrestled into ontological separations, thereby to assert the uniqueness of Christian love, *agapē.* This separation, as I will argue later, is no longer tenable.

Importantly, the standard of *agapē* was developed by Protestant theologians, specifically Lutheran and Reformed ones, who sought to renew engagement with biblical thought after the acids of historical criticism. They claimed to have found again the strange world of the Bible and this insight provided critical distance on the world in which they lived, a world scarred by two world wars. Entering the biblical world of thought they realized that the Christian vision centers on the absolute priority

---

7. Typological thinking has been used and developed by many thinkers interested in ethics (e.g., M. Weber, E. Troeltsch, H. R. Niebuhr, J. M. Gustafson). As often noted, a "type" does not exist in any empirical sense; they are ideal constructions. Any actual historical reality — say, any real Christian community or any real individual — will have features not specified by the "type." An ideal type is a scholarly, conceptual construct that aims to reveal a pattern of thought or life.

of God's action, even in the moral life. The double love command, to love God and one's neighbor as oneself (Mark 12:30–31; Matt. 22:34–40; Luke 10:25–28), means that the Christian exists not in self, but in others — namely, in the Divine Other and also in the neighbor, through love. This provided, as we will see, a powerful critique of tyrannous and totalitarian conceptions in which what is other is to be absorbed into the self or at the mercy of state powers.

What, then, is the standard account of *agapē?* Found in different versions among thinkers as diverse as Karl Barth, Anders Nygren, Paul Tillich, Joseph Fletcher, Reinhold Niebuhr, and Paul Ramsey, the basic move of this recognizable "type" of thinking was to contrast Christian love, or *agapē,* with other forms of human love.[8] While the verb *agapaō* is found in Greek thought from the time of Homer onwards, the noun appears almost exclusively in the Bible. The debate among these thinkers turned on the relations among loves. Tillich, for instance, argued that *agapē* and *erōs* must be related even though *agapē* is the depth and power of all forms of love; Nygren insisted on an absolute distinction. My interest is what these thinkers shared in claims about Christian love no matter what relation they believed obtained between it and other kinds of love.

Following these theologians, we can use the polysemy of "love" in its Greek forms to clarify the "type" and its aspects. Two of the contrasts (*erōs/agapē; philia/agapē*) are closely tied to the command of love as an action-guide and focus on the motivations and scope of Christian love; the third contrast (command/freedom) seeks to isolate the being of God that is disclosed in the command to love. I am going to use this hermeneutic of layered discourse or semantic fields in order to clarify the standard account of *agapē,* but also, finally, to transform those

8. See Karl Barth, *The Holy Spirit and the Christian Life: The Theological Basis of Ethics* (Louisville: Westminster John Knox, 1993); Anders Nygren, *Agapē and Erōs,* trans. Philip S. Watson (London: SPCK, 1957); Paul Tillich, *Morality and Beyond* (Louisville: Westminster John Knox, 1995); Joseph Fletcher, *Situation Ethics: The New Morality* (Louisville: Westminster John Knox, 1997); and Paul Ramsey, *Basic Christian Ethics* (Louisville: Westminster John Knox, 1993). A crucial background figure in this line of thought is the nineteenth-century Christian thinker Søren Kierkegaard. His books *Training in Christianity* and *Works of Love* outline many of the features of what I am calling the "standard account." While drawing inspiration from Kierkegaard, these twentieth-century theologians move the discussion of love into their ideas about the being of God and thereby, it seems to me, make the more radical case for *agapē.*

Christian claims. The move beyond the standard account, recall, will be undertaken by means of closer attention to the interlocking of the love commands found in Jesus' Torah teaching.

Erōs and Agapē

Agapē, it was argued by these twentieth-century Protestants, specifies God's utterly unmerited love of human beings, even in sin, made manifest in Christ and active in radical love for others, a love created, sustained, and motivated by God's love. Christians are called to love others as God has loved them (John 13:34). This means that *agapē* is not motivated by the goodness or beauty or lovability of its object; it is not a version of *erōs*. The god of human desire, a kind of apex of religious *erōs*, is a figment of the human imagination. It is not the God of the Bible, but, in reality, a symbol of fault or sin. God loved us while we yet sinners, as Paul put it (Rom. 5:8).[9] God's action could be specified or symbolized rightly in biblical terms: love is the reality of God *in actu* (1 John 4:8). It could also be articulated theologically in terms of the internal relations of the Divine Trinity where the Divine Persons exist in love. If human beings can and must act with *agapē*, then God must be the motive force. More pointedly, Christian love is not the cultivation or perfection of nascent human aspirations or desires. That was, for these thinkers, the fatal error of classical Hellenistic and Roman Catholic ethics. *Agapē* trumps human aspirations and, therefore, also claims about desires at the level of moral motivation.

Because *agapē* is not erotic, it is also nonpreferential. Insofar as the motive power of Christian love is the activity of God working in the moral agent, then authentically loving actions cannot be motivated by self-regard or the desire for a specific other over care *for all others*. A Christian cannot give priority to self over others, even in the case of the right to self-preservation, nor can she or he make special claims for those near and dear. While *for the sake of the neighbor,* one might care for oneself, this account of Christian love means that the self is not a

---

9. This passage was central to classical Reformation thinkers like Luther and Calvin insofar as it meant that the believer did not need to attain merits in order to gain salvation. God's free gift of grace and that alone is the power of salvation. On this see B. A. Gerrish, *Old Protestantism and the New: Essays on the Reformation Heritage* (Chicago: University of Chicago Press, 1982).

proper end of its own action, a good to be respected and enhanced. "Thus self-love," wrote Reinhold Niebuhr, "is never justified, but self-realization is allowed as the unintended but inevitable consequence of unselfish action."[10] Obedience to the command of love is neither motivated by human desire for flourishing nor aimed at the well-being of the Christian. In this way, *agapē* combats a primal human sin called concupiscence, the desire to draw all else into the self. Christian love, not driven by desire, seeks neither to possess nor to control its object, but, rather, to serve the neighbor. Christian faith is not about the perfection of human desire to a divine telos; the living God is not the object of human aspiration to happiness. The living God acts radically for the sake of sinners; the Christian exists by faith before God and is thereby moved to love in the same way.

While this idea of love seemingly breaks the tenacious grip of clinging and possessive desire in our lives, there are criticisms. The difficulty is that if *agapē* is motivated *solely* by the Divine and not by human aspirations, then the goods that surround basic human needs and inclinations receive little attention. Of course, God knows all human needs, as Barth might put it. But the question remains, ethically speaking, what it would mean for one human being to love another unmindful of needs and desires that shape life? This lends force to the criticism made by some nonreligious humanists that Christian claims are strangely otherworldly, focused on God rather than the living and breathing neighbor in her or his real needs. Christian love has the virtue of being extended to all people, but, ironically, it effaces distinction among individuals. As philosopher Tzvetan Todorov argues, Christian *agapē* is "a love of particular individuals, but a love whose objects are, indeed, interchangeable; enemies deserve it no less than friends." Even more forcefully he insists that for "Christians no less than for Plato...the adoration of the particular human person smacks of idolatry."[11]

---

10. Reinhold Niebuhr, *An Interpretation of Christian Ethics* (New York: Seabury, 1979), 33. These claims about the radical duty of Christian love were also developed by Paul Ramsey. See Paul Ramsey, *The Essential Paul Ramsey: A Collection*, ed. William Werpehowski and Stephen D. Crocco (New Haven: Yale University Press, 1994), esp. 25–40.

11. Tzvetan Todorov, *Imperfect Garden: The Legacy of Humanism* (Princeton: Princeton University Press, 2002), 119, 129.

For critics like Todorov and Martha Nussbaum the focus in ethics ought to be how love entangles persons with the joy and travail of other human beings.[12] The love of God is seen as the great detractor from the real business of life, which is attention to concrete, human others. Let religion be what it may, it cannot claim human love as its proper domain. What is needed, Nussbaum and Todorov aver, is innerworldly transcendence whose object is other people. In other words, Christian claims about love fail for two reasons. As an action-guide, Christian love detracts from concern for the particular human other. And, further, these beliefs about love imply a theistic metaphysics that is difficult, if not impossible, to sustain. Insofar as these two are connected, that is, an action-guide and its reality-condition in God's act, then rejection of one requires the rejection of the other claim as well.

Can that be right? If one situates the command to love in its biblical and narrative contexts, it is clear that Jesus' acts of healing, feeding, and forgiveness of tax collectors or an adulterous woman recognizes the particular other person in need! What is more, the reality condition disclosed in Jesus' teaching is hardly an otherworldly God; it is the very possibility of rightly loving finite life and thereby a means to stop the long journey on the road of hatred. Still, the critics have a point. In the hope of avoiding a vicious preferentialism limited to kin and clan, the modern Protestant account of *agapē* seems to have missed something important. What does it mean to love the neighbor if one does not attend to basic needs of real individuals? This brings us to the next contrast to arise out of the semantic field of love.

Agapē, Philia, and Justice

Unlike *erōs* or erotic love, Christian love on the standard account is radically nonpreferential. Whereas all forms of *erōs* specify the special desire and attraction for the object of love, making him, her, or it a unique focus of concern, *agapē*, modeled on God's love for sinners, neither

---

12. See Martha Nussbaum, *Love's Knowledge: Essays on Philosophy and Literature* (New York: Oxford University Press, 1990). For similar worries see Iris Murdoch, *Metaphysics as a Guide to Morals* (New York: Penguin, Allen, 1992); Raimond Gaita, *A Common Humanity: Thinking about Love and Truth and Justice* (New York: Routledge, 2000); and Irving Singer, *Meaning in Life: The Creation of Value* (New York: Free Press, 1992). Also see Darlene Weaver, *Self-Love and Christian Ethics* (Cambridge, UK: Cambridge University Press, 2002).

recognizes nor endows others with special status. Like modern, Kantian ideas about justice, *agapē* is nondiscriminatory and thereby works against all special relations. Yet, in a way more radical than claims about justice, Christian love, because it is divinely motivated, acts on behalf of even the sinner, the evildoer, the enemy (Matt. 5:44–46; Luke 6:27, 32). Whereas acts of justice on most accounts require that like be treated as like, *agapē*, so it was claimed, reaches out to care for those unlike the lover. *Agapē* is not defined by a logic of equivalence but, rather, by a logic of superabundance.[13] Christian love is not just nonpreferential, it is also *nonreciprocal*.[14]

While the term *philia* is used in the New Testament to denote mutual regard and friendship among people bound to each other through lineage and faith, *agapē*, on the standard account, is something more. The Christian acting in love for others does not rightly expect that the same love will be given to oneself or that one can make a rightful claimed on others for love. Christian love, ethically speaking, is focused not on an abstract "other" or even members of one's own clan and kind, but on neighbor love. The idea of the "neighbor" expands the scope of moral concern beyond the strict demands of justice or *philia*, both of which retain some idea of reciprocity. This is because the idea of "neighbor," despite Todorov's critique noted above, is specified not with reference to the object of just actions, but in terms of the *doer* of acts of love. As the parable of the Good Samaritan aptly shows, Jesus explodes the question, "Whose is my neighbor?" by transforming it into the question, "Am I a good neighbor to the suffering?" (compare Luke 10:29–37) The right relation to the living God is not via desire and its possible objects, as with the contrast between *erōs* and *agapē*. Rather, it is when the dictates of justice and its logic of equivalence are transgressed by the superabundant care of God's action in Christ.

---

13. See Paul Ricoeur, *Figuring the Sacred: Religion, Narrative, and Imagination,* ed. Mark I. Wallace, trans. David Pellauer (Minneapolis: Fortress Press, 1995). Also see *Paul Ricoeur and Contemporary Moral Thought,* ed. J. Wall, W. Schweiker, and W. D. Hall (New York: Routledge, 2002).

14. Gene Outka has helpfully nuanced these arguments. He notes that mutuality or reciprocity might be the ideal fruition of Christian love even if the logic of equivalence is not the condition for that love. See Gene Outka, *Agapē: An Ethical Analysis* (New Haven: Yale University Press, 1972).

Christian love so conceived stands against moral ideals, like *philia*, coming from ancient Greece that insist, as Aristotle would hold, that only like can love like. A friend is simply another self. Yet Christian love is also, and for the same reason, opposed to modern, Kantian-like conceptions of justice grounded in equality of consideration. Those ideals and conceptions are at best pale reflections of the radical claims of *agapē*. The encounter with the Divine is in an event in which justice is sustained even as divine mercy is revealed. That event is the cross of Christ and Christ's act of "atonement."[15] Christian love exceeds the law; one is justified by faith in this event of grace. But this also means that the standard account of Christian love was beyond the reach of Jewish Law. It was deeply informed by Paul's theology rather than derived from the New Testament Gospels.[16] Yet we must ask: is it really possible on biblical grounds to understand the love of neighbor without also delighting in the law of God? In making this claim about *agapē* beyond law and justice, theologians aborted any substantive project of reflexive self-transformation in and through engaging the life and witness of another religious communities, especially the Jewish community. That fact exposes another aspect of the standard account.

Command and Freedom to Love

Thus far I have tried to show how the standard account of *agapē* developed by twentieth-century Protestant theologians drew a categorical distinction between Christian love and other usual ways of connecting love to the moral life, namely, through desire for the Good or concrete others and also the kind of mutuality entailed in reciprocal relations of other-regard in justice and friendship. We have also seen that this argument upends usual ideas about the human relation to the Divine. God is not the highest object of human desires; God acts toward human beings in an event of unmerited love. God is not the God of justice alone, but

---

15. These ideas are longstanding in Christian thought and there are many theories of atonement. In this modern version of *agapē*, and the connection of justice and mercy, the key classical voice is St. Anselm's argument in *Cur Deus Homo*.

16. For a recent work that follows this radical Pauline line and in fact reduplicates many of these earlier twentieth-century theologians (though, of course, without acknowledging this fact), see Alain Badiou, *Saint Paul: The Foundation of Universalism*, trans. Ray Brassier (Stanford: Stanford University Press, 2003).

the God of a mercy that exceeds or transgresses the logic of equivalence and thereby other-turns friendship and justice. With that discussion in hand, it is possible now to isolate the reality condition that makes *agapē* possible, the reality of divine freedom.

It has long been noted that Christians are commanded to love. What does that mean? After the blistering modern critique of religious servitude by Nietzsche, Freud, and others, can one show that following Christ's precepts enacts freedom rather than bowing to a foreign will? In order to redress the charge, Tillich and other twentieth-century Protestant theologians coined a term for freedom in love, calling it "theonomous" existence. The Christian is not in the strict sense "autonomous," since, as noted above, the norm of one's action is not self-determination but the divine act of love. Yet this divine norm is not a heteronomous imposition of a foreign will on the self that demands blind obedience. What was taken away at the level of self-love is returned to human beings in terms of freedom. Human love has no divine analogue or even aspiration, but human freedom is grounded and measured by God.[17] God's freedom, not law or human aspiration or special relations or claims to justice, is the reality condition of the command of Christian love.

An action-guide is reality revealing. As Kant might put it, ought implies can, but, for these theologians, freedom is not noumenous; the reality of the "can," the reality of freedom, is the being of God. Freedom in love is nothing else than the very being of God.[18] Even the love of God — the bonds of the Triune being of God — is grasped through the utter freedom of God to be God. This overturns traditional strategies of theological thinking. No longer is the reality of God to be conceived along the lines of a "substance," as in classical Western thought. So, God is not the being of being, the highest substance, the object of our desire. The reality of God must be thought from when and where God freely gives God's self for thinking, namely, in the radical love of sinners

17. This is why Tillich could speak of ecstatic humanism and even Barth went on in later years to champion the humanity of God.

18. On this point, see Eberhard Jüngel, *God's Being Is in Becoming: The Trinitarian Being of God in the Theology of Karl Barth*, trans. and intro. John Webster (Edinburgh: T. & T. Clark, 2004); and Robert P. Scharlemann, *The Being of God: Theology and the Experience of Truth* (San Francisco: HarperSanFrancisco, 1984).

manifest in the Christ. This is why Christian love cannot be conceived with reference to human desire or the reciprocal relations of justice still immersed in ideas about being as substance. Christian love is the form that divine freedom takes in the world.

Reflection on the encounter with the Divine is of a special kind. Barth, for instance, claimed that the freedom of God to being God for us is the condition of the hearing of the divine Word and thus the permission to obey God's command. Tillich, in a different way, construes theonomous life as overcoming existential estrangement and thereby enacting true humanity under the conditions of existence.[19] The condition and depth of human freedom is found in God. The self is, we might say, not a source of freedom but in love a vehicle or medium for divine freedom in the world. Neither desire nor the logic of justice warrant theological reflection. Christian love focuses on the being of God as freedom.

And yet, here, too, the critic rightly raises a question. This construal of *agapē* as theonomous existence might render it difficult to impute or ascribe responsibility to individuals. If God is the real operative agent of love, the freedom that is the condition and motive for radical neighborly regard, then in any loving act it is God who is responsible and not human agents.[20] Theologically considered, this move ensures the absolute priority and gratuity of divine grace. No merit or works-righteousness could be claimed on behalf of a human being for genuinely loving actions. In a word, not only is the typical concept of *agapē* Pauline, rather than derived from the teachings of Jesus, it is also ardently Protestant insofar as it is linked to claims about salvation through grace and grace alone.

---

19. There are great differences between these thinkers. For Tillich, the Divine is the power of being as the depth structure of the self-world relation. This means that divine power is always mediated in the world and, accordingly, ontological structures and domains of culture become theologically important. Barth, conversely, is much more insistent that the divine freedom is not mediated by ontological structures but, rather, interrupts being and time. Still, most contemporary thinkers fail to grasp that Barth, Tillich, and others were making strikingly similar claims about the being of God as freedom.

20. There is a long history of worry about this point, usually around idea of predestination. For later Protestants in the seventeenth and eighteenth centuries, Luther and Calvin's insistence on the bondage of the will and God's predestination were not seen as doctrines of comfort, as Calvin and Luther held. These claims seemed to provoke profound anxiety because they seemed to imply that human beings do not even have a receptive freedom to respond to God's grace. Given this, later theologians, like Wesley and others, work to insist on some place of genuine human freedom in the religious and moral life.

How then is one to think about the proper domain of human responsibility? Does the critic's worry about Christian love being otherworldly return once we understand the reality condition of love as divine freedom? How can one preserve the ways in which human dignity is bound to imputations and self-ascriptions of responsibility?

Agapē's Appeal

By exploring the standard account of *agapē* developed by twentieth-century Protestant theologians we have unfolded a paradoxical hermeneutics of love. *Agapē* is the form divine freedom takes in the world in and through human agents and it thereby overturns commonsense notions of love rooted in desire and the reciprocal relations of friendship. As noted, an action-guide, a command, is reality revealing; it shows the being of God as the condition of human freedom. *Ought* (the command to love) reveals *is* (the being of God) as the condition of *can* (human, theonomous freedom). It is not difficult to see the attraction of this account of Christian love, especially in a time scared by world war, the fanatical love of blood and soil, and the madness of racist desire and lust. Internal to the biblical tradition, *agapē* places the accent in Christian conviction on God's freedom against all claims of desire, debts of justice, or religiously sanctioned obedience. The state, one's race, any ideology, or political institution could never claim ultimate obedience. By conceiving of the divine freedom as the reality condition of love, these theologians found a way to retain love as a guide for Christian action while breaking those bonds of human desire and affection that had come to horrific and bloody expression in the horror of war. Christian love ignites radical concern for the other rooted in the absolute freedom of God.

Importantly, the standard account of *agapē* helped to bring to an end a classical metaphysical account of God. God is not a being, even the highest and most glorious being, where "being" is conceived along the lines of a substance. God's being is freedom. The tenacious grip of desire, the logic of equivalence expressive of beliefs about self-worth, and the constraints of natural bonds of duty rooted in all-too-human loyalties to blood and soil cannot and do not define the being of God or the proper relation to the living God. This theological vision undercut the traditional onto-theology that backed structures of political, racial, and sexual power.[21] What was crucial for these Protestant theologians was, then, not the love commands as action-guides; what was crucial was the way in which Christian love opened a new vision of reality and the place of love, justice, and freedom in a world at war.[22] Who in good conscience could deny the force of these claims? Sad to say, too many Christians did!

However, the standard account is not without its problems. The picture of *agapē* makes a double move that teeters between some form of humanism and also, ironically, a kind of anti-humanism. On the one hand, *agapē* utterly dethrones and decenters the self, even from the heart of ethical reflection. The moral agent is not a rational and purposive being who decides to exercise powers of action in concert with others. Rather, the self is located in a complex field of nonhuman forces defined by the freedom and love of the Divine and bound through God's being to acknowledgment and care for others. As we have seen, this opens the standard account of Christian love to the charge that it is strangely inattentive to concrete human needs. On the other hand, the human agent is recentered as the locus of divine concern and activity in the world. The self is ecstatic, caught up, in the Divine Other and in this way one can and ought to speak, as Barth did, of the humanity of God. The distinctiveness of human existence is located within the freedom of God who graciously creates, redeems, and restores the broken.

One should not gainsay the achievements of what I have called the standard account of *agapē* in its various versions. Yet, in my judgment,

---

21. This was, of course, the implication of the Barmen Declaration. It is also why Barth attacked natural theology even while Bonhoeffer challenged ideas about the so-called orders of nature. Of course, one problem now facing Christian theology in an age of ecological endangerment is to rethink the attack on the "natural" in order to offer a robust understanding of the good of human life and also the moral considerability of nonhuman life. On this topic, see James M. Gustafson, *A Sense of the Divine: The Natural Environment from a Theocentric Perspective* (Cleveland: Pilgrim, 1994); Jürgen Moltmann, *The Spirit of Life: A Universal Affirmation*, trans. Margaret Kohl (Minneapolis: Fortress Press, 2001); Larry L. Rasmussen, *Earth Community, Earth Ethics* (Maryknoll, N.Y.: Orbis Books, 1998); and William Schweiker, *Theological Ethics and Global Dynamics: In the Time of Many Worlds* (Oxford: Blackwell, 2004).

22. What is surprising but never noted is that the main features of this idea of *agapē*, if not the idea itself or its Christian origins, has returned, always unacknowledged, under various guises of postmodern thought. It finds varied expression in claims by thinkers like Emmanuel Lévinas about "the other," Paul Ricoeur's ideas about the "gift," Alain Badiou's argument for universalism, and also nonmetaphysical conceptions of God beyond Being currently debated among French phenomenologists.

ambiguities in that account ought to give anyone pause. The position can unwittingly be exploited to further a quite anti-humanistic agenda that divests actual human beings of responsibility. Yet the account can teeter in the other way as well. It proposes an anthropocentrism in which human beings are the sole end of God's purposes. In the world marked by both massive human suffering and increasing ecological endangerment through the extension of human powers, neither of those options is any longer acceptable. When all forms of life are endangered, human beings must bear responsibility for the exercise and transformation of the capacities at their disposal, acknowledge human worth, and yet never limit the domain of value to human life. The human enemy and also "nature" as the age-old enemy of human striving now demand love if we are to leave the long road of hatred.[23] A different, if related, account of love beyond the standard account is needed. This is required not only in order to meet the criticisms of Christian love but also to face the challenges of our own day.

Love Commands and Ancient Humanism

The analysis of the standard account of *agapē* just undertaken has disclosed its conceptual power and also some of its problems. In order to avoid those problems, I propose to mediate theological claims about *agapē* in and through engaging the biblical texts that situate love within the actual travail of life. In this respect, I believe it is important to locate the discussion of Christian love within the trajectories of thought ignited by the Sermon on the Mount (Matthew 5–7) rather than the Lutheran/Reformed dogmatic stance of the standard account of *agapē*.

This "placement" of the question of love is most adequate for contemporary Christian theological ethics because it enables one to respond to the problems isolated in the standard account of *agapē*. First, insofar

23. On the problem of the status of nature in light of the extension of human power in our age see Hans Jonas, *The Imperative of Responsibility: In Search of an Ethics for the Technological Age*, trans. Hans Jonas and David Herr (Chicago: University of Chicago Press, 1984); Erazim Kohák, *The Embers and the Stars: A Philosophical Inquiry into the Moral Sense of Nature* (Chicago: University of Chicago Press, 1984); Langdon Gilkey, *Blue Twilight: Nature, Creationism, and American Religion* (Minneapolis: Fortress Press, 2001); and Gustafson, *A Sense of the Divine*.

as the Sermon opens with the so-called Beatitudes, one finds grounds for reflection on the relation between blessedness or happiness (*makarioi*) and the commands to love. This will allow us to reconsider the place of desire and human aspiration in ways otherwise than found in the standard account of *agapē*. Second, this placement of thought situates reflection in the context of Jesus' Torah teaching retained within an early Jewish Christian community. That enables us to trace the connection between Christian ideas and Jewish thought seemingly disallowed by the standard account's rejection of the "Law." Third, the Sermon sparks inquiry into the connection between love of enemy and "perfection" (*teleioi*). This connection enables one to explore the radical nature of Christian love in ways similar to the standard account but with different implications. What is revealed as the reality condition sustaining love is not an event of freedom, but, rather, the divine outpouring of the bounty of creation that constitutes the domain of human responsibility and the goodness of life itself. It is humanism without anthropocentrism.

Finally, focus on the Sermon on the Mount as the epitome of Jesus' teaching is central to strands of Christian tradition too often ignored in the standard account of *agapē*. For instance, John Wesley, writing within eighteenth-century England and drawing inspiration from the ancient Greek Fathers and also his own Anglican heritage, thought that the Sermon set forth Christ's "whole plan of religion," in which is found "the nature of that holiness without which no man shall see the Lord." The Sermon teaches nothing less than "the art of happiness." In this religion of the heart, God is the very "soul of the universe" and human life is restored to the image of God.[24] Placing the question of Christian love within the textual intersections of Jesus' Torah teaching rather than the semantic landscape of Greek terms for love makes a difference in understanding love in the moral life! It might provide some novel response to our situation when under the forces of global dynamics hatred is now also globalized.

A thorough engagement with the Sermon on the Mount is, of course, not possible in one essay. Granting that limitation, a few comments on

---

24. See Wesley's thirteen sermons on the *Sermon on the Mount* in his *Sermons on Several Occasions*, 201–380.

the text are needed in order to sustain my theological and ethical reflections. It is important, first, to note that a series of antitheses structures much of chapter 5 of the Sermon. The chapter concludes with what some scholars, notably Hans Dieter Betz, judge to be the keystone of the whole, namely, perfection as the imitation of God.[25] The antitheses continue the idea of an inversion in moral expectations found in the standard account of *agapē*, but, importantly enough, without denying human desires or relations. These desires and relations are intensified through a rhetorical trope. The antitheses, we can say, are the linguistic form within which the paradoxical work of the religious imagination comes to articulation. Jesus teaches like this:

> You have heard that it was said to those of ancient times, "You shall not murder."...But I say to you that if you are angry with your brother or sister, you will liable to judgment.... You have heard it was said, "You shall not commit adultery." But I say to you that everyone who looks at a woman with lust has already committed adultery with her in his heart.... "You have heard that it was said, "An eye for an eye and a tooth for a tooth." But I say to you, Do not resist the evildoer. (Matt. 5:21–22, 27–28, 38–39)

Not only is murder prohibited, but also hatred; not only adultery that rends asunder human bonds, but also pernicious, unconstrained lust. The logic of equivalence — an eye for an eye — is overturned with a demand of nonreciprocal resistance. Human desires that motivate actions are retained, intensified, and transformed.

The last antithesis in chapter 5 is also a negation of common sense but this time about the right object of neighbor love. "You have heard that it was said, 'You shall love your neighbor and hate your enemy.' But I say to you, Love your enemies and pray for those who persecute you" (Matt. 5:43–44). This command continues with a surprising, shocking connection to the Divine. Love and pray for the enemy so "that you may be children of your Father in heaven." This inversion focuses on Leviticus

---

25. Hans Dieter Betz, *The Sermon on the Mount: A Commentary on the Sermon on the Mount, Including the Sermon on the Plain (Matthew 5:3–7:27 and Luke 6:20–49)*, Hermeneia (Minneapolis: Fortress Press, 1995). I am greatly indebted to Betz's contribution to these points, both his written work and from several conversations.

19:18, found amid the so-called Holiness Code, and thus matters of ritual and moral holiness. The Torah text reads: "You shall not take vengeance or bear a grudge against any of your people, but you shall love your neighbor as yourself: I am the Lord." In Matthew's account, Jesus alters the text. He reads Leviticus *as if* it conjoins neighbor love limited to the people of Israel ("your people") with the hatred of enemy, and then he commands a love not just of one's own people but of the enemy. This rhetorical move poses the question, "Who is the neighbor?" It distances Jesus' interpretation of the command from any account that would place hatred of enemy coequal with neighbor love. What is more, the authority for this teaching rests not on divine commandment, "I am the Lord," as in the Torah. Jesus recasts the warrant for love from command to the action of God.

Betz has astutely noted that we must ask, How does God act toward God's own enemies, toward human beings bent on the destruction of life? Importantly, the passage under consideration (Matt. 5:45a) continues with a claim about God's actions. Jesus portrays the Divine pouring out the bounty of creation even on evildoers. God "sends rain on the righteous and on the unrighteous" (Matt. 5:45b). In a reassertion of the Noahide covenant, where after the flood God promises never again to destroy life in response to evil, the Divine is portrayed here as acting to sustain and further creation despite human vice and ingratitude. The divine act is a "yes" to human existence despite moral failure. To be a child of God means then to love as God loves, to be perfect as God is perfect (Matt. 5:48), and thus to love what is other, different, even hostile and not simply what returns love for love in bonds of sameness.

Of course, this "yes" to existence embodied in the enemy is not without its judgment. God acts to transform the "enemy," to evoke gratitude for life and thereby instill the intention to respect and enhance creation and all its creatures. One defeats an enemy if they are reconciled, made friends in common cause.[26] God's actions do not aim to leave in place the righteous and the unrighteous but, rather, to transform the unrighteous

---

26. One is reminded of Abraham Lincoln's response to a bystander who learned that he had appointed a former critic to be one of his cabinet secretaries: "Madam, do I not destroy my enemies when I make them my friends?" The remark is cited by Martin Luther King Jr. in *Strength to Love*, 53. King adds: "This is the power of redemptive love."

into the way of life and thus to vanquish the enemy. Human existence is set amid the Divine's working in and through creation in which human responsibility is evoked and demanded. What distinguishes the one who imitates the divine love is, then, that his or her acts of love are motivated by inclusion of others in the scope of love for life. By so acting, one is perfect "as your heavenly Father is perfect." God's will is done on earth as in heaven.

Many scholars note that the idea that one should not repay hatred with hatred or that one is not just to love friends and hate the enemy are widespread claims in the ancient world. They are not unique to Jesus' teaching, even if he gives them a distinctive expression. Socrates, in Plato's portrait, argued that one ought to suffer rather than to do wrong and that doing evil even to the wrongdoer is immoral (see *Republic* 1, 332d–336a and *Crito* 49a–e). The Epicureans and also Plutarch have similar teachings. Leviticus 19:17, the verse just prior to the contested one, condemns "hate in your heart" even as in Exodus 23:4–5 there is a concern for those who hate you. In these strands of thought, and others as well, there is concern to treat the enemy in a humane way, an "ancient humanism," as Betz calls it.

In this light, it seems clear that Jesus' teaching contributes to a humanistic agenda of finding human commonalities that extend moral concern even to wrongdoers and one's enemies. The distinctiveness of Jesus' teaching is not with respect to the enemy *qua* enemy. What is distinctive about Christian love, I submit, is its link between the problem of the enemy and God's action toward all creation. That is to say, the claim about the enemy is embedded in a construal of the context of all life ordered not just by natural processes but also by divine creative and redemptive action. The being of God remains the reality condition disclosed in the action-guide to love the enemy. But the divine reality is conceived not merely in terms of freedom. God's being is a self-transformation of retributive power manifest in the outpouring of life and, what is more, the outpouring of the Spirit in new life.[27] It is this

---

27. On this account of the divine reality see William Schweiker, *Responsibility and Christian Ethics*. On the outpouring of the Spirit, see Michael Welker, *God the Spirit: A Theology of the Holy Spirit*, trans. John F. Hoffmeyer (Minneapolis: Fortress Press, 1994).

divine power that vanquishes the enemy through restoration. The super-abundance of divine life rather than freedom or sheer power is the reality disclosed in Christian love. The abyss of God's power is grasped within the living being of God that creates the space of human responsibility.

Of course, the biblical texts leave open crucial questions. Why does the text in Matthew 5:43–44 shift from the claim not to hate the *"enemy,"* a singular, to the injunction to "Love your *enemies* and pray for those who persecute you," the plural? Is the persecutor the definition of the enemy? What are the forms hatred takes? Should they all be objects of forgiveness and mercy? Are there any limits to mercy and forgiveness?[28] Recall, the idea of love cannot do all the ethical work! Granted that further ethical reflection is needed, can we nevertheless rethink and retrieve something like that ancient humanism for our age? How might this enable a response to our moral and religious situation?

Interlocking Loves

In light of the above theological and textual reflections, my strategy now will be to focus on the interlocking commands of love beginning with the surprising, even shocking, connection between the love of enemy and a relation to God, the "Father in heaven." This is an exercise of Christian imagination wherein the meaning of faith and love are grasped in and through a seeming negation. My reason for undertaking this mode of thinking is not unlike that faced by those twentieth-century theologians explored above. Our world is also at war, in various ways. People long for some way to grasp human commonalities within the wild and wonderful and dangerous diversity of our species. Perhaps more than ever, we face the moral question of how to treat the enemy for the sake of the survival of our world.[29] That question poses a profound challenge to each of the world's religions to clarify the moral viability of beliefs about the Divine, the sacred. Religious people can ill afford to believe any longer that the object of their devotion commands hostility toward

---

28. On these questions see Jefferie G. Murphy and Jean Hampton, *Forgiveness and Mercy* (Cambridge: Cambridge University Press, 1988).

29. On this see Donald W. Shriver, *An Ethics for Enemies: Forgiveness in Politics* (New York: Oxford University Press, 1995).

others. Seen in the context of Jesus' Torah teaching, my claim is that the love commands disclose a structure of understanding, a way of perceiving and grasping the meaning of the human moral lot. The form of understanding instigated by the commands founds the moral adventure for Christians rather than providing every norm, rule, or directive needed to carry on with life.

The command to love the enemy is, paradoxically, bound to love of God insofar as it is meant to imitate the divine action. This upends common religious sensibilities where it is usually believed that one is obligated to hate and quell all that is opposed to God. Surely the godly thing to do is to hate the godless, the enemies of God! What would seem a negation of the love of God — that is, to love the enemy of God and what God has commanded one to love — is, surprisingly, linked to a right relation to the Divine. At the heart of a Christian conception of reality is, then, love as respect and enhancement of what is other and thus a transformation of power in light of what serves future life. From that insight flows the complexity of another command of love: the self is loved through what is other (the neighbor) and the other (neighbor) through the self, thereby holding power responsible for what is vulnerable to it.

What becomes apparent is the mutual entailment of the various commands to love (God; self/neighbor; enemy) even as these are presented in ways that seems to negate commonsense moral and religious conceptions of love. The command to love does not thereby constitute an ontologically distinct form of love. The standard account is simply wrong on that point. Rather, the love commands are a prism through which a vision of life must be factored if any love is to attain fullness. The command of love locates human life within a space defined by God's action to respect and enhance creation in the face of threats to life. It intensifies awareness and perception of the depth of moral reality. The love commands are hyperbolic demands that pierce consciousness and awaken one to the full reality of life. Stated otherwise, love requires that we affirm the great gift of life and labor to sustain all that is needed for its flourishing.

The commands to love in their interlocking forms instigate a kind of religious understanding in which finite being, even as threatened and threatening, is affirmed as good. This is how the commands are sense making. One has then a new way to specify the distinctiveness of Christian love as well as its relation to other moral and religious outlooks. Not only is the human other to be loved, but also all of life as the condition for our own existence, even though life threatens us with loss and suffering and death. Christian love thereby lends its voice to reclaiming "ancient humanism" about how to treat others by grounding that command not in aspirations to virtue or the demands of justice but gratitude for creation. Unlike the Greek and Roman philosophers for whom hatred and animosity are destructive of the virtue of one's own soul, the concern in Christian love is not only with self but really the sustaining conditions for life. Relatedly, Leviticus (19:17–18) demands one not to take vengeance, but the warrant for the demand is the so-called Golden Rule and thus the principle of reciprocity or justice, namely, to love your neighbor as yourself. If the philosophers reach the grand humanistic vision of not doing evil to the wrongdoer within the ambit of self-cultivation, then in the Leviticus texts it is the idea of equivalence that supports an analogous vision.

Christians are called to join anyone who struggles to invigorate the insights of that ancient humanism under present global realities and endangerments. They do so in a particular or distinctive way. Again, the command to love the enemy is not backed by ideas about self-cultivation or justice. It is about the conditions of life made apparent in a new form of understanding once this command is linked, as it is, to divine action toward creation and the enemy. The command, in other words, reveals a hidden blessing through its seeming negation, the blessing of life itself. It asks, in essence, this: In the face of whom could one will that the sustaining of life not continue? Is the enemy, and so threat to self and the breakdown of reciprocal relations, a necessary and sufficient condition to deny the love of life? Jesus confronts the listener with the decision God faced at the time of the "flood," and then bids the hearer to imitate not a warrior God but the God of new creation. The command to love the enemy is a rhetorical antithesis that intensifies to the breaking point commonsense moral and religious consciousness. Do we really love life? Can one love life, even more life, despite the fact that existence is marked by strife, conflict, loss, death, and sorrow?

Christian love is the means for the radical interpretation of the many forms of human love so that our loves enable an apprehension, a vision, of the goodness of life and thereby enables one to live in gratitude. Christian love is not a distinct form of love; it is not the ground and power of all love. The diagnostic force of the Matthean text, I suggest, is to display how human life can be situated in a bountiful created order that gives and sustains life and yet is also marked by animosity, disease, death, and hatred of life and others. Along with the chorus of our desires, the claims of justice, and the depths of freedom, human beings are situated morally in the world in our comportments of gratitude or hatred of the full ambiguity of life. The interlocking commands of love are to evoke gratitude for existence in the face of this ambiguity and hope that this same gratitude will arise in others, even in the enemy. Christian love is thereby the capacity to see through the violence and brokenness of human life so that we might not just live but actually love life. The love commands open the possibility for continued love of neighbor, self, and God amid the terror of human destructiveness.

The distinctiveness of Christian love, accordingly, is not that it is somehow nonerotic or nonsocial or nonworldly. It makes no *a priori* judgment about our desires, our friendships, and our temporal lives. Christian love even leaves open the possibility that, for the sake of sustaining life, some forms of aggression must be restrained and resisted. Untoward and unjust aggression against the innocent must be resisted, even with lethal force. As noted throughout this inquiry, love alone cannot and ought not do all the work in theological ethics. Nevertheless, resistance to evil cannot and ought not lead to a hatred of life, any life.[30] Human existence can and may and must express a gratitude for life even in the face of its brokenness. The command to love the enemy and its connection to the other love commands is a jarring inversion of normal perception meant to shock us into grateful awareness of the preciousness of finite life.

---

30. This is not the place to enter into a discussion of just-war theory, only to say that I judge the account of Christian love I am giving leaves that possibility open. And that was part of the force of my claim that a viable theological ethics cannot be built around one idea, even the idea of love.

The reality condition revealed in the commands is the being of God as that self-transforming power which evokes gratitude for existence, joy in life. Any form of love that does not manifest in its distinct way that awareness is surely at odds with itself. How often do erotic drives secretly turn to hate or friendships sadly conceal animosity and envy? And what then is desire or friendship? How often do the agents of justice deliver retribution that exceed the limits of justice and so thwart the cause of justice itself? The question is how to keep our desires, claims to justice, and our power from thwarting their own purposes. In order to do so, these capacities must be tested against their negation and inversion. This may well appear as a scandal to a conception of the moral life founded on justice or sheer folly to any ethics that focuses on self-cultivation. It means that the mark of love is the intensity of its gratitude for life in the face of all that can destroy and demean human and nonhuman existence.

Love and Theological Humanism

Christian love articulates a way in the world moved by gratitude for life. The imitation of the Divine enacts that image of God in the uniquely human form of gratitude that respects and enhances the integrity of life, even the "enemy." This does not deny or demean the other forms of love that cruise through human lives or those traditions that focus on those loves. Rather, this love situates life in a distinctive moral space defined by the divine action and demands concrete, decisive labor in the face of real and grave practical threats to the integrity of life. It opens the question of God in the very center of our moral vocation. Love does so not through some abstract other, but in the concreteness of any human encounter that threatens to overwhelm and destroy gratitude for life. This kind of love is purity of heart, and, thereby, to borrow again from Wesley, the way to see God in all things.

This kind of love is the important, even distinctive, contribution that Christian teaching can make to ethics in an age riddled with hatred and war, driven by wanton consumption, hopeless and ungrateful. The hatred of life besets too many among people worldwide; it is a blight upon the human project. Nothing but misery follows from that hatred since it pits one's being against finite life. Subtract "gratitude for life" and does love in all of its confusions really remain? I can only hope, even pray, that Christian reflections on love will be part of a wider movement of spirit that evokes gratitude for life in all its tenuousness and thereby helps to calm the fury of our troubled age.

Chapter 6

THE IMAGE, THE GLORY, AND THE HOLY

Aspects of Being Human in Biblical Thought

Tikva Frymer-Kensky

When one considers biblical ideas of humanity, the first thought to come
to mind is invariably the idea of humanity as *tselem 'Elohim,* the "image
of God." This idea became the template for much later Jewish thinking
about humankind and has a long and complex history in Christianity.[1]
It is therefore somewhat surprising to note that the term *tselem 'Elohim*
appears in the Hebrew Scriptures only in the primeval history of Genesis 1–11. The concept also may underlie the thinking of Ezekiel and the
author of the book of Ruth, but it is still a very restricted concept. Elsewhere in the Bible human beings are categorized as *nefesh hayyah* (living
being), a term they share with the animals, and as possessors of *kavod*
(glory), a characteristic they share with God. In addition to these first two
biblical ideas of humanity, other biblical texts express the obligation of
all of Israel to be *qadosh,* holy-like, or God-like. In what follows, I examine the meanings of these three biblical terms for central attributes of
humanity — being the *tselem 'Elohim,* "the image of God" (*imago Dei*),
having *kavod* ("glory"), and being *qadosh* ("holy") — within the context

---

1. For an excellent review and bibliography of the early Christian discussion and the
pre-1970 scholarly studies see David Clines, "Humanity as the Image of God," in *On the
Way to the Postmodern: Old Testament Essays 1967–1998,* vol. 2, Journal for the Study of
the Old Testament. Supplement series, 292 (Sheffield: Sheffield Academic Press, 1998), 447–
97; originally published as "The Image of God in Man," *Tyndale Bulletin* 19 (1968): 53–
103. For early Jewish development of the theme, see Yair Lorberbaum, *Imago Dei: Rabbinic
Literature, Maimonides and Nahmanides,* Ph.D. dissertation (Jerusalem Hebrew University of
Jerusalem, 1997), recently published by Magnes Press. For a theological review of this issue in
Christianitity, see Tikva Frymer-Kensky, "The Image: Religious Anthropology in Judaism and
Christianity" in *Christianity in Jewish Terms,* ed. Tikva Frymer-Kensky, et al. (Boulder, Colo.:
Westview, 2000), 321–36, 399.

of their political, social, and ritual thought worlds in the ancient Near East, and within the context of contemporary theology and religious anthropology.

The Image (*Tselem*)

The word *tselem* means "statue" and the idea that a human could be the statue of a God begins very early, in Egypt, in the eighteenth dynasty (ca. 1539–1295 B.C.E.), when the pharaoh, who was considered the very incarnation of a god, calls himself the "image" of that god, and he is followed by almost all succeeding pharaohs. It was particularly popular in the twenty-fifth dynasty (ca. 719–657 B.C.E.), when the pharaohs declared themselves the image of Horus or the image of Re. In Egyptian wisdom literature, in the "Wisdom of Meri-kare," the concept is extended to all human beings, all of us being statues of the gods.[2] The Assyrian texts are of particular interest both because Assyrian kings did not consider themselves gods and because the term that Tukulti-Ninurta I and later Assyrian kings used to call themselves "image of God" is *ṣalam ili,* clearly the same words as Genesis's *tselem 'Elohim.* "It is he" says the Tukulti-Ninurta Epic, "who is the eternal image of Enlil, attentive to the voice of the people, to the counsel of the land."[3] Other kings follow him, as does an *āšipu* priest identifying himself as "statue of Marduk" as he performed the rites that invoked Marduk's powers.[4]

To understand what the phrase "statue of a god" might have meant in the ancient world, it is important to look at the function of actual statues. Very early, we find, figurines were placed in the temple to appear before the god in permanent praise and petition. The early kings placed such statues of themselves in the temple;[5] they also established statues

---

2. For a review of the texts, see Otto Eberhard, "Der Mensch als Geschöpf und Bild Gottes in Ägypten," in *Probleme biblischer Theologie* (Munich: Kaiser Verlag, 1971), 335–48.

3. Tukulti Ninurta Epic I 18' (= A Obv.) numeration as in the English translation by Benjamin Foster, ed., *Before the Muses: An Anthology of Akkadian Literature,* vol. I (Bethesda, Md.: CDL Press, 1993), 209–30, esp. 210.

4. There is considerable literature on these Akkadian texts but, for convenience see Jeffrey Tigay, "The Image of God and the Flood: Some New Developments," in Shapiro, Alexander M. and Burton I. Cohen, eds, *Studies in Jewish Education and Judaica in Honor of Louis Newman* (New York: KTAV, 1984), 169–82.

5. See, for this question, William W. Hallo, "Cult Statue and Divine Image: A Preliminary Study," in William W. Hallo, et al., eds., *Scripture in Context II* (Winona Lake, Ind.:

in which they themselves were the object of veneration,[6] and statues
that they set up at the far-flung borders of the empire. Perhaps the most
impressive set of such statues are the many black diorite statues of King
Gudea of Lagas. One of the most complete texts declares that the statue
be set in a libation shrine and gives a list of foods with which it should be
provided.[7] As the statue is being brought into the temple, Gudea the *ensi*
(official) "puts the word" to Gudea the *alan* (statue): " 'Image, to my lord
[the god Ningursu] speak!' " (7:21–25). He then gives a list of his pious
deeds that his statue is to recite continually to the great god. Later, the
inscription informs the readers that Gudea installed this image so that
it might recite these words (7:37). During the making of the statue, its
installation in the shrine, and its dedication by the king, the statue has
become animated so that it can perform this duty of reciting the king's
great deeds.

As time went on, the statues of kings were overtaken in importance
by the cult statues of the gods themselves. The term *alan* ^{d}X, "statue
of the god X," comes from the Early Old Babylonian period (ca. 1900–
1600 B.C.E.), but in the late Sumerian period before this (ca. 2020 B.C.E.)
months were named after the travels of gods to their temples, and even
earlier (ca. 2300 B.C.E.), cylinder seals showed human-form gods rid-
ing on boats.[8] Statues were set up in the cellar of the temple, and were
clothed and fed by their worshipers.[9] In Babylonian mythology and ritual, they were brought in procession to the central shrine in Babylon so
that the gods would meet in sacred convocation.

Eisenbrauns, 1983), 1–17; idem, "Texts, Statues, and the Cult of the Divine King" *Vetus Testa-
mentum* 40 (1990): 54–66; and Irene Winter, " 'Idols of the King': Royal Images as Recipients
of Ritual Action in Ancient Mesopotamia" *Journal of Ritual Studies* 61 (1992): 15–42.

6. For this question, see Hallo, "Cult Statue and Divine Image"; idem, "Texts, Statues,
and the Cult of the Divine King."

7. Horst Steible, *Die Neusumerischen Bau und Weihinschriften*, Freiburger altoriental-
ische Studien 9, as cited in Winter, " 'Idols of the King,' " 21. For the Sumerian statues, see also
Agnès Spycket, *Les statues de culte dans les texts mésopotamiens des origins à la Ire. dynastie
de Babylone*, Cahiers de la Revue Biblique 9 (Paris: J. Gabalda et Cie, 1968).

8. See Michael B. Dick, "Prophetic Parodies of Making the Cult Image," in *Born in
Heaven, Made on Earth: The Making of the Cult Image in the Ancient Near East*, ed. Michael B.
Dick (Winona Lake, Ind.: Eisenbrauns, 1999), 1–54, esp. 33. Dick notes that Spycket, however,
holds that divine cult images first emerged in the Early Old Babylonian period.

9. See A. Leo Oppenheim, "The Care and Feeding of the Gods," in *Ancient Mesopotamia:
Portrait of a Dead Civilization* (Chicago: University of Chicago Press, 1964), 183–98.

Isaiah accurately relates the construction of a divine statue. The wood carver shaped it out of hardwood (in Mesopotamia, a special wood, mesu-wood). It was then brought to the various smiths and artisans who plated it with silver and gold, adorned it with jewels and stones, and finished painting and embellishing it. Isaiah is wrong, however (perhaps willfully wrong), when he describes the worshiper at this point saying to the statue, "my father, who created me." The statue remained an ordinary statue until it was connected to the god by means of special rituals, known in Mesopotamia as *mīs pî* and *pīt pî*, "mouth opening" and "mouth washing."[10] We have these elaborate consecration rituals from both Egypt and Mesopotamia, and they are strikingly different. In Egypt the ritual focused on the divine commission, direction, and sacralization of each of the artisans, so that the statue, which was commissioned, designed, and overseen by the gods, could be inhabited by the god.[11] The statue is thus the abode of the god, and this ritual has considerable similarity to the biblical account of the construction of YHWH's abode, the tabernacle in Exodus. God delivered the design to Moses, and God placed divine spirit and wisdom in Bezalel and in the artisans who worked with him. The tabernacle was then consecrated so that the divine *kavod* could enter and fill it.

The Mesopotamian *mīs pî* ritual was quite different. The human artisans are deemphasized; in fact, they are symbolically deprived of their powers by having their hands ritually cut off with a wooden knife. Instead, attention is focused on the parallel creation of the statue in heaven. As the craftsmen finish their work in the special workshop, the *bīt mummi*, up above the gods are giving birth to the statue so that, as a Mesopotamian text relates, the statue is "born on earth, born in heaven." When its heavenly birth is finished, the wood and metals of

---

10. See the articles in *Born in Heaven, Made on Earth*; and Christopher Walker and Michael Dick, *The Induction Of The Cult Image In Ancient Mesopotamia: The Mesopotamian Mīs Pî ritual* (Transliteration, translation, and commentary by Christopher Walker and Michael Dick). *State Archives of Assyria Literary Texts*, vol. 1 (Helsinki: Neo-Assyrian Text Corpus Project, Institute for Asian and African Studies, University of Helsinki, 2001).

11. David Lorton, "The Theology of Cult Statues in Ancient Egypt," in *Born in Heaven, Made on Earth*, ed. Michael B. Dick, 123–210. The aniconic stones could also be deified as habitations of the gods, attested by their names Bethel, Sakkun (from *škn*), Abnu, and Sulmu (from *šlm*). For these, see Karel Van Der Toorn, "Worshipping Stones: On the Deification of Cult Symbols," *Journal of Northwest Semitic Languages* 23 (1997): 1–15.

the earthly statue become the flesh of the god. The statue is thus transformed: to use the terminology familiar to us from discussions about the
Eucharist, the materials of the statue are transubstantiated or, at least,
consubstantiated with divine essence. This Mesopotamian conception
lies behind the use of all cult statues, whether of kings or of gods.

The statue incarnated and embodied the god, but it did not have any
claims to exclusive embodiment. Even though a statue could incarnate
only one god, there could be many statues of the god, and the god could
be present in all of them, while still transcendent in his/her position in
the cosmos or in the political running of the universe. Nevertheless, the
embodiment was not simply symbolic, for the statue was a channel of
divine presence, both radiating divine power (like the ark in the field of
Obed-Edom in 2 Samuel 6:11) and channeling human concerns to the
god (as Solomon's Temple was to bring them to God in 1 Kings 8:28–
53), while also influencing the whereabouts and behavior of the God.
Not all statues were equal: of the many statues of Marduk, none could
rival the main statue of Marduk in Esagila, his temple in Babylon. None
had a greater interface with Marduk.

To some extent, a divine statue is a little like a voodoo doll. When you
carry it by boat or wagon, the god comes with you. In just this way, when
the Philistines saw the ark, they were convinced that YHWH had come
to the battlefield. If the statue is destroyed, the god himself is portrayed
as falling ill or being captured. Moreover, if the temple is ruined, the
god may have to leave, either fleeing to safety or being captured and
taken away. This connection of the physical well-being of the statue
and the life of the god dates back at least to the early Third Dynasty
of Ur (ca. 2100–2000 B.C.E.), when Lagas was carried away to Elam
and the goddess Baba reached her final days, like humankind, lamenting
that "the storm" carried off her city.[12] Nevertheless, this connection of
the statue to the god is not entirely automatic. The god can cancel the

---

12. See Wolfgang Heimpel, "Der Tod der Göttin Baba von Lagas. Einer Beobachtung zum
sumerischen Götterglauben," in *Festschrift für Hermann Heimpel zum 79. Geburtstag am
19.9.71. Veröffentlichungen des Max-Planck Instituts für Geschichte* 36 (Göttingen: Vanden-
hoeck & Ruprecht, 1972). For a more recent study of this text, see Piotr Michalowski, *The
Lamentation over the Destruction of Sumer and Ur Mesopotamian Civilizations* 1 (Winona
Lake, Ind.: Eisenbrauns, 1989), 46f., with commentary.

relationship. If angry, he might refuse to stay in the statue, or might not allow a new "birth" on earth until he was ready.

During the long history of Mesopotamia, there were numerous occasions in which statues were broken or their connection to the god destroyed. Most illuminating are the adventures of the statues of Shamash and of Marduk. The great cult statue of Marduk in Babylon was carried off by invaders several times during Babylon's long history. The city of Babylon, its king, and its god came to prominence during the reign of King Hammurabi, the fourth king of his West Semitic dynasty and the consolidator of Babylon's power as the head of the Old Babylon Empire. The Empire didn't last long, and at some point in its embattled later period, the Haneans made a raid on Babylon, and carried off the great statue of Marduk. The Babylonians understood this conquest to have been the will of Marduk; for some time afterwards, King Agum-kakrime of Babylon records the events of his reign (1602–1585 B.C.E.). He relates that the gods decreed that Marduk should come back to Babylon. The king came to lament to Marduk that he should agree, and that he would love the king for helping him. When an oracle informed him that it was time, the king spoke to the Haneans and brought Marduk and his wife Ṣarpanitu back to Babylon and took them to a house that the oracle had pronounced suitable. The king then called in craftsmen to readorn the gods (i.e., their statues) with gold and precious stones.[13] Five hundred years later another king of Babylon, Nebuchadnezzar I (1124–1105 B.C.E.) also relates bringing back Marduk to Babylon from Elam, which had captured him. Like Agum-Kakrime, Nebuchadnezzar tells how he prayed to Marduk after the successful campaign against Elam so that Marduk would come back, which he did in great procession.[14] When Marduk's cult statue was taken by the Assyrians, however, there were two different explanations. Nabonidus reports that Marduk was angry at Babylon, that Sennacherib dealt harshly with Babylon to assuage Marduk's anger, but that Marduk still was angry and stayed

---

13. The text is in Jensen in Schrader, *Keilinschriftlichen Bibliothek* 3/1, 134–52. Discussed by Thorkild Jacobsen, "The Graven Image," in *Ancient Israelite Religion*, ed. Patrick D. Miller, Paul S. Hanson, and S. Dean McBride (Philadelphia: Fortress Press, 1987), 15–32, esp. 16.

14. Jacobsen, "The Graven Image," 29–30 n. 3 refers to IV R. pl. 20 no. 1.9–18 and then quotes the bilingual text.

twenty-one years in Assyria.[15] In a very different version of the events, it was not that Marduk had gone out of anger at Babylon, but rather that Marduk himself was in captivity, and could not come back until a later king restored (or rebuilt) the statue and returned it to Babylon.[16]

A different story is told about the great statue of Shamash, which the Suteans captured and effaced when they invaded Sippar. The Babylonian King Sinmassihu wanted to build a new statue and enquired by divination but the god Shamash "did not smile on him" and he could not build a statue. Instead, he roofed over the sun-disc that was in front of the temple and instituted regular offerings for it. He thus made the sun-disc, a nonanthropomorphic representation of Shamash, the central cult image.[17] Then, during the reign (888–855 b.c.e.) of the later king, Nabu-apla-iddina (whose inscription it is), Shamash stopped being angry at Babylonia and a "picture of his statue, a plaque of baked clay, of it and its attributes, was discovered on the other side of the Euphrates river, the west side" (iii:20–25). The king then happily had a cult statue built according to the model of the plaque.[18] The statue of Shamash could not be built until Shamash wanted it to be built.

Given these parameters of the statue, what does it mean to say that the king is a living statue of the God? Or to say that all people are such statues, as Egyptian and Babylonian wisdom and the book of Genesis teach us? The significance of this idea is carefully spelled out in Genesis 1–11. First, God created us in the divine image and commanded us to supervise the world. This "supervision" (*radah*) (Gen 1:28) is part of the famous biblical "democratization," in which features associated with Mesopotamian kings are attributed to all humanity. This included both ruling (supervision) and the idea of being the animated statue. It

---

15. Ibid., 30 n. 4 quotes the text from S. Langdon, *Die neubabylonische Königsinschriften* (Leipzig, 1912), 271 Nabonaid Nr. 8 I 14–25.

16. See Tikva Frymer-Kensky, "The Tribulations of Marduk: The So-called Marduk Ordeal Text," in *Essays in Honor of Samuel Noah Kramer, Journal of the American Oriental Society* 103 (1983): 131–41.

17. For the sun disc see Stephanie Dalley, "The God Salmu and the Winged Disk," *Iraq* XLVIII (1986): 85–102.

18. Text is published in I. W. King, *Babylonian Boundary Stones and Memorial Tablets in the British Museum* (London: British Museum, 1912), no. XXXVI. For a later treatment, see Katthryn Slanski, *The Babylonian Entitlement Narûs (Kudurrus): A Study in their Form and Function* (Boston: American Schools of Oriental Research, 2003), 196–221. This text is also discussed in Jacobsen, "The Graven Image," 20–24.

also explains why God receives consensus from the divine council. This, too, is originally attributed to the king, as the "myth of the creation of the king" depicts, for the god requests from the council that now that they have created human beings (*lullû-amēlu*), they should create a royal being (*māliku-amēlu*) who will be inherently superior.[19]

The creation of humans to rule the world in the divine image created its own problems for, as time went by, it became obvious that humans themselves needed administration and rule. In a world full of rulers, they descended into violence and polluted the world. The utter contamination of the earth made it necessary for God to bring a flood to purge the world, after which God instituted law to address the problem of human violence and control.[20] These laws reinforced human rule: despite the mistake humans had made, God still wanted humankind to run the world. Moreover, God made very clear the distinction between human beings and the other creatures, even those that also came from the earth on the sixth day. Humans were to have absolute power over animals, and have the right to kill and eat them, whereas nobody, animal or human, could kill a human being without forfeiting his or her life. The text quotes a very significant legal maxim, *shofek dam ha'adam, ba'adam damo yishafek ki betselem 'Elohim asah et ha'adam* — "whoever spills the blood of a human, by a human his blood must be shed, for in the image of God, God created humanity" (Gen 9:6). Later religions have paid much attention to the first part of this balanced phrase, the declaration of the sacrosanct nature and absolute inviolability of human life. But they have paid much less attention to the second half, even translating it *"for the sake of that human* his blood must be shed," a perhaps willful misinterpretation of the clause. Despite this unfortunate translation, this second clause is highly significant for our understanding of the Bible's idea of humanity: being created in the image of God does not only mean that we cannot be killed; it also means that we ourselves must act to prevent or at least deter such killing. Today, after thousands

19. See W. Mayer, "Ein Mythos von der Erschaffung des Menschen und des Königs," *Orientalia* 56 (1987): 55–68; and John von Seter, "The Creation of Man and the Creation of the King," *Zeitschrift für die alttestamentliche Wissenschaft* 101 (1989): 332–42.

20. Tikva Frymer-Kensky, "The Atrahasis Epic and its Significance for Understanding Genesis 2–9," *Biblical Archaeologist* 40 (1977): 147–55.

of years of experience, many of us disagree with the philosophical pre-
sumptions embedded in this demand for capital punishment, its belief
that the controlled violence against murderers will deter greater violence, much like a backfire stops a forest fire. Even two thousand years
ago, Rabbinic Judaism effectively did away with capital punishment by
extending the concept of humans as the image of God into an absolute
prohibition against taking the life of a human being, even for punishment.[21] Despite our disagreement as to how best to prevent violence
against human beings, the essence of the statement "by humans shall
his blood be spilled" remains unchanged: human beings must be the
ones responsible for making sure that human beings are not killed. God
will not act to save the threatened person or to wreak vengeance or bring
punishment on the killer. Instead, God established a system in which we,
the images of God, perform the divine task of preventing and punishing
murder.

Human beings are also in charge of preventing and punishing other
misbehavior. In the aftermath of the flood, the new order begins to resem-
ble the old. A drunken Noah passes out, immodestly exposed in his tent.
His actions are not laudable, but they are understandable in someone
who has gone through such trauma. There is no real wrongdoing here.
Nothing is really wrong until his son Ham sees him and then disgraces
his father by revealing to his brothers their father's overly revealed condition. But God does not act to punish Ham. Instead, Noah, as a human
charged with preserving and restoring both cosmic and human order,
acts to restore family hierarchy by cursing Canaan. Before the flood,
God cursed the serpent, the ground under Cain's feet, and the polluted
world. But now it is Noah who takes on the cursing role.

Noah's curse is not a high point in Noah's life. He began his story as
a righteous and innocent man. Now he has become drunk and humili-
ated and then pronounced a thoroughly questionable curse. Readers can
argue whether familial hierarchical order was so crucial to cosmic order
that it had to be reinforced by a curse; readers can question whether cursing was an appropriate response and why Canaan was cursed instead of

---

21. Rabbi Akiba declared that "whoever sheds blood cancels the image" (*tYev* 8) and Rabbi
Akiba and Rabbi Tarphon declared, "if we were in the Sanhedrin, no one would ever be killed"
(*mMak* 1:10).

Ham. We can, moreover, disapprove of a curse that introduced national rivalry and enmity into the newly reconstructed world. Noah has gone downhill, from the righteous companion of God to the drunken man, to the misguided curser, the nadir of his existence. Noah is, after all, a human being, not some superior flawless creature, but, with all our flaws, Noah and all humanity now run the world. God stays in heaven and does not come down until the technological achievement of the tower induced God to come and to bring human mastery to the entire earth.

The Glory (*Kavod*)

The Bible sees a pattern to the divine appearance in the world. In the primeval history, God began by actively planting a garden, walking in it, and conversing with Adam and Eve, and ended this period of human civilization in heaven, leaving the earthly field to humans. The next period, begun by the ancestor stories, shows the same progression. God starts intimately involved with Abraham, appears to Isaac only once, to Jacob only in dreams, and to Joseph not at all. Then the same thing happens in the salvation history of the people: God is intimate with Moses; the *kavod* is revealed to the people; but by the time of the judges, God appears only through "messengers" and the charismatic spirit of the judges. In the days of the ancestors, God constantly intervened to rescue Abraham's family; by the time of the judges, God is active in history, bringing and defeating foreign enemies, but God no longer intervenes in family matters. God saved Isaac from being sacrificed, but not Jephthah's daughter; Lot's angelic visitors saved him and his daughters, but the Levite and his concubine were on their own, with lethal result. The next period, that of the monarchy, shows the same progression: God is close to David and Solomon, but even they are usually approached by "angels," temporary emanations of divine essence; and then by prophets, human beings imbued with divine spirit. By the Persian period, even such indirect supervision by God through prophets is felt to have ended. The message is clear: people have the power, and they had better be careful how they use it. God is in the Temple, viewed in visions (as by Isaiah); however, out in the world prophets may offer guidance, but power and authority are in the hands of kings and officials and, locally, by

ordinary citizens. As prophets and scribes warn, all actions have consequences, but God will intervene only cataclysmically. The psalmists
praise God for supervising from heaven, petitioning God to do so, but
the storytellers do not relate any such activity. As a psalmist declares,
"the heavens are YHWH's and the earth He gave to human beings" (Ps.
115:16).

The book of Ruth indicates how the system was to work: God does
not act on the human plane in either Ruth or the story of Joseph; but in
the latter, God (say Joseph and the narrator) is actively manipulating and
directing events from behind the curtain, whereas in Ruth, God may not
do anything. People in Ruth are always talking about God, blessing each
other as a greeting formula, invoking divine power to ensure their promises, attributing to God misfortune (famine and death) and good fortune
(when people say God has provided food at the end of the drought). They
invoke God's aid and protection for others. But the narrator never tells
you that God did anything, except provide pregnancy. Even the serendip-
ity involved in Ruth's heading to Boaz's field to glean is not attributed
to Providence. Abraham's servant says to God *haqreh na'* — "make a
happening happen" (Gen 24:12) — as he asks that the girl who offers
hospitality should be the right one for Isaac. But the narrator in Ruth
says *wayyiqer miqreha:* "her happening happened" (Ruth 2:3), being
very careful not to indicate whether God arranged the meeting or not.
The narrator does not know whether coincidence or Providence brought
Ruth to Boaz's field. The people do not wait to find out: every time a
character wishes good for another character by invoking divine blessing,
that very character has to act to make sure that the blessing is carried
out. Naomi wishes "rest" for her widowed daughter-in-law in a new
husband's house; later, she herself sets out to provide this rest with her
plan for Ruth's nocturnal visit to Boaz. Boaz wished Ruth security and
reward for coming under the *kanaf* (wing) of God (Ruth 2:12); Ruth
then tells him to "put his money where his mouth was" by spreading his
kanaf (edge of robe) over her (Ruth 3:9). Readers of the book of Ruth
have often noted the benevolence of the characters; equally important
is their embrace of their human responsibility to make sure that society
and cosmos work right. They thus carry out their nature as "statues" of
God, channelers of divine might in the world.

The term *tselem* is restricted to Genesis, but not the ideas that the term conveys. The connection of human and divine agency in running the world is indicated elsewhere by the use of the word *kavod*, a term normally associated with God as God's "glory." The *kavod* of a God is visible. It is to be seen, ascribed to God in praise, and talked about among the peoples. Its basic form is a light phenomenon, a luminescence, not unlike the Mesopotamian *melammu*, the awesome aura that surrounds a god (Exod. 24:12). The *kavod* can appear in human form, as in the vision of Ezekiel, but the *kavod* is essentially formless. It fills the place in which it moves, whether that be the tent of meeting, the temple, or the whole earth. In the "*kavod* theology" of Israel's priests, this *kavod* has entered the temple and abides there, cloaked.

All divine beings have some amount of this *kavod:* when the angels in Sodom were attacked, they turned on their mega-wattage, thus blinding the people of Sodom so that they couldn't find the entrance (Gen. 19:11). Like the divine beings (though less), but unlike the animals, human beings have *kavod:* when God gave human beings the task of running the world, God crowned us with splendid aura, *kavod wehadar* (Ps. 8:6).

The different attributes of God contribute to the character of God's *kavod*. The *kavod* can be associated with splendor, with might, and with judgment, and with the wondrous deeds God has done, which are God's creation of the earth and the historical judgments on Israel and on its enemies. Most significantly, when Moses asks God to reveal God's *kavod*, and God accommodates, what God reveals at that point are the "thirteen attributes:" "YHWH, YHWH, a God merciful and gracious, slow to anger, and abounding in steadfast love and faithfulness, keeping steadfast love for the thousandth generation, forgiving iniquity and transgression and sin, yet by no means clearing the guilty, but visiting the iniquity of the parents upon the children and the children's children, to the third and the fourth generation" (Exod. 33:18; 34:6–7).

Like God's *kavod*, the aura of human beings is determined by their deeds and attributes. Israel has an additional component to its aura that comes from God. Other nations have specific attributes that contribute to their own distinctive national auras: the *kavod* of Moab is its multitudes (Isa. 16:14); of Lebanon its trees (Isa. 35:2; 60:13); Assyria's the might of its troops (Isa. 8:7). Individuals have their national *kavod*, and additional *kavod* comes from their status: parents have *kavod* by virtue of being parents and kings by their majesty. Joseph speaks of his *kavod* in Egypt (Gen. 45:13) and the psalmist celebrates how God grants the king blessings, places splendor upon him, and makes his *kavod* great (Ps. 21:6–7). Riches give a rich man *kavod* (Ps. 49:17; Isa. 22:18; Est. 1:4; 5:11); the wise achieve *kavod* through wisdom (Prov. 3:35); a woman through graciousness (Prov. 11:16); and the humble of spirit through humility (Prov. 15:33; 29:23). These components of *kavod* can be additive, as when God gives Solomon both riches and *kavod* even greater than his father's (1 Kgs. 3:13).

Kavod is fragile. National *kavod* can be destroyed, as God warns Aram and Kedar. The people can change it, as Israel exchanged its *kavod* for the image of an ox (Ps. 106:19–20) or for one who cannot help (Jer. 2:11). God can also change it, as God changed Israel's *kavod* for shame (Hos. 4:7); and *kavod* can be exiled, as when the Philistines took the ark (1 Sam. 4:21) or when the calf of Samaria is to be taken to Assyria (Hos. 10:5).[22] The consequences of losing divine *kavod* have practical effects. The loss of children and of births can be dire: when Ephraim's *kavod* flies away, there will be no births and the children will die (Hos. 9:11–12). *Kavod* can also be restored—just as God's *kavod* is increased and transformed by justice, as when all the nations will see Zion's justice, which is her *kavod* (Isa. 62:2).

Personal *kavod* is also fragile: it must be recognized by others and therefore depends on both the behavior of the one with *kavod* and the ones recognizing it. Parental *kavod* depends on the actions of children: Malachi relates God's complaint that since a son should give *kavod* ("honor") to his father, if God is Israel's father, where is his *kavod* (Mal. 1:6)? It also considers the reconciliation between fathers and sons an absolute prerequisite for the reconciliation of Israel and God (Mal. 3:24). Job remembers when his *kavod* was fresh, and people listened to him (Job 29:20–21), but he complains that God has stripped him

---

22. The verse *'al kevodo ki galah mimmennu* might indicate that the glory of the calf has departed from it, as most translations read. This would be a rather positive evaluation of the calf. However, the verse may also mean that the glory of Israel has departed from it, because it has to send its calf to Assyria as tribute.

of his *kavod* (Job 19:9). Ascription by others is crucial to *kavod;* even God is dependent on God's *kavod* being recognized. By killing Nadab and Abihum, God demonstrated the *gravitas* of divine commands and thereby increased divine *kavod* among the people (Lev. 10:3). King Saul entreated Samuel to stand with him so that the people would continue to show Saul *kavod* (1 Sam. 15:30). Balak declared that he desired to give such *kavod* to Balaam, but God prevented Balaam from acquiring any *kavod* (Num. 24:11).

Kavod can be sought (Prov. 25:27), and it can be given unwisely, as when people give *kavod* to a fool, an act as inappropriate as snow in the summer (Prov. 26:1), and as useless as binding a stone to a slingshot (Prov. 26:8). As Job learned, our *kavod* may not be permanent. At death, we leave it behind; it can be stripped from us by God, and we may even try to hide it in order to hide from God's judgment.[23]

We frequently translate *kavod* as "honor" or "dignity," but *kavod* is something palpable. It can be visible, and yet it can stand for the entire being, placed parallel to *nefesh* (Gen. 49:6) and to heart (Ps. 16:9; 108:2). It can have dimensions, for when God removes Israel's *kavod,* God makes the *kavod* lower and thins the flesh (Isa. 17:4), a graphic image of the aura occupying less and less space. The *kavod* can be in a resting state, to be awakened and set up to praise God (Ps. 57:9; 108:2), and it can be transformed into burning fire (Isa. 10:16), or into its opposite, disgrace (Hab. 2:16). Our actions as well as God's change the size and intensity of our *kavod.* Our *kavod* will look different if it has been constituted by misdeeds, which is why the oppressor tries to leave his *kavod* behind in order to escape God's justice. This outer aura, which also encompasses God's name (Ps. 79:9), can still retain the shape and components of the body, for we hear of the eyes of God (Isa. 3:8) and the nipples of Mother Jerusalem (Isa. 66:11)

Inside the aura of *kavod* is a living being, a *nefesh hayyah. Nefesh* is a complex term, referring to the whole being (the self); the life of the self that can be sought, risked, saved, or spared; the body; body and spirit;

---

23. Isaiah's question, "Where will you leave your *kavod?*" is usually translated as "Where will you deposit your riches?" (Isa. 10:1), but this doesn't make sense in connection with "To whom will you flee for help?" More appropriately, the evildoer who has profited by despoiling widows and orphans has to hide his *kavod,* like dimming his light in an attempt not to be recognized and caught.

to the spirit animating the body; to the spirit that "exits" at death (Gen. 35:18); and to the lifeless being itself. It is the site of emotions, bitterness (2 Kgs. 4:27), desire (Deut. 18:6), anguish (Gen. 42:21). It is also the site of appetite, of satiety, and of the inability to be satisfied; on a more anatomical plane, it is the throat itself (for example, Jon. 2:6), which consumes both food and air.

The spirit is intricately intertwined with the body, and it is almost a truism to say that biblical religion was "monistic," believing in a mind/body rather than in the dualist division between "matter" and "spirit" that is so well known from Greek-inspired Western thought. Like all truisms, this one needs to be nuanced, but such discussion of the relationship between the body and consciousness is not a major subject of interest for the Bible. However, the relationship of the human body to God is a matter of considerable interest and concern to the biblical authors, and it is to this that we should turn.

The Holy (*Qadosh*)

Humans are created in both the *tselem* and form (*demut*) of the divine beings. *Tselem* may refer to function, but *demut* clearly means likeness: we look like God and the host of heavenly beings, just as Adam's son looked like him (Gen. 5:3). The Bible is replete with anthropomorphic images of the hand, the finger, the foot, the face, the back, and the mouth of God. Occasionally there are hints that Israel and Zion may be represented theriomorphically, with the horns or hooves of a bull (for instance, Mic. 4:13), but the overwhelming image for them, too, is humanoid. Humans look like God and the heavenly council, but there is an essential difference between the host and humans, one that establishes the difference between "holiness," the realm of the Divine, and the created world. Human beings are also flesh: we live in material bodies that come from clay (*'afar*) and will return there in 120 years (Gen. 6:3) or in seventy or eighty (Ps. 90:10) or less. Our lives are short, like a passing shadow (Ps. 144:4), but even if we should live to two thousand years (Eccles. 6:6) it would not make a difference: In the end we all die. We are animal, no different from the animals over whom we rule: we all die.

The mortality of human beings marks an enormous difference between us and God, for we do not live in the eternal, unchanging realm of *qodesh,* "holiness," the realm of God. God, who had no beginning and has no end, lives in a divine eternity. God's Temple also doesn't move through time. It lives in eternal, cyclical time as it goes through sabbaths and festivals, with each *mo'ed* coming around the same as the year before, and the days and the seasons come and come again. It participates in the eternal round that God established for the seasons and for the rain (Gen. 8:22). Humanity is very different. Made in the image of God, possessing a God-like aura, bidden to act in God-like ways, we nevertheless live in an entirely different dimension of time. Even though we can glimpse eternity, our own lives trace a direct line between birth and death. We live in linear, biological time: we are born, we grow, we grow older, and we die. Our days, once past, do not return to us. Linear and cyclical time may touch tangentially for an instant: we can enter the eternal world tangentially by participating in the festivals and in the Sabbath, holy time in the nonholy world; and we can physically come into the fringes of the Temple, holy space in the ordinary world. But the two times, linear and cyclical, are essentially incompatible, like matter and antimatter. They cannot merge and must be buffered from each other. People can never survive intense unmediated contact with *qodesh,* and when we carry on us the traces of linear, biological time, we cannot even enter the safe, mediated *qodesh* realm of the Temple court.

The Bible expresses this separation with the category distinction between *tahor* and *tame',* which we normally translate as "pure" and "impure."[24] *Tahor* is the normal state of *khol,* the world of human culture and created beings, distinguished from *qodesh* precisely by not belonging to the divine realm. Humans who are *tahor* can approach the fringes of *qodesh* space — the least holy of the holy realms — as long as they carefully avoid boundaries that could be dangerous to them individually and to the whole established order. *Tame'* is a state that must

---

24. See Tikva Frymer-Kensky, "Pollution, Purification, and Purgation in Biblical Israel," in *The Word of the Lord Shall Go Forth: Essays in Honor of David Noel Freedman in Celebration of his Sixtieth Birthday,* Carol L. Meyers and M. O'Connor, eds. (Winona Lake, Ind.: Eisenbrauns, 1983), and the many articles by Jacob Milgrom.

always carefully be kept away from *qodesh*, because by its very nature it can destroy the categories of being that form the order of the cosmos.

The distinction between *tahor* and *tame'* is not a moral issue: one can become *tame'* through performing essential social acts such as giving birth, tending the dying, burying the dead; through sexual copulation and involuntary physical acts like menstruation, genital secretions, and nocturnal emission. Without these actions, there could be no human society, and yet, they make the doer *tame'*, for being *tame'* results from being intensely occupied with the basic acts of moving through life. The consequence of being *tame'* is clear: as long as one is *tame'*, one must avoid coming to the Temple. Moreover, approaching the boundary between death and life results in an intensive charge of carnality. These actions, such as giving birth, death dealing, or having the illness that is death-in-life, leprosy, leave one in the *tame'*-state for seven days. This intensive form is contagious: if one has contracted these carnality charges, one can make others *tame'* by coming into contact with them. The carrier of intensive carnality must avoid not only the holy, but people and things that are *tahor* until the charge dissipates over time. At that time they will be required to perform the "ritual of the red cow" if they have come in contact with the dead, and the "ritual of the doves" if they have been cured of leprosy; the Bible does not mention special rituals after menstruation or giving birth.

The Temple was designed to be a safe meeting point between humans and God, and contains a whole series of physical separations. Israel comes to the courtyard, the priests are inside, and one priest comes into the antechamber daily, dressed in a holiness-hazard suit. Only the High Priest, who never leaves the Temple, goes into the Holy of Holies, and that only once a year, on Yom Kippur, the day of purging the Temple. In effect, the Temple was one great containment system that allowed Israelites to experience a buffered, and therefore "safe," form of holiness. God, the source of power and blessing, lived behind the *parokhet*, providing well-being for Israel. Without the containment, God's power would incinerate the worshipers. At Sinai, God warned the people not to approach the mountain as long as God was there, lest God "erupt" (*parats*) against them. When Nadab and Abihu drew too close to God at the installation of the tabernacle, they died (Lev. 16:1); elsewhere their death is attributed to their bringing "strange fire" which they had not been commanded to bring; they died in the fire that erupted (Lev. 10:1–2). And Uzzah was incinerated just for touching the ark in order to prevent it from falling (2 Sam. 6: 4–6). But the containment field, the *parokhet*, prevented people in the Temple from being unintentionally incinerated.

God, the quintessence of *qodesh*, "holiness," cannot live in the presence of *tame'*, for the two of them, the attribute of godliness and the attribute of carnality, are like matter and anti-matter, and cannot coexist. If a *tame'* person is exposed unshielded to God's holiness, the sheer power of that holiness will destroy him. In the Temple, the space differentiations and the *parokhet* will prevent this from happening. So a *tame'* person can "cheat" and come to the Temple without first becoming *tahor*, "pure," with no worry about suddenly being struck dead. Nevertheless even though the Temple buffered people from the full force of divine holiness, there were serious consequences to coming to the Temple while *tame'*. God, present in the Temple, had to be buffered from biological, carnal time and God might not be able to stay in a Temple contaminated by the carnal and would have to leave. The Temple was purified on Yom Kippur, but nevertheless, if the accumulating charge of biological carnality was too great, the Temple might cease to be an appropriate home for Holiness. It is for this reason that people who are *tame'* had to avoid the Temple, for the charge of biology they carried was cumulative and could act to endanger the holiness of the Temple. People who were *tame'* in its most intense form had to avoid others for seven days to prevent the possibility that more and more people, dripping from contact with the essence of linear, finite, carnal life, would have to be kept away from God.

There was yet another danger. As any *Star Trek* viewer knows, if the containment field of the starship's anti-matter engine gets too weak, then "she going to blow, Captain." The *parokhet*, itself part of the Holiness system, was vulnerable to being weakened by contact with items or people that were in a *tame'* state, this cultic impurity that resulted from close contact with biological life. It could be weakened wherever people came to Temple carrying the contagion of life. Moreover, the *parokhet* could also be weakened by the miasma that attended moral misdeeds. Moral infractions actively polluted the created world ("the earth" and Israel) and the people who performed them. The miscreants and the land they contaminated were called "polluted," *nitma'*, using the nif'al form of the same verb whose stative was *tame'*.[25] Unlike the people who were *tame'*, contaminated with the charge of biological life, people who were *nitma'* (polluted by their own misdeeds) were not contagious — you could not become *nitma'* by touching someone who was. Moreover, again unlike *tame'* people, their condition was dangerous to themselves, for they would suffer the penalty for their misdeeds. It was also dangerous to the nation, which might be held collectively accountable. There was also a further danger, to the Temple and the people it served.[26] Unlike biological contamination, moral pollution could contaminate the Holy from afar. Just as a positive electrical charge attracts a negative charge, the holy attracts the *tame'*, its polar opposite, and that which can nullify it. As wrongdoing contains invisible quanta of pollution, they are attracted to the holy, and to the holiest of holies, where they can damage the *parokhet* and destroy the system. Unlike the biological *tame'*, the *nitma'* of moral wrongdoing operates at a distance, and one must therefore avoid becoming polluted and polluting one's environment. Guarding the boundary between *tum'ah* (contamination) and holiness was part of the priestly responsibility. All the people of Israel were charged to observe the distinctions and categories that maintain the cosmos. One was not expected to remain *tahor* — for life, illness, and death claim attention — but one could be expected to isolate biological *tum'ah* and to keep oneself clear from moral *tum'ah*.

The unholy realm of *tum'ah* had both a behavioral and nonbehavioral aspect. Similarly, there was both a stative and a behavioral aspect of Holiness, *qodesh*. God is Holy and that which belongs to God is Holy, like the Temple and the Sabbath are holy; all of Israel had the obligation to maintain this distinction. They also had the obligation to be *qadosh*, holy-like, or God-like. As emphasized by the famed Holiness school, and as assumed by the prophets, in order to be *qadosh*,

25. See Frymer-Kensky, "Pollution, Purification, and Purgation."

26. Tikva Frymer-Kensky, "The Metaphysics of Pollution," forthcoming; originally "Pollution and Sacrifice: An Homage to Jacob Milgrom," presented at the Society for Biblical Literature, 2001.

"holy," it was not enough to behave in correct ways toward the Holy, the *qodesh:* observing the Sabbath or praying will not make one Holy. Holiness requires behaving in God-like behavior toward the world and toward other human beings. The absence of moral pollution is necessary, but certainly not enough: abstaining from misdeeds makes one pure, *tahor,* and even *tamim,* but not *qadosh.* That requires positive action to behave toward other people like divine beings and to create a society that could please the preeminent Holy One of Israel, the paradigm for Israel's behavior, God.

All of these attributes of humanity: being the *tselem 'Elohim,* the image of God" (*imago Dei*), having *kavod* ("glory"), and being *qadosh* ("holy") refer to behavior. But what about the physical body? It would be easy to conclude that the carnal, *tame',* world, the opposite of Holy, was somehow not only non-Holy, but evil, and that the Bible taught this idea that was so important in later Gnosticism and a constant danger to Christian thinking. But this most emphatically was not the Bible's position. God created the material world, the earth, and created the humans beings from the earth in order to create a non-Holy world. Even though the Bible never tells us why God wanted such a material world, it shows us God pronouncing each stage of creation "good." Matter, the earth and the body, is the arena in which the biblical divine drama plays out, and it is clear that God created it all as an act of will. The importance of the material body is further indicated by Divine anthropomorphisms, and such rabbinic thinkers as Hillel used the concept of "image of God" precisely to encourage burnishing the statue, that is, going to bathhouses and taking care of the body.[27] As time went on, and anthropomorphisms were more and more avoided, even the "likeness" began to suggest intellectual rather than corporeal likeness. But rather than conclude that the human body was therefore not a sacred object, Jewish thinking turned to another aspect of God: the name of God, which, they held, was placed in the human body. The Midrash *Tanhuma* tells us that God placed God's name *Shaddai* (usually translated the "Almighty") on the human form:

27. *Abot de Rabbi Nathan B (ARNB)* 30. For an English translation, see Anthony J. Saldarini, ed. and trans., *The Fathers According to Rabbi Nathan (Abot de Rabbi Nathan) Version B: A Translation and Commentary.* Studies in Judaism in Late Antiquity, vol. 11. (Leiden: Brill, 1975).

the *shin* is the humanoid nose that sticks out from the face; the *dalet* the arm with bending elbow and the hand with opposite thumb; and the *yod* the genitalia (penis and clitoris) that create human sexuality.[28] In this way, even after people no longer thought of God as having a body, the human body retained both its God-like nature and the aura that surrounded it. Each human being comes both in the image of God and in God's name to be God's agent on earth.

The implication of such thinking for faith in the twenty-first century is very great, for this biblical language and thinking provides an alternative to the long use of the language of self-abnegation and submission. While ostensibly preaching humbleness, this language has provided a rationale and justification for ignoring human responsibility for the world and for each other. The Bible's triple concepts of *kavod, qadosh,* and, above all, the *tselem 'Elohim,* demand that human beings fulfill their destiny as images of God to treat others as they would treat God. All human beings are sacrosanct and must not be killed. That is the barest minimum of righteous action. To that we add our responsibility to supervise the world to ensure its well-being, and then we behave in such a way as to "grow" our *kavod* and to be *qadosh.* We are the presence and face of God in this world. That is both our nature and our challenge.

---

28. *Midrash Tanhuma* 11. For English translation see, *Midrash Tanhuma,* trans. John T. Townsend (Hoboken, N.J.: Ktav, 1989–1997). For a modern theological extension of this midrash, see Tikva Frymer-Kensky, *Motherprayer: The Pregnant Woman's Spiritual Companion* (New York: G. P. Putnam Sons, 1995), 52–58 and notes.

Chapter 7

CREATION AND INITIATIVE
A Reading of Ricoeur's
Ethics of Originary Affirmation
Michael A. Johnson

*When the theologians [of the early Church] elaborated the doctrine
of man that is summarized in the startling expression of the first
chapter of Genesis — "Let us make man in our image and likeness" — they certainly did not master at once all its implicit wealth
of meaning.... We readily believe that the image of God is simply
an imprint like the worker's trademark: we then discuss among ourselves in order to know whether, in the economy of sin, this mark
has worn away and to what degree, and whether only lightly or
totally. But what should happen if we should invert the metaphor,
if we should see the image of God not as an imposed mark but
as the striking power of human creativity; if we treat it not as the
residual trace of a craftsman who has abandoned his work to the
ravages of time, but as a continuous act in the creative movement
of history and duration?*[1]

At the beginning of the third millennium, the world is beset by problems
on two major fronts: cultural and political conflict on a global scale, and

I wish to express my gratitude to the tireless dedication and good sense of Kevin Jung in
co-organizing the D. R. Sharpe Lectures of 2003 conference and to William Schweiker, who
offered constant and excellent guidance for the conference at each step along the way. I also
thank each of them for their insightful comments on the argument and shape of this essay.

1. Paul Ricoeur, "The Image of God and the Epic of Man," in *History and Truth*, ed.
Charles A. Kelbley (Evanston, Ill.: Northwestern University Press, 1965), 110–11.

industrial and technological endangerment of ecosystems on a planetary-wide basis. Certain theological or ecological perspectives may see the power of human creativity as threatening the order of creation upon which it depends and from which it originates. Rather than simply faulting human creativity as inherently destructive, however, another, perhaps more fruitful, approach may be found in reflection upon the ways in which human creativity participates in the power and goodness of creation itself and the imperative to reestablish such participation in the creative ground of the universe.

Through an exploration of the thought of the hermeneutical philosopher Paul Ricoeur, I attempt to uncover a "fundamental ethic," embedded in what he calls "originary affirmation" that is related to biblical symbols of covenant and creation. Part and parcel of this ethics of originary affirmation is an emphasis on a living tension between a "logic of superabundance" and a "logic of equivalence." The former relates to the Christian theme of grace, too often regarded as an extrinsic addition to the created order that interrupts finite human existence. Contrary to this tendency, Ricoeur, through a reading of the Genesis narratives, grounds this logic of superabundance in creation itself. This is important, since, on my reading, Ricoeur includes human initiative and meaning-creation under the general category of creation. Human beings participate in creation through the power to initiate new beginnings in time, history, and culture.

Throughout his long career, Ricoeur tended to keep his philosophical writings separate from his exegesis of biblical texts, narratives, and symbols. This methodological division sometimes renders obscure the possible connections between his philosophical studies and biblical analyses. I intend here to correlate concepts drawn from these two sets of writings that circulate around the Ricoeurian thematics of creation and initiative. My thesis is that there are conceptual clusters present in each group of texts that, when juxtaposed, resonate with each other to a remarkable degree. These terms create a productive network of inter-signification within the thought of Ricoeur. Ricoeur himself does not, to my knowledge, relate together this network of meanings in any explicit manner, so this represents my own constructive contribution to some degree. In my view, however, there exists such a wealth of potential conceptual interconnections as to render this correlation extremely fruit-ful. I draw on the rich exegetical and philosophical resources in Ricoeur's writings in order to construct a theory of human creative activity — a fundamental ethics of originary affirmation — oriented to a vision of religious humanism that affirms rather than denigrates human power and capability. My central concern throughout is to develop a reading of Ricoeur's theories of meaning-creation and initiative that provides a robust way to understand how human beings participate in creation in responsible community with human and nonhuman life.

This reconstructive reading of Ricoeur's fundamental ethics will pro-ceed in several steps that build upon each other. First, I examine Ricoeur's exegesis of two senses of beginning embedded in the creation narra-tives of Genesis. Next I connect this idea of creation with the concept of originary affirmation that grounds his fundamental ethics. Third, I examine Ricoeur's hermeneutics of human selfhood and identity with an eye toward drawing very precise connections between human cre-ativity in action with the energy of creation. Fourth, I turn to Ricoeur's exegesis of the biblical themes of love and justice, and its connection with the logic of superabundance that he links to the biblical senses of creation. I next turn to explore a way to understand Ricoeur's theory of meaning-creation (initiative/culture-creation) as an expression of the thematics developed earlier — that is, human creativity as participatory in the power of creation itself. I conclude with a reflection on the phe-nomenon of conscience as the most primordial intersection of originary affirmation with the self.

Thinking Creation: Two Types of Beginning in the Exegesis of the Biblical Creation Narratives

In an exegetical study of the of the idea of creation in the Old Testa-ment entitled "Thinking Creation," Ricoeur finds a "broad dynamism" at work between concepts of creation in "primordial narratives of cre-ation" and those of narratives of early history in the Hebrew Bible.[2] I

---

2. André LaCocque and Paul Ricoeur, *Thinking Biblically: Exegetical and Hermeneutical Studies* (Chicago: University of Chicago Press, 1998), 31.

want to focus on two senses of beginning and the complex intersignification in play among these senses that Ricoeur finds at work within this
dynamic concept of creation. Conceptually, Ricoeur distinguishes these
two senses as an "absolute beginning" of creation (which he also calls
"origin") and "relative beginnings" (also called "founding events") in
the creation narratives and their continuation in the history recounted
in the Hebrew Bible. Ricoeur claims that these "founding events" participate in and continue the "absolute beginning," or origin.[3] According
to Ricoeur, the senses of the two terms have a circular relationship such
that they can really only be understood together. This is important for
the later part of my argument since "founding events" primarily refer to
events in human history.

On the one hand, we have beginnings in the sense of first beginnings,
or "original creations" of Genesis 3: "creation of the world; creation of
humanity; creation/discreation of evil."[4] God withdraws and separates
Godself from this original creation in primordial time, and history, the
time of relative first beginnings, begins. We, then, on the other hand,
encounter the narratives of "relative beginnings": the flood; tower of
Babel; birth of Israel as a people; call of Abraham; escape from captivity
in Egypt; giving of the Law to Moses on Sinai, and so on.[5]

At an earlier stage in his career, the main focus of Ricoeur's biblical exegesis was upon the symbolism of evil and redemption and not the symbolism of creation.[6] In a 1999 address, however, Ricoeur implies that his new
insight into the two senses of beginning described above allows him to shift
his focus from radical evil and a theology of redemption to the grounding
of human creativity in the originary goodness and energy of creation.

> My reflections [referring to his more recent work] are close to
> Rosenzweig's *Star of Redemption* concerning creation around the

---

3. Ibid., 48ff.
4. Ibid., 47.
5. Ibid., 48.
6. In the 1960s, Ricoeur's main preoccupation in biblical interpretation was with the
symbolism of evil and theological ideas of redemption built around a "philosophy of hope."
This philosophy of hope was informed by Kantian idealism and the eschatological theology of
Jürgen Moltmann. Significantly, in light of his later theory of selfhood, Ricoeur developed his
philosophy of hope around Moltmann's theological interpretation of biblical ideas of covenant
and promise.

concept of origin, *Ursprung,* which has its correlates in Greek thought under the term *arche.* I tried to show that there is a dialectics between beginning and origin, beginning as a starting point in time and origin as the always-already-there of rising reality.... To underline the difference between origin and beginning, I tried to show that the notion of origin has itself its own temporal development along the lines of founding events transmitting the energy of the origin. I now think that there is a philosophical side of creation that allows us ... to help the theologian not to cover over too quickly a theology of creation by a theology and Christology of redemption. This reminds us that creativeness comes before law, guilt, and even redemption.[7]

Thus, there is an original energy of creation that continues in "founding events transmitting the energy of the origin."[8] Ricoeur here grounds his ethics of the capable person in an ontology based on the biblical sense of beginnings, an ontology that rejects a static substance view of metaphysics in favor of an ontology of being as act (actuality-potentiality).[9] In the same address, Ricoeur asserts that "as radical as evil may be, it will never be more originary than goodness, which is the *Ursprung* in the field of ethics, the orientation to the good as being rooted in the structure of the human being, or in biblical terms, creation, createdness."[10] Ricoeur seems to suggest here that the new conceptual repertoire centered on the notion of two beginnings gives him a means to shift attention from human fault and evil to the human orientation to and participation in the original power and goodness of creation.

Ricoeur contends that the intersignification between the absolute and relative beginnings sets up a "circular relation" between the pair that

---

7. Paul Ricoeur, "Ethics and Human Capability," in *Paul Ricoeur and Contemporary Moral Thought,* ed. John Wall, W. David Hall, and William Schweiker (New York: Routledge, 2002), 283.

8. On the influence of Rosenzweig's *The Star of Redemption* on Ricoeur's two senses of beginning, see his discussion in LaCocque and Ricoeur, *Thinking Biblically,* 65–67, 120.

9. See the Tenth Study of Paul Ricoeur, *Oneself as Another,* trans. Kathleen Blamey (Chicago: University of Chicago Press, 1992), "Tenth Study," 297–356.

10. Ricoeur, "Ethics and Human Capability," 284.

"tends to wipe out the distinction" between them.[11] The concept of creation as an absolute beginning not preceded by any prior events was "foreign . . . to the cultures of the Near East."[12] He then inverts the point: every "beginning is ab-solute, in the most basic sense of the not being bound to what preceded it."[13] How should this be understood? Every new beginning receives its energy from the "first creation," and thus they all participate in the original creation. For example, the narrative depictions of prophetic callings of the Hebrew people or individuals within the nation of Israel reenact this first creation. Turning this around dialectically, however, the sense of the original creation may be seen as given *after the fact* by reflection on the meanings of the multiplicity of founding events in which the energy of the first creation has continuance. Founding events have a "temporal thickness" that require unfolding through a narrative. Ricoeur states that "the very idea of Creation emerges enriched from this kind of proliferation of original events."[14] How? The initial sense of a "founding event" is that "in it is expressed what we can call the energy of beginning." But what then "circulates among all the beginnings, thanks to the relation of intersignification, and thanks to the circular relation brought about by the initial events, is the initial, inaugural, founding power of *a* beginning."[15] The *single* "sense" of the first beginning is given content through the *multiplicity* of founding events.

Thus, the energy and meaning of the first creation is known by reflection upon its propagation through the myriad but analogous founding events. However, this continuance of the first creation is distributed not just among the different founding events but also *within* the inaugural events, each of which has its own specific continuance. Fundamentally connected to the two senses of beginnings, Ricoeur introduces a novel notion of temporal continuation or permanence in time that he relates to biblical themes of the promise or covenant.

Ricoeur's later exegesis of the biblical symbols of creation and covenant expands an interpretation he worked out at an earlier stage in his career. At that time, he inscribed his reading of the biblical symbols of

11. LaCocque and Ricoeur, *Thinking Biblically*, 49.
12. Ibid.
13. Ibid.
14. Ibid.
15. Ibid.

the covenant and promise within a metaphorics of seeing and not see-ing, intuition and sign (word), and expectation and fulfillment.[16] Here he followed a reading of the Hebrew Bible partly inspired by the dialogical philosophy of Martin Buber, who insisted "on the massive opposition between the God of the promise — the God of the desert, of the wander-ing — and the gods of the 'epiphanic' religions."[17] Ricoeur schematized this division between the gods of nature and the God of the covenant and history by means of an opposition between "the Name and the idol."[18] In the *encounter* with the Hebrew people, God identifies God's Name with the promise to build a nation from the children of Abraham. This promise is an event *in* history that sets up a narrative "tension of his-tory."[19] Whereas idols manifest themselves in specific, static locations, God does not. God is known in history and covenant. In the covenant, God promises a new kind of social being, an "increase in being" yet to come. But this is not a one-way covenant because God also gives laws to the Hebrew people to follow. As part of the covenant, the Hebrew people are to walk in the ways of the Lord and create God's justice on earth. This obedience to the Law enables not only life but also the form-ing of the communal bonds of a just society. In this way, the purpose for obedience to the Law is not simply to placate the capricious and harsh demands of a tyrant deity modeled on the kings of Babylon but rather the fulfillment of the creation begun in the Genesis story.

In "Thinking Creation," these earlier interpretations of the prom-ise/covenant reemerge but now in the new context of the intersignifying senses of creation in the various kinds of beginnings. A new beginning, an event of founding, is always the beginning of an unfulfilled task or expec-tation; this task unfolds through narrative into a "temporal thickness."[20]

---

16. In so doing, he blended together themes from Husserlian phenomenology with ideas drawn from Jürgen Moltmann's eschatological theology in his *The Theology of Hope: On the Ground and the Implications of a Christian Eschatology,* trans. James W. Leitch (London: SCM, 1967).

17. Paul Ricoeur, "Freedom in the Light of Hope," in *The Conflict of Interpretations,* ed. Don Ihde, Northwestern University Studies in Phenomenology and Existential Philosophy (Evanston, Ill.: Northwestern University Press, 1974), 404.

18. Paul Ricoeur, "Hope and the Structure of Philosophical Systems," in *Figuring the Sacred: Religion, Narrative, and Imagination,* trans. David Pellauer, ed. Mark I. Wallace (Minneapolis: Fortress Press, 1995), 204.

19. Ricoeur, "Freedom in the Light of Hope," 405.

20. LaCocque and Ricoeur, *Thinking Biblically,* 49.

An event of founding is radically creative in a double sense. First, it does not simply aim at the actualization of already existing possibilities; it creates new possibilities for existence and aims toward the realization of these. Second, this project continues through and develops over time and becomes more concrete as it develops. Thus, creativity of the founding event continues in the process of achieving its fundamental aim and through reversals and resistances to its realization. The promise is a "demand" for continuation and completion despite changes or setbacks in circumstances or even infidelity by one of the partners of the covenant. In general, a founding event seeks to bring into finite temporal conditions (the real) an unconditional Idea (the ideal) that exceeds the human capacity to represent it within objectifying thought. This is because the absolute "first beginning ... is ... ungraspable."[21] The first beginning is known after the fact, as it were, in the later relative beginnings that are its continuance. The "energy of the origin," or first beginning, expresses itself in the relative beginnings, even while these expressions remain inadequate to the surplus of its full causality. We remain faithful to the promise to achieve this synthesis of the ideal and the real in time, even as God, the source of the energy of the first beginning remains faithful to God's people in their effort. "This promise and this demand for a continuation are redoubled by the assurance that what God has begun will be continued though his grace. What the Bible calls God's faithfulness constitutes the veritable principle of continuity for the history inaugurated by the founding events."[22] In this sense, God's self-constancy becomes the ground for the narrative history of all the biblical inaugural events that continue and realize the original creation.

Originary Affirmation and Creation

The second step in my reconstruction of Ricoeur's idea of creation is to connect the idea of the first beginning (origin; *Ursprung*) with a concept

21. Ibid., 51.
22. Ibid., 50. "Here is where a reflection on the pair 'to begin' and 'to continue' can take place. This is called for here all the more because in the Bible beginning is always to some degree the promise or at least the demand for a continuation: the promise of an orderly world, or a responsible humanity, of many descendants, of a common identity, of a land in which to dwell; a demand in the form of a mission, in the call narratives.... "

that long nourished Ricoeur's thinking, mediating for him the tradition of reflexive philosophy in German idealism with a hermeneutical variant of Husserlian phenomenology. This is the concept of "originary affirmation" (*affirmation originaire*) that Ricoeur appropriates from the French reflexive philosopher Jean Nabert, who wrote in the first half of the twentieth century.[23]

Originary affirmation is an "original causality" at work in the "human desire and effort to exist."[24] Originary affirmation comes to expression in each act of human power. Each of these acts actualizes originary affirmation to a greater or lesser degree but the originary affirmation always exceeds its realization in each specific act. The self knows itself by reflecting on its acts that objectify this effort to exist. For example, I require a body for movement and as the locus of natural inclinations and motives for action. It provides my finite opening or perspective on the world.[25] These tendencies for action are diverse and disunified, but they are susceptible to ordering into unified autonomous action by rational reflection on my actions. In an Aristotelian vocabulary, I put reason into passion and appetite.

The human person experiences the causality of originary affirmation in two ways. First, there is an inchoate awareness of the interior feeling of the "effort to exist" in the power of action. According to Nabert, there is a dialectic between the "inner operation" of the effort to exist that produces these actions and the manifestation of these efforts in objectification. We lack a pure or direct intuition (in phenomenological terms) of the more primordial effort. Rather, we see the finished products of this effort from the outside, as it were. These "acts" become objects for consciousness and food for thought. On the one hand, our bodily desires and psychological motivations appear as subject to the laws of natural causality, completely conditioned and determined. On the other hand, we also seem to be able to corral these inclinations into rational action

---

23. Among other works, see especially Jean Nabert, *Elements for an Ethic*, trans. William J. Petrek (Evanston, Ill.: Northwestern University Press, 1969). This is the seminal work for Ricoeur in his development of a fundamental ethics based on originary affirmation.

24. For the following paragraphs, see Paul Ricoeur, "Nabert on Act and Sign," in *The Conflict of Interpretations*, 219–22.

25. See Paul Ricoeur, *Fallible Man*, trans. Charles A. Kelbley (New York: Fordham University Press, 1986).

and subject them to a different law, a law that we give to ourselves as rational agents (that is, the Kantian categorical imperative). From the perspective of consciousness, the original causality bifurcates into natural causality and noumenal freedom. "Creation springs up like a stream of time, a *durée;* but it is as time itself that works are deposited behind the stream of time and remain inert, offered to the eye as objects of contemplation or as essences for imitation."[26]

Original causality requires objectification for actualization, but these objectifications tend to dissolve into different moments the total movement of its operation. Consequently, Nabert's idea of originary affirmation requires a process of radical reflection on the various objectifications of selfhood in the effort to exist in order to conjoin through reflection what objectifying consciousness can only experience disjunctively. We must "decipher" these acts as "signs" of our effort to exist. We interpret our acts as we would a text. Indeed, Ricoeur's later theory of hermeneutics flows out of his attempt to appropriate Nabert's concept of radical reflection. This radical reflection provides the "assurance" of our effort to exist as responding to the originary affirmation even as it remains (partially) inadequate to it. In the effort to exist, the self experiences a difference within itself between what it is and what it ought to be.

> Because we do not enjoy immediate self-possession and always lack perfect self-identity, because . . . we never produce the total act that we gather up and project in the ideal of an absolute choice, we must endlessly appropriate what we are through the mediation of the multiple expressions of our desire to be. The detour by way of the phenomenon, then, is based on the very structure of original affirmation.[27]

Based on this idea of originary affirmation, Ricoeur seeks to develop a "fundamental ethics" of human desire that is teleological in a radical sense.[28] According to my reconstruction of Ricoeur's biblical exegesis of

---

26. Ricoeur, "Nabert on Act and Sign," 221.

27. Ibid., 222.

28. On the term and conceptualization of a "fundamental ethic," see Paul Ricoeur, "The Demythization of Accusation," in *The Conflict of Interpretations*, 340. In this essay, and many others, Ricoeur connects the idea of originary affirmation to a fundamental ethics based on an expanded notion of human desire somewhat akin to Spinoza's idea of the *conatus*. Because of

the symbols of creation, in the location of "origin," or the ever-present energy that begins and continues creation, we can view Ricoeur as placing Nabert's idea of "originary affirmation" as a type of causality that drives creation and the self's "effort to exist" expressed individually and communally in the biblical narratives as an intersignifying network of "founding events." Ricoeur's theory of originary affirmation, when fully developed and rendered explicit, thus already contains the two intersignifying senses of beginning that he discovers in the biblical narratives of creation and founding events.

Thinking Human Capability:
Originary Affirmation and Initiative
in the Hermeneutics of the Self

So far I have demonstrated a way to correlate the two senses of beginning expressed in the biblical narratives with two senses of action in Ricoeur's theory of originary affirmation. The third step in my reconstruction is to show how the meanings of the biblical triad — origin/founding events/ covenant (or absolute beginning/relative beginning/continuation) — resonate with a triad of concepts to be found in *Oneself as Another*, where Ricoeur develops his hermeneutics of the capable person centered around narrative identity. This triad can be labeled: originary affirmation/initiative/promising. I will use the two patterns of thinking to interpret one another mutually.

Having discussed the concept of originary affirmation in the previous section, here I will focus mostly on the pair of concepts in *Oneself as Another* that correspond to the last two terms of the biblical triad: initiative and promising.[29] With the category of initiative, we reach a

---

the logic of originary affirmation and radical reflection just described, Ricoeur argues that he can incorporate the Kantian *formalism* in morality as a moment in an overall teleological ethic of actualizing the original goodness of human existence toward which originary affirmation strives.

29. To be clear, I am correlating the triad of categories (originary affirmation/initiative/ promising) in *Oneself as Another* with the triad (origin/founding events/covenant) found in his biblical exegesis conducted separately. Ricoeur develops the concept of initiative in other places as well. See Paul Ricoeur, "Initiative," in *From Text to Action: Essays in Hermeneutics, II*, ed. Kathleen Blamey and John B. Thompson (Evanston, Ill.: Northwestern University Press, 1991), 209. There he explains initiative as the synthetic moment that connects the point-like instant (of cosmological time) and the living present (of phenomenological time). The concept

pivotal point in my argument. It is one thing to show that the "founding events" of the biblical narratives participate in and propagate the energy of creation. It is quite another thing to argue that this power of creation propagates through human action, initiative, and meaning-creation outside of "biblical time." Showing that the idea of creation can be understood this way through a constructive reading of concepts drawn from different writings of Ricoeur is the principal task of this essay.

A. Initiative

Ricoeur crafts the category of initiative in order to answer the question, What is meant by the "power to act?"[30] This relates to the question of how it makes sense to *ascribe* an action to an agent as the cause of the action, even as we *describe* human desires, motivations, and firing of brain synapses as being subject to natural causality. In ascription of an action to its agent, we say that an action *depends* on the person: it is "in her power." We have another concern as well, since we want to see our desires and motivations as related to the principle of action. Following Aristotle, we want to say we are embodied, desiring creatures in the world, but also, again with Aristotle, that we are able to put reason into our desires and dispositions for action. For Ricoeur this "power to act" is a "primitive datum" (*fait primitif*), but one which (*à la* Nabert) we can assert only after the effort of hermeneutical reflection on the paradoxes of action.[31] In this respect, the causality of initiative (power to act) can only be understood dialectically, in conjunction with the two types of causality (natural/noumenal). Here we encounter a rare explicit reference to the "causality" of originary affirmation in *Oneself as Another,* despite the pervasive presence of this notion operating behind the scenes.[32] Ricoeur writes that it is "necessary to coordinate in a synergistic way the original causality of the agent with the other forms

---

of "initiative" is thus his reworking of the Husserlian concept of the "living present." I am trying in this essay to draw out the implicit connections between this reworked concept of the "living present" with Ricoeur's other concepts of "living metaphor," on the one hand, and "new creation," "promising," and "*ipse*-identity," on the other hand.

30. Ricoeur, *Oneself as Another,* 101.

31. Ibid.

32. The reason for the conspicuous absence of this term is that Ricoeur came to substitute the term of "human capability" in all its forms (power to speak, power to act, power to narrate, power to be the subject of moral-ethical action, etc.) for the category of originary affirmation. However, on the interpretation being developed in this essay, he means the same

of causality."[33] In seeing their interaction in the power to act, we can then recognize the primitive datum of initiative.

Throughout this discussion Ricoeur has in mind Kant's "third antinomy" or "conflict of the transcendental ideas." The antinomy results from the fact that two apparently contradictory statements about causality in the "world of appearances" seem equally sound. The "thesis" asserts that not all appearances in the world operate in accordance with the laws of nature and that some can only be explained through a "causality through freedom."[34] The "antithesis" asserts the contrary proposition. The main issue is whether there can be observed in appearances a cause with "absolute spontaneity," that is, the power to begin from itself. Ricoeur observes that we use such a notion all the time in the practical field. Ricoeur recalls here the idea of a "basic action" discussed by analytic philosophers "which require[s] no other intermediary action one would have had to perform in order to do this or that."[35] This represents a kind of causality that depends on no other causes.

We have, then, a kind of primitive *attestation* of this power to inaugurate a new chain of events in the world. Yet the "antithesis" in Kant's antinomy says this is impossible. The series of causes in appearances is "interminable." An "absolute spontaneity" is an "illegitimate exemption from laws" of nature.[36] Kant's well-known solution to the third antinomy is that both thesis and antithesis can be true if they are seen as applying to different worlds, the phenomenal and the noumenal. Human freedom (spontaneous cause) happens in the world. When we view the person as a denizen of the noumenal world, we ascribe the action to the person. Our search for a responsible cause terminates in the "who?" to whom we impute the origin of the action. In contrast, when we describe

---

thing. Indeed, Ricoeur's term for the epistemological correlate of originary affirmation, "attestation," is used throughout *Oneself as Another*. (Attestation is the type of certainty that, as both non-verificationist and non-intuitionist in nature, is appropriate to the hermeneutics of human action, or, in terms of the argument being developed here, the hermeneutics of originary affirmation.)

33. Ricoeur, *Oneself as Another*, 102.

34. Immanuel Kant, *Critique of Pure Reason*, ed. and trans. Paul Guyer and Allen W. Wood, The Cambridge Edition of the Works of Immanuel Kant (Cambridge: Cambridge University Press, 1997), 484.

35. Ricoeur, *Oneself as Another*, 103.

36. Ibid., 104.

the person as a body in the world, our search for causal origin of action is "interminable."[37]

Assuming that my earlier reconstructive reading of Ricoeur's idea of creation is compelling, Ricoeur's way of framing Kant's third antinomy in relation to the category of initiative should be of considerable interest to us. Ricoeur picks up on the fact that what is really at issue for Kant involves *a distinction between two types of beginning*. Ricoeur writes that "Kant distinguishes two types of beginning: one which would be the beginning of the world, the other which is the beginning in the midst of the world."[38] On the one hand, a spontaneous cause may refer to an "absolute beginning" of the complete causal nexus of all reality. On the other hand, the spontaneous causality may simply refer to a "relatively first beginning," a beginning *in* time and not *of* time or causality itself.[39] Is this not the same idea underlying the causality of "founding events" we saw before? Even if Ricoeur did not directly draw this connection, I believe we are permitted to do so by the extreme similarity between the logics involved in each context (that is, absolute vs. relative beginnings).

Nevertheless, because of the constraints of his transcendental idealism, Kant can only assert that there exists no contradiction between the two theses. He can give no *positive* notion of an interweaving of physical causality (human desire) with rational freedom, the involuntary and the voluntary, our being-in-the-world, which is Ricoeur's ultimate aim. Indeed, as long as we remain on the level of abstract predicates of actions — whether as determined by noumenal or phenomenal laws — we skirt the issue of how we individuate or personalize the "who?" upon which the action depends. On the one hand, if I am determined by noumenal freedom alone, the causality of each action can only be ascribed in a complete vacuum — that is, without reference to other actions by the same agent across different times. Human identity dissolves as the inexorable result of Kant's pure formalism that dominates his theory of morality. On the other hand, if my identity is described through the abstract predicates of natural causality, then "who I am"

---

37. Of course, Kant's "solution" remains aporetical and continues to vex Kant scholars — a point to which I return below.

38. Ricoeur, *Oneself as Another*, 105.

39. Ibid., 108: "[F]reedom as a pure transcendental idea, without any connection to appearances, constitutes the ultimate sense of the faculty of beginning a causal series oneself."

changes according to various causes outside myself that condition me. Furthermore, I cannot be responsible for my actions in this case, since the search for the cause is interminable on the descriptive level alone.

In order to escape such dilemmas, Ricoeur believes that we must assert the category of initiative as responding to the primitive datum of the power to act. In contrast to Kant's solution, Ricoeur sees initiative as working through the interweaving, or synthesis, of the two types of causality. This synthesis is grounded in the original causality of originary affirmation, a kind of causality that cannot be observed objectively but is known through hermeneutical reflection upon the conditions of the human power to act. "Could one not say, in a nonphenomenalist sense of the term 'appearance'...the phenomenon or appearance of acting requires the union of thesis and antithesis in a phenomenon...specific to the practical field, which could be termed *initiative*."[40] Ricoeur concludes that the "primitive datum of the power to act [in initiative] is part of a constellation of primitive data that belong to the ontology of the self."[41]

B. Promising and *Ipse*-Identity

Ricoeur fuses the concept of initiative together with an ethical and ontological interpretation of the act of promising. Promising adds the ethical, ontological, and temporal senses of "self-constancy" to the act that initiative begins. In fact, as we saw in the case of the biblical sense of continuation of the founding events, initiative only truly appears in the temporal thickness that the self-constancy of promising makes possible. Promising connects together past and present in the living present of initiative.[42] In the act of promising a new possibility is brought into being. It aims at a "not-yet" reality but something I can and will make real. And a promise connects to the past, because promising is always a response to a concrete other.[43]

---

40. Ibid., 109.
41. Ibid., 112.
42. On the connection of initiative to Ricoeur's theory of "human time," see n. 29 above.
43. See Ricoeur, *Oneself as Another*, 266. Ricoeur argues that promising in the abstract is not possible, for a promise must be made to someone. I can make a contract with a business corporation; I can make a promise only to a concrete person.

In *Oneself as Another,* Ricoeur also develops another idea very central to the hermeneutics and temporality of selfhood, what he calls "*ipse*-identity."[44] Ricoeur defines "*ipse*-identity" as a type of permanence of the self through time that does not depend upon unchanging objective predicates of sameness, the kind of predicates that we would use to reidentify the permanence through time of a substantial object like a table or a tree. He labels the latter type of identity (or permanence through time) "*idem*-identity." In contrast, *ipse*-identity is a "self-constancy" based not on the impersonal predicates of substances but on *personal* predicates (irreducible to abstract impersonal predicates) that are essentially related to human acts in time, acts that are responses to radical affections that themselves cannot be described in objectifying terms. Ricoeur is thus explaining the origin in passivity that motivates the synthetic process that initiative brings to fruition. Promising provides the temporal tension that completes the process. Self-constancy in promising is the continuance of the promising. This grounds the notion of *ipse*-identity for Ricoeur.

It is through the idea of promising, not in the bare performative or grammatical sense described by speech-act theory, but in the sense of a real fidelity of the self to remain constant to the word of promise that the self has given to the other person in attention to his or her concrete actuality that provides the permanence-in-time of *ipse*-identity. Whether or not the *idem*-predicates attached to either the self (the maker of the promise) or the other (the recipient of the promise) undergo alteration, as they inevitably do, the self-constancy to the word one has given grounds a duration through time of a new beginning that predicates appropriate to a substance ontology cannot encapsulate or adequately describe.

Still, as we saw in the concept of initiative, it is impossible to remove all corporeal anchorage and still be able to "see" instances of *ipse*-identity in the world.[45] For this reason, Ricoeur develops along with *ipse*-identity and *idem*-identity another "mixed" category of identity, which he calls "character." In character, *ipse*-identity and *idem*-identity overlap and interweave to some degree. From the point of view of other

---

44. Ibid., 118ff.
45. Ibid., 132.

agents, the self acts and responds to other actions upon the self in characteristic ways that result from the sedimentation of habits. Through this overlapping of *idem*-identity and *ipse*-identity in character, Ricoeur develops a hermeneutical theory capable of showing how we "see" *ipse*-identity, or make it appear.

In *Time and Narrative,* Ricoeur works out a complex notion of narrative as the "mimesis" or imitation of human action in stories that functions to configure and give intelligibility to human action, initiative, and identity.[46] A narrative is a temporal unfolding that interweaves change (events) with the relative unchanging (that is, the stable world of the narrative). In telling stories, we understand characters only in the dialectical relation of their development to the plotting of the story, a plot displaying a narrative arc of a beginning, middle, and end. In this way, the configuring of human action by narrative serves to provide one means for the closure of the causal chains of human action for which we were searching in the earlier discussion of initiative. A narrative is like a dynamic metaphor that holds together discordant elements through time. The plot sets up a tension or expectation that demands completion and unity but it must negotiate events, contradictions, character development, and reversals of fortunes. The very reversals and surprises in the plot make possible the transformation of the situation depicted at the beginning to the new situation at the end of the story. But a good narrative is not arbitrary; it makes sense after the fact. A narrative, as a discordant concordance, makes "possible an ordered transformation from an initial situation to a terminal situation."[47]

In extreme cases, we can imagine a character in a story that remains constant to a promise despite radical change from her or his initial state or situation. We can imagine a near-total loss of *idem*-identity for a character in a narrative and still retain some intelligible sense of this character's selfhood. "My thesis is that, set back in the framework of

---

46. It is important to realize that Ricoeur intends only that our understandings of characters acting in stories serve to configure our own identity outside of stories; our actual identities are never completely subsumed within a particular narrative as some recent narrative ethics would have it. See Paul Ricoeur, *Time and Narrative,* vol. I, trans. Kathleen McLaughlin and David Pellauer (Chicago: University of Chicago Press, 1984).

47. Ricoeur, *Oneself as Another,* 141. In the interplay between *ipse* and *idem* senses of identity in narrative, we encounter in Ricoeur's thought something akin to the dialectic of the Name and the idols that we saw at work in his analysis of the biblical covenant narratives.

idem and *ipse*, these unsettling cases of narrativity can be reinterpreted as exposing selfhood by taking away the support of sameness."[48] Narrative configuration fills in the "interval of sense" opened up in "opposing the sameness of character to the constancy of self in promising."[49]

Thus, like the biblical narratives that unfold the temporal thickness of the founding events, it is finally only in narrative that we see the self-constancy of *ipse*-identity displayed in a meaningful way. The character of a story involves an interweaving of the two types of identity (and the two types of predicates). A character in a story can remain true to a promise even though "Everything has changed!"[50] My acquired dispositions, desires, habits, and motivations may all undergo radical transformation; nevertheless, I remain (or do not remain) true to my commitment. Narrative configures human identity and time, although it does not constitute it.

C. Passivity and Affection

So we now have in hand a thicker, more developed sense of our triad of fundamental ideas of creation and beginnings that grounds the fundamental ethics of originary affirmation I have been develop-ing. The enriched notion now incorporates the senses gathered up from Ricoeur's exegesis of the idea of creation in the Hebrew Bible, on the one hand, and the hermeneutics of the capable person, on the other hand: origin (creation/originary affirmation); relative new beginning (found-ing events/initiative); and temporal continuation (covenant/promising). Where does that leave us?

The next step in the reconstruction of the fundamental ethics based in a dynamic vision of creation is to look at the role of passivity and affec-tion in the constitution of various senses of creation. Human initiative is a moment of creative activity in several senses: (*a*) meaning- or culture-making; (*b*) human action in building its social world and responding to its environment; and (*c*) the radical ontological sense of becoming

---

48. Ibid., 149.
49. Ibid., 125.
50. This is not to say that there are never conditions for breaking a promise. What we are interested in here is the temporality structure the self-constancy of promising makes possible in human action, time, and narrative.

a self in responsible relations to the world, other persons, and the creative ground of being. This fundamental ethic is based on a humanistic affirmation of the power of human beings to create something of new significance. But this power could be misunderstood as a radically arbitrary creativity, even as a kind of Nietzschean will-to-power in which the self imposes its vision on the world without regard to the other persons or the environment that it affects. On the contrary, meaning-creation related to initiative is not arbitrary or coercive. Rather, it is always a response to radical affection by the power of original affirmation (that is, creation). Meaning-creation in initiative is the attempt of the self to respond to this causality and bring what it demands into being. In initiative, human beings create in order to uncover something about the world. As Ricoeur states, within his theory of metaphorical meaning-creation, "we invent in order to discover." We invent meaning because we are affected by and responding to something not yet given meaning but that needs to be articulated. As an expression of original affirmation, meaning-creation is not merely a linguistic process going on at the higher levels of consciousness but goes to the very bottom of our existence. My claim here is that meaning-making should be understood in both hermeneutical and ontological senses. (In a later section, I will describe the relation of passivity and affection in the activation of the metaphorical process as integrally related to the power of initiative.)

Initiative, we then realize, must have both active and passive sides. So far I have placed greater emphasis on human creativity as *activity,* alluding only in passing to issues of radical affection or *passivity* at the heart of originary affirmation in initiative. What I now want to suggest is that originary affirmation orients us to a telos, that is, of aiming at bringing about an ideal society of justice that affects us as a demand. In theological terminology, this is the kingdom of God as a radical call. Ricoeur articulates this idea philosophically by means of the Kantian Rational Idea of the Kingdom of Ends. We can "think" this Idea abstractly, but apprehending the fullness of it requires an affection that exceeds our finite conditions of intuition. Nevertheless, we are affected by it and strive to bring it into actuality.

The idea behind my reading is simply as follows. Ricoeur holds that the idea of the kingdom of God cannot be presented (by finite intuition) as knowledge (similar here to the way Kant's "Rational Idea" of the Kingdom of Ends cannot), but, also on strictly Kantian grounds, we can meaningfully *think* it and *hope* for its fulfillment.[51] However, we may still wish to inquire, does such a status relegate the idea to the realm of the Ideal as an ever-unrealized possibility? In other words, is it real, is it ever fulfilled? I believe that Ricoeur's answer is that indeed it is real insofar as it affects us and actualizes the power of human freedom to make it so. Thus, although there is no "certainty" in terms of epistemological verification of its "presence," there is an "attestation" of its reality in the power of human "initiative" to create new beginnings in the world that then bring the divine economy of justice into the world. It depends on human effort and creativity, but this human effort is the sign, or testimony, of the effort to make it real. The kingdom of God is present, not in terms of usual epistemological criteria of knowledge, but in terms acceptable to a hermeneutical epistemology of "attestation."[52]

Ricoeur concludes *Oneself as Another* by developing an ontology of selfhood based on act/potentiality (rather than substance) that includes a triad of experiences of radical passivity corresponding to predicates of otherness in his hermeneutical investigation into the moral-ethical predicates of human action.[53] Commentary on Ricoeur appears to ignore a remarkable fact, namely, that these sites of radical affection correspond precisely to the three main symbols of evil of his earlier work, *The Symbolism of Evil,* in which the affections of the self by originary affirmation somehow have gone askew.[54] In *Oneself as Another,* these

---

51. See Ricoeur, "Freedom in the Light of Hope." Ricoeur builds upon Kant's critically important distinction between *Erkennen* and *Denken.* The technical contrast here between "knowing" and "thinking" is Kantian. In the former, a priori concepts can find objective "presentation" within empirical intuition within the finite limits and conditions of the human form of sensibility, whereas, in the latter, cognition seeks to go beyond the limits of such intuition and produces Ideas without objective content. We can "know" events and things in the phenomenal world based on "constitutive concepts"; beyond this we are led into a Dialectic of Rational Ideas and possible "transcendental illusion." However, there are some "regulative Ideas of Reason" that we can legitimately "think" even if we cannot know them, and these are given content through the Kantian practical philosophy. Because Ricoeur is a hermeneutical thinker, who builds fundamental ontology not solely by reflection on things (substances) but on human action, he ultimately rejects the idea of an absolute separation between the theoretical and the practical.

52. On this category of "attestation," see Ricoeur's discussion in *Oneself as Another,* 21–23.

53. Ibid., 317–56.

54. Paul Ricoeur, *The Symbolism of Evil,* trans. Emerson Buchanan (Boston: Beacon, 1972). For reasons of space, I do not pursue these aspects of *Oneself as Another* in this essay. Ricoeur

three loci of radical passivity are the ownness of the body, the alterity of the other person, and experience of attestation and injunction by otherness in conscience.[55] These correspond to the three relations of self-world, self-other, and self-self respectively. According to Ricoeur, these fundamental relations are mediated by a fundamental "passive synthesis" that makes the active consciousness of these relations possible. In other words, in each of these moments of passivity, the self is affected by aspects of the relation, an affection that exceeds the capacity of the finite understanding to represent.[56] I will deal in detail only with the phenomenon of conscience here.

Ricoeur describes conscience as a modality of affection by otherness irreducible to bodily otherness and the otherness of other persons, "namely *being enjoined as the structure of selfhood.*"[57] In conscience, the inner voice of my moral self is fused with the calling voice of the other. We can thus identify the fundamental sense of conscience as the demand of originary affirmation on us in all its mediated forms. This capacity to be affected by the call of originary affirmation opens the self to the other kinds of otherness. Ricoeur also says that conscience is both "attestation" and "injunction." Attestation "can be defined as the *assurance of being oneself acting and suffering.*"[58] Ricoeur conceives attestation as a nonverificationist form of certainty appropriate to a hermeneutics of the selfhood.[59] To the degree that the self succeeds in manifesting originary affirmation in initiative responding to radical affection by original affirmation (goodness) with integrity and self-constancy, then it has an assurance of being oneself — there is "attestation" of the capability.

---

lays out this ethics in Studies 7–9 of *Oneself as Another.* The triad of passivity forms the positive counterpart in his hermeneutics of human capability to the three primary symbols of evil in his hermeneutics of human fallibility and fault. Presentation of these connections would form an essential part of a more complete presentation of my reconstruction of Ricoeur's fundamental ethics of originary affirmation.

55. Ibid., 318.

56. Perhaps not surprisingly, a close examination of the triad of passivity shows that it can be mapped onto the temporal triad we have discovered undergirding Ricoeur's fundamental ethic. This is only to state in a different way my earlier claim that the activation of the self's response to original affirmation (creation) in its three senses is mediated by forms of radical affection. The major difficulty is how the self does so with integrity and maintains its own activity. My thesis is that this self-constancy in integrity is achieved through conscience.

57. Ibid., 354 (italics in original).

58. Ibid., 22 (italics in original).

59. Ibid., 21.

But to the degree that the self becomes aware that the acts that are the signs of its effort to exist remain not fully adequate to the full affirmative causality, conscience becomes "injunction." Thus, conscience is the form of radical self-affection that relates the self of consciousness to the deeper self.

In the concept of original sin, however, something "goes wrong" in the response to affection by originary affirmation, something external or anterior to the self (the involuntary), but also something the self does and for which he or she is responsible (the voluntary). It is in terms of this dialectic of the voluntary and involuntary, on the one hand, and interiority and exteriority, on the other hand, that Ricoeur develops his hermeneutics of the three main symbols of evil — stain or defilement, violation of the Covenant with God and consequent wandering or captivity of the nation of the Hebrew people, and guilt (or the bad conscience).[60] In evil, the passive synthesis of the self needed to actualize the human power and freedom to live well together in communal existence somehow fails and constricts into self-love and false justice.

Through comparative exegesis and analysis of Augustine's attempt to rationalize these primary symbols into his concept of "original evil" with the Kantian account of "radical evil," which has an inscrutable origin temporally anterior to all actions of the self, Ricoeur attempts to lay bare the dynamics of the failure to actualize the full power of selfhood.[61] What Ricoeur shows is that Kant's Idea of the *Summum Bonum* (highest good) is the actualization of the Kingdom of Ends in which happiness corresponds to the worthiness to be happy. This is the highest "demand" of practical reason in the Kantian critical philosophy, what Ricoeur calls the complete determination of the object of the will. It is a Rational Idea that we can think (*Denken*) but cannot know (*Erkennen*) because, like all Kantian Rational Ideas, it would require the production of an intuition of an unconditioned object within phenomenal experience, and because of the conditioned form of our sensibility, this remains the impossible. Nevertheless, for Ricoeur, the highest good signifies the full actualization

---

60. See Paul Ricoeur, "The Hermeneutics of Symbols and Philosophical Reflection, I," in *The Conflict of Interpretations*, 289–96; and Ricoeur, *The Symbolism of Evil*.
61. See Paul Ricoeur, "The Hermeneutics of Symbols and Philosophical Reflection, I," in *The Conflict of Interpretations*, 301–14.

of both reason and desire and thus equates to some degree with the telos of originary affirmation. It remains an idea in the making, becoming a reality to the degree that we render it efficacious in human power and initiative. Like the network of passivities, it cannot be directly experienced in consciousness, but it still affects us to the degree that originary affirmation pushes us to its actualization.

The Idea of the Highest Good lies not only beyond the "limits of the understanding." It also places a check on the pretensions of human power. Whenever Ricoeur discusses *Kant's Religion within the Limits of Reason Alone,* he makes the following observations.[62] First, radical evil is not reducible to a specific act violating the Kantian moral law. Rather, it is an affection by evil of the power of human choice that leads it to choose the dispositional maxim of self-love over respect for the moral law as the meta-maxim for all other maxims of action. Thus, evil is not a matter of natural inclination gone wild; it is something that we take on voluntarily. Nevertheless, its origin is "inscrutable," because, while in some sense taking place in the intelligible (noumenal) realm, it is itself nonrational. In various essays on this subject of the Kantian idea of radical evil, in discussing the avowal of radical evil Ricoeur always speaks of an accompanying experience of *negativity,* a primal affect that exceeds the more restricted negativity commensurate with the degree of culpability present in the failure to live up to individual laws in specific acts. In the very negation of human power and freedom in the experience of original sin, the excess of negative emotion signifies an affection by the telos of originary affirmation that we have failed to actualize. In this connection, Ricoeur frequently conceptualizes this excessive negative affect through two notions gleaned from Spinoza's *Ethics:* every finite being expresses an ontological desire or "effort to exist" (*conatus*), and failure to fully actualize this desire elicits "ontological sadness."[63] In sum, radical evil is something that goes wrong in the self's affection by originary affirmation and causes its expression in initiative to abort

---

62. See, for example, the following essays in *The Conflict of Interpretations:* "The Demythization of Accusation," 335–53; "Freedom in the Light of Hope," 402–24; "The Hermeneutics of Symbols and Philosophical Reflection, I," 287–314. See also, in *Figuring the Sacred,* the following two essays: "Hope and the Structure of Philosophical Systems," 203–16; "A Philosophical Hermeneutics of Religion: Kant," 75–92.

63. For example, see *Oneself as Another,* 315–17.

in mid-action. The human choice of the meta-maxim of self-love is a *constriction* of human power that cuts itself off from its affection by and grounding in originary affirmation and the energy of creation. Here ethics must pass to religion in order to affirm that the ground of originary affirmation in creation is real despite the existence of radical evil.

The Economy of Superabundance and the Economy of Equivalence

We can see this same dynamic at work in Ricoeur's theory of the relation between love and justice, and his reading of the commandments to love in the Gospels. In his later writings, Ricoeur consistently relates the idea of creation to an "economy of superabundance." This is especially evident in his use of Rosenzweig's philosophy of religion in *The Star of Redemption*, which devises a novel way to reinterpret the relation of Creation, Revelation, and Redemption, centered on the Divine Command to "Love me!" which Rosenzweig locates in the *Song of Songs*.[64] So I turn next to Ricoeur's analysis of the relation of love and justice, and how he uses this relation to reinterpret the economy of superabundance.

In later discussions of the economy of the gift, Ricoeur views the gift, while opening or awakening the self to otherness, as interrupting human activity, initiative, and culture (meaning-creation). In *Totality and Infinity*, Emmanuel Lévinas describes the encounter with the "face of the other" in similar terms. The face of the other summons the self to an infinite responsibility to which no human response is ever sufficient. In the face of the other, we encounter infinity, a trace of a Good beyond being, that interrupts human freedom and our attempt to limit the scope of responsibility by claims of just reciprocity based on our ontological notions (totality).

According to my reading, Ricoeur's idea of the economy of superabundance is very different. He sees the economy of the gift as awakening the affections (love) that make justice real. Rather than the two economies being in conflict, a productive, living tension exists between them. In the

---

64. See, for example, Paul Ricoeur, "Love and Justice," in *Figuring the Sacred*, 315–29; and *Oneself as Another*, 351. Franz Rosenzweig, *The Star of Redemption*, trans. William W. Hallo (Notre Dame, Ind.: University of Notre Dame Press, 1985), 199.

final analysis, both logics require one another. He argues that a morality of reciprocity based solely on a pure Kantian formalism fails. Still, he wants to hold onto the Kantian imperative. He argues that the Golden Rule expresses the necessary reciprocity but does so with proper attention to the concrete other that Kantian morality seeks to respect as an end-in-itself. Jesus' commandment to love the enemy prevents both the Golden Rule and the Kantian imperative from constricting into an empty formalism disguising self-love.

Ricoeur describes the creation of the sense of morality (and justice) as a three-stage process: first, affection by originary goodness inclusive of otherness at the fundamental level of the experience; second, a passage from this base level to a meaning-structure (the Golden Rule) that recognizes sameness in otherness; and finally, a formalization of the Golden Rule into a rule of reciprocity (for instance, morality or justice). When we turn to the discussion of the metaphorical process of meaning-creation we will see the same process at work. Both processes describe a passage from affection by alterity at a basic level of experience and the creation of a novel meaning through a passive synthesis not totally within the self's conscious activity. In both processes, this is the affection and constitution of the self's being through the superabundant causality and goodness of creation (that is, original affirmation).

Ricoeur draws out his idea of the logic of superabundance, or gift economy, from various biblical texts and genres. This ranges from topics of creation and the liberation of the Hebrew people from Egyptian captivity, in the Old Testament, to Jesus' parables and Pauline discussions of grace, in the New Testament. Here I will focus on the "living tension" Ricoeur details between the "logic of equivalence" and the "logic of superabundance."[65] Ricoeur associates the Kantian imperative and ideas of justice (especially as formulated by the political philosopher John Rawls) with the logic of equivalence. In a hermeneutical investigation of a set of passages from the Sermon on the Plain (Luke 6), he finds resources to elaborate how this living tension is productive of meaning and motivation and not simply two sets of incommensurable logics. Ricoeur identifies the principle of the morality with the Golden Rule as

---

65. Ricoeur, "Love and Justice," 328.

formulated by Hillel: "Do not do to the neighbor what you would hate
to have done to you." In *Oneself as Another*, Ricoeur seeks to show how
this identification forms a bridge between an ethics in the style of an Aristotelian "rational desire" and the formalism of the Kantian morality of
duty, which seeks to constrain desire, not to render it rational. This is
so, Ricoeur contends, because the other formulation of the Golden Rule
is the commandment to love the neighbor as oneself (Matt. 22:39). In
this way, Ricoeur retrieves the second formulation of the Kantian categorical imperative, the Respect for Humanity formula. But this is only
half the story.

Ricoeur discovers a plurality of senses, or "polysemy," both among
kinds of love and among the various commandments to love. It is this
very polysemy that allows for what he calls the "poetic use of the
commandment."[66] He detects a "gap" between the poetic use of the
commandment and its properly ethical sense (in the Golden Rule). But it
is in terms of this gap that he undertakes to develop a "dialectic centered
on the economy of the gift."[67] Underlying this polysemic *semantic* field
of kinds of love and the different commandments of love, Ricoeur also
perceives a level of affect in which different *affective* modes of love are
in play. The different types of desire interact; they are distinguishable but
not radically discontinuous. Nor does Ricoeur want to declare either an
absolute distinction or sameness among the different kinds of love (*erōs*;
friendship; *agapē*; or some form of love as pure other-regard). Instead,
he perceives a "process of metaphorization" on the linguistic plane that
responds to and interacts with the field of different affective modes of
love. He sees the "production of a vast field of analogies among the affective modes of love, thanks to which they mutually signify one another."[68]
It is this analogy of love that drives the logic of superabundance and
renders it productive of new meaning.

In addition to this interplay of affects and analogy between kinds
of love, Ricoeur also discovers a tension displayed in the love commandments themselves. Ricoeur draws attention to a set of passages
in the Sermon on the Plain in Luke where the Golden Rule and the

66. Ibid., 320.
67. Ibid.
68. Ibid.

commandment to love the neighbor are brought into a "strange contiguity."[69] In the clash of meaning, Ricoeur sees the production of new meaning.[70] Ricoeur focuses on a series of passages in the text in which Jesus apparently condemns the Golden Rule: even sinners follow the Golden Rule since they give in order to receive (Luke 6:32–34). The implication appears to be that if the meaning of the Golden Rule funds the logic of the Kantian imperative, but even the Golden Rule can base itself surreptitiously on the love of self, then a morality based on formalistic notion of reciprocity can fall under radical suspicion. In other words, the "golden rule, given over to itself, sinks into the rank of a utilitarian maxim."[71] Ricoeur points out that this apparent condemnation is quickly followed by the commandment to love one's enemies in Luke 6:27–30. In Ricoeur's reading, this tension between the Golden Rule (and its apparent condemnation) and the commandment to love the enemy sets up a logic of generosity, superabundance, and gift that forestalls utilitarian distortions of the Golden Rule. The commandment to love the enemy intensifies the Golden Rule into a "hyperethical" commandment that prevents self-love from being the motivation. The commandment to love one's enemies places a check on perverse interpretations of the Golden Rule. But "the commandment to love one's enemies is not sufficient by itself [that is, in isolation]; rather, it is the hyperethical expression of a broader economy of the gift, which has many other modes of expression."[72]

It is the living tension between the logic of the gift and the logic of reciprocity that allows Ricoeur both to employ the formalisms of the Kantian imperatives and the Rawlsian imaginative reconstruction of the hypothetical original social contract (behind the veil of ignorance), while also escaping their usual pitfalls. Ricoeur bases his discussion of the idea of justice on the classical Aristotelean definition of just distribution, to each his or her due. But this formalism of reciprocity and equality, while not invalid on its own proper level, does not guarantee true morality or justice, in Ricoeur's view. True justice depends on a disinterested respect

---

69. Ibid., 324.
70. Ibid.
71. Ibid., 328.
72. Ibid., 320. This essay is trying to draw out some of these connections.

for the equal rights and needs of all affected. Suspicion, however, can always be cast upon any actual concrete application of this mere formalism. In terms similar to the Hegelian criticism of Kant's abstract *Moralität,* morality is empty without its actualization within concrete ethical life, or *Sittlichkeit.* Suspicion can always be cast on the material principles of justice that result from a purely formal procedure.

But this is not to say that justice should be simply supplanted by Christian love: "But what kind of bond is thereby instituted between social partners? My own suggestion would be that the highest point the idea of justice can envision is that of a society in which the feeling of mutual dependence — even of mutual indebtedness — remains subordinate to the idea of mutual disinterest."[73] So thus, from the other side, the formalism of the Kantian morality and the Rawlsian idea of justice serve also as a check on false expressions of the hyperethical command to love one enemies: "If the hypermoral is not to turn into the nonmoral — not to say the immoral, for example, cowardice — it has to pass through the principle of morality, summed up in the golden rule and formalized by the rule of justice."[74]

Ricoeur also sees this reinterpretation of the Kantian imperative in terms of the dialectic of love and justice as providing the means to respond to Emmanuel Lévinas's critique of everyday morality. In Lévinas's account, the "face of the other" places the self under a demand of infinite responsibility.[75] There is no limit to my responsibility, because any placing of a limit formalizes my relation to the other and denies my true concern — the very feeling of responsibility that funds all morality. In reinterpreting the Respect for Humanity formulation of the Kantian imperative by the Golden Rule (in living tension with the hyperethical command), Ricoeur can avoid the Lévinasian challenge while responding to the core of it: moral action is a response to the concrete other. Formalism in Kantian morality can degenerate into violence to the other when it becomes infected by a utilitarian self-love. "Underlying the [golden] rule is the presupposition that to act is already to begin to exercise a power

---

73. Ibid., 323.
74. Ibid., 328.
75. Emmanuel Lévinas, *Totality and Infinity: An Essay on Exteriority,* trans. Alphonso Lingis (The Hague: M. Nijhoff Publishers, 1979).

over others, with the risk of treating them as docile and at worst as non-consenting victims."[76] On Ricoeur's account, all morality begins with an affection by the concrete other in all his or her otherness. Human interaction can become a mere "power-over" the other. The primitive intuition underlying morality is the affective response of indignation we feel in perverted forms of "power-over," the indignation in face of innocent suffering at the hands of the stronger or more powerful.

In sum, Ricoeur argues that there exists a deeper fundamental ethics underlying morality and justice, which aims at a telos that "evil ought not to be" and that its contrary should be brought into being. This fundamental ethic draws on the intersignification between the interpretation of the creation narratives, the idea of originary affirmation, and the concepts of initiative.

Thinking Affectivity: Passive Synthesis and the Metaphorical Process of Meaning-Creation

It is my claim that Ricoeur builds his theory of the metaphorical process of meaning-creation on the basis of a concept of "passive synthesis" (borrowed from the phenomenologist Edmund Husserl).[77] In making this claim, I am proposing a link between central aspects of his hermeneutics of the self with that of his theory of the interpretation of texts. Ricoeur never renders this linkage quite explicit, but I believe the logic of passive synthesis, so much in evidence in *Oneself as Another,* is the common term between these two aspects of Ricoeurian thought. Ricoeur's remarkable innovation is to extend the idea of passive synthesis simultaneously into his analyses of meaning-creation in language and of human initiative. Ricoeur worked out his theory of the metaphorical process in order to account for affection by the self by original affirmation. His theory of narrative and narrative identity is an extension of this effort and accomplishment. Thus, we must understand his hermeneutics

---

76. Ricoeur, "Love and Justice," 295.
77. On the following discussion of passive synthesis, see Edmund Husserl, *Analyses Concerning Passive and Active Syntheses: Lectures on Transcendental Logic,* trans. Anthony J. Steinbock (Dordrecht: Kluwer Academic Publishers, 2001).

of creation, selfhood, texts, and narratives as seeking to describe different facets of the same phenomenon of creativity.

The linkage of meaning-creation in language (the metaphorical process) and human initiative in action is displayed most fully in his account of narrative emplotment (Ricoeur's term, *Time and Narrative*), which Ricoeur views as a metaphorical process configuring human action and identity through time. Narrative and metaphor are creations of new meaning that allow human beings to configure initiative, the new beginning in time. Language, in what Ricoeur calls "the living metaphor," is part and parcel of the creative uprising (*Ursprung*) of being itself (*phusis*). Metaphor, or the creation of new meanings in general, allows the novelty of new beginnings in time to emerge into view as new crystallizations of sense.

As I mentioned earlier, I see a moment of affection and passive synthesis intervening between the *Ursprung* of Creation and new beginnings in time. In *Oneself as Another,* Ricoeur describes each of the three types of radical passivity also as sites of "unparalleled" passive syntheses.[78] It is well known that Husserlian phenomenology interprets consciousness as being a kind of activity through which the subject constitutes the object of experience utilizing a stock of sense-meanings. But there are aspects of experience toward which the self is relatively passive. The phenomenological theory of passive synthesis supplies an answer to the question of how what is before and outside of conscious awareness may nevertheless become part of awareness.

Husserl held that we do not possess from eternity our entire stock of ideas and meanings that we use to interpret experience. Rather, Husserl speaks of a "genesis" of these concepts through our participation in time, language, and the life-world. The paradox here is that the ego lacks the means to focus attention on objects of experience whose corresponding meanings have yet to be acquired. In this context, Husserl speaks of the foreground and background horizons of experience. We are only dimly aware of the fringes of experience. They affect us but do not automatically enter into the ego's awareness. How then does Husserl explain conscious awareness of those things for which the ego lacks a meaning?

---

78. Ibid., 325.

Husserl explains: through a law of association, similar to Hume's analysis of the production of ideas, certain constellations of "somethings" effect an "affective allure" that awakens the ego's attention.[79] When this process is carried to completion, there takes place a "primordial constitution" of sense. This sense then becomes habitually available to the ego. The self's synthesis of the objects of experience emerges out of this process of passive genesis.[80]

While Ricoeur regards the "metaphorical process" as taking place on the semantic level, he clearly sees this as emerging out a process of passive synthesis of meaning. He is always careful to note that the creation of metaphors does not take place in the absence of feeling or affectivity. Ricoeur writes that the theory of metaphor is "incomplete if it does not give an account of the place and role of feeling in the metaphorical process."[81]

In his semantic theory of metaphor, he rejects a simple substitution theory that sees metaphor as merely placing the meaning of two words in tension. Rather, metaphor, for Ricoeur, is the coming to expression of something that is felt as rising to awareness and needing articulation to be fully grasped. In opposition to the substitution theory of metaphor, he views the metaphorical process as taking place only in the "event of discourse," in which a person uses a full sentence (subject-verb-predicate)

79. In the Humean theory, ideas result from a *psychological* law of association modeled on the Newtonian law of gravitation brought about by resemblance, contiguity, and constant conjunction. In Husserl's *transcendental* appropriation of the Hume's *psychological* theory of association, these processes are reconceived as taking place on a level prior to sense-giving and consciousness. The ego is affected by elements of the field of experience that are "below the radar," so to speak, of consciousness. But through the laws of association these unconscious givens effect an "apperceptive transfer of sense" (Husserl) among each other and begin to beg for attention ("affective allure"); prior to this stage, attention to these "somethings" is at a zero-point. At some point, the degree of affective allure reaches a critical threshold and the ego awakens to and turns its gaze toward the nascent object with a newly acquired sense-intention—that is, a crystallization of sense precipitates out of this process of passive synthesis. Note that this synthesis is also critical to the constitution of the ego itself since there is no ego without the habituated activities of active synthesis of noematic sense.

80. We can note that, without going into more detail here, there are, for Husserl, several very important primordial passive syntheses: the sense of the corporeal ownness of the self as "paired" with sense of the alterity of other persons; the internal experience of time in which the living present trails off into the past in primary memory ("retention") and stretches into the future in anticipation ("protention"); and the experience of the ownness of the self in corporeal existence. To this list of primordially passive syntheses, Ricoeur would add the affection of the self by self in the experience of conscience.

81. Paul Ricoeur, "The Metaphorical Process of Cognition, Imagination, and Feeling," *Critical Inquiry* (Autumn 1978), 155.

to assert something (predicate) about something (subject) in the world (verb/being). Metaphor takes place in the tension created when a sentence combines meanings borrowed from two semantic fields of sense that are incongruent or do not normally belong together.

Ricoeur also borrows from Kant's idea of the "productive imagination," which provides a matrix of rules for meaning-creation that is not merely the mental reproduction of images of things no longer or not yet present. The imagination, for Ricoeur, invents new concepts to describe novel realities to which meanings borrowed from our existing semantic stock are inadequate.

For example, in the sentence, "Time is a thief," the subject *time* is placed into the alien semantic field of *human* exchange and feelings of loss. Ricoeur sees this as a process of both semantic deviance and finding new congruence: out of the literal incongruence a new "pertinence" or congruence is created. Ricoeur argues that this process of meaning-creation arising from the tension of semantic deviance across the whole sentence is not simply the work of psychological association by resemblance (as in the Humean theory of association). In the metaphorical process, a new insight into reality is achieved.[82] Indeed, ultimately for Ricoeur, all meaning arises out of the metaphorical process. Metaphor brings to thought the inchoate affective level of experience through which originary affirmation operates.

Conscience

Throughout the essay, the theme of creation has been explored through the concept of originary affirmation. The most important locus for the expression of originary affirmation is conscience. As we saw, for Ricoeur, conscience is the site of a passivity in the relation of the self to itself. In his account of conscience, Ricoeur combines attestation and injunction in the power to respond to the "voice of the other" in the self. It is *attestation* of the self's effort to exist to the extent that originary affirmation is realized (partially) in initiative and meaning-creation; it is *injunction* by the voice of the other to the degree this effort to exist fails. Here the

---

82. Ibid., 148.

self finds itself becoming other to itself, that is, "oneself as another." Drawing upon Martin Heidegger and Lévinas in their accounts of the phenomenon of conscience (being-toward-death; summons to responsibility by the other), Ricoeur allows an intersection between contrary models of the limits of selfhood. Both Heidegger and Lévinas speak of impossibility in relation to death that defines the self's own-most possibility. Heidegger calls death the possibility of impossibility in relation to the self. Lévinas inverts this formulation and regards the death of the other as the impossibility of possibility, the limit of the ego's power of comprehension. True subjectivity, for Lévinas, is the impossible relation of infinite responsibility to the other. Responding to anxiety in the face of death, conscience, in Heidegger's analysis, is the self's call to itself in attestation of its authentic self. Lévinas speaks of the injunction issuing from the face of the other which interrupts the ego's indifference. Ricoeur permits an intersection of these reciprocal accounts of conscience and their complementary aporias. In the end, both accounts result in a similar conclusion: the impossibility of the self to ethically *respond* to the other ontologically (on the basis of finite human power and capability). Ricoeur, in contrast, views the ethical confrontation with alterity as the key to the *actualization* and opening up of the capacity for responsible selfhood in its full scope. Conscience, for Ricoeur, is the attestation of self-constancy in the face of otherness. In the final analysis, the originary affirmation to which the self attests in its effort to exist is a voice of the other in the self. In Lévinas, the infinite responsibility that demands "substitution" of oneself for the other is experienced as accusation and persecution. In Ricoeur's eyes, however, attestation empowers the capability to respond to the other in the recognition of oneself as another in the voice of conscience. In this way, the power to become and remain a responsible self arises out of an experience of alterity, not despite it. Seeing oneself as another entails the creation of meaning at the most fundamental level of the self's power to be. In a very real sense, the self is a living metaphor. Ricoeur's juxtaposition of Heidegger and Lévinas enables him to chart a way through the impasses in their respective analyses.

As we have seen, in Ricoeur's view, ethical selfhood requires the capacity to keep promises and the power to respond to the concrete other despite changing circumstances and even substantial alterations in oneself. We have attempted to show how meaning-creation is essential to this capability to achieve a type of permanence in time not based on substance metaphysics. But this binding of time may have a paradoxical result. The temptation to found self-identity on factors within the control of the self produces the paradox of the self-binding will. By attempting to establish the enduring self through a process of "buying time" in the logic of exchange, the very power to remain self-constant over time is undermined. A kind of "powerless power" results, for example, through the substitution of technological means, force, or even violence for the power of initiative inherent in human action.

Ultimately, this power consists in the capacity to make promises and to found the bonds of community. In biblical terms, this capability consists in the power to form and keep covenants. Ricoeur points to the paradox of self-binding power in his concept of the servile will, the phenomena of the guilty conscience that he explored in *The Symbolism of Evil*. The flipside to the figure of fault represented by the guilty conscience is found in *Oneself as Another*. Ricoeur regards conscience as the power of attestation that detects in the excess of sadness over fallibility an indication of affection by the originary affirmation underlying human capability.

As part of the "little ethics" Ricoeur develops in *Oneself as Another*, he formulates the "ethical intention" of "*aiming at the 'good life' with and for others, in just institutions.*"[83] In light of my derivation in this essay of a fundamental ethics of originary affirmation in which human creativity participates in the power and goodness of creation itself, we can slightly revise Ricoeur's perhaps overly anthropocentric imperative and extend it in a more theocentric direction. The imperative of the fundamental ethics is to reestablish in conscience and integrity the participation of creative human initiative in the creative ground of the universe.

---

83. Ricoeur, *Oneself as Another*, 172 (italics in original).

Part Two

Humanity in Creation

Chapter 8

THE HUMANISTIC ETHIC
Jewish Reflections
Paul Mendes-Flohr

"Religion without power is mere philosophy."[1] This sapient observation by the Indian Muslim poet Muhammad Iqbal (1877–1938) boldly thrusts all discussion of religion and ethical humanism in critical perspective. It is a perspective that informs this essay. Modern Jewish thought, the exposition of which is my bread and butter — or, if you wish, bagel and cream cheese — abounds in philosophical and theological constructions of a Jewish ethic in support of a humanistic vision. The reflections that follow are prompted by a parenthetical remark of a colleague, who, in the midst of an impassioned conversation in the corridors of the University of Chicago's Divinity School, paused and with a deeply pensive gaze, looked at me — or perhaps she was actually looking at the angels above us — and with a soft, almost remorseful voice mused: "As a Catholic, indeed, as a passionate and devoted member of my church, I belong to a community that lays claim to privileged knowledge. Can I be a believing member of my faith community without being exclusive? Can I *truly* [her emphasis] embrace the Other as a fellow human being without compromising my conception of God's Word? Can I truly reach out to the Other without vitiating the values and institutions of the religious tradition that nourish my soul and furnish the fabric of my family life?"

As a Jew, I have analogous concerns. I, too, am torn by an anxiety that my particularistic fidelities are at odds with the humanistic ethic

---

1. Cited in Daniel Pipes, *In the Path of God: Islam and Political Power* (New York: Basic Books, 1983), 1.

to which I am beholden with a passion equal to that of my love of my people and its traditions. Sigmund Freud once observed that a Jew is a person who has more than one passport. In fact, I have two passports with an option for a third. But Freud also meant that a Jew — surely the modern Jew — inhabits many cultures and travels between different cognitive landscapes. Indeed, this is a condition — I dare say, privilege — of many denizens of the modern world, Jews and non-Jewish alike. The ethical implications of our multiple cultural citizenship were perhaps best captured by Jean-Paul Sartre. Modernity, the French philosopher noted, has transformed our notion of fraternity; we now sense a solidarity with persons "whose face we do not recognize." We identify with others whom we do not recognize as belonging to our circle of acquaintances; we are bound morally to persons who inhabit neither the same communal nor cultural space we do. Indeed, the bonds of human solidarity stretch beyond the limits of our group, religion, nation, or universe of discourse. Unleashing centrifugal forces, modernity has expanded not only the boundaries of knowledge but also our sense of community.

I am a Jew, but my moral, and *a fortiori* political, community is not confined to my fellow Jews. The modern, indeed, humanistic configuration of the multiple, overlapping communities of intellect, imagination, and moral sentiment gained terse but vigorous expression in a *cri de coeur* of the Bulgarian-Jewish writer Elias Canetti. Writing in the midst of the horrific events that so brutally sought to sever the Jews from their fellow human beings — the events we now call the Holocaust — this Nobel laureate for literature exclaimed: "Should I harden myself against the Russians because [they persecute the] Jews, against the Chinese because they are far away, against the Germans because they are possessed by the devil? Can't I still belong to all of them, as before, and nevertheless be a Jew?"[2]

As a citizen of the State of Israel I am witness to an ever-increasing shrinkage of the cosmopolitan and humanistic horizons of my fellow Jews. To be sure, when one's community is under siege, it is difficult to reach out to the Other across the barriers of enmity. It is thus not

2. Elias Canetti, *The Human Province*, trans. Joachim Neugroschel (New York: Deutsch, 1978), 51.

surprising that in the grips of a fierce and seemingly intractable political and territorial conflict with our neighbors, many of my fellow Jews in Israel yield to base emotions and subscribe to political views that hardly conform to a humanistic ethic of embracing and confirming the Other. National conflicts, especially when inflamed by the savagery of tanks and suicide bombers, are inherently Manichaean, casting one's adversaries as incorrigible beasts, embodying all evil. War polarizes and dehumanizes the Other. This is tragic, indeed. What is disturbing, however, is that the rabbis — as the Imams — are seemingly incapable of transcending this Manichaean divide. Sadly, they are often at the frontline leading the forces that seek to deepen the divide. They do so by a studied conflation of religious teachings with national interests, rendering faith in effect a vehicle of patriotism and myopic nationalism. To be sure, most of the rabbis — as the majority of Imams — are disinclined to join the ranks of their patriotic colleagues, and prefer to stand silently on the sidelines. By their silence they countenance outrages that theists should condemn as reprehensible transgressions of God's law.[3]

The Danger of *Sacro Egoismo*

Of course, one may retort that these rabbis misinterpret the teachings of the tradition. Or one may point to the political-sociology of the State of Israel, and argue that the rabbis feel themselves obliged to vie with the secular authorities and forces in society to gain sway over the "soul" of the people, and thus calculatedly wed religious values and doctrines to the nation's political agenda. This analysis would only underscore our misgivings about the failure of the rabbis to assume a transcendent perspective illuminating a horizon beyond the fray. Moreover, by identifying the tenets of Torah with a politically circumscribed (perhaps more correctly "circumcised") understanding of Jewry's collective interests, no matter how one assesses those interests in strict secular and political terms, they, the rabbis, lend a given policy a seal of sanctity. Their theological endorsement of patriotic politics thereby exacerbates

3. There are notable exceptions, such as *Rabbis for Human Rights*, an Israeli organization concerned specifically with giving a voice to the Jewish tradition of respect for human rights within the context of Israel's occupation of Palestinian territories.

the danger of a *"sacro egoismo"* — that is, a sacred egoism — that is inherent in all expressions of patriotism, certainly in its more febrile articulations. While a nation's egoistic regard for its own interests is natural and, in certain circumstances, surely by any moral standard, in order, patriotism, especially in its more hyperbolic manifestations, tends to view those interests as sacrosanct and hence as ethically self-justifying and nonnegotiable.

By exalting the nation's interests to be sacred, *sacro egoismo* not only negates the legitimacy of the interests of the nation's adversaries, but also serves to blind the nation to the human reality of its adversaries. Even more lamentable, *sacro egoismo* also allows — nay, enjoins — a nation to commit acts that one would otherwise regard as morally reprehensible. Under the command of *sacro egoismo*, the citizens of a state (or any political community, however constituted), who in their personal lives may be utterly decent and upright, kill and plunder. When blessed by the custodians of divinely revealed truths, the state — which, after all, is a human, hence a fallible, institution — becomes a veritable Moloch. As Martin Buber noted, "in the realm of Moloch honest men lie and compassionate men torture. And they really and truly believe that brother-murder will prepare the way for brotherhood!"[4] This is a bizarre and frightening dialectic. The perverse fantasy of "redemptive sin" informs the political judgment, alas, not only of Oriental nations, but all nations, even those privileged to dwell in the enlightened West, that regard themselves as charged with a divinely appointed task to cleanse the world of evil, the alleged agents of who are, after all, their fellow human beings.

One may conclude, as a good old-fashioned liberal I surely do, that religion should at all cost be kept apart from the corridors of political power. But then we are confronted once again with Muhammed Iqbal's dictum that "religion without power is mere philosophy." If I understand Iqbal correctly, a religion's quest for power in and of itself is not a vice. Indeed, he would argue that the pursuit of political power is, in fact, a theological duty. After all, biblical faith is born of a vision of the common good, a vision that, when inflected with the remonstrations of

---

4. "On the Suspension of the Ethical," in *The Eclipse of God: Studies in the Relation between Religion and Philosophy*, (New York: Harper, 1952), 156.

the prophets, demands social and political justice.[5] But this vision, as I have suggested, becomes blurred and profoundly distorted when it is associated with the political, and thus parochial, interests of a particular polity, nation, or community of faith.

The Challenge of Secular Humanism

There is yet another dimension to the religious quest for political power that Iqbal seems to have had in mind. The possession of power is a test of the efficacy of a particular faith's teachings; only by passing through the fire of such a test can these teachings be authenticated. Sermons, theological disquisitions, systematic or constructed, remain, indeed, but mere philosophy when relegated to the precincts of our houses of worship and learning and solely ensconced in our hearts. While concurring with Iqbal that religion must embrace the quotidian realm of public life and thus perforce requires power, one may question whether this power need be political. I shall return presently to consider alternative modalities of power that religious faith may assume.

The failure of the rabbis of the State of Israel to distinguish what type of power may be appropriate to their calling and to provide the state with moral leadership is often ascribed to the fact that most of them have yet to experience the purgatory of the Enlightenment and a Western education. The apologia is telling, for it implicitly acknowledges that the religious humanism that we wish to celebrate is a construct born of a response to secular humanism. My colleague's anguished concerns cited at the beginning of my reflections—namely, how one can be a believing Christian without being supersessionist and exclusive—reflects the fact

5. Cf. "I think it is a mistake to suppose that the idea of state is more dominant and rules all other ideas embodied in the [religio-political] system of Islam. In Islam the spiritual and the temporal are not two distinct domains.... In Islam it is the same reality that appears as Church looked at from one point of view and the State from another.... The truth, however, is that matter is spirit in space-time reference. The unity called man is body when you look at it as acting in regard to what we call the external world; it is mind or soul when you look at it as acting in regard to the ultimate aim and ideal of such acting.... The state, from the Islamic standpoint, is an endeavor to transform these ideal principles into space-time forces, an aspiration to realize them in a definite human organization.... The ultimate reality, according to the Quran, is spiritual, and its life consists in its temporal activity. The spirit finds its opportunities in the natural, the material, the secular." Mohammad Iqbal, *The Reconstruction of Religious Thought in Islam* (London: Oxford University Press, 1934), 146f.

that her faith commitments, as are mine, are challenged by a source from without our respective religious communities and traditions. Our faith commitments are challenged by secular humanism, especially as elaborated by its so-called postmodern articulations calling upon us to honor alterity and affirm the integrity of the "otherness of the Other," while reaching out to her or him as a fellow human being.

To be sure, the secular humanist vision has its roots in the biblical affirmation of the oneness of God as the presupposition of the unity of the human family. The great hymn of secular humanism, Beethoven's jubilant "Ode to Joy" as sung by the chorus of his Ninth Symphony, evokes the divine source of the universal fraternity to be forged by secular wisdom and ethical reflexes:

Freude, schöner Götterfunken	Joy, lovely divine spark,
Tochter aus Elysium,	Daughter of Elysium,
Wir betreten feuertrunken,	Drunk with fire, we enter,
Himmlische, dein Heiligtum!	Heavenly one, your shrine!
Deine Zauber binden wieder	Your magic spells reunite
Was die Mode streng geteilt.	What convention has rough sundered;
Alle Menschen werden Brüder,	All men will become brothers
wo dein sanfter Flügel weilt.	At the gentle touch of your wing.

The Ode to Joy became the veritable anthem of secular humanism. As the novelist Robert Musil describes its impact, "millions sank . . . awestruck in the dust; hostile boundaries shattered; the gospel of world harmony reconciled and unified the sundered."[6] The Ode to Joy attained a delightful simplicity but compelling poignancy, highlighting its universal message, in its Yiddish rendition by the poet Y. L Peretz:

Alle Menschen zeinen brider:	All human beings are brothers and sisters:
braune, gelbe, schwartze un weisse. . . .	brown, yellow, black and white. . . .
Alle Menschen zeinen brider,	We are all brothers and sisters,
fon ein Taten, fon ein Mamen.[7]	from one papa, from one mama.

Despite the religious resonance of the secular humanist vision, it challenges theistic faith precisely because it is secular and thus not dependent on a privileged access to saving truths. To be sure, the humanistic ethos could be amplified and perhaps even strengthened by theological insights

6. Robert Musil, *The Man without Qualities*, trans. Sophie Wilkins (New York: Vintage Books, 1996), 1:45.

7. Y. L. Peretz, "Brider," in idem, *Ale vork*, ed. Central Yiddish Cultural Organization (New York: CYCO Bicher-Verlag, 1947), 1:96–97.

and doctrines, but nonetheless one must acknowledge that the challenge to our respective faiths to affirm humanism has come in good measure from the secular vision. I underscore this as a caveat against theological arrogance, against theistic superciliousness. Religious faiths have not brought healing to a world lacerated by the antagonisms engendered by human differences, by diverse cultures, religions, traditions, memories, axiological and political systems. The secularists, of course, have also failed miserably, although they have often tried gallantly to liberate the human family from some of its more invidious divisions. The ignominious collapse of communism and the full realization that under its proletarian banner humanism was rendered a tyrannical creed has left secular humanists bewildered and in nigh-utter disarray.

Into the resulting vacuum, the purveyors of a new ecumenical gospel have rushed in to proclaim the salvific gifts of cybernetic and consumer globalization. The floundering vision of a world united by moral solidarity has been replaced by the promise of one happy human family bonded by the shared fantasy of a market economy providing one and all an abundance of consumer goods and electronic wizardry. One should not, of course, gainsay the blessings of economic well-being and its attendant educational, technological, and medical benefits. Moreover, it would be profoundly hypocritical of us who live in well-heated homes, graced with the latest amenities provided by the market economy, not to speak of access to fine educational and health facilities, to deny to our disinherited neighbors, distant and far, the same possibilities. What is questioned is whether the transformation of the world into one massive conglomerate of shopping malls and fast-food eateries will usher in the *eschaton* in which poverty and misery will be abolished from the face of the earth. Forgive me if I cite Buber once again, albeit by paraphrase. Should poverty be abolished, and material need no longer blight our global village, and all have ample cash in their pockets to buy computers, DVDs, and consume more food than our physicians tell us is necessary or healthy, the real ethical task will still remain — indeed, "would become wholly visible for the first time."[8]

8. See Martin Buber, "Replies to My Critics," *The Philosophy of Martin Buber,* eds. Paul Arthur Schilpp and Maurice Friedman, The Library of Living Philosophers, vol. 12 (LaSalle, Ill.: Open Court, 1967), 723.

The vast majority of our fellow human beings are, of course, still abysmally poor and deprived. The disinherited are not only in distant lands; they are within blocks of many of us, or even closer. Our ethical task is still defined by the exigent need to clothe the naked and feed the hungry, although we are cognizant that moral solicitude does not cease with that action. We all know that the divisions that fracture the human family will not be healed by economic abundance and opportunity alone. Genuine moral solidarity goes deeper than the reaches of a McDonald's hamburger or a Macintosh computer.

Biblical faith speaks of love, and the limits of love are not only set by a commitment to alleviate the material want of the stranger and one's neighbor. Love includes such concerns, but much more. Secular and religious humanists alike are bound by the knowledge that love of the stranger and one's neighbor requires a caring attentiveness to all that constitutes their spiritual — as well as psychic and cultural — reality, indeed, all that makes them human. Duly alarmed that the superficial and ultimately chimerical promises of globalization and the gospel of the market economy may lead us to complacency and stupefy our moral judgment, and terrified by the ever-mounting threat of Moloch subverting the rule of God the Creator, religious and secular humanists should resolve to join forces and revalorize the humanistic vision of a moral solidarity grounded in love.

Love, of course, cannot be taught, at least not catechistically. Like the humanistic ethos, which it is to animate, love is a sensibility that must be cultivated; it is an attitude, nay, a spiritual orientation, that must be nurtured. Focusing on a notion that has shaped both religious and secular Jewish ethical sensibility, I conclude my thoughts by illustrating what constitutes the humanistic ethos. Christians and Muslims will undoubtedly recognize analogies in their own traditions.

Doing a *Mitzveh*

In Yiddish one speaks of "doing a *mitzveh*." The term defies easy and fast definition; its semantic fullness can only be spelt out by illustration, and ultimately by its performative reality. "Doing a *mitzveh*" means, roughly, to perform a good deed, but it signifies eminently more than that. It entails being alert to the needs of others and acting upon one's apprehension of those needs. Performing a *mitzveh* takes one beyond mere compassion. As the Swiss Jewish writer Margrette Susmann averred, "compassion is empty and vain as long as I have not taken upon myself the other's suffering and made it my own."[9] In a similar vein, a Hasidic master told of a conversation he overheard in a tavern between two slightly inebriated peasants. With a glass of vodka in his hand, one peasant turned to other, and asked, "Tell me, do you love me?" "Sure, I love you." "No," retorted the first peasant. "Yes, I do love you," protested the second peasant. Whereupon, the first peasant imbibed his vodka and, looking his drinking partner in the eyes, declared, "If you really loved me, you would know what pains me."[10]

In her masterful essay "Regarding the Pain of Others," the late Susan Sontag concluded that "compassion is an unstable emotion. It needs to be translated into action, or it withers." And she continues to pose the question regarding what one "is to do with the feelings that have been aroused, the knowledge that has been communicated. If one feels that there is nothing 'we' can — but who is that 'we' — and nothing 'they' can do either — then one starts to get bored, cynical, apathetic."[11] Sontag's understandable misgivings about the limits of compassion are unintelligible for one borne by the consciousness beseeching him or her to perform a *mitzveh,* for the *mitzveh* is not assigned to a "we" or a "they" to perform. The performative axis of *mitzveh* is the individual deed and resolve to reach out to those in need. We may regard *mitzveh* performance as proactive humanism.

One familiar with Hebrew and the lexicon of traditional Judaism will readily recognize that the concept of *mitzveh* performance has religious origins. The precepts of the Torah are *mitzvoth,* the plural of *mitzvah.* Indeed, the term *mitzvah* is derived from the Hebrew for command: *Ha-Shem mitsaveh mitsvot:* God commands *mitzvoth.* But to perform a *mitzveh* — I emphasize the Yiddish inflection in order to highlight the difference of nuance — is a commandment not legislated directly or

9. M. Susmann, "God the Creator," in Nahum N. Glatzer, ed., *Dimensions of Job: A Study and Selected Texts* (New York: Schocken, 1969), 87.
10. Cited by Martin Buber, *The Tales of the Hasidim: The Later Masters,* trans. Olga Marx (New York: Schocken, 1948), 86.
11. Susan Sontag, *Regarding the Pain of Others* (New York: Picador, 2004), 101.

explicitly by God. It is a supererogatory deed one performs in anticipation of God's commandment or, rather, God's love. To perform a *mitzveh* is, if you will, a form of *imitatio Dei*. In performing *mitzvehs* religious and secular Jews meet, and share in a proactive humanism. It is in the cultivation of this ethos, I submit, that religion is to seek its true power.

One must acknowledge, of course, that the parameters of such a proactive humanism may be limited to one's family, tribe, or polis. Any anthropologist would be quick to remind us of this. Anthropologists speak of "familial amoralism," of the fact that the members of a particular group may treat one another with remarkable humanity, but behave toward those who dwell beyond the walls of the community with moral indifference, if not contempt. Cognizant of the danger that one's ethical and religious principles may very well be delimited to tribal affiliation, Franz Rosenzweig once quipped, "God created the world, not religion."[12] With this theological *obiter dictum* he sought to point to the foundational belief of biblical faith and humanism alike: reflecting the oneness of God, creation marks the oneness of life and the human life. Creation is inclusive; religion is, alas, all too often exclusive. God created the World, and "saw all that He had made, and found it very good" (Gen. 1:31) — if, and only if, we share in the work of Creation.[13]

---

12. Rosenzweig, "The New Thinking," in N. N. Glatzer, ed., *The Life and Thought of Franz Rosenzweig*, 3rd ed., with new foreword by Paul Mendes-Flohr (Indianapolis: Hackett, 1998), 201.

13. Cf. "There was a time when the various religions and the many schools of thought filled the world with the noise of their disputes. Today, in the light of the common danger of destruction and the total decline of humanism, the time has come [that the religions of the world] will seek that which is common to them all: [The work of Creation.]...'You have created us that we might meet you,' says St. Augustine. A humanism that seeks to be true humanism...must necessarily be a believing humanism, based on the covenant between God and man. From this, a new perspective on the human is derived. Man is called upon to participate in Creation, to bring to consummation, as it were, the process of creation on earth that has not yet been completed. Man is called upon to be a partner [of God]." Samuel Hugo Bergman, *The Quality of Faith: Essays on Judaism and Morality*, trans. from the Hebrew by Y. Hanegbi (Jerusalem: World Zionist Organization, 1970), 85–88.

Chapter 9

COMMON MORALITY, PREMORAL GOODS, AND RELIGION

Kevin Jung

The idea of a universal morality and the civilization to be built on this idea are often attributed to the Enlightenment project. But, for quite some time now, this idea has been under increasing philosophical scrutiny and suspicion. In fact, it would not be an exaggeration to characterize the current climate in moral philosophy as that of uneasy attitude toward any claims to universality. Certainly, the increasing recognition of moral and cultural diversity has added weight to such suspicion. In what is called the "Information Age," peoples from different cultures have become more acutely aware of differences among their moral beliefs and cultural practices than ever. In contrast, ironically, there is a growing sensitivity to violations of human rights. The idea of human rights is invoked not only in law but also in many other spheres of society such as politics, medicine, and religion. So pervasive and powerful this idea has become, that many are now even willing to accept some measure of humanitarian intervention into nations to prevent human rights atrocities from occurring, as witnessed in places such as Kosovo and East Timor, which would have been seen as an illegal infringement of national sovereignty not many decades ago.

For many moral philosophers, this raises an interesting question: How can we talk about common morality, much less human rights, if we admit the plurality of values and value-systems? For our purposes, this

I am very grateful to Michael A. Johnson and William Schweiker for their extensive and insightful criticisms of an earlier draft.

185

question can be slightly modified as the following: Given the moral and religious pluralism in our world, how can religious ethics or monotheistic religions affirm both moral pluralism and common morality? In the following pages, I will locate four "sites" where a different "house" is located, each site representing one of the competing formulations of how to understand the problem of value and how best to resolve or approach the problem. After gaining some insight into the problem by comparing and contrasting these sites, I will propose that, despite the pessimism looming about the idea of a common morality in contemporary discourse, we can and should endorse the idea of such a common morality. It is my thesis that we need to reformulate the idea of common morality through a careful reflection on the place of premoral goods in moral judgment. This reformulation will specify important aspects in which a discourse of common morality informed by the notion of premoral goods is preferable to other options in contemporary moral and social theories, as I consider the notion of premoral goods an important part, though not all, of value theory.[1] In particular, I will explore how the discussion of premoral goods may also advance the contemporary debate on the role of tradition and religion in the public sphere.

Four "Model Houses" of Value

Site 1: A House Divided

There are particularists in moral epistemology who are so disillusioned with the modern pursuit of objective knowledge and the Enlightenment view of morality that they want to revert to a premodern, or countermodern, notion of tradition-defined morality. Alasdair MacIntyre, a key representative of this view, argues that rationality is meaningful only within the tradition that gave its birth and nourished its development. Our present world has fallen into a grave state of disarray because our

---

1. It must be clear at the outset that this essay is meant to be a limited exercise in value theory. While this essay focuses on the notion of premoral goods, especially those in relation to our bodily and psychological needs, in order to demonstrate the possibility of common morality, it is by no means my position to argue that all premoral goods are directly related to or can be abstractly derived from such physical or psychological needs. It is very important to note that while premoral goods themselves (e.g., freedom of thought, sociality, and equality) are not historically or culturally contingent, the interpretations of these goods often take various temporal and relational forms in history and intersubjectivity.

current languages of morality are incapable of adjudicating their differences and unable to offer common rational criteria for objective morality. The Enlightenment that promised a universal morality stands virtually paralyzed, as it has lost the historical worlds of meaning that once made our moral concepts intelligible and coherent. Modern moral philosophy, social science, and everyday people use a jumble of moral terms and concepts in our moral judgments that turn out to be remnants of older, coherent moral vocabulary. This moral vocabulary once made sense within a community that shared a common narrative and practices aimed at human flourishing: virtue-creating practices and a historically embedded tradition of moral inquiry to back them. This vocabulary makes no sense without this framework of narrative, virtue, and practice. Modern attempts to justify a universal morality thus result in various theories of emotivism, which holds that moral judgments are mere expressive assertions of our emotions and preferences. Theories in modern moral philosophy have failed precisely because they have sought to understand rationality independently of its historical and social origins.

To understand these origins is also to find a unity that narrative history furnishes in one's selfhood and renders one's actions intelligible. As MacIntyre puts it, "the unity of a virtue in someone's life is intelligible only as a characteristic of a unitary life, a life that can be conceived and evaluated as a whole."[2] Just as one's actions are intelligible only within one's personal history, the narrative structure of human life illumines standards of practices concerning both internal and external goods of individuals who share the narrative tradition. In other words, morality is dependent upon traditions.

In fairness to MacIntyre, two things need to be noted with respect to the charge of relativism. First, his incommensurability thesis does allow room for the possibility of some understanding between rival traditions. He writes,

> If two moral traditions are able to recognize each other as advancing rival contentions on issues of importance, then necessarily they

---

2. Alasdair MacIntyre, *After Virtue: A Study in Moral Theory* (Notre Dame, Ind.: University of Notre Dame Press, 1984), 205.

must share some common features.... Issues on which the adherents of the rival tradition will appeal to standards which are simply incommensurable with those appealed to by adherents of the rival tradition will not be and could not be the only kinds of issues to arise in such a situation. It will thus sometimes at least be possible for adherents of each tradition to understand and to evaluate — by their own standards — the characterizations of their positions advanced by their rivals.... Indeed nothing precludes the discovery that the rival tradition offers cogent explanations of weaknesses, of inabilities to formulate or solve problems adequately, of a variety of incoherences in one's own tradition for which the resources of one's own tradition had not been able to offer a convincing account.[3]

Every tradition confronts knowingly or unknowingly a state of epistemological crisis which compels its adherents to evaluate its own standards of rational justifications but also those of the other tradition.[4] As a result, it may be possible that the response from the other tradition to this crisis is judged more adequate by the adherents. Thus, MacIntyre does not concede that the incommensurability of rational standards excludes any meaningful debate between rival traditions.

Second, as Gene Outka notes rightly, MacIntyre's theory does not necessarily admit relativism, at least for the participants in traditions.[5] For these participants will still make their own truth-claims about reality, though these claims are not believed to be intelligible to others outside the traditions. Even epistemological virtues of understanding and judging well must be formed within a tradition. Particularists, for example, hold true their moral claims about justice but consider the criteria for such claims to be tradition-immanent. They will not be recognized by a person whose practices of judging are not formed within a tradition that possesses truth-conducive practices. This is what William Schweiker

3. Ibid., 276–77.
4. Alasdair MacIntyre, *Whose Justice? Which Rationality?* (Notre Dame, Ind.: University of Notre Dame Press, 1988), 364–66.
5. Gene Outka, "The Particularist Turn in Theological and Philosophical Ethics," in *Christian Ethics: Problems and Prospects*, ed. James F. Childress (Cleveland: Pilgrim, 1996), 102.

calls "internal realism" in ethics, a view shared by a number of Christian thinkers such as Stanley Hauerwas.[6]

Thus, while tradition-dependent morality should not be equated to a kind of relativism that says "Every opinion is as good as another," it does lack the basis for appeals to universal principles whose validity can be recognized independently of a tradition. Many deem such tradition-transcendent principles as necessary to sustain a pluralistic society. Yet, it seems to me that the real question is not so much about the epistemic possibility of truth as about the possibility of a stable politics in a pluralistic society. If people want to adhere to their own truth-claims and disregard those of others, how can there be any agreement to orient action and choices within a society that comprises many traditions? Though MacIntyre says that it is possible to have a meaningful debate between traditions and even to acknowledge the superiority of the rival tradition, it is not all clear how feasible this is in a pluralistic society. If, for example, each local or religious community wants to create and enforce (irreconcilable) laws based on its own truth-claims and standards of rationality, the possibility of reaching some agreement among these communities just seems remote, if not unrealistic. In a sense, the situation may be compared to a house divided within itself. Can such a house divided still sustain itself? Picture the scene where different people in the same house appeal to different sets of rules to settle their differences. Will it work?

Site 2: A House under De(con)struction

Picture now a house that is being constantly demolished for a never-ending renovation. My next model house of value may fit this picture. The residents in this house, the theorists known as deconstructionists, espouse the view that a complete presence of truth is never possible, not to mention the possibility of a universal morality. They hold that what is argued for in the name of universal morality is at best a tenuous and arbitrary claim of the modern solipsistic subject that is far from being objective. Putative objective moral values that are allegedly built into the structures and foundation of the world represent only

---

6. William Schweiker, *Power, Value, and Conviction: Theological Ethics in the Postmodern Age* (Cleveland: Pilgrim, 1998), 64–65.

the thought-horizon of the subject to which others must conform and under which they are subsumed. These thought-structures are rickety and full of drafts. What is worse, sometimes claims to universality can be unmasked as nothing more than façades, ingenuous schemes to manipulate and dominate others, like the infamous Potemkin village, erected to both disguise and impose one's will-to-power. The task of postmodern philosophy is to debunk the myth of universality espoused by traditional philosophy as *epistēmē* and to welcome new possibilities of knowledge overshadowed by the previous philosophy.

John Caputo, in his *Against Ethics,* maintains in typical Derridean tone that there is no origin or foundation of ethics, by which he means that there is no ground of universality, metaphysical or empirical, that generates our moral obligation. Rather, obligation simply happens as an event in the interaction of the self with the "other" when the alterity of the other disrupts the self in an ever-ambiguous claim against the self's imposition of its own value schemes. Paradoxically, obligation happens in an encounter that interrupts and limits our usual value-schemes or conception of universal principles. Such a happening should be unfamiliar to no one because it is a facticity of life. Caputo claims that his ethics of deconstruction is to appreciate "the tenuous and delicate situation of judgment addressed by undecidability,"[7] which denies the absolute nature of obligation (based on universal principles) while affirming the binding nature of obligation as such.

Now what are these deconstructionists trying to deconstruct and why? The deconstruction here in question is aimed at both classical and modern metaphysics. First, their deconstruction is a critique of classical (or premodern) metaphysics. The work of deconstruction takes up the task of the *Destruktion* of classical metaphysics begun by Heidegger but in a more radical form. Heidegger complains that the classical philosophers understand the question of being primarily in terms of presence (*ousia*).[8] Jacques Derrida goes further in arguing that there are no fixed

---

7. John D. Caputo, *Against Ethics: Contributions to a Poetics of Obligation with Constant Reference to Deconstruction* (Bloomington: Indiana University Press, 1993), 3.

8. Martin Heidegger, *Being and Time,* trans. Joan Stambaugh (Albany: State University of New York Press, 1996), 22.

centers that are always present behind beings or objects of thought. Derrida's reworking of Husserlian phenomenology is just to make this point. Derrida denies Husserl's claim of an *a priori* correlation between the "what" and the "that" of experience, driving a wedge between the signifier and the signified. Against Husserl, he seeks to problematize the relation between signification and intuition, claiming that expressions (for instance, language, words, or signs) can bear signification with or without the "fulfilling" intuition of the objects referred to. Contrary to Husserl, Derrida contends that a theory of signification can do away with fulfilling intuition as a necessary condition of meaning. Derrida thinks that he can exhibit — through the endless work of deconstruction — how every text, including, or perhaps especially, "metaphysical" texts, depends on significations that defy fulfillment by intuition, or rather, significations whose fulfillment by intuition ("presence") remains ever undecidable.

The denial of intuition, however, does not lead to the loss of meaning. For him, the field of meaning — and the apparent correlation of signification and intuition — is rather an effect (not a condition) of the play of presence and absence, a play of the substitution of signs in which the final presence or fixed center or totalization of meaning in any given text is constantly promised and deferred.[9] This means that a new meaning is always possible on the basis of what he calls "undecidability" between presence and absence. It is neither affirmation nor negation of full presence of a sign but the "supplementarity" of the sign that permits the constant replacing of the center.[10] On this account, meaning is constituted not by presence but by a play of presence and absence, not by identity but by *différance,* that is, the never-present condition of the possibility of play. The undecidability or what he calls "trace" of sign is this constant oscillation between presence and absence or between spatial and temporal differences of the sign.

Deconstruction is also a critique of modern metaphysics and the Enlightenment. Modern metaphysics since Descartes posits the human

---

9. Jacques Derrida, *Writing and Difference,* trans. Alan Bass (Chicago: University of Chicago Press, 1978), 292.
10. Ibid., 289.

subject as the subject of modern philosophy. That is to say, the metaphysical foundation is no longer sought in a changeless form or telos but in the conscious thinking thing (*res cogitans*) or in the ego by which other entities become intelligible.[11] *À la* Emmanuel Lévinas, both Caputo and Derrida question modern philosophy's obsession with the subject. What they all share in common is the belief that the origin of subjectivity does not reside in the subject but rather comes from the (wholly) other. They also agree that the other is not an entity that can be simply thematized or measured by the subject or the ego's intentionality (projections of meaning). For such a thematization silences or reduces the heterogeneity of the other into the same, once again into an object whose *presence* is now grasped by the subject; otherness is reduced by comprehension and thematization. This mastery of self over the otherness of the other concerns all of these thinkers of radical ethics. For Derrida, the basis of the post-deconstructive subjectivity is the result of the *impossibility* of fulfilling intuition.[12] It means that the other as the signifier is never fully given to the intuition of the subject, always already escaping fulfillment. It is this impossibility of fulfilling intuition that liberates the signifier, that is, the other, from the self.

In short, the universal reason that the Enlightenment promised to deliver is nothing but the echo of the subject whose autonomy and self-legislation disguises itself as the voice of universal reason. As John Caputo puts it, "The law that reason obeys is reason's own law, so it does not, ultimately, finally, bend its knee to anything 'other' (*heteros*) but offers its respects to itself (*autos*), like a man bowing to himself in the mirror. Even when it honors the Other as an end in itself, it does so in virtue of the Law, which is Reason, which is itself; so it respects itself as an end in itself."[13] The result is the silence of the Other, the heteronomous Other. Against such a backdrop of the modern metaphysics, deconstruction seeks to destroy the false images of universal morality and to welcome new possibilities of knowledge where not sameness but

---

11. Simon Critchley, *Ethics-Politics-Subjectivity: Essays on Derrida, Lévinas and Contemporary French Thought* (New York: Verso, 1999), 53.

12. John D. Caputo and Michael J. Scanlon, "Introduction," in *God, the Gift, and Postmodernism*, ed. Michael J. Scanlon (Bloomington: Indiana University Press, 1999), 6.

13. John D. Caputo, *Against Ethics*, 13. Kant, however, would argue that this is precisely the power of reason that obeys the moral law.

differánce is the key to knowledge. Postmodern deconstructionists, in this sense, live in a house they are constantly destroying and rebuilding. As Simon Critchley puts it, "each decision is necessarily different, each time I decide I have to *invent* a new rule, a new rule, a new norm, which must be absolutely singular in relation to the other's infinite demand made on me and the finite context within which this demand arises."[14]

Now what is the problem with this house under deconstruction? The problem is simply this: How can we rebuild a house without any manual or supervision, while we keep wrecking any remaining structures? Can we save the house?

Site 3: A Good-Enough House

Among those who share the view that there is no ahistorical, philosophical metanarrative that ought to govern human action, some opt for the value vocabulary of liberal democracy as a historically contingent yet by far best of all possible choices. The sense of the term "best choice" is ironic here because what makes it best "for us" is our historically contingent inheritance of the vocabulary of liberal democracy we use to express our moral standards. Richard Rorty, who has been an outspoken proponent of this option, is well aware of the problem of pluralism in a modern liberal democratic society and the challenges it brings to politics. While Rorty shares with many communitarians the view that there are no moral languages divorced from historical communities, he is not eager to join the counter-moderns in their chorus of distrusting the ability of modern democratic institutions. Whereas communitarians believe that liberal institutions and culture cannot survive without a strong moral community, the shared practices of moral judgment that support their values, and also the thick historical character of the self that identifies itself with the community, Rorty does not think that politics requires antecedent philosophical grounds.[15]

Steering a course between realism and antirealism, Rorty's pragmatism not only severs the connection between truth and ontology but also rejects philosophy's traditional emphasis on epistemology. He wants to

14. Critchley, *Ethics-Politics-Subjectivity,* 277.
15. Richard Rorty, *Objectivity, Relativism, and Truth: Philosophical Papers. Vol. I* (New York: Cambridge University Press, 1991), 178–79.

cut through modern debates between "realist" and "antirealist" theories of truth. On the one hand, the realist holds that truth is a property of propositions that correspond to the objective world. On the other hand, the antirealist holds that we can only understand a proposition's being true relative to the knowing the conditions of justification that would make it true for a finite, human knower. With the antirealist, Rorty holds that our contingently acquired moral language does not *represent* or *correspond* to the world, and therefore any truth claims based on the nature of being are futile. We human beings do not have a God's-eye view. But against the antirealist, Rorty asserts that the meaning of truth does not depend on the "assertability-conditions" of our truth claims, to use Michael Dummett's term for the subject-relative conditions of justification under which a statement can be claimed to be true. He rejects the supposition endorsed by antirealists and realists alike: that there is a property that defines Truth. This is not a debate about what is true or knowable but about the very "meaning of truth." Rorty finds the debates between realism and antirealism and between objectivism and relativism pointless because we need not presuppose that there is a property of truth (whether subject-relative or subject-independent) that explains the big concept of Truth with a capital "T." To state it otherwise, truth itself does not prove that a statement is true, but it is the details of how a statement or claim works in our everday and scientific practices and vocabularies that makes it true.[16] A kind of skeptical pragmatist, Rorty wants to jettison ideas of the meaning of truth that "do no work" in our everyday judgments. In this way, he evades both antirealist and realist theories of truth as both stemming from the urge to itch the same senseless question, as Wittgenstein would say.

To illustrate how Rorty's more general views about epistemology and meaning are applied to contemporary society, we return to our previous problem: pluralism. Rorty wants to *replace* philosophy's obsession with epistemology with politics, as the former is no longer viewed capable of discovering truth, its own self-appointed job description. Politics, or more specifically, what he calls "postmodernist bourgeois liberalism," allows individuals to communicate freely with each other in the task

16. Ibid., 140.

of solving the problems they face together without appeals to any purported transcultural and ahistorical rationality.[17] Truth, in this sense, may be historically contingent but not without merits. People from different groups and traditions will debate their rationality, avoiding assuming the language of any privileged epistemological vantage point outside of time and any practical concerns.

On this view, the self is not a self-legislating law-giver, independent of social practices and moral beliefs of her fellows in historical communities. Nor is it the other who issues moral obligation. In the Rortyan vision, the self may be best described as an *adaptive* being who adjusts and readjusts its beliefs and vocabularies to the needs of its environment, often measuring its views against those of others. With communitarians, Rorty agrees that traditions shape our understanding of morality, but he is not so inclined to hold the incommensurability thesis of some communitarians that the structure of rationality of a tradition is incommensurate with that of another tradition. Rorty holds open the possibility that one vocabulary might just seem better than another. Much less is he disposed to discredit modern liberal democratic institutions, disagreeing again with them over the benefits and harms of liberal democracy. For the purpose of politics, there is no need to justify every truth-claim according to unrealistic epistemological standards. Politics requires no metaphysical claims about the nature and the essence of the human person. We only need to acknowledge the priority of democracy to philosophy. To use the language of my typology, the residents in this house must find a way to live together by utilizing things at hand; if the house works, it is good enough for now. A house is built for living and not the other way around. Morality should be about what members of a political community come to view as acceptable and agreeable practices under their historical and social circumstances.

Rorty is not alone in holding such a view. John Rawls, who differs from Rorty in many other respects, also voices a similar line of thought. Like Rorty, Rawls believes that what is important is not a meaningless and endless debate on what constitutes the meaning of the human person or what is the nature of good but what is the "overlapping consensus"

17. Ibid., 198–99.

of our basic sense of justice among the citizens in a well-ordered political society, or what he calls a modern constitutional democratic society. For instance, Rawls's primary goods represent the goods that *reasonable* democratic citizens would accept as a basis of measuring social justice and of reaching their mutual agreement. According to Rawls, such acceptance requires neither an *a priori* nor a tradition-based agreement about ultimate comprehensive moral visions of the good that may find allegiance by different groups of reasonable citizens. Because it is almost impossible to find a shared idea of good in a pluralistic society, the conception of primary goods must be independent of any comprehensive doctrines and be understandable on "a practicable public basis of interpersonal comparisons based on objective features of citizens' social circumstances open to view."[18] Such objective features are to be based not on some comprehensive doctrine of good but on "a conception of citizen's needs — that is, of person's needs as citizens" where the fulfillment of their needs can be "publicly accepted as advantageous and thus counted as improving the circumstances of citizens for the purpose of political justice."[19] On this account, primary goods such as liberty, income and wealth, self-respect, health, and intelligence are affirmed not because they contain intrinsic value but because they are what people *de facto* want in a modern constitutional democratic society. A "political conception" of the relation of justice and primary goods replaces any comprehensive conception in the public ("reasonable") discourse of a democratic society.

Rawls's idea (and also ideal) of public reason well captures his view of morality in such a society. This is the form of reason required for the reasonable comprehensive doctrines in a society, that is, those doctrines that allow a reasonable political discourse. Public reason specifies basic moral and political values that are needed to coordinate and satisfy the criteria of reciprocity among the citizens. This does not mean that the public reason precludes any expression of comprehensive doctrines as long as they operate within the bounds set by the law of peoples. Rawls makes it clear that the idea of public reason "neither criticizes nor attacks

---

18. John Rawls, *Political Liberalism* (New York: Columbia University Press, 1996), 181.
19. Ibid., 179.

any comprehensive doctrine, religious or nonreligious, except insofar as that doctrine is incompatible with the essentials of public reason and a democratic polity. The basic requirement is that a reasonable doctrine accepts a constitutional democratic regime and its companion idea of legitimate law."[20]

Rawls and Rorty will not endorse or prescribe the ideas of universal morality and tradition-dependent morality. These two options appear equally problematic to these thinkers. If the former morality is epistemologically impossible, the latter is *practically* unacceptable for a pluralistic modern democratic society, or so would they argue. In a way, Rorty and Rawls are saying that we have found the good-enough house for which we have long searched, good enough at least for now and at least for us (that is, those who live in a liberal democratic society). Though we may have to share the same space with other residents, most of them are committed to the idea of civilized coexistence under the same roof, as being "reasonable" enough to compromise in times when basic needs of one person or group conflict with those of others. If others want to join the reasonable residents to live in the house, they will have to accept the house rules. So far, so good, it may seem.

There are, however, three possible rejoinders to this view. The first may be formulated in the following terms: How do we know whether this is the good-enough house we have *all* been waiting for? Dissatisfaction is the human lot. Unless there is some means to compare houses, the grass will always seem greener on the other side of the fence. Yet, this question already assumes the primacy of epistemology and objective criteria that these liberal theorists refuse to accept. The second is a question often raised by many communitarians and some religious ethicists: Do the residents in this house (that is, the citizens in the liberal democratic society) have what it takes for them to be the kind of people this house purports to have? In other words, do the residents of this house have the very moral capacity or resources within themselves that enable them to manifest and support the ideals of public reason? The third question may be stated in this manner: What motivates the residents

20. John Rawls, *The Law of Peoples* (Cambridge: Harvard University Press, 1999), 132.

to cooperate each other? Is it a sheer Hobbesian fear, Machiavellian necessity, or something else?

After looking into three different types of housing for the understanding of value, there is one last stop to make on our tour: the "house of organic needs." As we will see, there are similarities and dissimilarities between this house and other houses that we have explored so far. Before we get there, some sketch of this house is in order.

Site 4: A House of Organic Needs

In recent years there have been some thinkers who wanted to synthesize insights garnered from a wider range of disciplines than philosophy alone in order to reach a better understanding of morality. These disciplines are as diverse as psychology, biology, neuroscience, philosophy, theology, and ethics. Not all of these thinkers reach the same conclusion. Some take a reductive course, often arguing for a kind of ethical naturalism without fully realizing that is what they are doing. Others develop an approach that seeks to avoid such reductionism. In this regard, Don Browning's recent work represents the latter course. Browning, who has been investigating connections between science, especially moral psychologies, and religious ethics, maintains that both have much to learn from each other with respect to the question of value.

According to Browning, science brings a wealth of empirical data that support the view that practical reason is both motivated and constrained by a wide range of what he and others call premoral goods.[21] Premoral goods, in distinction from moral goods, are things we experience as valuable objects to pursue. "Premoral goods are not directly moral goods because we do not attribute moral qualities to them as such, but we do indeed see them as objects or experiences good to pursue and, in this sense, relevant to any theory of ethics."[22] Examples of

---

21. Among those who explore the ethical implications of premoral goods for Christian ethics is William Schweiker. Schweiker specifies three different types of goods, which are broadly referred as premoral in this essay: premoral, social, and reflective goods. See his *Responsibility and Christian Ethics,* New Studies in Christian Ethics (Cambridge: Cambridge University Press, 1999), 117–22. For the purpose of this essay, I have intentionally avoided a more extensive account of value.

22. Don S. Browning and Terry D. Cooper, *Religious Thought and the Modern Psychologies,* 2nd ed. (Minneapolis: Fortress Press, 2004), 141.

premoral goods include life, health, friendship, food, education, and cultural values among others. Premoral goods then are contrasted with what Louis Janssens calls "ontic evil," any act that thwarts or impedes the attainment of premoral goods.[23] Many types of modern psychology, for instance, help us understand the teleological foundations of premoral goods, as they help discover the sources and the extent of these goods in the biological and social needs of our being.[24] Thus, Browning shares Janssens's view that an important part of the ethical task is to preserve and enhance premoral goods (or, in Janssens's term, ontic goods).[25]

One will find a similar argument in Martha Nussbaum's "capabilities approach." While Nussbaum is not as keen as Browning in her understanding of the role of hermeneutics, she and Browning share the view that, despite many cultural and historical differences among people, there is a list of goods that are required for human functions and capabilities. Her list includes life, bodily health and integrity, bodily integrity (autonomy), senses, imagination, thought (freedom of speech), emotions, practical reasons, and so on.[26] The list indicates that no matter how one describes his or her life-goal, some basic and common needs of human beings must be acknowledged and respected.

Yet, our use of science must be welcomed with a caution, according to Browning. In the philosophical tradition of hermeneutics, represented by Hans-Georg Gadamer and Paul Ricoeur, Browning submits that scientific knowledge is not always value free. More importantly, he demonstrates that scientific investigation into human needs and motivation

---

23. See Louis Janssens, ed., *Ontic Evil and Moral Evil: Readings in Moral Theology No. 1* (New York: Paulist, 1979).

24. For instance, Browning refers to *Hardwired to Connect: The New Scientific Case for Authoritative Communities,* A Report to the Nation from the Commission on Children at Risk and co-sponsored by YMCA of the USA, Dartmouth Medical School, and Institute for American Values (New York: Institute for American Values, 2003), a collaborated study by 33 leading American scholars on the well-being of children and youth. In this study, researchers from different fields, including developmental psychology, neuroscience, evolutionary psychology, biology, and sociology, diagnose and analyze many personal and social problems of today's youth. The study is an example of how modern psychologies help us clarify the deep needs of the young people with regard to their hardwired attachment to the family, community, and meaning.

25. According to Janssens's interpretation of Aquinas, an action becomes a moral evil when the final end of the action does not conform to the measure of reason and eternal law *and* when the external or material means of the action is not proportionate to its final end.

26. Martha C. Nussbaum, "Women and Cultural Universals," in *Sex and Social Justice* (New York: Oxford University Press, 1999), 41.

must be placed within preempirical and philosophical model of human experience or *praxis* in order for its relevance to morality to be understood. While science can show the biological and psychological grounds of our needs and desires, it is unable to explain the ways in which each person pursues the goods we desire. The answer may lie in the dialectic in the will between the voluntary and the involuntary, to use Ricoeurian language, that is, the free will and the body that is a source of our motives, an organ of our movement, and a locus of our necessity. In Ricoeur's thought there is a dialectical relationship between the voluntary and the involuntary to the extent that as much as our bodily needs motivate and our body limits our action, our will has the power to regulate and overcome the involuntary in choosing, accepting, or rejecting our needs and desires.

Part of this functioning of the involuntary has to do with how the self understands its action with regard to his or her "lifeworld," the term phenomenologists use to describe the world understood through the meanings and motivations of everyday actions. In the lifeworld human needs, desire, action, and the perception of the desirable (premoral goods) are always linked together. Phenomenologists and hermeneutical thinkers assert the ontological reality of the lifeworld, whereas natural scientists, and some social scientists, want to question this. Important, in this respect, is the fact that we do not simply follow our bodily desires. Rather, our actions and desires are patterned after pre-encoded meanings in the practices we engage in through ideals and narratives in our tradition. This pre-encoded patterning of action precedes our pursuit of goods. Various cultures and beliefs interpret our needs differently and arrange them into different orderings of value. The objects of our needs or goods thus are always mediated to us through the hierarchy of meanings encoded in the language patterns and practices of traditions. Thus, Browning goes as far as to say, "We first come to know our moral and premoral goods by interpreting a tradition; science can then play a secondary diagnostic role helping us clarify goods and threats to them when conflicts and obscurities within our cultural and religious traditions require additional testing."[27] The function of science may be

---

27. Don S. Browning, *Moral Psychology and Christian Ethics* (Grand Rapids, Mich.: Eerdmans, forthcoming).

said to be analogous to the process of *diagnosis* in the case of a doctor.[28] If a patient can explain his symptoms and express his subjective experience in a language that is part of his tradition, empirical science may use the knowledge of the patient in analyzing the symptoms but may also discover the functional disorder or the involuntary needs of the patient. Here the meaning of a practice is decoded or interpreted internally through its history and tradition, while the same practice then is illumined externally by scientific studies that disclose its psychological and biological substratum.

Browning emphasizes the role of traditions in *describing, narrating,* and *prescribing* practices. To be more specific, with Ricoeur, Browning argues that a tradition can help science by *describing* our pursuit of goods discovered in our tradition's social practices. Yet, the meanings of the social practices concerning these goods would not be fully intelligible until we *narrate* the thick history of the practices and the goods within a unity of larger narratives that give intelligibility. It entails careful interpretation of narratives. Yet, a move called *prescribing* is going beyond describing and narrating; a tradition should test its own narratives and social practices by its own deontological elements (tests of universalizability, for example) as well as help practical wisdom to adjudicate possible conflicts of goods in concrete situations.

This does not mean, however, that we should simply accept our conventional practices as in tradition-dependent morality. Unlike communitarians, Browning adds that we need to constantly *interpret, critique,* and *test* the practices and narratives of our communities that surround us. As the moral life is concerned with the teleological orientation of life in its plural forms, we should not lose sight of the fact that the goods that we pursue inevitably come into conflict, often resulting in various forms of violence. Thus, we need to test our ethical strivings of the goods of life by employing what Ricoeur calls the "deontological test." This test is essentially the application of the principle of universalization that Browning finds in Kant's categorical imperatives, the Golden Rule, or Christian *agapē* as equal regard. For Ricoeur and Browning, the deontological test does not conclude the moral deliberation but moves

28. Paul Ricoeur, *Freedom and Nature: The Voluntary and the Involuntary,* trans. Erazim V. Kohak (Evanston, Ill.: Northwestern University Press, 1966), 13.

to the next moment in moral reflection, the return to *Sittlichkeit* where the conflict of goods is brought under the judgment of practical reason in actual situations. One must attend to the specific context of the moral decision in integrating and ordering conflicting goods. This acknowledges the fact that some sacrifice of goods may be necessary, however tragic it may be.[29]

While I agree fully with Browning about the role of tradition in mediating our needs and goods, I may have some minor disagreement with him about (1) the extent to which they are mediated and (2) the relationship between tradition and science. In my view, it is true that we often choose between different goods, as our self-identity formed by the narratives of our own tradition shapes and helps the pattern of our choices. Yet, the individual also has his or her own self-consciousness whose expression can defy the understanding of goods as formulated in his or her narratives *with* or *without* some deontological test. It is neither that we do not need a deontological test nor that religious traditions do not furnish such a deontological principle, but we sometimes choose to act against the directives of our narratives for various reasons. Put otherwise, the voluntary is not in the sole possession of our tradition, however great the latter's influence on us may be.

I also acknowledge that science functions as a diagnostic tool, explaining and clarifying our needs. But it seems that science can also play more than a diagnostic role; it can also provide some knowledge into premoral goods. Discovery of viruses and vaccines inform us of the importance of hygiene and immunization in a way the knowledge of a religious tradition cannot. A tradition may teach that AIDS (Acquired Immune Deficiency Syndrome) is a Western science scam, rather than caused by HIV (Human Immunodeficiency Virus) usually obtained through an unsafe sexual act. Normally, we do not expect that traditions will teach us about the benefits of vitamins for our health. Yet, there are also limits to what science can do. While science can tell us how to make a nuclear bomb, it cannot tell us how to make peace. Likewise, science can help

---

29. Here Browning differs from people like Finnis and Grisez at least in the latter's insistence on (1) the absolute nature of these human goods as exceptionless moral obligations, and (2) the incommensurability of the goods to reason, meaning that basic goods are incommensurable. See John Finnis, *Fundamentals of Ethics* (Washington, D.C.: Georgetown University Press, 1983), 45.

make biological weapons beyond inventing vaccines. My point here is that there are areas in which science can indeed be a source of our knowledge about premoral goods, just as a tradition could be a source of the same and other premoral goods. In this regard, what we need is not so much either tradition or science but a dialectical debate between science and tradition in helping understand the importance of premoral goods.

To continue in the vein of my typology, I have named the fourth house the "house of organic needs" to highlight the feature that the values we discover at this site are not abstract or arbitrary but real and concrete needs related to our biological, psychological, contemplative, and social life. Our desires for life, pleasure, joy, thinking, or relationship are fundamental to who we are as human beings; they are what make human beings human. In this house, the residents respect others' rights to their premoral goods not because their otherness from us demands such respect or because that is simply the rule of the house, but because the residents and nonresidents alike share a common vulnerability to losing these goods or possessing them in a disintegrating fashion and duly recognize the significance of these goods for all of us. In other words, a common morality is formed among the residents and nonresidents of this house as they understand basic needs of others as their own.

Premoral Good, Human Rights, and Religion

Allow me now to consider some advantages of the notion of a theory of ethical value grounded in premoral goods over the other accounts of value. First, unlike communitarians and other historicists, we do not have to give up the idea of universal values. Communitarians are quick to disavow the idea of universal values partly because they see value as derivative of tradition-dependent rationality. For them, values are inseparable from the practices formed internally to the narratives of traditions. Yet, they overlook not only the fact that many enduring and tested narratives, such as Jewish and Christian traditions, contain elements of universal significance (for example, deontological injunctions), but also the fact that these narratives themselves strongly affirm the basic goods of life that we have called premoral. Thus, it is not difficult to find the injunction of love in many religious narratives as functioning to integrate both deontology and the actualization of goods, whereby love is a joyful obligation of the believer to respect and care for others beyond the self and to condemn willful indifference to their suffering. These narratives tend to affirm life over death, joy over sadness, and love over hate. Put otherwise, the particularist errs in understanding traditions solely as disparate and incommensurable epistemological domains rather than as resourceful witnesses that attest to shared human experience. To use my own typological images, when the particularist enters a mansion, he sees only different rooms. But try living in the house. The same rooms will appear not merely as separate rooms but as the rooms that are connected to each other through hallways. Premoral goods are the passageways to other ways of dwelling in the world.

I also disagree with postmodern deconstructionists and historicists as regards the dynamics of language. Their insight that value is a creative play of language is only partially true when language is viewed as an arbitrary composition of heterological points of view. On the contrary, we can hold that language reveals layers of shared meanings captured and encoded by people who pursue a plurality of goods in life. The fact that we are historical and social beings does not necessarily entail that every idea and activity we engage in must be historically contingent. Bread, spoons, and dishes may have evolved in tandem with different tastes, colors, and shapes, but we still need these utensils (or something like them). We may lie about our age, but our age cannot lie to us. Freedom has been denied to many people for various reasons and the enslaved often accepted this social injustice, but this does not prove that these people did not want their freedom. All of this is to make the point that not all values are arbitrary or contingent. True, there may be important differences in ways and in degrees as to how individuals and communities treat particular goods, but to deny human beings any shared features of biological and social existence seems neither commonsensical nor reasonable.

In this respect, I would argue that it is not a sufficient or even workable argument to say that morality should be conditioned upon an overlapping consensus within a society or among different societies. It may take such a consensus to put morality into a law, but what makes something a morality should not be the same as what makes the law. I consider such a historicist argument not a statement of epistemic humility but of intellectual arrogance. How can the condemnation of torture, for instance, be conditioned by the consensus of a particular society? Such a view will only lead to kinds of practices we have seen at the prisons of Abu Ghraib or Guantanamo. Unless basic human nature or the human condition becomes fundamentally altered, *basic* human needs and the objects of these needs, namely premoral goods, must be also the same across cultures, races, and communities.

The second advantage that comes into view when we consider premoral goods is the defense of common morality without the dangers of foundationalism and antiscience. In contemporary moral discourse, the alarm bells go off whenever one speaks of universal values, alerting all to the ever-present danger of foundationalism. The cries of foundationalism, that one is trying to build knowledge based on empirical evidence or first principles that guarantee objective certainty, are a false alarm here. I have not argued in this essay that we could and should grasp premoral goods by science alone. Quite contrary, both science and tradition are in need of one another. I consider the debate on which one comes first futile, only comparable to that of "chicken or egg." Science can help a tradition to gain insight into the needs, states, and problems of our bodily and social life and critique the practices allowed in the tradition when the latter arbitrarily ignores or destroys, rather than respects, our natural processes. Concomitantly, a tradition may also serve as a source of knowledge for premoral goods, as it helps us understand not only basic natural human inclinations but also the complex and multidimensional aspects of human life where basic human needs and goods extend beyond mere physical or psychological ones. Unfortunately, I cannot elaborate on this in this essay.

Perhaps, more importantly, claims of science must be checked by moral insights of traditions, as traditions should inform and guide science by way of disclosing a wider and deeper view of reality and adjudicating possible conflicts of goods. We have to be wary of natural reductionism where natural claims are erroneously given the weight of moral imperative. Premoral goods are called "premoral" precisely because they can be overridden by other moral considerations (for example, the morally legitimate use of force by the public authority against criminals such as rapists). Rather, premoral goods are significant for their *relevance* to morality insofar as the latter seeks to respect and protect the former against any morally indiscriminate harm (for instance, ethnic cleansing or torture). Thus, it is not a matter of either/or but both/and. The moral self needs to make critical use of both science and tradition to better understand its needs and the practices related to them.

Third, the notion of premoral goods as conceived by Browning addresses the important role of religion (referring to Western religions in this essay) in addressing the problem of common morality. Liberals such as Rorty and Rawls often doubt the place of religion in the debate on common morality, arguing that religious beliefs are either simply irrelevant to civic virtues or obstacles to any civic consensus. The presence of various sorts of religious fundamentalists in our society may help prove their point. Nevertheless, we should not come to the hasty conclusion that religion cannot contribute to common morality. After all, our understanding of value has an important relationship with our self-understanding through various narratives within our communities, including religious ones. Individuals in a modern liberal state are also members of various communities where their understanding of value is informed by the practices and narratives of these communities. To underestimate such sources of morality is to forget the very sources of the moral self.[30] To be sure, the primacy of some religious narratives or doctrines, when they are incongruent with the ideas and ideals of the public reason, can be unhelpful and even dangerous for the welfare of our pluralistic society. Yet, it would be overreaching to argue that religion should therefore be precluded from any public discourse. As I have argued, our knowledge of premoral goods comes through various sources including our tradition and science. That is to say, we come to understand something as good not merely through our senses but also through the medium of the meaning attached to it in a tradition. In this sense, it would be premature to separate a religious tradition from other traditions that shape our lifeworld.

---

30. See Charles Taylor, *Sources of the Self: The Making of Modern Identity* (Cambridge: Harvard University Press, 1989)

Moreover, it should be noted that many religious narratives and the moral beliefs furnished by them have constantly appropriated insights from nonreligious sources of morality. For instance, in its most significant thinkers, ranging from Augustine who used Plato and Cicero to Aquinas who incorporated Aristotle's moral and social ideas as well as his biology, Christianity has been in close, constructive conversation with other sources of morality. That is, Christian thinkers have often accepted, amended, and built upon the moral insights found in nonreligious sources. As Browning says in the words of Johannes A. van der Van: "religion integrates, orients, and criticizes nonreligious morality."[31] What this means is that religion represents a rich resource of moral reflection rather than claiming to be the exclusive source of unadulterated morality. Thus, to dismiss religion from the discussion of common morality will be a grave mistake. It follows that religious ethics has a legitimate place in participating in and contributing to the discussion of common morality.

Conclusion

I have thus far tried to show how the notion of premoral goods can help us affirm the idea of common morality and why this fares better than the other contemporary options. As much as our contemporary world has enjoyed the expansion of individual freedom and technological development, we have also watched in horror an unprecedented, sophisticated level of violence aimed at innocent people. From mass murder to mass rape and from totalitarianism to terrorism, people's basic goods have been violated and taken away against their will. As Ricoeur notes, we form some of our most primitive moral intuitions in the feeling of indignation rising up when confronted by innocent suffering of a human being caused by the violence of others. Unfortunately, there is too much confusion in the field of ethics as how to account for such violence and what to do about it. This essay, in this regard, has attempted to make a compelling case that the protection of premoral goods ought to become a central concern for contemporary ethics, both religious and

31. Browning, *Moral Psychology and Christian Ethics.*

nonreligious, including those of the monotheistic faiths. Informed by scientific knowledge about real and concrete human needs and critical reflection on moral traditions, we have many good reasons to affirm the importance of premoral goods and their significance for the possibility of common morality, despite the deeply entrenched cynicism and skepticism in contemporary ethics. The four model houses we visited thus may serve as comparison points in making our prudent choice among the current "value" houses in moral theories.

Chapter 10

NATURAL-LAW JUDAISM?

The Genesis of Bioethics in
Hans Jonas, Leo Strauss, and Leon Kass

Lawrence Vogel

The shadow of Martin Heidegger looms large over his most original Jewish students. Each offers a philosophical diagnosis of their mentor's moral failings. Emmanuel Lévinas follows Martin Buber's criticism that Heidegger forgets the Thou or *Other* in his account of authenticity. Hannah Arendt and Leo Strauss accuse Heidegger's "politics of Being" of distorting a more human *politics*. And Hans Jonas develops Karl Löwith's charge that Heidegger fails to do justice to *nature* as what gives rise to life and the *body* as the medium of our existence.

The University of Chicago's Leon Kass is the most important bioethicist writing out of the work of Hans Jonas today and was, during his tenure as chair of President George W. Bush's Council on Bioethics, the most politically powerful. Though Jonas has a Jewish theology that supplements his ontological vision of nature, his ethic does not depend on revelation. For Kass, on the other hand, a satisfactory account of human dignity must go *beyond* what "unaided reason" can tell us about human nature. He offers an interpretation of sexuality and reproduction based on the biblical book of Genesis to "correct" Jonas's philosophy

Thanks to audiences at the University of Chicago, Trinity College, and Dartmouth College for helpful responses to earlier drafts of this paper, originally given as one of the 2003 D. R. Sharpe Lectures at the University of Chicago Divinity School. Another version of this essay will be published in *The Hastings Center Report*.

of nature. And given what Genesis teaches him about living "worthily in God's image," Kass adopts a far more broad-sweeping conservatism than the stance Jonas officially held.

Kass's appropriation of Jonas is deeply influenced by the work of another Jewish thinker of University of Chicago fame, Leo Strauss. One gets a glimmer of this in Kass's critique of "the postmoral ambience" of modern liberal democracies and his remark that because conservative moral views rooted in "natural hierarchy" will never be popular with more than a few, "we should put our trust neither in nature nor in philosophy but in our religious traditions."[1] For his part, Jonas did not want religious argument to be used in the service of public, ethical debates. In any case, it is not clear that Jewish sources should be read as justifying the sort of "hierarchy" that Kass apparently thinks they do when he defends "patriarchy" as "the primary innovation of the new Israelite way."[2]

That Kass's work has heretofore been of less interest to Jewish commentators than to the Bush administration should not conceal the fact that, by blending American-style neoconservatism with Judaism, Leon Kass has become the most influential public Jewish intellectual on matters bioethical. His understanding of Judaism, however, supports a position quite close to what William Galston has called the "Catholic-evangelical entente."[3] Halakhic Judaism, according to Galston, tends to be much more accommodating than "the Catholic-evangelical entente" on issues like stem-cell research, new reproductive technologies, abortion, and euthanasia. If this is correct, then Kass is really outside of the Jewish mainstream, and we must ask whether he is a reliable transmitter of Jewish values on these matters. Or, to put it bluntly, is he driven by a natural-law perspective through which he filters his readings of Torah so that they end up supporting a position closer to the Pope or even Jerry Falwell than the rabbis?

---

1. Leon R. Kass, "The Troubled Dream of Nature as a Moral Guide," in *Hastings Center Report* (November–December 1996), 24.
2. Leon R. Kass, *The Beginning of Wisdom: Reading Genesis* (New York: Free Press, 2003), 249.
3. William A. Galston, "What's at stake in biotech?," *The Public Interest* (Fall 2002), 106.

But before turning to Kass we need to consider the thinker Kass calls "my first real teacher in philosophical biology," Hans Jonas.[4]

Jonas on Contemporary Ethics from a Jewish Perspective

In 1968, Hans Jonas saw the biotechnological wave on the horizon and posed a challenge as relevant today as it was then: "If we are Jews — and a corresponding question Christians and Muslims must ask themselves — what counsel can we take" from our tradition in the face of "the pressing dilemma of our time"?[5] The dilemma stems from the explosion of our technological powers coupled with the demotion of our metaphysical rank within nature. If the Copernican revolution left "the nature of things, reduced to the aimlessness of their atoms and causes, with no dignity of its own," then revolutions in evolutionary biology, psychoanalysis, and the social sciences left us with no image of our own higher nature, nothing analogous to the biblical idea that we are created in the image of God.[6] If we *can* manufacture new and improved versions of ourselves, then *why not* — for example — screen fetuses to weed out the "unhealthy" or even unwanted, genetically engineer healthier babies, clone desirable individuals, forestall the aging process so that people can have much more of a good thing, harvest the organs of brain-dead patients to save potentially flourishing people, and let doctors gently kill when their patients have ceased to lead meaningful lives?

Confronting the Pandora's box of biotechnology, Jonas raises a question still pertinent today:

> Can we afford the happy-go-lucky contingency of subjective ends and preferences when (to put it in Jewish language) the whole future of the divine creation and the very survival of the image of God have

---

4. Leon R. Kass, "Appreciating *The Phenomenon of Life*," *Hastings Center Report* (Special Issue: The Legacy of Hans Jonas, 1995), 4.

5. Hans Jonas, "Contemporary Problems in Ethics from a Jewish Perspective," *Philosophical Essays: From Contemporary Creed to Technological Man* (Chicago: University of Chicago Press, 1974), 178.

6. Ibid., 173.

come to be placed in our fickle hands?...We need wisdom when we believe in it least.[7]

But, Jonas contends, science does not "refute" the symbolic meanings of four key biblical propositions: that God (1) created heaven and earth, (2) saw God's creation was good, (3) created humanity in God's own image, and (4) makes known to humanity what is good because God's word is written in our hearts. And these meanings, he states, *must* be preserved "if we are still to be Jews."[8] Jonas sets out not to *prove* the truth of these propositions, but only to *articulate* the wisdom that can be gleaned from "the Jewish stance" on the relation between power and responsibility.

On the *negative* side, Torah teaches us "modesty in estimating our own cleverness in relation to our forebears."[9] And caution rooted in modesty "requires that we go slow in discarding old taboos, on brushing aside in our projects the sacrosanctity of certain domains hitherto surrounded by a sense of mystery, awe and shame."[10] On the *positive* side, the idea of creation sanctions an attitude of reverence for "inviolable integrities." Torah, according to Jonas, teaches us to be responsible caretakers of the integrity of the lifeworld. "While Biblical piety saw nature's dependence on God's creative and sustaining will, we now also know its vulnerability to the interferences of our developed powers." Respect for the phenomenon of life on earth demands that we cry out "an unconditional 'no' to the depletion of the six-day's plenitude — and also, we might add, to its perversion by man-made genetic monstrosities."[11]

Torah teaches us not only reverence for nature but also for our human nature, for we are "made in God's image." The main meaning of *imago Dei,* according to Jonas, is our ability to distinguish between good and evil and our responsibility for promoting the good, symbolized by the commandment, "Be ye holy, for I am holy, the Lord your God." Jonas concludes that respect for the mystery of human freedom should make

7. Ibid., 176, 178.
8. Ibid., 177.
9. Ibid., 178.
10. Ibid., 179.

us seek the improvement of character through education, not genetic manipulation, and prefer persuasion under conditions of freedom to psychological manipulation in the hands of behavioral engineers. Finally, Jonas contends that biblical wisdom teaches us to balance a love of life with an acceptance of mortality, for "the birth of new life is life's answer to mortality," and if we abolished death, we would have to abolish the birth of new life, too. The upshot of the psalmist's words — "Teach us to number our days that we may gain a heart of wisdom" (Ps. 90:10–12) — is that medicine should not be transformed into the Promethean effort to eliminate imperfection or to prolong life at all costs.[12]

So Hans Jonas speaks as a Jew about how veneration for humanity under God might help us resist the tide of "modern reason," which holds that there is no human essence, for revelation gives us an "image of man" sufficient to put ethical limits on what we have the right to do to ourselves in the name of bettering our God-given nature. In his role as a philosopher, however, Jonas insists that his imperative of responsibility can be "ontologically" grounded without appealing to theistic premises, for "an image of man" is rooted in "the integrity of nature," even if nature is *not* God's creation. This grounding depends on a description of "the phenomenon of life" at odds with the assumptions of modern materialism.

Jonas's Ontological Grounding of an Imperative of Responsibility

Jonas uses Heidegger's own *existential* categories to subvert the modern credo that human being is the origin of all value. He provides "an existential interpretation of the biological facts" that lets us see, in the spirit of Aristotle's psychology and against Cartesian dualism, how all organisms, not only humans, have "concern for their own being." Value and disvalue are not human creations but are essential to life itself. Every living thing has a share in life's "needful freedom" and "harbors within

---

12. For other references in Jonas's work to the image of God motif, see Hans Jonas, *Mortality and Morality: A Search for the Good after Auschwitz,* ed. Lawrence Vogel (Evanston, Ill.: Northwestern University Press, 1996), 75 and 178.

itself an inner horizon of transcendence," for each organism must reach out to its environment in order to stay alive.[13]

The extension of *psyche* or self-concern to all organisms enables Jonas to venture two *ontological* conjectures that cannot be proven but are consistent with the biological facts, existentially interpreted: (1) that matter's feat of organizing itself for life attests to latent organic tendencies in the depths of Being; and (2) that the emergence of the human mind does not mark a great divide within nature, but elaborates what is prefigured throughout the lifeworld. And these two points make room for a third speculation with dramatic *ethical* consequences: (3) insofar as we see ourselves, with our capacity for reflecting Being in knowledge, as "a 'coming to itself' of original substance," we should understand ourselves as being called by nature, our own source, to be her guardian. By extending the category of "existence" to all organisms, Jonas makes possible a radical conversion of modern thought: "a principle of ethics which is ultimately grounded neither in the authority of the self nor the needs of the community, but in an objective assignment by the nature of things."[14]

But the primary focus of our responsibility ought to be humanity itself.

> Since in [man] the principle of purposiveness has reached its highest and most dangerous peak through the freedom to set himself ends and the power to carry them out, he himself becomes, in the name of that principle, the first object of his obligation, which we expressed in our "first imperative": not to ruin, as he well can do, what nature has achieved in him by the way of his using it.[15]

Unlike Plato's eternal Form of the Good, the good-in-itself of living nature is at the mercy of our actions. Our primary duty is to protect the future of humanity because we are "executor[s] of a trust which only [w]e can see, but did not create."[16] Jonas's precautionary imperative enabled him to level early criticisms of environmental degradation,

---

13. For his most complete account of "an existential interpretation of biological facts," see Hans Jonas, *The Phenomenon of Life* (Evanston, Ill.: Northwestern University Press, 2001).
14. Ibid., 283.
15. Hans Jonas, *The Imperative of Responsibility: In Search of an Ethics for the Technological Age* (Chicago: University of Chicago Press, 1984), 129.
16. Jonas, *The Phenomenon of Life,* 283.

human cloning, germline genetic engineering, crude forms of behavior control, and the immortality project on the grounds that these risk closing "the horizon of possibilities which in the case of man is given with the existence of the species as such and—as we must hope from the promise of the *imago Dei*—will always offer a new chance to the human essence."[17]

In effect, Jonas claims to have found an ontological analogue to the theological idea that we are created in the image of God. Once the prejudice of modern reason—materialism—has been challenged by Jonas's "existential interpretation of the biological facts," he can defend three biblical propositions *without* recourse to the premise at the heart of the biblical tradition: that God created heaven and earth. In each case, we must be able to translate a theological proposition into a naturalistic one. First, "God saw that His creation was good" gets reinterpreted in Jonas's metaphysics as the good-in-itself of living nature whose very being imposes an "ought-to-be" whenever a responsible agent is there to appreciate it. Second, "God created man in His own image" gets recast as the notion that "the Idea of Humanity" is an event of cosmic importance because our power to reflect Being in knowledge and to put our imprint on nature is constrained by our responsibility for the good-in-itself: the transcendent measure of our cognitive and technical powers. Finally, "God makes known to man what is good because His word is written in our hearts" gets translated into the idea that the objective imperative of responsibility is answered by our subjective capacity to feel responsible for the totality, continuity, and futurity of the fragile object that commands our respect: namely, the existence and essence of humanity on planet Earth.[18]

Though nature *may* be God's creation, there is no *need* to ground ontology in theology, for nature is purposive even if there is no "purposer." The goodness of life must speak for itself. If it falls silent, Jonas contends, theology cannot rescue it from the nihilist's protest that "the whole toilsome and terrible drama isn't worth the trouble."[19]

---

17. Jonas, *The Imperative of Responsibility*, 140.

18. For Jonas on "the fundamental biblical propositions" negated by contemporary ethical theory, see Section II in "Contemporary Problems of Ethics in a Jewish Perspective."

19. For Jonas's argument that the response to "nihilism" must be ontological, not theological, see Jonas, *The Imperative of Responsibility*, 47–48.

The outcome of Jonas's philosophy is a defense of the biblical idea that "the human essence" lies in "our ability to distinguish between good and evil, which is said to be the main meaning of the phrase, 'imago Dei.' "[20] But the means of this defense — an ontological grounding of the imperative of responsibility — is true to the Greek idea that the human mind shares in the Divine because reason is able to grasp the good-in-itself. It remains unclear, therefore, whether Jonas is a philosopher of nature whose project is informed by Judaism — or rather a philosopher who happens to be Jewish. The question is particularly pressing in the face of Leo Strauss's claim that the Hebrew people had no concept of nature as a measure available to human reason: a standard in light of which we might evaluate the variety of human conventions.[21] Must not Jonas's project be seen as an essentially "Athenian" move — *contrary* to the temper of "Jerusalem"? To be sure, Jonas develops a theology, most forcefully presented in his essay, "The Concept of God after Auschwitz: a Jewish Voice."[22] And he does speak to a religious audience as a Jew about how the idea that we are created "in God's image" might help us address quandaries in bioethics. Nonetheless, in his role as philosopher, Jonas insists that ontology is likely to provide a more universal footing for ethics than theology and that appeals to revelation too easily place irrational dogmas on higher ground.

Kass's "Correction" of Jonas:
Why Accounting for Human Sexuality and
Reproduction Requires Returning to Genesis

In his essay "Appreciating *The Phenomenon of Life*," Leon Kass applauds Jonas's attempt "to think nonreductively about living nature."[23] Jonas seeks to bypass "the quarrel between the ancients and moderns" by showing how the modern view that "mind even on its highest reaches

20. Jonas, "Tool, Image and Grave: On What Is Beyond the Animal in Man," *Mortality and Morality*, 75.
    21. Leo Strauss, "Progress or Return," *The Rebirth of Classical Political Rationalism*, ed. Thomas L. Pangle (Chicago: University of Chicago Press, 1989), 253.
    22. Jonas, "The Concept of God after Auschwitz: A Jewish Voice," *Mortality and Morality*, chap. 6.
    23. Kass, "Appreciating *The Phenomenon of Life*," 3–4.

remains part of the organic" need *not* preclude the ancient credo that "the organic even in its lowest forms prefigures mind." By Kass's lights, Jonas "succeeds" in demonstrating (1) that and how every organism is a psychophysical unity, "the living concretion of embodied awareness or of feeling-and-striving body," (2) that the form of an organism is causally primary, (3) that life-forms are hierarchically ordered with the human animal possessing "unquestionable [ontological] superiority" over merely nutritive and sensitive souls, and (4) that teleological notions are indispensable to an explanation of life that is true to both the functioning of organisms and the upward trajectory of evolution.[24]

Yet Kass finds "something missing from this otherwise truthful account of rising individuality" which tells us how "animals, and especially the higher animals, are more pronounced selves who live in a more pronounced world." The missing ingredient is "the specially focused kind of desire...rooted in sexual difference."[25] Though Jonas brilliantly describes how metabolism is a defining power of life, he admits, when Kass challenges him, to giving short shrift to sexuality and reproduction. And he concurs with Kass's diagnosis: that Jonas remains in the grip of his mentor, Martin Heidegger, who viewed existence as a struggle between the solitary, mortal individual and an inhospitable world.

Kass speculates on where "a corrected teaching" on the phenomenon of life might lead. For hunger, the world comprises prey, predators, and a vast sea of indifference. But for *erōs* the world contains "some very special, related but complementary beings: members of the same kind but opposite sex towards whom one reaches out with special interest and intensity." In sex, Kass says, life is not self-centered individuality but self-sacrifice: "unbeknownst to themselves animals desire their own replacement, voting with their genitalia for their replacement." Still, the full truth of sexuality is not so self-denying. In reproduction life offers to life a kind of transcendence, for organisms have the chance to leave behind another like themselves — "participating in the eternal in the only way they can." To conceive of life apart from its reproductive

24. Ibid., 4–5.
25. Ibid., 11.

whence and whither, as Jonas following Heidegger tends to do, is "to homogenize the outer world and exaggerate its loneliness."[26]

Kass concedes that "the wisdom of finitude and the redemptive possibility of now-precarious perpetuation comprise the cornerstone of Jonas's teaching on responsibility."[27] Jonas, after all, calls the parent-child relationship "the archetype of all responsibility," for a parent is responsible for the "totality, continuity and futurity" of the child, on the basis not of a revocable contract, but the unconditional, one-sided claim of the vulnerable object. In this respect parental responsibility is a precursor to our obligation to protect the future of humanity as such, for this, too, calls for total, continuous, and future-oriented care-taking. But whereas the desire to protect one's own is "implanted in us by nature," Jonas's imperative requires a level of veneration for "the Idea of humanity" that does not come naturally, for it calls on us to control our present-centered inclinations for the sake of a distant future that will not serve our own happiness.[28]

Kass alleges, however, that Jonas's wisdom regarding how "children provide life's (partial) answer to mortality" derives not from Heidegger or even Aristotle, but from his Jewish heritage, "a more loving and just tradition" whose anthropology is anchored in Genesis.[29] Though Jonas "knew all this in his bones," according to Kass, he does not go far enough in spelling out the meaning of sexuality, for Jonas treats the parent-child relationship in a *gender-neutral* way, and uses it as a vehicle for an *ontological* grounding of an imperative of responsibility in an *intellectual* intuition of a good-in-itself speaking through nature. Kass's Genesis, on the other hand, understands the ultimate meaning of "generative love" in terms of the *heterosexual* difference between male and female. The telos of this difference is realized, Kass tells us, in the institutions of *marriage* and *patriarchy* that, because they are "somewhat against the grain of nature," must be authorized by *revelation*.[30] It is worth considering *The Beginning of Wisdom*, Kass's 700-page interpretation of Genesis, as an

26. Ibid., 12.
27. Ibid.
28. For a comparison of the responsibilities of parents and statesmen, see Jonas, *The Imperative of Responsibility*, chap. 4, sec. III.
29. Kass, "Appreciating *The Phenomenon of Life*," 12.
30. Kass, *The Beginning of Wisdom*, 250.

elaboration of his "correction" of Jonas: a midrash on what his teacher failed to acknowledge, but supposedly "knew in his bones" all along. My purpose is not to retrace the twists and turns of Kass's long argument, but to elicit its basic structure so that we can see how his reading of *Genesis* serves as both a reply to Jonas and a lever for Kass's critique of modernity.

Kass on *Genesis:*
The Way of Right Replaces the Way of Nature

Kass holds that Genesis offers a philosophical anthropology: an account of "the timeless psychic and social principles...of human life...in all their ambiguity."[31] This anthropology provides the basis for an ethics and politics, for it shows how "it is possible to find, institute and preserve a way of life, responsive both to the promise and the peril of the human creature, that accords with man's true standing in the world and that serves to perfect his god-like possibilities"[32] In one respect, the Bible anticipates modern natural science, for it "recognizes the silence of the heavens and the earth regarding the human good and, therefore, emphasizes the incompetence of human reason, thinking only about nature, to find a decent and righteous way to live." But, unlike science, the Bible compensates for the deficiencies of nature and reason with revelation: "a teaching for human life that, though *accessible* to human reason, is apparently not *available* to unaided human reason as it ponders the natural world."[33] Because biblical stories dramatize and codify the meaning of human *erōs* in a way unavailable to unaided reason, Kass concludes, what it means to live "worthily in God's image" cannot be gleaned, Jonas notwithstanding, from an ontological vision of nature alone.[34]

In the creation stories Kass identifies "two crucial strands of our emerging humanity": the linguistic (or rational) and the sexual (or social). The linguistic/rational strand culminates in the Noahide code, whereby "man uses his freedom and reason to promulgate moral and

31. Ibid., 10.
32. Ibid., 11.
33. Ibid., 6.
34. Ibid., 294.

legal rules and to pass moral and legal judgments, first among which is
the judgment that manslaughter is to be punished in kind because it violates the dignity of such a moral being." The Noahide code founds civil
society on rudimentary but explicit notions of law and justice rooted in
the idea that all human beings are created equally in God's image. "God's
image is tied to blood," the high depends on the low, for "human elevation is achieved only through a law that reminds the god-like man to
honor and defend his precarious, animal-like mortal existence."[35] Kass
claims that belief in the *covenant* is as important to the new civil society
as belief in the code of law, for "God's covenant... overcomes by agreement nature's indifference, not to say hostility, to human aspiration,"
and so supports our hope for a future that will redeem the exercise of
our "higher" possibilities.[36]

The sexual/social strand of human nature, however, is crucial to *per-
petuating* this new civil order across generations. Generative love, rooted
in the difference between male and female, shows how we are *unlike*
God, but in ways that bear on the idea that we are created in God's
image. The Bible's genius, according to Kass, is to make the rational and
sexual strands of human nature inextricable. For Genesis (and against
Heidegger) man became man when he became conscious of his own
sexuality, not mortality.

> Human *erōs*... takes wings from the recognition that there are
> higher possibilities for man than finally unfulfilling acts of bodily
> union, among which is the establishment of long-lived familial soci-
> eties, grounded in the awareness that sex means children, human
> children need long-term rearing for sociality, morality and love, and
> children are life's (partial) answer to mortality.[37]

The story of the Garden of Eden shows that "gender-neutral humanity
is an abstraction or, at most, a condition of childhood."[38] Furthermore, the "primordial story of man and woman" Kass contends, "hints
that... complementarity — the *heterosexual* difference — and not just

35. Ibid., 186.
36. Ibid., 188.
37. Kass, "Appreciating *The Phenomenon of Life*," 12.
38. Kass, *The Beginning of Wisdom*, 98.

doubleness...may point the way to human flourishing altogether."[39] God's later legislative efforts (in Leviticus), Kass states, will codify what became clear at Sodom: that acts of incest and sodomy embody unjust principles of "love of like, aversion to unlike" and "sexual selfishness."[40] Sodomy in particular shows what happens, Kass avers, when "city dwellers, devoted both to political unity and immediate self-satisfaction, and indifferent to their vulnerability and need for replacement, take nonprocreative sex to its logical and sterile conclusion."[41]

Division of labor, inequality, and rule and authority enter the sexual picture in Genesis 3 with the coming of children: the woman's desire, God predicted, would be to her man, and he would rule over her; he, in turn, would toil and trouble to provide for her and her children (3:16–19).[42] Kass interprets Genesis from chapter 12 on as a story about what it takes to educate young men to become worthy husbands and fathers — against the wayward tendency of their male nature, for "most men, left to their own devices, do not readily leap to this task," pursuing instead ways of life devoted to wealth and pleasure, power and domination, or even heroic quests for personal honor and glory.

"Law, custom and instruction are everywhere needed to shape and transform the natural attractions between man and woman into the social and moral relations of husband and wife."[43] Though "the Noahide code is silent on this subject," Kass states, God Himself supports all three elements of the marital bond: (1) respect for woman's chastity and marital sexual fidelity, which anticipates (2) the gift of children within marriage, which makes necessary (3) the right ordering of the household, with the husband endorsing his wife's devotion to the well-being of their children.[44] This by no means diminishes the role of women, Kass tells us, for "it takes the right women to attach their husbands to the high-minded and reverent rearing of the next generation."[45]

39. Ibid., 121.
40. Ibid., 294–95.
41. Ibid., 329–30.
42. Ibid., 270.
43. Ibid., 268.
44. Ibid., 292.
45. Ibid., 266.

Though Kass describes a "true wife" as "an equal partner," he states that "the primary — not the last but the first — innovation of the Israelite new way" is "patriarchy."[46] He admits that "patriarchy" has become "a dirty word" today because it is thought to refer to "the hegemonic and arbitrary rule of men over women and children, justified simply because they are men."[47] But he insists that

> patriarchy properly understood turns out to be the cure for patri-archy properly condemned. The biblical sort of patriarchy is meant to provide a remedy for arbitrary and unjust male dominance and self-aggrandizement, for the mistreatment of women, and for the neglect of children.... [And] patriarchy properly understood..., depends on marriage rightly understood, [and both are] essential element[s] in promoting holiness and justice. [But] they are hardly the natural ways of humankind. They have to be learned — to begin with, somewhat against the grain.[48]

"Abraham must learn that founding and leading a great nation depends on woman, whose generative power holds the key to the future."[49] Like most men, Abraham needs more instruction than women in tending to the family because women as childbearers are naturally closer to the claims of "generative love." And Abraham must learn that proper founding and rule, like proper fatherhood, requires a reverent orientation to "the fatherhood of God." Abraham, Kass claims, is "the model father of his family and his people because he loves God more than his own."[50] All fathers, states Kass, "sacrifice" their sons to some "god" by what they respect and teach in their homes. We rear our children not for ourselves but to do without us, to take our place, to aspire to righteous and holy ways. The "true father" is even willing to part with his son altogether — witness Isaac — recognizing him rather as a gift and blessing from God. This anticipates the "true founder's" acceptance of the fact that his own innocent sons must suf-

---

46. Ibid., 291.
47. Ibid., 249.
48. Ibid., 250.
49. Ibid., 266.
50. Ibid., 348.

fer for the sake of the righteous community, that one's own life is not worth living if there is nothing more sacred for which one will sacrifice oneself.[51]

The psychological structure of what Kass calls "proper patriarchy" is clear enough. Future generations provide life's answer to mortality. Women must lure men away from their lustful and worldly exploits and get them to acknowledge their dependence on women's reproductive powers, but out of pious regard for the transcendent imperative "to be fruitful and multiply." Parents, however, owe their children not only life but a good life, and the "true father," more independent as he is than mother from the natural connection to "one's own," is better able and duty-bound to transform "family values" into a civic piety oriented by devotion to what is higher than politics altogether. Though women as wives and mothers initiate and ground the transformation from animal lust to human *erōs*, men must complete the transformation as fathers and leaders whose patriarchal authority is oriented by "fear of the Lord."

Kass claims, in effect, that important aspects of what it means to "live worthily in God's image" are not captured by Jonas's philosophical biology, oblivious as it is to the place of sexuality in the meaning of life. Jonas — with his ontological analogue to the idea of humanity in the image of God — fails to appreciate the depth of the tension between Athens and Jerusalem, reason and revelation, nature and right. His gender-neutral interpretation of the *imago Dei* motif overemphasizes equality at the expense of heterosexual difference and "natural hierarchy." "God's instruction consists in replacing the way of nature with the way of right," Kass tells us, for "natural sexual impulses will not by themselves establish the proper institutional forms."[52] Revelation allows for a "completion" of Jonas's "more natural science," but one with serious implications for Kass's whole view of bioethics, which now goes well beyond (in its specificity concerning our "proper" limits) Jonas's quite general "imperative of responsibility."

51. Ibid., 350.
52. Ibid., 294.

Kass on Genesis and the Crisis of Bioethics:
From the End of Courtship to the Beginning of Cloning

Kass's reading of Genesis is the lever for his critique of the "postmoral ambience" of modern liberal democracies. At the end of his discussion of the tower of Babel, Kass describes modernity as a return to the Babylonian vision. The language of Cartesian mathematics and method, he states, promises that the world might become a cosmopolitan city devoted to universal "equality in freedom," a city made ever more comfortable by the conquest of nature for the relief of man's estate. As an antidote to the proliferation of opposing nations, "our modern Babel constructs the United Nations, the worldwide web, the globalized economy, and the biomedical project to recreate human nature without imperfections." Kass suggests, however, that modern Babel falls prey to the same failures as its ancient predecessor. Its inhabitants — we — know no reverence, are inhospitable to procreation and childrearing, lack nonarbitrary and nonartificial standards for human conduct, and are unable to be self-critical. "The city is back," Kass laments, "and so, too, is Sodom, babbling and dissipating away."[53]

In his essay "The End of Courtship," Kass indicts liberal democracy and modernity for "hamper[ing] courtship and marriage" by destroying "cultural gravity about sex, marriage and the life-cycle."[54] Liberal principles were, for the Founding Fathers, "narrowly political"; morals and mores were informed by biblical religion. But as our nation became more pluralistic and secularized — and as rights became the sole coinage of moral discourse — liberal principles became "corrupted by expansion and exaggeration."[55] "The right ordering of family relations" is lost on "democratic man" for whom "all hierarchy is suspect, all distinctions are odious, and all claims on his modesty and respect are confining." Announcing himself liberated from archaic and stultifying norms, "democratic man" asserts, "We're all pals now." Filial piety and paternal excellence are precarious virtues, Kass notes, and "the supply may be shorter than ever." Evidence of our moral decline lies

---

53. Ibid., 242–43.
54. Leon R. Kass, "The End of Courtship," *The Public Interest* (Winter 1997), 44.
55. Leon R. Kass, "Introduction," *Life, Liberty and the Defense of Dignity: The Challenge for Bioethics* (San Francisco: Encounter Books, 2002), 13.

in "the sins that unfatherly fathers visit upon their sons and grand-sons." Kass avers that "Canaan is again cursed to live slavishly like a pagan."[56]

But the brunt of Kass's critique falls upon unmotherly women who are all-too-willing accomplices in the decline of traditional family values. The "most devastating" social outgrowth of the Enlightenment, according to Kass, is the sexual revolution, "facilitated by cheap and effective birth control."[57] Liberated from the generative consequences of sexual activity, a woman can declare herself free from "the teleological meaning of her sexuality — as free as a man appears to be from his."[58] The first casualty of the sexual revolution is "the supreme virtue of the virtuous woman" — modesty — "a necessary condition of transforming a man's lust into love...." But immodesty is endorsed by public sex education that promotes "safe sex," treats contraception as a morally neutral tool, and regards "offspring and disease as equally avoidable side-effects of sex, whose primary purpose is pleasure."[59]

Fueled by the sexual revolution, feminism turns against marriage by radically attacking sex roles: in particular, "the worth of mother-hood and the vanishing art of homemaking."[60] Equal education tempts women to put career above marriage, and the legitimate quest for mean-ingful work can lead to a "disordering of loves" in which economic independence — "no asset for marital stability" — comes at the price of a commitment to husband and children.[61] "Without powerful non-liberal cultural forces, such as traditional biblical religion, that defend sex-linked roles, androgyny in education and employment is the likely outcome."[62]

With the rise of out-of-wedlock births and divorce, the stable, monog-amous marriage is no longer the accepted cultural norm. As Kass puts it, "new family forms allow children to have between zero and four parents." In the meantime, the feminist and the gay rights movements

56. Kass, *The Beginning of Wisdom*, 215–16.
57. Kass, "The End of Courtship," 44.
58. Ibid., 45.
59. Ibid., 46.
60. Ibid., 49.
61. Ibid., 50–51.
62. Ibid., 53.

have pushed for the reproductive "rights" of single women, homosexual men, and lesbians, treating natural heterosexual difference and its pre-eminence as "matters of cultural construction." "With adultery almost as American as apple pie, few appreciate the awe-ful shame of the Scarlet Letter. And the sexual abominations of Leviticus — incest, bestiality, and homosexuality — are going the way of all flesh: homosexuality with religious blessings, no less!"[63] These social changes are the "bittersweet fruits" of the successes of modern democratic cultures that value freedom, equality, and universal, secularized education and are characterized by prosperity, mobility, and progress in science and technology.[64]

Kass's diagnosis of the demise of courtship contains the kernel of his critique of contemporary *bioethics*. The "postmoral ambience" of modern liberal democracies explains both why marriage has become so troubled and why, in matters bioethical, "we are getting used to everything," for " 'human nature' is dead in the water as a moral guide."[65] When contraception is justified as part of a woman's right to privacy, abortion as belonging to a woman's right over her body, and procreation as a matter of a woman's right to reproduce, Kass tells us, it is hard to make sense of the biblical understanding of male and female as "unavoidably complete and dependent children of the Lord" ordered "to be fruitful and multiply."[66] The easy availability of contraception and abortion bespeaks our "anti-natalist" belief that all children should be wanted: a belief implying, according to Kass, that "only children who fulfill our wants will be fully acceptable."[67] We are on a slippery slope to genetic engineering. Furthermore, contraception and abortion violate women's "generative nature," for, by separating sex from its serious consequences, they foster the irresponsible and ultimately dehumanizing view that sex primarily means self-gratification. And, having abandoned the idea that babies have a necessary connection to sex, "it must seem

63. Ibid., 56.
64. Ibid., 53.
65. For Kass's reference to "the postmoral ambience in which we now live," see "Cloning and the Posthuman Future" in *Life, Liberty and the Defense of Dignity*, 144. For his suggestion that in this environment "human nature is dead in the water as a moral guide," see "The Troubled Dream of Nature as a Moral Guide," 24.
66. Kass, "The End of Courtship," 53.
67. Ibid., 62.

anachronistic to fight, in the name of nature, against IVF and surrogate pregnancy."[68]

Finally, in spite of official opposition to human cloning, the prospect offers "the perfect embodiment of the ruling opinions of the new age: the ultimate single-parent child."[69] Cloning symbolizes our desire to control the future but not to be subject to any control ourselves. Kass warns of "a posthuman future" in which we prevent all genetic disease but only by turning procreation into manufacture, promote safe and shame-free sex but at the expense of romance and lasting intimacy, create "happy souls" but people who want and know only chemically induced satisfactions, and aspire to "ageless bodies" that house people who cannot remember why they want to live for so long.[70]

Because these developments are facilitated by our liberal-democratic values of life (welfare) and liberty (autonomy), we "are slow to recognize" them *as* threats to human dignity. But we are naïve to believe that "the evils we fear can be avoided by compassion, respect for autonomy, and regulation." Kass searches for "nonarbitrary standards" based on "unalterable human nature" and known by way of our "repugnance" toward these violations of natural limits.[71] To avoid a posthuman future we need to be devoted not primarily to life and liberty but to a "higher" image of "dignity" rooted in "richer ways of doing, feeling and being." Convinced of the insufficiency of nature for ethics, Kass turns to the idea of "living worthily in God's image" to reveal "our proper standing."[72] Perhaps, he suggests, "we should pay attention to the plan God adopted as an alternative to Babel, walking with Father Abraham."[73]

Kass wants to retrieve what he takes to be "the [biblical] core of our culture's wisdom" that, until the post-War era, comprised "a common and respectful understanding" of sexuality, procreation, nascent life, family, the meanings of mother and father, and links between

68. Kass, "The Troubled Dream of Nature as a Moral Guide," 24.
69. Kass, "Cloning and the Posthuman Future," 143–44.
70. Leon R. Kass, "Ageless Bodies, Happy Souls," *The New Atlantis* (Spring 2003).
71. Kass, "The Age of Genetic Technology Arrives," *Life, Liberty and the Defense of Dignity,* 132, 138.
72. Kass, "The Permanent Limitations of Biology," *Life, Liberty and the Defense of Dignity,* 297.
73. Kass, *The Beginning of Wisdom,* 243.

generations.[74] This would demand, Kass states, the restigmatization of promiscuity and illegitimacy, the reversal of anti-natalist prejudices implicit in the practice of abortion, the correction of anti-generative sex education, and the revalorization of marriage as an ideal, including the encouragement of earlier marriage and child-bearing and the postponement of the training of women for careers. But these reforms would depend on restoring the conditions for successful courtship, especially the virtue of female modesty. But in the age of "democratic man," Kass predicts, the likelihood of this is slim.[75]

"Leo-conservatism": The Influence of Leo Strauss on Leon Kass

I hope it is clear how Kass's Judaic "correction" of Hans Jonas makes Kass at home in the company of the so-called "traditional family values" and "right-to-life" crowd in Washington today. But it would be mistaken to dismiss Kass as a Republican ideologue who tailored his ideas to please the powers-that-be so that he could break out of the ivory tower and into halls of power. His views germinated during thirty years of teaching, first in the early '70s at the "great books" program of St. John's College in Annapolis, where he crossed paths with Leo Strauss, and then at the University of Chicago, where Strauss himself had taught for two decades and exerted such an influence, especially through his student Allan Bloom.

Let me suggest that if Jonas was Kass's first teacher in philosophical biology, then Strauss was Kass's professor of philosophical anthropology and theology. Kass's ethical stance is not a calculating power-grab, but, whether one likes it or not, a logical outgrowth of Strauss's misgivings about modernity in general and America in particular. Strauss's leading idea is that modernity is essentially "nihilistic." No longer believing that humanity belongs to a sacred order of creation or an objective order of essences in the totality of nature, moderns think of humanity as "freely projecting existence" who must create values on the basis of

74. Kass, "Cloning and the Posthuman Future," *Life, Liberty and the Defense of Dignity,* 143.
75. Kass, "The End of Courtship," 62–63.

nothing but the shifting soil of history. Values, as we have come to say, are "social constructions"; there is no natural or God-given standard of right. According to Strauss, "German historical relativism," epitomized by Heidegger, is the culmination of the modern tenor.[76]

Strauss bids us to return to "Athens" and "Jerusalem" as antidotes to the nihilism and relativism of modernity. But there is a problem. Athens (philosophy) and Jerusalem (the way of Torah) are at loggerheads and cannot be "synthesized." *Philosophy* depends on unaided reason, and presupposes the possibility that the human mind can autonomously comprehend "the whole," although, at the end of the day, reason must admit its own finitude and remain open to the infinity of reality and so to the possibility of divine transcendence. *Torah* presupposes the incomprehensibility of the whole to our intellect and so our need for "obedience" to law through faith in a mysterious but omnipotent Creator, although religious piety, too, should admit that it may have given up on reason too soon. Though these two ways of life are incompatible, their irresoluble conflict, according to Strauss, comprises "the secret of the vitality of Western civilization." Neither can prove the other wrong, and yet, because Socrates and the Hebrew Bible provide alternatives to the "nihilism" of modernity, Strauss hopes that they can cohabitate in creative tension.[77]

Although Greek philosophy and the Bible "proceed in entirely different ways" — reason versus revelation — Strauss makes the stunning claim that they agree about "the essential content of morality": that "murder, theft, adultery, etc., are unqualifiedly bad" and that "the proper framework of morality is the patriarchal family, which is, or tends to be, monogamous, and which forms the cell of a society in which the free adult males, and especially the old ones, [properly] dominate" because "the male sex is in principle superior."[78] While Greek philosophy allegedly grounds human patriarchy in natural hierarchy known to reason, the Bible traces human patriarchy to law obeyed out of love of the divine patriarch. Philosophy, however, "weakens the majesty of the

---

76. See Leo Strauss, "An Introduction to Heideggerian Existentialism," chap. in *The Rebirth of Classical Political Rationalism.*
77. Strauss, "Progress or Return?," *The Rebirth of Classical Political Rationalism,* 270.
78. Ibid., 246–47.

moral demands [because they are not backed up by the promises and omnipotence of God]."[79] For this reason, Strauss states, "[divine law] is accepted by Greek philosophy for the education of the many," although "not as something which stands independently."[80]

Though Strauss never quite puts his cards on the table, I conclude that he sides with Socrates over Torah. One cannot preclude the possibility of revelation, but Strauss puts his trust in reason since a believing Jew's faith in revelation ultimately calls for a "childlike obedience" that Strauss, devotee of Socrates that he is, cannot muster.[81] Yet he still insists that "it is impossible [for a Jew] not to remain a Jew," because it is impossible, even for an unbeliever, "to get rid of one's past by wishing it away."[82]

For the Socratic political philosopher like Strauss, "fear of the Lord" cannot be ruled out as a valid attitude, but revelation must be considered "a noble lie" from the perspective of the philosopher's love of wisdom and faith in reason. But even if biblical religion is false, Strauss suggests, it plays an important role in liberal societies because, left to their own devices, the "hoi polloi," when loosed from "sacred restraints" and allowed to philosophize, tend to end up hedonists, relativists, or nihilists: the "democratic men" described by Kass. So "the many" need the stabilizing "structure" of religion in order to reinforce civic piety. But "the wise" are able to recognize on the basis of reason alone "the natural hierarchy" that ought to inform the good society.[83]

Kass shares Strauss's critique of modernity: a critique foreshadowed by Plato's worries about democracy in his *Republic*. Liberal pluralism produces "souls without longing": a desire for comfort and freedom, but no "high" aspirations and, ultimately, a belief that truth is "relative" and that life is for pleasure — in other words, a version of Plato's democratic soul whose culmination is Nietzsche's "last man." Strauss calls "liberal tolerance" a cover for "nonjudgmental relativism": a commitment

79. Ibid., 252.
80. Ibid.
81. Ibid., 257.
82. Leo Strauss, "Why We Remain Jews," in *Jewish Philosophy and the Crisis of Modernity*, ed. K. H. Green (Albany: State University of New York Press, 1997), 317.
83. For Strauss on the role of "divine law" in Greek philosophy, see "Progress or Return?," *The Rebirth of Classical Political Rationalism*, 256.

to equality ("I'm OK, you're OK") that leads to a refusal to make distinctions between good and evil or to condemn anything absolutely.[84]

Strauss's core idea (elaborated by Allan Bloom) is that "the American mind" is becoming "closed" to the possibility of "higher Truth" — in the name of a liberal, tolerant, and ultimately relativistic "openness to diversity." He worries that the United States (and especially its liberal universities) is infected by the very "German historical relativism" that left Weimar with no intellectual defense against Nazism.[85] This leads him to return to Athens and Jerusalem as alternatives to the elements of liberal modernity that incline it toward doom.

Kass purports to side with Jerusalem over Athens, Abraham over Socrates. He wants to believe that revelation conveys the Truth, not merely a "noble lie" that serves political ends. Kass is trying to take "the leap" that Strauss, who remained a "zetetic skeptic" like Socrates, seemed unable to take.[86] Though Kass claims to speak from "Jerusalem," I shall argue that he really arrives at his conclusions on Straussian, that is, philosophical, grounds. But practically speaking, it doesn't matter, for his social agenda converges with Strauss's claim that the moral substance of Greek philosophy and the Bible is the same: the second table of the Decalogue and patriarchy.

Kass's Natural-Law Judaism and Neoconservative Politics

Earlier I argued that Hans Jonas's invocation of "humanity in the image of God" owes a greater debt to ontology than to theology. Jonas, taking his cue from Kant's "enlightened" effort to defend "religion within the limits of reason," fashions a rapprochement between Athens and Jerusalem: an ontology of nature that can — but need not — be supplemented by a theology of creation. Jonas is a kind of "natural theologian"

---

84. See Strauss's critique of the liberalism of Isaiah Berlin in "Relativism," chap. 2 in *The Rebirth of Classical Political Rationalism*.

85. For Strauss's argument that the United States faces a philosophical peril similar to the relativism that weakened Weimar Germany's resistance to Nazism, see Strauss's classic *Natural Right and History* (Chicago: University of Chicago Press, 1950).

86. For the interpretation of Strauss as a "zetetic skeptic," see the writings of Steven Smith of Yale University.

whose imperative of responsibility comprises "natural law." For just this reason, Leon Kass finds Jonas's defense of our responsibility for future generations to be untrue to Jonas's own Jewish heritage. A satisfactory account of the meaning of human sexuality and reproduction, according to Kass, requires that the way of nature — and Jonas's path, too — be "corrected" by revelation and divine legislation. But does Kass's account depend on his reading of Genesis — or is it an outgrowth of his "more natural science"?[87]

When Kass speaks of the "more loving and just tradition" embodied by Genesis, it is not clear that he is speaking as a Jew, and this for several reasons. First, Kass reads Genesis without seriously engaging the other four books of the Pentateuch, not to mention the vast corpus of rabbinic and post-rabbinic interpretation that, according to Rabbi Soloveitchik, defines what "Torah" — or revelation — is. Second, Kass admits to approaching Genesis as a humanities professor: not on the basis of "a leap of faith or commitment in advance to the truth of the biblical story, but, rather, [through] a suspension of disbelief."[88] He holds himself open to glean what lessons he can from what the biblical tales offer him, reading the text in the "wisdom-seeking spirit of philosophy." But, as Leo Strauss puts it, "By saying that we wish to hear first and then to act to decide, we have already decided in favor of Athens against Jerusalem."[89]

Finally, Kass acknowledges how closely his view approximates a natural-law perspective. The Noahide code, he states, stands on ontological ground more solid than the needs of society, the will of the victim, or even the authority of divine commandment.[90] Though Kass contends that "the most important insights on which decent society rests — for example, the taboos against incest, cannibalism, murder and adultery — are too important to be imperiled by reason's poor power to give them convincing defense," he also reminds us, echoing Strauss, that "the entire

87. For Kass's fullest development of Jonas's idea of "an existential interpretation of biological facts," see Leon R. Kass, *Toward a More Natural Science: Biology and Human Affairs* (New York: Free Press, 1985).

88. Kass, *The Beginning of Wisdom*, 17.

89. Leo Strauss, "Jerusalem and Athens: Some Preliminary Reflections," in *Jewish Philosophy and the Crisis of Modernity*, ed. K. H. Green, 380.

90. Kass, *The Beginning of Wisdom*, 174, 178.

second table of the Decalogue propounds not so much divine law but natural law, suitable for man as man, not only for Jew or Christian."[91] And these "reasons immanent in the nature of things" were evident even to pagans like Aristotle, though the vehicle of our discernment of these taboos is not pure reason, but, as Kass calls it, "the wisdom of repugnance."[92] Regarding the Noahide covenant, political philosophy can at most show the "utility, even the necessity" of faith in divine providence. But even if "decent human life requires a belief in a secure future and in the justice of law and the sureness of punishment," and these beliefs are "considerably more stable in the presence of a belief in divine backing," this impulse, Kass concedes, "may originate, without external cause, entirely from within the human soul."[93]

As for the erotic side of human nature, Kass admits to embracing the idea, associated with the natural-law tradition and "a more ancient and teleological understanding of nature," that "a proper understanding of the inner procreative meaning of ... human sexuality points exactly to the institution of exogamous, monogamous [and heterosexual] marriage as the institution best suited to rearing decent and upright children, that is, children who are truly human (or, as our text might put it, worthily in God's image)."[94] Kass, to be sure, states that "since moral views rooted in natural hierarchy will never be popular with more than a few, we should put our trust neither in nature nor philosophy, but in our religious traditions."[95] But in saying this, he *seems* to side with Strauss's pagan defense of piety: that although "natural hierarchy" can be defended on philosophical grounds, the wise man's reasons will fail to persuade "the many" in a democratic culture, and so the promotion of "family values" and patriarchy in particular are better left in the hands of religion.

When Kass refers to the insufficiency of nature and reason for ethics, however, he claims to speak not merely from a political perspective, but from belief in the superiority of revelation over philosophy, Jerusalem

---

91. Kass, "Death with Dignity and the Sanctity of Life," in *Life, Liberty and the Defense of Dignity,* 236, 239.

92. Kass, *The Beginning of Wisdom,* 187. For Kass on "the wisdom of repugnance," see "Cloning and the Posthuman Future."

93. Kass, *The Beginning of Wisdom,* 194–95.

94. Ibid., 274–75.

95. Kass, "The Troubled Dream of Nature as a Moral Guide," 24.

over Athens. Here he goes beyond Leo Strauss's Socratic or "zetetic" skepticism. For Kass concludes that "only with the Bible's help" could he have discovered the truths he thinks he has found, and so "my sympathies have shifted toward the biblical pole of the age-old tension between Athens and Jerusalem," for "I am no longer confident of the sufficiency of unaided human reason. I find congenial the moral sensibilities and demands of the Torah, though I must confess that my practice is still wanting."[96]

Nature is an insufficient guide, for the heavens don't teach us how to live and, although sex has "inner procreative meaning," proper marriage and patriarchy do not come naturally, especially given males' "inborn polygamous nature."[97] And philosophy is inadequate because even though the Bible's lessons are available to "the wisdom-seeking mind," the inaccessibility of these lessons to reason unaided by revelation indicates "the presence of some higher yet mysterious cosmic power to which human beings can and should be open."[98] In short, "the right ordering of loves" requires revelation, for "natural sexual impulses will not by themselves establish the proper institutional forms."[99]

Kass's claim is puzzling, for an advocate of natural law or natural theology need not hold that we are immediately inclined, regardless of the quality of our education, to apprehend moral truths or develop moral virtue. Human nature requires cultivation if we are to have any hope of understanding or actualizing our potential. The real question is whether the ends, the proper goals of culture and education, can be discerned on the basis of reasonable inquiry into the human condition. Kass's protests notwithstanding, one senses that the truths he traces to revelation are forgone conclusions based on his own philosophical stance toward life. God's manifest wisdom in structuring human nature the way God has, not God's incomprehensibility, comprises the ground of Kass's faith in revelation. And, as Strauss, puts it, "natural theology . . . is the forgotten basis of modern free thought."[100]

96. Kass, *The Beginning of Wisdom*, xiv.
97. Ibid., 250.
98. Ibid., 195.
99. Ibid., 194, 250, 294.
100. Strauss, "Progress or Return?," *The Rebirth of Classical Political Rationalism*, 267.

If Kass is really a natural philosopher wearing the mantle of Judaism, then his arguments about the moral norms that follow from human nature must be addressed in philosophical terms. I think that Hans Jonas's reluctance to deduce moral norms like heterosexuality, gender roles, the nuclear family, and patriarchy from his "existential interpretation of the biological facts" proves to be an asset, not a liability. Though his imperative of responsibility — "Don't do what risks jeopardizing the existence or essence of humanity" — may seem too "thin" and lacking in content from Kass's perspective, Jonas might reply that Kass projects his own moral and social judgments onto nature and so ends up with norms that are all too "thick" to be universal. The question for bioethics is, At what point should a possible intervention be prohibited on the grounds that it violates what Jonas calls "the integrity of the human essence" or, in a biblical key, the *imago Dei?*

Jonas's imperative gives us a direction or orientation, but no decision-procedure leading from "the human essence" to what is right in any particular case. Still, it puts us on guard against nightmares lurking within the utopian dream of manufacturing a "new and improved" humanity. This is the *conservatism* in Jonas that resonates so deeply with Kass. But Jonas never launches into the full-scale critique of liberal democratic culture that Kass, following Leo Strauss and Allan Bloom, does. On their view of modernity, the liberal values of freedom and equality cease to be "narrowly political" and instead masquerade as the ultimate ends of human life, thereby corrupting culture as a whole. "Democratic man" has a shallow soul: hollowed out by the relativism inherent in the view that all choices are equally good so long as they are freely chosen. And the promise of radical autonomy tempts moderns with the fantasy of technological liberation from "merely natural" constraints.

Kass extends the Straussian critique of modernity to the sphere of bioethics. "The wisdom of repugnance" before the prospect of human cloning awakens Kass's antipathies toward a whole set of social changes that allegedly pave the way to cloning because they overextend the values of freedom and equality and comprise "violations of human nature": feminism, the sexual revolution (spurred on by the availability of safe and effective contraception), the pro-choice movement on abortion, the gay rights movement, and the acceptance of divorce and arrangements other than the "traditional nuclear family." So-called women's liberation is the root of the "postmoral ambience" into which "cloning fits perfectly." This makes Kass sympathetic to the "family values" agenda of the neoconservative movement. Hans Jonas, so far as I can tell, neither anticipates nor shares this expansion of his critique of biotechnology. Kass's "correction" of Jonas, facilitated by his reading of Genesis, opens up a far more broad-sweeping conservatism.

If Kass's case for revelation is really a version of natural theology, then his position confronts the familiar criticisms of natural-law ethics, and, I have argued, Jonas's minimalist version of natural-law fares better. But given that Kass professes to speak from "the biblical pole of the age-old tension between Athens and Jerusalem," he must address William Galston's claim that one should hesitate to refer, as neoconservatives including Kass tend to do, to "biblical religion." For "Judaism (including Jewish orthodoxy, which makes common cause with Catholics and evangelicals on other matters) is much more accommodating" about the legitimate uses of biotechnology than "the Catholic-evangelical entente." Galston writes:

> Judaism accords a very high value to reproduction and healing, and less value to the status of nonimplanted pre-embryos. It also sets forth an activist vision of human beings as co-creators of the world. These basic features of the Jewish outlook lead it to embrace many applications of biotechnology.[101]

I am not qualified to assess Galston's claim, but hope to open it up for dialogue among those who are, for only then can Jews judge whether Kass's normative pronouncements fulfill what David Hartman calls the teaching of the rabbis: namely, that "the Sinai moment of revelation, as mediated by ongoing discussion in the tradition, does not require passive obedience and submission to the wisdom of the past," but instead requires Jews to "live by the Torah as if it had been given in [our] own time."[102] For Leo Strauss "Jerusalem" was a symbol for the recovery of Jewish identity — a kind of "inner Judaism" in his own case — against

---

101. Galston, "What's at stake in biotech?," 106.
102. David Hartman, *A Living Covenant: The Innovative Spirit in Traditional Judaism* (Woodstock, Vt.: Jewish Lights Publishing, 1997), 8–9.

a modernity whose "enlightened" solution to "the Jewish question" — namely, assimilation — had proven to be a disaster. How ironic it is that Kass's return to "Jerusalem" allows him to assimilate into the civil religion espoused by the Bush administration. Though halakhic Jews may find Kass's reliance on Genesis so restricted that he shouldn't be taken seriously as a Jewish voice, the fact remains that in Leon Kass the White House has found its official standard-bearer for the neoconservative agenda in bioethics, thereby promoting its arguably evangelical aims in the guise of an inclusive "biblical morality."

Chapter 11

DIVINE JUSTICE AND THE HUMAN ORDER

An Islamic Perspective

Azizah Y. al-Hibri

The Qur'anic worldview is a seamless web of ideas that begins with *tawḥīd* (the belief in a single God) and permeates various aspects of Qur'anic teaching from creation and the nature of the universe to ethics, social relations, and commercial and constitutional matters.[1] By ignoring the systematic worldview of the Qur'an, we risk impoverishing, even distorting, the various concepts that govern the Qur'anic approach to specific areas of human existence. Yet many of us, including some Muslims, believe that we can understand the Qur'an by discussing it one verse or passage at a time. This essay will argue that there is a unified worldview that permeates the Qur'an, and that makes it a seamless web of ideas, so that each verse cannot be properly understood without reference to others. In one sense, this is not a new argument, because ancient jurists have already stated that passages in the Qur'an explain each other.[2]

1. In this article, I use the famous translation of Yusuf Ali, entitled *The Holy Qur'an: Text, Translation, and Commentary* (Brentwood, Md.: Amana Press, 1992). I have revised it in some cases to modernize archaic language (such as to use "you" instead of "thee"). More importantly, I have replaced the word "Allah" with the word "God," since "God" is the proper English translation of the word "Allah." The God of Islam is the same God of the other Abrahamic faiths. Using the Arabic word for "God" clouds that fact. Finally, in a couple of places I changed a word in order to make the translation more accurate. For example, "al-nas" includes men and women, as 'Ā'isha, the wife of the Prophet, pointed out. So "people" is a better translation of this word than "mankind."

2. See, e.g., Badr al-Dīn al-Zarkashi, *Al-Burhān fī 'Ulum al-Qur'ān* (Beirut: Dār al-Jīl, 1988), 2:175.

I will argue that *tawḥīd*, whose object is an All-Merciful and All-Compassionate Abrahamic God, leads to a particular Qur'anic philosophy that is reflected throughout the universe, including both spheres of the world, inanimate and animate. But the operation of this philosophy is not the same in the two spheres. In the first sphere, its operation is determined through the laws of nature. In the second, it is not, because God has endowed humans with free will. That difference has often led most jurists to discuss the basic principles of each sphere separately, as if they were totally independent from each other. I shall argue that such an approach leads to a fragmented understanding of the world that goes counter to Qur'anic philosophy. Further, it leads at times to error in understanding such important Qur'anic concepts, as *al-mīzān* and *al-'adl*. These concepts represent overarching principles that flow between and within the two spheres, and cannot be understood in their fullness without the recognition of their overarching character. Misunderstanding or misconstruing these principles diminishes our ability to pursue the Islamic ideal in the various areas of human life.

For example, principles such as those governing gender relations in the family and constitutional rights in the state have often been treated in isolation from the overall Islamic worldview. As a result, they became subject to political and personal whims, and in the process created confusion among the Muslim masses. Tying these principles to the Islamic worldview and positioning them securely within it will eliminate problems of error, distortion, and confusion.

The Role of *Tawḥīd*

Central to the Islamic worldview is the concept of a single supreme being, namely God. This concept is the lynchpin of all Islamic beliefs and reverberates throughout the Islamic worldview. The Qur'an clearly states that the God of Islam is the same God as that of Christianity and Judaism, calling followers of these two religions "People of the Book" (Qur'an 3:64). But the Qur'anic revelation, while accepting Jesus as a major prophet of Islam, rejects the concept of the Trinity, a position I refer to as "deep monotheism." *Surat al-Ikhlas* (chapter 112) of the Qur'an is dedicated in its entirety to articulating this position. It states:

> Say: He is God, The One and Only
> God the Eternal, Absolute,
> He begetteth not, Nor is He begotten
> And there is none Like unto Him.[3]

This deep monotheism, called *tawḥīd*, has significant consequences for the Human Order on earth. Because God is the Supreme Being, it follows that there is no will superior to God's. To deny this by word or action is to fall into *shirk*, that is, associating partners with God. Iblīs (Satan) attempted to do just that and suffered dire results. According to the Qur'an, after God created Adam and taught him the names, God ordered the angels and Iblīs to bow to Adam. The angels obeyed God's order although they had misgivings about the violent nature of human beings (2:30–34). Iblīs, on the other hand simply refused to obey God's order. When questioned by God about his disobedience, Iblīs answered that he could not possibly bow to Adam for "I am better than he is" (7:12). God then cursed Iblīs, describing him as arrogant (7:13; 15:33–35; 38:74–78). Arrogance, therefore, appears very early on in Islamic thought as a major sin. It is, after all, arrogance that led Iblīs to disobey God, an act that posited Iblīs's will as superior to that of God. By doing so, Iblīs fell into *shirk*, the only sin God tells us in the Qur'an God would not forgive (4:48, 116).

After his fall, Iblīs asked God for respite until Judgment Day. He wanted to prove to God that the children of Adam were no better than him. In other words, Iblīs still "did not get it." He continued his old arrogant ways of thinking in terms of competitive hierarchies. God gave Iblīs the respite, but warned, "O children of Adam! Do not let Satan seduce you" (7:27).

The medieval scholar al-Ghazali found the story of Iblīs to be quite significant, arguing that it should be understood within the context of our society. He noted that a rich man who believes that he is better than a poor man, or a white man who thinks he is better than a red or black man, succumbs to Iblīsī logic. All actions that reflect a commitment to

---

3. While linguistically the Qur'an uses the masculine gender to denote God, as is the Arabic language convention, it makes clear at the same time that God is neither male nor female because "there is nothing like unto Him" (Qur'an 42:11).

a hierarchy of humans based on various worldly factors reflect the same kind of logic used by Iblīs. This is why humility becomes such an important virtue in Islam (31:18). It recognizes the fundamental equality of all humans, and eschews vain hierarchies. It is this humility that permitted renowned medieval Muslim jurists to shy away from claiming the truth of their conclusions. Instead, they always concluded their arguments with the phrase *wa-Allāhu aʿlam* (God knows best) and developed an etiquette of difference among them that resulted in a free and active market of ideas, where scholarly critiques could be quite incisive, yet respectful and humble.

Thus, the story of Iblīs points to two ways of being in the world: (1) a vain way based on worldly hierarchies rooted in differences such as those of wealth, race, ethnicity, or gender, and (2) a humble way based on the recognition that we are all God's creatures. The Qur'an recognizes differences and the problems they create among humans when it states:

> It is He Who has made you (His) agents, inheritors of the earth: He has raised you in ranks, some above others: that He may try you in the gifts He has given you. (6:165)

In other words, those among us who feel superior to others because of our worldly goods succumb to Iblīsī logic and fail the test of God. So, Adam's original predicament of having to choose between what is desirable and what is right continues to be replayed on earth in the life of Adam's descendants until the Day of Judgment. As we shall see later, this is partly due to Adam's choice to have a free will.

The second way of being is emphasized in the Qur'an when it tells us repeatedly that we were all created from the same *nafs* (soul) (4:1; 7:189; 31:28; 39:6). A repetitive thought in the Qur'an usually indicates a basic principle, and this principle of original equality is quite basic to the Islamic worldview. I will refer to it henceforth as the Equality Principle.

Other passages in the Qur'an explain the sameness of origin of all humans in greater detail, pointing to the pious path for understanding difference. The most famous one is the following:

O People! We created you from a single (pair) of a male and female, and made you into nations and tribes, that you may know each other. Verily, the most honored of you in the sight of God is (the one who is) the most righteous of you. (49:13)

This verse reveals difference in the world as an occasion for friendly communication, not conflict and domination. It then accepts a hierarchy in terms of closeness to God, making the standard one of righteousness, something any one of us can strive for and achieve. The Qur'an also articulates the nature of the one and only God. He is the Abrahamic God who is All-Powerful, All-Good, and All-Knowing (2:165; 18:39; 59:23; 2:54; 3:26; 2:163; 32:6; 49:16; 87:7; 40:19).

If God wills something into being, it materializes instantaneously (3:47). Since God's attributes are inseparable one from the other, God's creation of humans puzzles the angels. Knowing that God is All-Good, they question God's creation of Adam: "Will you place therein one who will make mischief therein and shed blood?" and God answers: "I know what you do not know" (2:30). Thus, the apparent problem of evil in the world is part of the design of an All-Good God who knows more than we or the angels know.

The most salient attribute of this God in Islam is His compassion, for God is the All-Merciful, the All-Compassionate. We know that this is the most salient of God's attributes because every chapter in the Qur'an starts with this description. Further, every prayer by Muslims must start with the statement, "In the name of God the All-Merciful, the All-Compassionate," a statement that is repeated many times during prayer. It is also a statement that Muslims utter when they begin an important (or even unimportant) activity. So, while every Muslim knows that his or her God is All-Powerful, All-Knowing, and All-Good, the focus of the Qur'an is specifically on God's compassion and mercy, not God's power or knowledge.

As proof of God's mercy, the Qur'an tells us that God forgave Adam after he ate from the forbidden tree of immortality and eternal power (2:35–37; 7:19–24; 20:117–22). But then, Adam's sin was not of the same order as that of Iblīs. Adam's disobedience was not based on arrogance but on weakness (20:115). So, Adam was forgiven and given another chance on earth to rectify his behavior. As a result, each person is born without the burden of the Original Sin. Instead, he or she is a *tabula rasa* that is defined by their life choices and actions.

Because God is All-Merciful, All-Compassionate, it stands to reason that God would order the universe in accordance with a principle that reflects this salient attribute. This principle, as articulated in the Qur'an, is described by the concept of *al-mīzān*.

The Universal Ordering Principle and the Concept of *al-Mīzān*

God's creation, the Qur'an tells us, was never haphazard (25:2). Everything God created was created in accordance with *al-mīzān* (due balance). In one verse we are told that the "firmament was raised high and He set up *al-mīzān*, so that you may not transgress *al-mīzān*" (55:7–9). In another passage, the natural laws of *al-mīzān* are described further: neither the sun is permitted to overtake the moon, nor the night may outstrip the day, and each swims along in its own orbit (36:40). Closer to home, the Qur'an tells us that "the earth we have spread out (like a carpet); set thereon mountains firm and immovable; and produced therein all kinds of things in due balance" (15:19).

Thus, the mathematical features that govern the constellations, gravity, and other similar forces of attraction and repulsion that stabilize the heavenly bodies are all part of God's overarching design, for it balances and harmonizes the universe into a beautifully integrated whole. In other words, God's principle of *al-mīzān* permeates the heavens and the earth. This is why the Qur'an repeatedly states that all of God's creations, even fruits, vegetation, and the sea and its contents, are signs for those who ponder (55:11–13, 19–23). It exhorts us to look at nature and admire God's creation, for God's miracles are evident to those who ponder (55:5–25; 16:65–69; 29:43; 23:12–22). This Qur'anic worldview gave rise to the golden age of Islamic science and philosophy in medieval times, and led to the invention of algebra and algorithm, significant advances in medicine, physics, and astronomy, and ultimately to the development of alchemy, the predecessor of chemistry.[4]

This unity between physics and metaphysics, inanimate and animate, is thus crucial for the Islamic worldview. There is no schism between the spiritual and the material, between science and religion. One leads to the other; all are ways of knowing God. This state of affairs is a direct consequence of *tawḥīd,* since the unicity of the universal ordering principle reflects the unicity of God Himself. This argument is suggested in the Qur'an itself when we are told that had there been more than one god, each god would have set his creation apart from those of the others, and some gods would have acted superior to other gods (23:91). The result would be a universe radically different from ours, one which is at best fragmented, and at worst in continuous conflict or chaos.

On the other hand, the Qur'anic worldview anchored in *tawḥīd* gives us a single standard — *al-mīzān,* the overarching divine ordering principle that provides our universe with balance and harmony. It is clear from the various Qur'anic verses that *al-mīzān* according to which the heavens and earth were created is the same *al-mīzān* that is supposed to govern human relationships. The very verse quoted above about the firmament being raised high moves directly from talking about *al-mīzān* in the context of nature to talking about it in human context. It enjoins us humans not to "transgress *al-mīzān.*" Indeed, the word *al-mīzān* was repeated twice in that short passage, once for each context for emphasis. Clearly then, according to the Qur'an, a single concept of balance and harmony orders the whole universe of creation from the grandest to the most humble.

As an ordering principle, *al-mīzān* manifests itself differently in different contexts. For example, in nature, it manifests itself as laws of nature; but in the human context, where people are endowed with free will, it becomes an ethical ideal to be achieved through a free will that is subject to temptation. Commitment to this ideal becomes the measure of the person in the second and final test of humanity after the fall. On the Day of Judgment, our deeds will be measured by *al-mīzān.* We are told

---

4. For more on this, see Seyyed Hossein Nasr, *Science and Civilization in Islam* (New York: Barnes & Noble, 1992), esp. 21–29; 92–285.

that the one who has light weights (for lack of adequate good deeds) will be among the losers (7:9).

According to the Qur'an, this test of human free will was not imposed on us, but was rather the direct result of our own choice. It informs us that at the time of creation, "We did indeed offer the Trust to the Heavens and Earth, and the Mountains, but they refused to carry it and were fearful of accepting it, but the Human Being carried it . . . " (33:72). The trust referred to in this verse is the trust of a free will, one that would have the responsibility of fostering *al-mīzān* in its own surroundings. This is a heavy trust, especially in light of the Iblīsi challenge (7:16; 15:39; 38:82). But humans were willing to accept it. The Qur'an refers to the human being as both foolish for accepting such a heavy trust, and as God's vicegerent on earth (33:72; 2:30).

The angels were concerned because the human being would spill blood on earth (2:30). But the "pious will" delivers the Trust by fostering a world order that reflects God's design of harmony and balance on earth. This is why God responded to the angels' concern with the simple answer: "I know what you do not know." This answer gives humanity hope that, in God's vast knowledge, in the end we will do what is right. We will opt for a human world order that fosters balance and harmony, rather than bloodshed and conflict. This world order, according to the Qur'an, is one of *al-'adl* (balance, justice). We now turn to the study of this concept.

In one passage, the Qur'an addresses Prophet David specifically, stating: "O David! We did indeed make you a vicegerent on earth, so judge thou among people in truth and justice, and do not follow your desires, for they will mislead you from God's path" (38:26). In another, it addresses the believers generally, saying:

> "O you who believe! Stand out firmly for God, as witnesses to fair dealing, and let not the hatred of others towards you make you swerve away from justice. Be just! That is next to piety: and fear God for God is well-acquainted with all that you do." (5:8)

The contrast in these verses is between one's inclinations and desires on the one hand, and God's path of truth and justice. This path is a difficult one, but if the human being is to shoulder his divine trust, then he must rise above his inclinations to follow the path of *al-ʿadl*. The Qurʾanic concept of *al-mīzān* is so intertwined with this concept that many commentators and translators use them interchangeably.[5] Nevertheless, there is a subtle difference between the two concepts. The first concept, namely *al-mīzān*, refers to God's ordering principle in God's creation. But the second concept, namely *al-ʿadl*, when applied to human contexts, refers to the choice of the pious free will of a human being to realize the state of *al-mīzān* in the arena of free human action.

Thus, in the domain of free will, *al-mīzān* becomes an ideal choice achievable through the pursuit of *al-ʿadl*. But the Islamic concept of *al-ʿadl* is not one of basic retributive justice; otherwise it would not foster balance and harmony. Rather, it is a full-bodied concept that includes, in the final analysis, forgiveness and restorative justice, elements that can in fact result in a balanced and harmonious world. *Al-ʿadl* in the human context becomes the means by which *al-mīzān* is fostered. It extends this principle to society, the state, family, and self. It reaches down even into our daily transactions and governs them with rules of ethics, so that we may not "transgress the balance."

According to the Qurʾan, God transmitted these rules of ethics to us repeatedly through past messengers who came with the Book and *al-mīzān*, so that people may stand forth in justice (57:25). Ignoring these messages and upsetting *al-mīzān* creates chaos, imbalance, injustice, and oppression. This is why the Qurʾan is very succinct in its directive: "God orders you to be just" (5:8). Furthermore, "if you judge among people, then judge justly" (4:58), even if one of the parties involved is a relative of yours (6:152). Upsetting the balance creates catastrophes in the natural world, and oppression and tyranny in society. Thus, we must strive for the proper balance in each case, to avoid wreaking havoc on our lives and those of others.

In the rest of this essay, I will articulate the concept of *al-ʿadl* as it affects various aspects of the human condition.

---

5. See, e.g., Ibn Manthūr, *Lisān al-ʿArab* (Reprint; Beirut: Dār Ihyāʾ al-Turāth al-ʿArabī, 1992), vol. 15, 290–91; see also, Fakhr al-Dīn al-Rāzī, *Al-Tafsīr al-Kabir* (Reprint; Beirut: Dār al-Kutub al-ʿIlmīyyah, 2000), vol. 15, 80–81.

The Concept of *al-ʿAdl* in Society, the State, and the Family

Society. From the above discussion, we can distinguish several meanings of the concept *al-ʿadl*. One important general meaning is that of balance and proportionality. This meaning is most salient when we discuss the concept of *al-mīzān* in its universal manifestation. For example, this is the meaning implicit in the saying: "With *al-ʿadl* were the Heavens and Earth erected."[6] A more specific meaning is that of justice as fairness, or giving each his due.[7] This meaning arises uniquely within the human context because humans have free will and could choose to be unjust. In other words, *al-ʿadl* in its specific meaning does not articulate a binding law of nature. Rather, it offers an ideal for a free human will that may fall short of this ideal.

In society, *al-ʿadl* is manifested in large part through the Equality Principle. This was the lesson of the story of Iblīs. Iblīsī logic dictates behavior that would create hierarchy, oppression, and conflict, and hence chaos in the world, by positing false hierarchies among humans. Qur'anic logic, however, is best expressed by the above-quoted verse, which states that all people were created from the same *nafs*, and ranks people in terms of their righteousness, not outward worldly difference (49:13).

The logic of this verse dictates a principle of original equality that leaves room for difference, but original equality is subject to human free choice, and hence human relations could be forced to move away from equality through bad choices. For example, Iblīsī logic is based on a radically different principle, namely that of a hierarchy which emphasizes and magnifies difference as adequate justification for inequality. If espoused, Iblīsī logic is a suitable foundation for an authoritarian, racist, classist, or patriarchal society in which conflict is rampant. Our earthly world took the first turn toward that logic when Cain killed Abel, his righteous brother. Cain was the elder, yet God accepted Abel's sacrifice and rejected Cain's. Upset by this situation, Cain "resolved" it by

---

6. A saying attributed to Imam ʿAlī Ibn Ābī Ṭālib; see, al-Imām ʿĀlī Ibn Ābī Ṭālib, *Rawaʾiʿ Nahj al-Balāgha* (Reprint; Beirut: Dār al-Shurūq, 1975), 38.

7. See Muṭahharī Murtaḍā, *Al-ʿAdl al-Ilāhī* (Qum: al-Dār al-Islāmiyya li al-Nashr, n.d.), 66–68.

killing Abel. In other words, he asserted his superiority over Abel by wiping him off the face of the earth. Thus, he became one of the "losers" who espoused Iblīsī logic (5:30). But Cain soon discovered the futility of his victory (5:31). Yet, because of the human condition, we continue to repeat Cain's mistake either by killing the Other or superceding the Other's will through the use of economic, military, or other types of oppressive force. Often, we discover the error of our ways after the fact, as Cain did; yet humanity continues to repeat these errors. Over time, the world we live in has become quite troubled and human relations have frayed at the edges. The question becomes, How do we now change a world of defective human relationships into one that satisfies *al-mīzān?* This is a question that the Qur'anic revelation addressed when it was revealed about fifteen hundred years ago.

The Qur'an answers this question not by calling for a revolution, that is, change through the use of force, but by calling for gradual change, or change through persuasion. To help this change along, it provides incentives, rationales, and injunctions. This approach gives humans time to reconsider their views and change their hearts. An imposed change would only lead to frustration, resentment, and ultimately further conflict, a situation contradictory to the ideal of *al-mīzān.*

This Qur'anic approach is best illustrated by its call for change with respect to the treatment of three of the most vulnerable segments of the population: orphans, women, and slaves. The Qur'an encourages Muslims to treat these three groups with special kindness, and provides protections for orphans and women as well as significant incentives for freeing slaves.[8] Further, it introduces a principle of mutual responsibility according to which everyone is responsible for those less fortunate than him or her. The line of responsibility is described in detail so that those closest to the disadvantaged person will have the strongest responsibility initially, but if they and others down the line fail or are unable to

---

8. For verses encouraging and praising those who take care of orphans, *see,* Qur'an 2:83, 177, 215, 220; 4:36; see also Muhammad Abu Zahrah, *Tanẓīm al-Islām li al-Mujtamaʿ* (n.p., Dār al-Fikr al-ʿArabī, n.d.), 50–51 [hereinafter, Abu Zahrah, *Tanẓīm al-Islām*]; on women, see Qur'an 4:127; and for verses that recommend Muslims to take good care of slaves and give incentives for freeing slaves, see Qur'an 4:92; 5:89; 58:3; 90:13; and see also Abu Zahrah, *Tanẓīm al-Islām*, 27, 28.

help, then in the end the state becomes responsible for helping its citizens.[9] In this system, no person is left behind, and everyone's humanity is recognized.

Additionally, the system of *zakāt* (tithing) provides the underpinning of this arrangement, and is further enhanced by the concept of *ṣadaqa* (or alms). While the Qur'an recognizes private property, and the fact that God gives some of us much more than others, it is very emphatic about the importance of sharing our financial blessings with others (2:177; 51:19; 70:24–25; 93:10).[10] It calls the *ṣadaqa* a loan to God, and asks: "Who is he that will loan God a beautiful loan [that is, one without interest]? For God would increase it many folds to his credit and he will have [also] a liberal reward?" (57:11).

In fact, a major rationale for the prohibition of usury appears to be that of preventing the oppression of the poor, and the exploitation of their need for personal gain. While usury may be financially rewarding, it does foster frustration and enmity within society, as opposed to cooperation, balance, and harmony; that is, a state of *al-ʿadl*. The Qur'an reminds us that humans tend to be stingy and unwilling to readily part with their money, even for good deeds (4:37; 47:38; 57:24; 59:9; 64:16). It teaches that those who are able to protect against their stingy selves are the successful ones (59:9; 64:16). For these reasons, and in the spirit of fostering equal human dignity, Muslim jurists recommended that a *ṣadaqa* be given secretly, so that neither the giver nor the recipient knows the other's identity. In today's world, such modesty is becoming under our laws increasingly impossible.[11]

The State. The Islamic state is also founded on the Equality Principle, because it is based on the consent of the people, extensive consultation with the people or their representatives, and constitutionalism that binds the ruler and defines his or her powers in light of a collectively agreed-upon charter.

The earliest model of an Islamic state was the one established by the Prophet Muhammad in Madinah. The Qur'an tells us that a delegation

9. See, e.g., Abu Zahrah, *Tanẓīm al-Islām*, 140–47.
10. Ibid., 40; 148–58 (explaining at length the system of *Zakāt* in Islam) and 164–66 on the Qur'anic injunction to give charity and share wealth with disadvantaged people.
11. If money ends up in the wrong hands, the donor may become legally liable.

of women gave their *bay'a* (vote, consent) to the Prophet as the leader of their community (60:12). The Prophet accepted this *bay'a* but only after he conversed with the women about the basis of their vote, and hence established the basis of the relationship between the leader and the people.[12] The same discussion took place when the men came (with some other women) to give their *bay'a*.[13] These events do not only establish the principle that the people choose their own leader in a Muslim state, but it also shows that Muslim women are an integral part of this process.

The head of the Muslim state is also bound by the principle of *shūrā* (consultation). He cannot govern unilaterally against the will of the people, for in Islam the *umma* (singular, meaning "the people") is the highest authority in the political system (*ḥakimiyyat al-umma*).[14] In fact, the Qur'an mentions *shūrā* alongside prayer and *zakāt,* and in one passage orders the Prophet to engage in *shūrā* because it soothes the heart of the people.[15] Further, the head of state is bound by Qur'an and the constitution of the state.[16] He may not violate either.

In the city of Madinah, the Prophet concluded a charter with the people of Madinah, both Muslims and Jews, articulating in it the rights of each group to mutual defense and freedom of belief.[17] It also articulated the obligations of the two groups and called them collectively "one *umma.*"[18] As such, the Madinah charter is perhaps the earliest document in history that establishes a constitutionally-based multifaith

---

12. Zayd Ibn ʿĀlī al-Wazīr, *Al-Fardiyya: Baḥth fī Azmāt al-Fiqh al-Fardī al-Siyāsī ʿind al-Muslimīn* (Virginia: Yemen Heritage and Research Center, 2000), 49.

13. Ibid., 13.

14. See, e.g., Muhammad Diyāʾ al-Dīn al-Rayyis, *Al-Naẓariyyat al-Siyāsiyya al-Islāmiyya* (6th ed.; Cairo: Dār al-Turāth, 1976), 175–76; 220; 229–35; 239–42; Munīr Ḥāmid al-Bayātī, *Al-Niẓām al-Islāmī al-Siyāsī* (Amman: Dār al-Bashīr, 1994), 332–35.

15. "Those who hearken to their Lord, and establish regular prayer; who (conduct) their affairs by mutual consultation; who spend out of what We bestow on them for sustenance," Qur'an 42:38; "It is part of the Mercy of God that thou dost deal gently with them. Wert thou severe or harsh-hearted, they would have broken away from about thee: so pass over (their faults), and ask for ([God])'s forgiveness for them; and consult them in affairs (of moment)," 3:159. See also 48:10; 48:18.

16. See al-Hibri, "Islamic Constitutionalism and The Concept of Democracy," *Case Western Reserve Journal of International Law,* 24, no. 1 (1992): 21–26; see also A. al-Hibri, "Islamic and American Constitutional Law: Borrowing Possibilities or a History of Borrowing?" *University of Pennsylvania Journal of Constitutional Law* 1, no. 3 (1999): 505–11.

17. Akram Diyāʾ al-ʿUmarī, *Al-Sīra al-Nabawiyya al-Ṣaḥīḥa* [the Correct Account of the Life of the Prophet] (al-Madinah al-Munawwarah: Maktabat al-ʿUlūm wa al-Ḥikam, 1994) [hereinafter *Al-Sīra*] cls. 25 and 37 (b), at 285.

18. Al-ʿUmarī, *Al-Sīra,* cls. 2, 25–35, at 282–84.

society, where the various faiths are protected in the exercise of their beliefs. This document contains various other important principles, such as equality before the law and the rejection of guilt by association. Thus, majority does not translate into coercion in an ideal Islamic society, especially in matters of faith. As the Qur'an states it, "there is no coercion in religion" (2:256). If coercion is used, then we will be only repeating Cain's mistake in some other form, for what does it benefit a person if one gains the whole world but loses oneself?

Muslim jurists understood this lesson very well. Indeed, when al-Khalīfa al-Mansūr proposed to make Maliki jurisprudence the official school of thought for his Abbasi Empire, Imam Malik resisted the idea.[19] Malik was concerned about using the arm of the state to propagate his views. Generally, until the later days of the Ottoman Empire, Muslims were free to choose the religious school of thought they wanted to follow without interference from the state, and other religious minorities were subject to their own courts of law.[20] With the advent of modernization and the rush to codify laws, this situation changed. Muslim rulers selected official schools of religious thought for their countries.[21]

Other changes in Muslim countries have been even more significant, and took place much earlier. The most significant is the rise of illegitimate authoritarian rule based on economic power and the use of force. This new rule has suppressed the will of the people, and marginalized the *shūrā* process. It has also led to instability, bloodshed, and chaos. The solution to this corrupt state of affairs is for us Muslims to divorce ourselves from Iblīsī logic and return to the logic of the Qur'an. We can rebuild through persuasion, thoughtfulness, and piety a new society in which every person counts, and the principle of *al-mīzān* is restored. There are serious hurdles facing this approach, because we live in a world in which Iblīsī logic is rampant. So, how can one group decide to live by divine logic and eschew the use of force when the rest of the world does

---

19. Subḥī Mahmasānī, *Al-Awḍāʿ al-Tashrīʿiyya fī al-Duwal al-ʿArabiyya* [*Legal Systems in the Arab World*] (3d ed.; Beirut: Dār al-ʿIlm li al-Malāyīn, 1965) [hereafter *Al-Awḍāʾ*], 159; see also Azizah al-Hibri, "Islam, Law and Custom: Redefining Muslim Women's Rights," *American University Journal of International Law and Policy*, 12, no. 1 (1997): 8–9.

20. Subhi Mahmassani, *Al-Awḍāʾ*, 171–78.

21. Non-Muslim minorities, however, continue to be governed by their own faith-based courts.

not? That was the dilemma Abel faced, but he answered his aggressing brother:

> If thou dost stretch thy hand against me, to slay me, it is not for me to stretch my hand against thee to slay thee; for I do fear God, the Cherisher of the worlds. (5:28)

But Abel was a special person, and he ended up dead, an example that not many of us rush to emulate. Further, a Muslim is charged with the duty of enjoining the good and repelling evil, and is permitted the right to self-defense (3:104; 9:71).[22] The problem becomes this: How do we balance all these elements, and choose a course of action that does not fall into the Iblīsī trap? This is the eternal challenge for the children of Adam. But today it has reached a critical stage. A new jurisprudence on the matter, which takes into account the specificity of today's risks and possibilities, as well as understands the heart of the Qur'anic principle of *al-mīzān*, is urgently needed.

The Family. The family relationship, from the Qur'anic point of view, is a prime example of *al-mīzān* on earth. It is a relationship between two independent beings who are created from the same *nafs*. Thus, the Qur'an includes gender in asserting the original equality of human beings. Further, the Qur'an tells us:

> And among His Signs is this, that He created for you mates from among yourselves, that ye may dwell in tranquility with them, and He has put love, and mercy between your [hearts]; verily in that are Signs for those who reflect. (30:21)

Thus, the Qur'anic view of the spousal relationship is one of love, tranquility, and affection, not domination, patriarchy, and oppression.

The married life, from the Qur'anic point of view, reflects the same safeguards required for establishing the legitimacy of government and its proper operation within the state. For example, no marriage may

---

22. See also Abu Zahrah, *Tanẓīm al-Islām*, 22–24 (stating the importance of the Islamic principle of enjoining the good and repelling evil); and 57 (listing the fundamental right to protect one's own life and defend it).

be validly formed without the free and informed consent of both parties.[23] Also, the spouses are expected to consult each other on family matters.[24] When serious differences arise between them, the Qur'an prescribes mediation. Divorce is entertained as a last resort, and is yet one more expression of the Qur'anic aversion to coercion. Harm or abuse, even if it is verbal and not physical, are legitimate reasons for seeking divorce.[25] In fact, strong dislike without more suffices for the woman to leave her husband without his consent. This form of divorce is called *khul'* and has only recently been properly recognized in Muslim courts despite its existence since the days of the Prophet.

It is worth noting that when the early Muslim state was going through turbulent times, Imam 'Alī, the last *khalīfa* and cousin of the Prophet, proposed mediation to resolve the conflict. He argued that if God required us to resolve familial conflicts through mediation, then it is even more urgent to use mediation to resolve conflicts within the *umma*.[26] This position illustrates Imam 'Alī's consciousness of the fact that a unifying overarching principle permeated all aspects of human life, and that since the state and the family have much in common, Qur'anic solutions from one area can be applied to another.

Historically, the demise of egalitarian relations within the family went hand in hand with the demise of the will of the people in matters of state, and its replacement with authoritarian rule. So, just as Qur'anic logic is overarching and indivisible, so is Iblīsī logic. It starts in one area and then spreads to others. Today, many Muslims have moved away from the Qur'anic ideals of the state and the family and are taking actions that are in direct contradiction to them. In many Muslim countries women are often treated as inferior, their rights are often difficult to obtain even through the court system, and culturally defined duties are assigned to

23. 'Alī M. A. al-Qurra Daghi, *Mabda' al-Ridā fī al-'Uqūd* (Beirut: Dār al-Bashā'ir al-Islāmiya, 1985) (henceforth, *Mabda' al-Ridā*). vol. 2, 1016–17; see also 'Abd al-Hamid Maḥmūd al-Ba'lī, *Dawabit al-'Uqūd* (Cairo: Maktabat Wihba, 1989), 19–22.

24. For a discussion of consultation within the family, see 'Abd al-Halīm Abū Shuqqa, *Taḥrīr al-Mar'a fī 'Aṣr al-Risāla*, 6 vols. (Kuwait: Dār al-Qalam, 1990), vol. 5, 104–9.

25. In fact, certain Personal Codes in the Muslim world explicitly specify that verbal abuse is grounds for granting the wife judicial divorce. See, for example, Jordanian Code, Personal Status Code, Provisional Law No. 61 (1976), ch. 10, Art. 132, and Kuwaiti Code, Personal Status Code, Pt. 1, Bk. 2, Tit. 3, Art. 126.

26. Ibn Kathīr, *Al-Bidāya wa al-Nihāya* (Beirut: Maktabat al-Ma'ārif, 1974 [14th century]), vol. 7, 281.

them as wives and mothers despite the clear position of the Qur'an to the contrary.

For example, Muslim women are not obligated to nurse their children except as a last resort.[27] They are not expected to perform housework, nor may anyone, even their fathers and husbands, touch their property and wealth. Yet, the Muslim woman today is often expected to perform housework, nurse her children, and share her wealth with her husband. In fact, many modern Muslim men have treated their wives' wealth as their own. Upon divorce, some men have tried to take back the marital gift they gave their wives, despite a clear injunction by the Qur'an not to do so (4:21).

Final Observation

This state of affairs, where some Muslim men and governments are ignoring Qur'anic principles in favor of oppressive cultural customs and patriarchal interests, may be attributed to a decline in piety in the Muslim society as a whole. Contemporary Muslim societies have tolerated forms of individual and collective oppression that are unthinkable within the Qur'anic worldview. Yet Muslim societies continue to claim and believe that they are being guided by the light of the Qur'an. One possible explanation for this discrepancy is that they are engaging in self-deception; another is the historical and compounded ignorance of the Qur'an. For centuries, authoritarian Muslim rulers hired jurists to provide distorted interpretations of Qur'anic verses that served their interests. These jurists were referred to as "the Sultans' jurists." They were willing to please the ruler, even at the cost of distorting the word of God. As such, they engaged in *shirk* (associating partners with God), for they allowed the ruler's will to supercede that of God. After all, God has warned us that

> Those who conceal the clear (Signs) We have sent down, and the Guidance, after We have made it clear for the people in the Book — on them shall be God's curse, and the curse of those entitled to curse. (2:159)

27. ʿAbd al-Karīm Zaydān, *Al-Marʾa Bayn al-Dīn wa al-Mujtamaʿ* (Cairo: n.p., 1977) vol. 9, 475–80, stating that Hanafis, Shafiʾis, and Hanbalis, with minor qualifications, do not require the mother to nurse her child. Malikis do, unless the wife is from an upper class.

So, in appeasing the rulers, these jurists succumbed to Iblīsī logic, and, as a result, created a great deal of confusion and pain among the people.

Later, colonialism, a major historical manifestation of Iblīsī logic, separated many Muslims from the language of the Qur'an. Orientalists who came along and wrote about Islam brought their own biases and worldviews into their tainted research. These developments compounded the initial problem of ignorance, and led to a generation of Muslims who want to be pious but just do not know how. It also led to global misunderstanding that has generated a great deal of strife, bloodshed, and hatred in the world.

This essay has taken a deep look at the Qur'anic worldview, especially its twin principles of *al-mīzān* and *al-ʿadl*. It has shown that these principles permeate every aspect of our life. It has also underscored the problems resulting from ignoring them. We continue to live in a world where we are endowed with free will that allows us to define and redefine our existence. We have also been endowed with reason. We have Qur'anic verses and a rich historical record that detail the consequences in the world and the Afterlife of succumbing to Iblīsī logic. Are we ready yet to determine the path we ought to follow?

Chapter 12

RELIGION, HUMAN RIGHTS, AND SECULARISM

Preliminary Clarifications and Some Islamic, Jewish, and Christian Responses

David Little

An-Na'im's Proposal

Abdullahi An-Na'im,[1] the courageous and creative Sudanese Muslim thinker and human rights scholar, produced in 2003 a paper on the interdependence of religion, human rights, and secularism, with special reference to Islamic societies.[2] The paper's two-stage argument, in broad outline, is, first, that each of these notions, correctly considered, depends on the others. Religion, capable of inspiring intense, if strongly particularistic loyalties, may well affect a domineering attitude toward both adherents and outsiders if it is not disciplined by the principles of secularism and human rights. Secularism restrains such domineering tendencies by "deregulating" religion, and thereby encouraging a healthy diversity and pluralism within and among religious communities. Human rights, as enshrined in the growing collection of post–World War II international

1. Abdullahi An-Na'im is Charles Howard Candler Professor of Law, Emory University, Atlanta, Georgia.

2. "The Synergy and Interdependence of Human Rights, Religion, and Secularism: Prospects for Islamic Societies," which is very much still in draft form, and which the author kindly sent me, and graciously allowed me to quote from in writing this paper. Professor An-Na'im and I, along with Professors Michael Ignatieff and Frank Vogel, as well as other participants, had an opportunity to discuss the paper at length at a fruitful session sponsored by the Carr Center for Human Rights held at the Kennedy School of Government, Harvard University, on October 16, 2003. That discussion, for which I am very grateful, strengthened my conviction of the need for the sort of "clarification" I am proposing in this paper.

documents, constrains religions by imposing basic, universal individual and group protections, including provisions for especially vulnerable groups like women and minorities.

At the same time, the principle of secularism is likely to be enfeebled and severely beleaguered without religious support, especially in those parts of the world where initial antipathy on the part of religious groups toward the whole idea of secularism might be deep and widespread. Furthermore, the principle of secularism, properly understood, is historically and culturally contingent and variable. Though, in An-Na'im's words, the notion contains "certain minimum requirements," and encourages adherence to a "certain civic ethos"[3] (neither of which he elucidates), the term emphatically may *not* be taken, he says, to have one essential meaning. For example, the familiar definition of secularism found in the *Short Oxford Dictionary,* which An-Na'im cites — namely, a doctrine of morality oriented toward human earthly well-being "to the exclusion of all considerations" of religious belief, is not congenial to his purposes, since it rules out by definition any possible conceptual overlap between religion and the idea of secularism. For An-Na'im, what secularism means will have to be negotiated in different legal, political, and cultural settings. Consequently, local religious dispositions in belief and practice will, among other things, have both to be "considered" and, up to some point, accommodated by any proper understanding of secularism.

Essentially, the same points apply to human rights. The idea that human rights, as formulated, remain abstract, remote, and uninspiring, absent the fervency and commitment religion can generate, is a familiar point of An-Na'im's.[4] Given the influence of religion, especially in certain places, these limitations, he reiterates, "are unlikely to be overcome without solidarity and cooperation among different religious communities."[5] Without drawing a vital connection between human rights and indigenous religious predispositions, different peoples around the world

3. Ibid., 8.
4. See, for example, Abdullahi An-Na'im, "Islamic Foundations of Religious Human Rights," in John Witte Jr. and Johan D. van der Vyver, *Religious Human Rights in Global Perspective: Religious Perspectives* (The Hague: Martinus Nijhoff Publishers, 1996), 337–59.
5. An-Na'im, "Synergy and Interdependence of Human Rights, Religion, and Secularism," 6.

will not feel that they themselves "own" human rights, and will not, accordingly, be motivated to do much about them.

But human rights standards are also abstract in another sense. They are not self-applying. Like all general codes, they require contextual interpretation and adjustment, and consequently various provisions will have to be negotiated in reference to diverse cultural and religious settings. And not only that; as they stand, human rights documents contain a rich complexity of very different protections — from ensuring bodily and psychological integrity to guaranteeing civil, political, economic, social, and cultural freedoms and opportunities — all of which, given local variations, cannot help their being coordinated in different ways. Again, acute cultural and religious sensitivity is called for.

Finally, secularism and human rights, on An-Na'im's account, cannot get along without each other either. Unchecked, the doctrine of secularism, based as it is on the principles of the independent sovereignty of modern nation-states, and of their right to a monopoly of legitimate force over the inhabitants of a given territory, can incline, An-Na'im implies, toward a "totalizing" and dominating pattern of control over the ideals and practices of citizens. Here, an "international human rights regime" can represent an imposing system of transnational accountability. Conversely, human rights are ineffective and unproductive unless they are implemented by actual governments, operating within the limits of a duly regulated doctrine of secularism.

In the second stage of his argument, An-Na'im briefly applies this interdependent or "synergistic" view of religion, human rights, and secularism to Islamic societies. It is with these that he, as a practicing Muslim, is existentially most concerned. He takes up the cases of Egypt, Sudan, and Iran in passing.

A key underlying assumption of the entire approach is that, at bottom, a religion like Islam is indeed compatible with human rights and a doctrine of secularism, such that it can simultaneously profit from the interaction with them, and, in turn, contribute to their proper interpretation and application. If that were not conceded, the whole argument would collapse. According to An-Na'im, it is precisely the interaction with human rights and secularism — of course, in the right combination and with the right understanding — that induces an "internal transformation" of Islam that is long overdue, and that, in effect, helps to restore certain core essentials of Islamic faith.[6]

There are two essentials of special importance. One is *the principle of pluralism* — namely, the fundamental legitimacy of and respect for expressing and living by "competing interpretations" of Islam.[7] The second might be called *the principle of adjusted interpretation* — namely, the legitimacy (and unavoidability) of adapting the teachings of the Qur'an and the Sunna to variable historical circumstances "in concrete time and place," and to be done, as An-Na'im puts it in an arresting statement, "by human beings who share the same basic qualities, and are influenced by the same concerns, of human beings everywhere."[8]

These principles work together to support both a doctrine of secularism and the standards of human rights, whereby religion is "deregulated" by the state, and the "universal" rights of religious freedom and nondiscrimination, along with the rights of religious minorities, are protected. An-Na'im could hardly be clearer or more provocative on this matter:

> It is commonly claimed that Islam mandates the establishment of an "Islamic state" which will implement and enforce Sharī'a . . . as the normative law of the land. But in my view, the notion of an Islamic state is a contradiction in terms because whatever principles of Sharī'a are enacted by the state as positive law cease to be the normative system of Islam by the very act of enacting it as the law to be enforced by the state. Since there is so much diversity of opinion among Islamic schools of thought and scholars, . . . any enactment of Sharī'a principles as law would have to select some opinions over others, thereby denying believers their freedom of choice among equally legitimate competing opinions. . . . I also argue that the implementation of Sharī'a as the official state law is also untenable in economic and political terms for the modern nation-state in its present economic and political context.[9]

6. Ibid., 21.
7. Ibid., 22.
8. Ibid.
9. Ibid., 24.

Secularism and human rights are, for example, of considerable aid and comfort to the women's movement in Egypt. By restricting the capacity of the state to enforce religion, and by guaranteeing the rights of religious freedom and nondiscrimination to all citizens, these principles work together to assure that those women seeking equality will have the freedom, if they so desire, to identify with and rally around those interpretations of Islam that are most compatible with their cause. On the same principle, women, not similarly inclined, would likewise be guaranteed the right to reject Islam altogether, if they wish, and to associate themselves with non-Islamic justifications for their cause. "It is critical for the integrity of the religious tradition itself," says An-Na'im, "that people are free to stay or leave the community at will, instead of being forced or intimidated into the hypocritical pretense of believing in a religion."[10] He adds that contrary to the present practices of the Egyptian government, observing the same principles will more likely contribute to peace and stability in a country consisting of "a diversity of beliefs among the members of the Muslim majority," as well as of a sizeable Christian minority.

In the case of Sudan, a basic cause of the continuing civil war there, An-Na'im suggests, is the illicit domination of the National Islamic Front government, which has enforced its version of *Sharī'a* as the law of the land on a country with "profound religious and cultural diversity." "The imposition of a particular understanding of Islam...violates the human rights of Muslim as well as of non-Muslim citizens of the country."[11]

An-Na'im levels similar criticisms against the effort in Iran, since the revolution in 1979, to create an Islamic state. Like Sudan, he says, Iran has not only subverted the proper relation between religion and government, and consequently violated the fundamental religious and other rights of all Iranian citizens, but the experiment also failed dismally in other respects, including being subject to "devastating international isolation." The "sad experience" of Iran, from which much can be learned, is, according to An-Na'im, that "a secular space between religion and

10. Ibid., 26.
11. Ibid., 28.

state is critically important for the political stability, social and economic development, and general well-being of Islamic societies."[12]

An-Naʻim's proposal is, it seems to me, very appealing, and has broad significance. It is of course of obvious importance to the current, and often heated, discussions of the political interpretation and application of Islam. As such, the thesis is consonant with similar stimulating proposals being put forward by other contemporary liberal Muslim thinkers like Abdulaziz Sachedina and Abdolkarim Soroush.[13] As with An-Naʻim, both these authors explicitly endorse the indispensability of duly secular governments, largely compliant with human rights standards, for encouraging authentic Islam — namely, Islam that is open to the free and equal expression of many voices, both Islamic and non-Islamic, within the same political community. Also, as with An-Naʻim, both authors believe that a properly chastened Islam can make a helpful contribution to a richer and fuller understanding of both secularism and human rights, one that is truly intercultural, rather than being the product of just one tradition (that is, the West).

But, surely the pertinence of the thesis extends beyond Islam alone, and could usefully be applied to other religions as well. That, at least, will be my hypothesis in what follows. I shall draw out some brief connections between An-Naʻim's thesis and Judaism and Christianity, as well as Islam. How might "religion," "human rights," and "secularism" work together in regard to these three religions?

Given the limitations of space, however, we need to confine the subject somewhat. I intend to focus my attention here on trying to clarify and specify, a bit more than An-Naʻim is able to do, just what it means to claim that secularism and human rights ought in some way "to condition" or "constrain" religions like Islam, Judaism, or Christianity. Even if, as An-Naʻim suggests, secularism and human rights will have to be adjusted contextually, there must, nevertheless, also be some irreducible "fixed features" associated with these two notions that can, so to speak, be "brought to the table," and offered as *general outside constraints or*

---

12. Ibid., 29.
13. See especially, Abdulaziz Sachedina, *The Islamic Roots of Democratic Pluralism* (New York: Oxford University Press, 2001); Abdolkarim Soroush, *Reason, Freedom, and Democracy in Islam* (New York: Oxford University Press, 2000).

limits on religious thought and behavior. Otherwise, each of the three terms might be in danger of losing all distinctiveness or "definition" in an interminable and inconclusive process of mutual or "synergistic" readjustment of meaning.

We shall also briefly consider how religions like Judaism, Christianity, and Islam might go about embracing and affirming whatever outside constraints we are able to identify.

Objections: The Contrary View of Talal Asad

To help this process of clarification along, I shall take up an approach to religion, secularism, and human rights that is, if I am not mistaken, very nearly antithetical to An-Naʿim's proposal. The approach is contained in the forceful book by Talal Asad, *Formations of the Secular: Christianity, Islam, and Modernity*,[14] the central argument of which will have to be addressed and answered if claims by An-Naʿim and others in favor of a constructive interdependence among the ideas of religion, secularism, and human rights are to be sustained. Indeed, it is a fair assumption that Asad's position on these matters encapsulates a widespread suspicion, if not antagonism, inside and outside scholarly circles, toward proposals like An-Naʿim's that take a generally favorable attitude toward "modernity," and associated ideas of the modern state, secularism, and human rights as they bear on religion.

For Asad, "the unprecedented powers and ambitions of the modern state and the forces of the capitalist economy have been central to the great transformation of our time."[15] Even though he occasionally disclaims any intention to ascribe blame, or to make moral judgments about this "great transformation," his analysis is by no means value free. His account of the profound interconnection of nationalism, the modern nation-state, and the idea of secularism can only be characterized, from his point of view, as morally and religiously ominous. "Nationalism,"

---

14. Talal Asad, *Formations of the Secular: Christianity, Islam, and Modernity* (Stanford: Stanford University Press, 2003). I am deeply grateful to Ms. Atalia Omer, a graduate assistant at Harvard University, for calling my attention to this book by Talal Asad, as well as to the book by Yeshayahu Leibowitz, *Judaism, Human Values, and the Jewish State* (Cambridge: Harvard University Press, 1992), to which I shall be referring below (see n. 53).

15. Ibid., 253.

he writes, "with its vision of a universe of national *societies* (the state being thought of as necessary to their full articulation) in which individuals live their worldly existence requires the concept of the secular to make sense. The loyalty that the individual nationalist owes is directly and exclusively to the nation."[16]

This view of the "centralizing state,"[17] which is oriented toward "worldly existence" and rests "on coercion" (or what Asad also calls "the exercise of violence"[18]) and which is regarded as the ultimate, exclusive, and all-determining authority, not only over politics and economic affairs, but also over the place and character of morality and religion, suggests the very "totalizing" and dominating image of the secular state that An-Na'im himself fears, absent appropriate checks and balances. As Asad puts it, "the nation-state is not a generous agent and its law does not deal in persuasion."[19]

On Asad's view, the doctrine of "secular nationalism" arose in Europe and was closely connected to colonialism. The process of investing the modern state with supreme authority requires, first, the experience of "disenchantment," according to which modern techniques of production, political organization, education, warfare, travel, entertainment, medicine, and so forth imply "direct access to reality" — without recourse, that is, to supernatural assumptions.[20] Traditionally understood ideas of religion, myth, magic, and the sacred become radically redefined and recategorized so as to be subject to secular political regulation. Such an arrangement does not necessarily mean rejecting or dispensing with religious or "sacred" symbols altogether, but simply controlling and reshaping them for secularly defined purposes. The second step on the part of the Europeans was to try to "globalize" this system of understanding and practice by transplanting it among colonized peoples. "In their attempt to outlaw customs the European rulers considered cruel it was not the concern with indigenous suffering that *dominated* their thinking, but the desire to impose what they considered

16. Ibid., 193. Emphasis in the original.
17. Ibid., 227.
18. Ibid., 256.
19. Ibid., 6.
20. Ibid., 13.

civilized standards of justice and humanity on a subject population —
that is, the desire to create new human subjects."[21]

At present, it is the American model of secular nationalism, with its
universal hegemonic aspirations, and its now unrivaled military, political, and economic capabilities, that is regnant, and therefore, to Asad's
mind, particularly threatening. Asad's description is not complimentary.
American secular nationalism has, in effect, expanded the European
pattern of hegemonic domination, although, in keeping with its traditions, it has cast its mission of spreading secular political and economic
values in a distinctly religious, and therefore particularly high-handed,
mode. "Americans are likely to see enemies not just as opponents but as
evil." And because of the same domineering inclinations, "the repeated
explosions of intolerance in American history . . . are entirely compatible
(indeed intertwined) with secularism in a highly modern society."[22]

In the same spirit, Asad believes that the "myth of liberalism," together
with the constitutive idea of "universalizing reason," which underlies this
Euro-American secularist construct, actually "go[es] against the grain of
human and social nature," and, consequently, must be violently imposed
and maintained. He invokes the image of a garden constantly threatened
by a surrounding jungle that may only be held back by policies of perpetual
violence and destruction. "For to make an enlightened space, the liberal
must continually attack the darkness of the outside world that threatens
to overwhelm that space."[23]

Of special interest for our concerns is Asad's treatment of "a secular
system like human rights,"[24] as he calls it. Rather than representing a
transnational system of accountability, *à la* An-Na'im, Asad concludes
that international human rights are little more than biased instruments
in the service of the existing nation-state system. Human rights are, he
says, "floating signifiers that can be attached to or detached from various
subjects and classes constituted by the market principle and by the most
powerful nation-states."[25] Asad is very explicit on this point:

21. Ibid., 110.
22. Ibid., 7. The first citation is a quotation from the historian, Eric Foner.
23. Ibid., 59.
24. Ibid., 129.
25. Ibid., 158.

The American secular language of redemption, for all its particularity, now works as a force in the field of foreign relations to
globalize human rights. For that language does, after all, draw on
the idea that "freedom" and "America" are virtually interchangeable — that American political culture is (as the Bible says of the
Chosen People) "a light unto the nations." Hence, "democracy,"
"human rights," and "being free" are integral to the universalizing moral project of the American nation-state — the project
of humanizing the world — and an important part of the way
very many Americans see themselves in contrast to their "evil"
opponents.[26]

The basic argument appears to be that since international human
rights documents address themselves to "Member States" or "States
Parties,"[27] we may conclude that the only licit and effective authority
for interpreting and enforcing human rights are independent sovereign
nation-states themselves. It is states alone, according to Asad, that have
"exclusive jurisdiction" to "decide the fate" of individual citizens.[28]
Furthermore, he claims that human rights are not concerned with the
"civil status" of citizens, but only with what he calls their "natural
being,"[29] something he takes to be entirely independent of citizenship.
Consequently, "the identification and application of human rights law
has no meaning independent of the judicial institutions that belong
to individual nation-states...and the remedies that these institutions
supply."[30]

Commenting on the statement in the Preamble to the Universal Declaration, that unless human rights are "protected by the rule of law"
human beings will be "compelled to have recourse, as a last resort, to

26. Ibid., 147.
27. The Universal Declaration (which technically is not a treaty or convention) uses the term
"Member States," whereas documents like the International Covenant on Civil and Political
Rights, which are treaties or conventions, use the term "States Parties." However, it should
be noted that both these documents (and others) refer, in addition, to "the peoples of the
United Nations" (Preamble, Universal Declaration) or to "all peoples" (International Covenant
on Civil and Political Rights, art. 1). Very significantly, *peoples as well as states* are directly
addressed by international human rights documents. This point should be born in mind in the
light of our critique of Asad's view, below.
28. Ibid., 137.
29. Ibid., 129.
30. Ibid., 129.

rebellion against tyranny and oppression," Asad repeats the same point. He argues in part[31] that this reference is circular since whether or not human rights are in given cases protected by the "rule of law" is itself determined by the judicial institutions of the individual nation-states. There is also the further problem, he seems to suggest, that since human rights standards are definitively interpreted by national courts, there is no possibility in practice of distinguishing human rights standards from particular court rulings concerning what is lawful.

Asad slightly qualifies his arguments about the supremacy of national courts by mentioning transnational human rights institutions, such as the European Court. However, he contends that such institutions do not do much, in the final analysis, to alter the domineering status of the nation-state. Either the transnational institutions simply "act as larger proto-states" (presumably with the same "totalizing" effects as individual nation-states have) or they do not require that member states give up much of their authority, after all.[32]

Response to Asad

We should begin by affirming some of what Asad argues for, particularly in regard to the centrality of the modern nation-state system in influencing the terms of contemporary understanding and practice, including religious understanding and practice. He does touch on a few problem areas in the current formulation and administration of human rights and humanitarian law. And he is especially insightful when it comes to identifying the capacity for dominance on the part of the more powerful nations, like the United States, and for arranging things, often unfairly and highhandedly, in their own interest. At precisely this time in American history, governed as the country is by an administration that is officially committed to a foreign policy of preemptive unilateralism, and of ignoring or disabling international initiatives and institutions in favor

---

31. In addition, on p. 138 Asad makes an additional point about a convergence between the idea of "rule of law" and a doctrine of "social justice" that excludes rights, that is, frankly, not easy to understand.
32. Ibid., 129, 139.

of promoting and extending "our values" around the world, we are compelled to acknowledge at least part of Asad's dour description of where we stand.

But, ironically, our very readiness to agree on these points, and to concede that the United States, particularly under its present government, does conform to the pattern of domination Asad associates with the modern secular nation-state system, gives us a reason for concluding that Asad *can only be partly right,* and that An-Na'im's proposal, properly understood, has merit after all.

For we cannot have it both ways. We cannot, on the one hand, criticize current American behavior in the way Asad does for its high-handedness, and for its readiness to pursue unilaterally its own "secular" economic, military, and strategic interests under a self-serving banner of religion, and simultaneously embrace Asad's view that *all* national and international standards that enshrine the ideas of secularism and human rights, among other things, are *nothing but* the tools of self-serving nation-states. The reason is that the criticism itself rests on holding current American behavior accountable according to these very national and international standards.

Most of the objection to American policy in Iraq, at home and abroad, rests on the assumption that the United States has violated or is in danger of violating, both domestically and internationally, the "rule of law," as well as obligations to human rights and humanitarian law, as well as the United Nations Charter.[33] Moreover, most critics of U.S. policy do not consider the capacity of the American government to enforce its policies, either through the national courts at home, or by the use of military might abroad, *to end* the debate over the legitimacy of these policies. That suggests that Asad goes too far in contending that contemporary beliefs about right understanding and practice are determined finally by the "exercise of violence" on the part of the nation-state. It is, in fact, such "exercises of violence" that very often trigger the loudest objection and criticism within the United States and elsewhere, with what appear, fairly frequently, to be very significant political consequences.

33. David Little, "Terrorism, Public Emergency, and International Order," in *Human Rights, Democracy and Religion,* ed. Lars Binderup and Tim Jensen (Odense: University of Southern Denmark Press, 2005), 126–55.

Clarifications

Over against Asad, I want to suggest that objections and criticisms of this sort rest on firm ground, and that, even with all the possibilities for misunderstanding, the ideas of human rights and secularism nevertheless offer some standards of transnational accountability, including several important and usable "fixed features," and "outside constraints," which we need to develop. I shall consider the ideas of human rights and secularism in order, sketching in along the way some thoughts on the role of religion, and in particular, of Christianity, Judaism, and Islam.

Human Rights

Although Asad notes briefly the stimulus of German fascism and the record of German atrocities committed during World War II as the basis for drafting and adopting the Universal Declaration of Human Rights (and subsequent documents),[34] he does not grasp the full significance of those experiences, nor does he understand, therefore, the true character and implications of the human rights system that was inaugurated in 1948. Above all, human rights were formulated in direct and self-conscious response to a "modern secular nation-state," or to an example of "modern secular nationalism," gone radically pathological. Fascist Germany is the paradigm case of Asad's image of the modern secular nation-state. Under Hitler, the state asserted the supreme authority both to define the "true interests" and "true ideals" of all citizens, including what is an acceptable understanding of religion and morality, and to impose that "totalizing vision" by means of relentless "exercises of violence" that depended completely on the state's "exclusive jurisdiction."

The very word *Nazism,* of course, is short for "German *National* Socialism," and it has come to symbolize in explicit and vivid detail everything the human rights system was created to prevent ever after. This point is made with great force by Johannes Morsink in his indispensable volume on the drafting of the Universal Declaration.[35] That

34. Ibid., 57, 138–39.
35. Johannes Morsink, *The Universal Declaration of Human Rights: Origins, Drafting, and Intent* (Philadelphia: University of Pennsylvania Press, 1999).

means, first and foremost, that the idea of human rights, as Morsink shows, is grounded in a feeling of "shared moral revulsion"[36] against the record of atrocities perpetrated by the Nazis at home and abroad in the 1920s, '30s, and '40s. Such a feeling was unanimously assumed by the drafters to constitute *a universal, indubitable, and unavoidable standard of moral appraisal of the behavior of nation-states.*

This point about the assumed moral basis of human rights suggests two things. One is that the status of the crimes human rights standards are designed to condemn and prevent is, in an important sense, "self-justifying," and as such is "fixed" and nonnegotiable. Different religious and other groups may find a variety of grounds for supporting the judgment, *but whatever their responses may be, that judgment is understood to rest on independent and universally accessible moral grounds.* The second thing is that when the Preamble to the Universal Declaration pronounces that certain "barbarous acts...have outraged the conscience of mankind," the understanding is that *this judgment exists prior to and independent of the action of states.* In a word, states are creatures, not creators, of human rights — contrary to Asad's position.

Second, the fact that the provisions of the Universal Declaration (and thereafter of all subsequent human rights documents, which reiterate the original language) were composed against the background of particular acts of mistreatment by the Nazis, means that the provisions are not purely abstract or formal, but in fact prohibit *certain specifiable kinds of behavior.* For example, the provision against discrimination based on such indications as race, language, gender, religion, national or social origin, or birth or other status (Article 2) should be understood to ban *the kinds of discrimination actually practiced by the Nazis.* Similarly, "the experience of the war had reinforced the belief [of the drafters] that the cluster of rights spelled out in Articles 18, 19, 20, and 21 [freedom of thought, conscience, and religion, of opinion and expression, of association, or of participation in government] are universally the first ones dictators will seek to deny and destroy."[37] In short, preventing specific

36. Ibid., xiv. On pp. xiii–xiv, Morsink announces that "without the delegates' shared moral revulsion against ['the absolutely crucial factor of the Holocaust'] the Declaration would never have been written."
37. Ibid., 69.

kinds of acts that were practiced before and during World War II, and that profoundly informed the drafting of the Declaration, was understood by the drafters to be absolutely indispensable to thwarting future forms of "pathological nationalism."

Third, again contrary to Asad, human rights protections are in fact crucially aimed at the "civil status" of individual citizens. Nearly one-fourth of the articles of the Universal Declaration concern legal rights because, as Morsink points out, "the drafters were aware of how far the nazification of the German legal system had gone," and how important it was to make sure such conditions were not allowed to repeat themselves.[38] Nor is it the case, as Asad argues, that the determination of the civil rights of citizens in legal and other respects depends on the "exclusive jurisdiction" of the sovereign nation-state. Indeed, such a conclusion profoundly misunderstands the actual impact of the human rights system. "The cumulative effect of the legal provisions of the Charter, of the Universal Declaration and other instruments, and of subsequent state practice, is that human rights are no longer matters of domestic jurisdiction alone. They have become internationalized both politically and in law."[39]

Fourth, when it comes to the legal ratification of human rights conventions, it is true, in line with Asad's point of view, that "States Parties" do retain a certain amount of discretion by means of the prerogative, for example, to enter special "reservations" and "understandings" upon the act of adherence. By such devices, states are able to qualify their obligations to uphold certain provisions of a human rights convention or treaty by so declaring. While such privileges do weaken universal compliance, state discretion is by no means as unlimited as Asad implies. An-Na'im rightly points out that "even when a state refuses to commit to a positive international law obligation, as embodied in a treaty, the nation-state may still be bound to uphold the law if it is believed to be *jus cogens* [namely, part of a set of overriding peremptory legal

---

38. Ibid., 43.
39. Dennis J. Driscoll, "The Development of Human Rights in International Law," in Walter Laquer and Barry Rubin, eds., *Human Rights Reader* (New York: New American Library, 1979), 44.

principles]. These principles of international law, which may not be dero-gated from, include proscriptions [against] slavery, genocide, torture, and apartheid. Claims of state sovereignty are [in this respect subordi-nated] to *jus cogens* [principles]."[40] Furthermore, even during conditions of emergency, when it is permitted to derogate from certain (though not all) rights, states are nevertheless held accountable to the United Nations both to verify the existence of an emergency, and to prove the need to respond to it as they intend, and for how long.[41]

Fifth, Asad would seem to be completely mistaken concerning his interpretation of the reference in the Preamble to the Declaration about the need for human beings to be "protected by the rule of law," lest they be "compelled to have recourse, as a last resort, to rebellion against tyranny and oppression." In the light of the legislative history of this ref-erence, the meaning is rather clear. To avoid "understandable rebellion," which could result should states fail to enforce human rights, states are obligated to implement human rights by means of national laws in such a way that those laws comply with human rights standards.[42] Given the point we have been making, that human rights represent an independent standard in respect to national laws, there is nothing circular here, as Asad claims there is.

Sixth, while, as we conceded, there are at present extensive and sometimes grave violations and impermissible evasions of human rights standards by modern nation-states, prominently including the United States, charges concerning such violations and evasions are only pos-sible because human rights exist as a set of standards that is independent of the rulings of national courts and legislatures. Nor, by any means, are charges of human rights violation and evasion by this or that state utterly inoperative or ineffective under present conditions. In fact, there exists a multiplicity of international and national governmental and non-governmental institutions, organizations and "civil society" associations, together with the media and so forth, that act to monitor state human

---

40. An-Na'im, "Synergy and Interdependence of Human Rights, Religion, and Secularism," 16.

41. See article 4 of the International Covenant on Civil and Political Rights. It is not clear what An-Na'im means by his ensuing qualification that "with most international human rights, state sovereignty is elevated above human dignity concerns."

42. Morsink, *Universal Declaration of Human Rights*, 307–12.

rights performance the world around, and to do that with considerable, if variable, success. That can be verified, among other things, by observing the lengths to which states frequently go to avoid public scrutiny and criticism. While the monitoring system is far from perfect, it is certainly incorrect to describe it as nonexistent or without effect.[43]

Of special importance in this regard is the newly-formed International Criminal Court. The key element, as President Clinton emphasized when he signed the founding document in December 2000, is the importance of "international accountability for bringing to justice perpetrators of genocide, war crimes and crimes against humanity."[44] Such a court was part of the vision born of the horrors of the Nazi experience, and was, consequently, anticipated in the Genocide Treaty, which came into force in 1951.[45] There can be little doubt that, in the long run, "the new permanent court...is going to exist,"[46] and is going irreversibly to advance the ideal of universal legality, despite the resolute efforts of the current Bush administration to disable it. What remains unclear is exactly when the United States is going to recover "the tradition of moral leadership" that is committed to these ideals.[47]

Finally, Asad's claim that religious and moral understanding and practice is totally at the mercy of the modern nation-state is greatly overstated. By way of confirmation, we have only to invoke the argument of An-Na'im in favor of a constructive connection between religion and human rights. The idea is that religion can be shown to exert its own independent influence on human rights thinking, or on support for it,

---

43. Since Asad does not mention the range of human rights problems attending transnational corporations and others, I have not taken up that problem here. Still, this area of concern, which is receiving increasing attention, shows further that while the nation-state is not disappearing or by any means of small significance in regard to human rights difficulties, it is by no means the end-all of such difficulties.

44. Cited by David J. Scheffer, "Staying the Course with the International Criminal Court," *Cornell International Law Journal* 35 (Nov. 2001–Feb. 2002): 63.

45. See Convention on the Punishment of the Crime of Genocide, article VI: "Persons charged with genocide...shall be tried by a competent tribunal in the State of the territory of which the act was committed, or by such international penal tribunal as may have jurisdiction with respect to those Contracting Parties which shall have accepted its jurisdiction."

46. David J. Scheffer, "A Treaty Bush Shouldn't Unsign," *New York Times* (April 6, 2002), A27.

47. Part of Clinton's comment upon signing the Rome Treaty, cited in Scheffer, "Staying the Course with the International Court," 63.

rather than simply being told by the state what to think and do, as Asad believes.

An-Naʿim, along with other scholars like Sachedina and Soroush, mentioned earlier, apply the point to Islam. As we saw, An-Naʿim takes the position that the recent policies of the Sudanese and Iranian governments have unquestionably violated the human rights protections of all citizens (Muslim and non-Muslim) against the infringement of religious freedom and discrimination "based on conscience, religion or belief," and, by implication, have simultaneously violated the fundaments of authentic Islamic faith. Sachedina and Soroush would undoubtedly agree. Here we have an example of finding Islamic grounds for affirming the "outside constraints" on religious understanding and practice represented by human rights.

The same point can be applied to Christianity as well, however. Thanks to the definitive work of Brian Tierney, we now have abundant historical evidence regarding the constructive connection between Christianity and the modern development of human rights.[48] The key ideas, born of theological and legal disputes beginning in twelfth-century Roman Catholicism, were of a fundamental "subjective right" to self-defense naturally and inalienably claimable by every human being simply by virtue of being human. "In the last resort one could exercise [this] inherent natural right ... [,] that no human law could take away[,] against any oppressive authority, even an oppressive pope."[49] By elaborating certain notions of conscience found in the Pauline epistles, and combining them by the seventeenth century with this doctrine of a natural right to self-defense, freedom of conscience and religion came, according to Tierney, "to be seen as one of the natural [human] rights."[50]

That these rights were considered "natural" means not only that they were believed to be equally and universally available to all human beings. It also means that the rights are considered to be justified *independent of religious conviction.* The whole idea (as with the drafters of the Universal Declaration) is that there exists *a universal, indubitable, and unavoidable*

48. See Brian Tierney, *The Idea of Natural Rights: Studies on Natural Rights, Natural Law and Church Law, 1150–1625* (Atlanta: Scholars Press, 1997).

49. Brian Tierney, "Religious Rights: An Historical Perspective," in Witte and van der Vyver, eds., *Religious Human Rights in Global Perspective,* 29.

50. Ibid., 42.

standard of moral appraisal of the behavior of authorities of all kinds, including state authorities. In other words, we have here a powerful example of the way in which a religious tradition like Christianity finds a way to embrace and affirm a set of independent "outside constraints" on religious understanding and practice that eventually becomes associated with the concept of human rights.[51]

Incidentally, these points should cause An-Na'im to revise the widely affirmed, but mistaken, assertion that the concept of human rights was "premised on the Enlightenment," and that Christianity simply "reconciled itself" to the idea over time.[52] Tierney's exhaustive work renders that view out of date.

While the writings of the Jewish religious thinker Yeshayahu Leibowitz, in his compelling volume *Judaism, Human Values, and the Jewish State,*[53] deal more with the subject of secularism than human rights, his passing remarks on human rights are nevertheless interesting as an example of Jewish religious reflection on the question. Some of Leibowitz's strongest theological apprehensions arise in response to the policies of the state of Israel in regard to the occupied territories.

> As for the "religious" arguments for the annexation of the territories, these are only an expression, subconsciously or perhaps overtly hypocritical, of the transformation of the Jewish religion into a camouflage for Israeli nationalism. Counterfeit religion identifies national interests with the service of God and imputes to the state —

---

51. Asad's claim, in an obscure excursus on natural rights (130ff.), that the ideas of natural and human rights "depend on" "national rights" (135), and thus on the prior existence of "a strong, secular state" capable of enforcing its will by violent means, is completely insupportable, if he means by that that a state's interpretations of rights are accepted as ultimately determinative.

52. An-Na'im, "Synergy and Interdependence of Human Rights, Religion, and Secularism," 5. This is not, of course, to suggest that the Enlightenment (along with other intellectual movements) did not contribute to the evolution of human rights thinking. But it is to suggest — most emphatically — that the process of development did not *begin* in the eighteenth century. Incidentally, it is also to suggest that the Enlightenment itself is a much more complex historical movement than is typically acknowledged, with, therefore, quite variable implications for human rights thinking, variations that still obtain today. One has in mind the fact that the Enlightenment had British, French, and German versions, and that they did not all come to the same conclusions about the nature, basis and scope of rights or about religion and state, or about other subjects, as well. It is time simplistic references to "the Enlightenment project" were called into question or, as they say, "problematized."

53. Leibowitz, *Judaism, Human Values, and the Jewish State.*

which is only an instrument serving human needs — supreme value from a religious standpoint.[54]

Leibowitz claims that the State of Israel was dramatically transformed by the occupation of the West Bank and Gaza during the 1967 War:

> The change was not simply of quantity but of substance. Its significance consists not in the increase of the number of Arabs subject to Jewish rule . . . , but in the denial of the right of independence to the Palestinian people. Israel ceased to be the state of the Jewish people and became an apparatus of coercive control of Jews over another people. What many call "the undivided Land of Israel" is not, and never can be, the state of the Jewish people, but only a Jewish regime of force. *The state of Israel today is neither a democracy nor a state abiding by the rule of law, since it rules over a million and a half people deprived of civil and political rights.*[55]

> [W]e are able to maintain our rule over the rebellious people only by actions regarded the world-over as criminal. We refer to this as "policy" rather than "terror" because it is conducted by a duly constituted government and its regular army. The "aberrant cases" of necessity became the rule, since they are not incidental to a conquering regime but essential to it.[56]

Here, in short, is a suggestion from a Jewish theological perspective that basic, universal standards of proper treatment — fundamental human rights, it would seem — constitute an appropriate "outside constraint" on religious understanding and practice.

54. Ibid., 226,

55. Ibid., 243 (emphasis added). Elsewhere, Leibowitz dismisses the relevance of "rights talk" to the question of land allocation as between Israel and the Palestinians (see 241–42). However, one has the impression that he has here something different in mind from what he thinks are the valid rights claims Palestinians may properly make as victims of Israeli rule, which he mentions in the above quotation.

56. Ibid., 244. Of some relevance to Leibowitz's discussion is a point Asad makes. It is that the idea of "military necessity," permitted by the laws of armed combat, "can be extended indefinitely" in the interests of achieving victory (or protecting national security). Therefore, he says, any measure whatsoever can, in the end, be justified (118) and, consequently, the idea of effective restraints on force and suffering in time of war are for all practical purposes undermined. While this is certainly going too far, it must be admitted that this is a very worrying point, particularly because of the difficulties at present of the international enforcement of humanitarian law against offending states.

Secularism

The human rights documents themselves begin to help clarify the notion of "secularism," as distinguished from religious understanding and practice, by means of the way the "freedom to manifest one's religion or beliefs" gets elaborated. Paragraph 3 of Article 18 of the International Covenant on Civil and Political Rights states that the freedom of religion or belief "may be subject only to such *limitations* as are *prescribed by law* and *are necessary to protect public safety, order, health, or morals or the fundamental rights and freedoms of others*" (emphasis added).

Five things are notable about the terminology this statement uses to elaborate the "freedom to manifest one's religion or beliefs":

1. The use of the word *manifest* refers to public expression or practice and not simply to the holding of a belief.

2. The term *belief*, as in the phrase "religion or belief," refers to a philosophical belief that has the same fundamental or "conscientious" status that a religious belief has for a believer.

3. The reference to "safety, order, health, or morals" are all modified by the word *public*, suggesting that these terms refer to "goods" to which all citizens of a given state share a common claim and in which they all share a common interest.

4. Since appropriate measures to protect these "public goods" are regarded as possible "limitations" (or "outside constraints") on the public expression or practice of religion or belief, the basis for understanding and interpretation *must not be necessarily attached to or dependent upon particular religions or beliefs*. In other words, there is implied here the idea of what is called "public reason" — a set of norms and procedures of justification that are *publicly available, or assumed to be held in common*.

5. The phrase "prescribed by law" implies that the state's "legal function" — namely, the formulation and enforcement of law backed by coercion — applies authoritatively to this sphere of public goods, something we might call *the domain of the secular*. In cases of conflict between religion or belief and the domain of the secular, the state has the right to enforce its determinations, but always and

only, be it noted, so long as it does not exceed the boundaries of its domain, and acts in accord with the "fundamental rights and freedoms of others," as required.

These five observations sharpen our understanding of "secularism." The central idea of "deregulating religion," mentioned earlier in relation to An-Na'im's account, falls into place. State and religious authority are *differentiated*,[57] particularly in respect to the coercive or enforcement function of the state, and all religions (or beliefs) are given a free and equal chance to manifest their convictions within the "limitations" or "outside constraints" imposed by the domain of the secular.

In keeping with the human rights requirements of nondiscrimination, benefits and burdens in the public sphere may not be apportioned simply on the basis of race, gender, religion, national or social origin, or birth, and so forth. That is precisely because such indications are not what all citizens of a given society hold in common. They do not all have the same religious beliefs, nor the same race or gender. On the other hand, they all do share a common material interest in public health, safety, order, and morals, and it is therefore acceptable on the part of the state, acting in the service of that common interest, to impose restrictions in regard to protecting it.

When it comes, for example, to the meaning of the elusive term "public morals," the Human Rights Committee, which is authorized by the International Covenant on Civil and Political Rights to interpret the document, emphasizes that the term must be understood in a *pluralistic* fashion. "The Committee observes that the concept of morals derives from many social, philosophical, and religious traditions." Consequently, it concludes, "limitations on the freedom to manifest a religion or belief for the purpose of protecting morals must be based on principles not deriving exclusively from a single tradition."[58] The implication is that the same would apply to the other public goods as well. In implementing limitations for the purpose of protecting public health, safety,

---

57. José Casanova, *Public Religions in the Modern World* (Chicago: University of Chicago Press, 1994), 20–39.

58. General Comment Adopted by the Human Rights Committee under Article 40, Paragraph 4, of the International Covenant on Civil and Political Rights, UN Doc. CCPR/c/21/Rev.1/Add.4, September 27, 1993, para. 8, p. 3.

and order, as well as morals, the state would be obliged *to search, where possible, for the common denominator* among the various traditions of religion or belief represented among the citizenry. Where not possible, the state, through its duly constituted legal and political procedures, must make the best judgment it can, based on what are assumed to be publicly shared and accessible standards of reason.

Accordingly, the principle of pluralism, which was, we noted, so important in An-Na'im's proposal, can be seen to apply to our subject in two ways. One is, as we have just pointed out, in understanding and applying the limitations or outside constraints on the manifestation of religion or belief that are associated with the domain of the secular. Judgments in that regard must be plural and public in the appropriate sense. The other is aimed at An-Na'im's chief concern: the free play of many divergent beliefs and practices present within and among different religious and other traditions that may be manifested *inside the limits* imposed by the domain of the secular.

For one thing, the human rights documents fully endorse such pluralism. I have argued elsewhere that far from being indifferent to or having no interest in religion and similar beliefs, human rights law is, in fact, *deferent* to such concerns.[59] Part of that deference is guaranteeing free, equal, and open expression and practice consistent with the authorized limits we have discussed. For another, the authorized limits would decidedly not exclude religious or philosophical commentary on public affairs, including the domain of the secular. José Casanova's fascinating discussion of the prominent, and generally permissible role of Roman Catholic social and economic advocacy within the public arena, is a good example.[60] The only proviso is that when it comes to passing laws or rendering judicial decisions in the public arena, the actions must rest on "public reason" rather than particular religions or beliefs.

The next step is to consider examples of religious support from the three traditions for this outline of the idea of secularism. The underlying

59. David Little, "Studying 'Religious Human Rights': Methodological Foundations," in Witte and van der Vyver, eds., *Religious Human Rights in Global Perspective,* 52.
60. Casanova, *Public Religions in the Modern World,* chap. 7, "Catholicism in the United States: From Private to Public Denomination."

argument, again contrary to Asad, is that insofar as respectable exemplars of the three religions can be shown to embrace this outline, it is not correct to claim that religious interests as such are totally and inalterably opposed to the "modern secular nation-state."

We already know of An-Na'im's support for something close to this interpretation. Along similar lines, Sachedina says:

> The thesis that Islam does not make a distinction between the religious and the political requires revision in the light of what has been argued in this volume. Even the all-comprehensive sacred law of Islam, the Sharī'a, presupposes the distinction between spiritual and temporal, as it categorized God-human and interhuman relationships respectively. God-human relations are founded upon individual autonomy and moral agency regulated by a sense of accountability to God alone for any acts of omission or commission. Interhuman relations, in contrast, are founded on an individual and collective social-political life.... This latter category... has customarily provided Muslim governments with the principle of functional secularity that allows them to regulate all matters pertaining to interpersonal justice. The same principle rules out the authority of Muslim governments to regulate religious matters except when the free exercise of religion for any individual is in danger.... The foundation of a civil society in Islam is based on the equality in creation in which the privilege in citizenry attaches equally to Muslim and non-Muslim, entailing inclusive political, civil, and social membership in the community.[61]

From the perspective of Judaism, Leibowitz comes to comparable conclusions. His conclusions are couched in terms that are highly critical of the existing Israeli state for not being secular enough, and consequently for corrupting both religion and state:

> The demand for separation of religion from the existing secular state derives from the vital religious need to prevent religion from

---

61. Sachedina, *Islamic Roots of Democratic Pluralism*, 137. I am not assuming that there are no significant differences between An-Na'im and Sachedina (or Soroush, either). I simply emphasize the obvious and important overlap of views regarding the affirmation of "secular space" from several explicitly Islamic points of view.

becoming a political tool, a function of the governmental bureau-
cracy, which "keeps" religion and religious institutions not for
religious reasons but as a concession to pressure groups in the
interest of ephemeral power-considerations. Religion as an adjunct
of secular authority is the antithesis of true religion. It hinders
religious education of the community at large and constricts the
religious influence on its way of life. From a religious standpoint,
there is no greater abomination than an atheistic-clerical regime.
At present we have a state — secular in essence and most of its
manifestations — which recognizes religious institutions as state
agencies, supports them with its funds, and, by administrative
means, imposes, not religion, but certain religious provisions chosen arbitrarily by political negotiation.... The secular state and
society should be stripped of their false religious veneer.[62]

The function of the state is essentially secular. It is not service of
God.... Religion, that is man's recognition of his duty to serve God,
cannot be integrated with the machinery of government. The political organization, necessary as a condition of survival, merely sets
the ground for the struggle for religion, which is by its very nature
an eternal struggle that will never end in victory. The state of Israel
of our day has no religious significance, because no such struggle is
being conducted in it.... The state, as such, has no religious value.
No state ever had.[63]

Lastly, a Christian example. One of the most interesting illustrations
of this pro-secularist perspective in the history of Christianity is the
seventeenth-century New England Puritan Roger Williams.[64] Williams
was a fervent and, in many ways, orthodox Calvinist. As one of the
founders of the Rhode Island colony, he is particularly well known for
participating in the establishment of "the first commonwealth in modern
history to make religious liberty...a cardinal principle of its corporate existence and to maintain the separation of church and state on

---

62. Leibowitz, *Judaism, Human Values and the Jewish State*, 176–77.
63. Ibid., 215–16.
64. While Williams is not a contemporary representative of his religion, as are the other
figures we have cited, he nevertheless does have, it can be argued, profound "contemporary
significance."

these grounds."[65] A crucial feature of his resolute support for freedom of conscience and separation of political and religious authority was his unflinchingly "secularist" attitude toward the state. He could hardly have been clearer on this point.

While, he says, the general institution of earthly government is authorized by God "for the preservation of mankind in civil order and peace," particular governments derive their legitimacy exclusively from the human constituents who make up "the commonwealth, the body of people and the civil state," and who "communicate" authority "unto [the magistrates], and [en]trust them with it."

> All lawful magistrates in the world, both before the coming of Christ Jesus and since [with the temporary exception of the government of Biblical Israel] are but derivatives and agents, immediately derived and employed as eyes and hands, serving for the good of the whole. Hence, they can have no more power than fundamentally lies in the bodies or [constituencies] themselves, *which power, might, or authority is not religious, Christian, etc., but natural, humane, and civil.*[66]

Williams supports this interpretation by arguing that when Paul speaks of the lawful functions of government in Romans 13, he mentions only the "second table" of the Decalogue, which applies to interhuman relations, and not to the "first table," which concerns Divine-human relations.[67]

> What imprudence and indiscretion is it . . . to conceive that emperors, kings, and rulers of the earth must not only be qualified with political and state abilities to make and execute the civil laws which may concern *common rights, peace and safety* (which is work and business, load and burden enough for the ablest shoulders of the commonweal), but also furnished with such spiritual and heavenly

65. Sydney E. Ahlstrom, *A Religious History of the American People* (New Haven: Yale University Press, 1972), 172.
66. Roger Williams, *Complete Writings* (New York: Russell & Russell, 1963), 3:398 (emphasis added). I have here and there modernized Williams's prose to make it more readable.
67. Ibid., 3:151.

abilities to govern the spiritual and heavenly abilities and Christian commonweal, the flock and church of Christ, *to pull down, and set up religion, to judge, determine and punish in spiritual controversies, even to death and banishment.*[68]

There is a recurring emphasis in all the examples on what looks like a commitment to or a belief in the propriety of an independent sphere of secular jurisdiction, a "domain of the secular," that is, in each of the three cases, encouraged from a religious point of view. The fact that the domain of the secular is understood — albeit, with very limited jurisdiction — as the object of commitment and belief, suggests a reason for using the term "secular-*ism*" after all. If an "ism" can be a distinctive doctrine or theory, then it seems that just such a doctrine or theory is implied in the statements we quoted respectively from Muslim, Jewish, and Christian thinkers. Even though religious believers recommend such a doctrine, the doctrine itself is understood as publicly or commonly accessible, and thus need not be "necessarily attached to or dependent upon particular religions or beliefs," as stated above. It goes without saying that if we do use the term, we should use it very advisedly — that is, strictly according to the outline of thinking proposed above.

Conclusion

It is important to establish a set of limits or outside constraints with regard to human rights and secularism in order that various public manifestations of religious thought and practice be effectively restrained. The effort to identify a set of constraints may be thought of as an elaboration and clarification of Abdullahi An-Na'im's important suggestion

---

68. Ibid., 366 (emphasis added). As is clear from this passage, Roger Williams employs "rights language," contrary to the mistaken assertion of Brian Tierney. According to Tierney, "Williams has been called an extreme exponent of natural rights because of his all-embracing argument for freedom of conscience, but this seems to me a misunderstanding of his position. I do not think Williams ever used the language of natural rights" ("Religious Rights: An Historical Perspective," 42). Apart from the above quotation, Williams calls upon such language when, for example, he discusses the need for civil order independent of religious privilege. The civil order does not work well, he says, when "civil places" are "monopolized into the hands of church-members (who sometimes are not best fitted for them) and others deprived and despoiled of their *natural and civil rights and liberties.*" *Collected Writings,* 4:365 (original emphasis).

about the interdependence of religion, human rights, and secularism. In keeping with the spirit of An-Na'im's proposal, it should now be clear that a commitment to a set of constraints is by no means foreign to religious traditions like Judaism, Christianity, and Islam, but, in fact, finds eloquent resonance and support in at least some parts of such traditions. To demonstrate that fact greatly strengthens An-Na'im's proposal, for it proves that significant common ground does indeed exist for promoting the objectives An-Na'im seeks.

What I have attempted here is only a first step, however. It remains to look comparatively and in detail at what we might call the "sore points" of confrontation between religion and the "domain of the secular." How are courts and legislatures in different countries, respectively influenced by Judaism, Christianity, and Islam (to begin with), undertaking to adjudicate competing claims between the right to "freedom of religion or belief" and the prescribed "limitations" imposed by the universal need, to protect "public health, order, safety, and morals"? It is only as we begin systematically to examine decisions and laws in that context that we can begin to see how the relations among "religion, human rights, and secularism" are being negotiated in practice. And it is, in turn, only when we have that information, based on comparative legal investigation carried out in the light of the set of constraints we have proposed, that we may begin to construct some general and intercultural guidelines regarding how, in practical terms, religion, human rights, and secularism *ought to be* related to each other.

Chapter 13

ARMED FORCE AND POLITICAL RESPONSIBILITY

Justification and Resort to War in Abrahamic Traditions

John Kelsay

I should begin by easing the reader's mind. This is not a comprehensive treatment of the ways Judaism, Christianity, and Islam speak about armed force and political responsibility. Rather, this essay focuses on one case: the crisis engendered for contemporary Islam by the claims and tactics of Al-Qaeda. As I shall indicate, one might speak of this crisis in terms of an argument about the relationship between the "new" *jihād* advocated by Al-Qaeda and related groups, and historic Islamic political thought.

It is worth noting, however, that the political-military aspects of Judaism and Christianity are also at a moment of crisis. These aspects, which certainly constitute one way the Abrahamic faiths construe the human responsibility for justice, are at a moment that calls for careful deliberation. Thus, James Turner Johnson writes of the just war tradition as "broken."[1] George Wilkes writes of strains in halakhic debate regarding obligatory and permitted war.[2] In Islam, we find extensive debate regarding the use of "martyrdom operations" in Palestine/Israel,

---

1. See James Turner Johnson, "Just War I: The Broken Tradition," in *The National Interest* 45 (Fall, 1996): 27–36.
2. George Wilkes, "Judaism and Justice in War," in Paul Robinson, ed., *Just War in Comparative Perspective* (Hampshire, UK: Ashgate, 2003), 9–23.

as well as with respect to our current topic.[3] The crisis in religious traditions with respect to armed force and political responsibility is thus a matter of broad concern.

The Problem

The date is October 21, 2001.[4] In response to the attacks on New York and Washington, D.C., an international coalition led by the United States is engaged in a military campaign aimed at eliminating Al-Qaeda bases in Afghanistan. On this occasion, the Arabic-language news station Aljazeera releases a statement from Usama bin Ladin, who declares:

> Here is the United States. It was filled with terror from its north to its south and its east to its west. Praise be to God. What the United States tastes today is a very small thing compared with what we have tasted for tens of years. Our nation has been tasting this humiliation and contempt for more than eighty years. Its sons are being killed, its blood is being shed, its holy places are being attacked, and it is not being ruled according to what God has decreed.

Bin Ladin continues, speaking of those who carried out attacks on U.S. targets as a "convoy . . . the vanguard of Islam." He prays that God will elevate them to the status of martyrs, and that they will enjoy heavenly rewards.

During these last few years, the terms bin Ladin employs have become familiar. They set the context for this essay. Let us speak of the course of action advocated here and elsewhere as the "new" *jihād*. The qualifier is fitting, in the sense that this *jihād*, or struggle, is up to date or recent. Bin Ladin and other Al-Qaeda representatives want people to understand that the struggle in which they engage is the latest chapter in a conflict as old as humanity; namely, *the* struggle between *al-islām*, that submission

---

3. Cf. my article, "Suicide Bombers," in *The Christian Century* 119, no. 7 (August 14–27, 2002): 22–25.

4. The material that follows is covered in somewhat different form in my articles on "The New Jihad and Islamic Tradition," available at http://www.fpri.org, and on "Islam, Politics, and War," in *Sewanee Theological Review* 47, no. 1 (Christmas 2003): 11–19; "Democratic Virtue, Comparative Ethics, and Contemporary Islam," in *Journal of Religious Ethics* 33, no. 4 (December 2005): 697–708.

to the will of God which constitutes the natural religion of humanity, and *al-jāhiliyya,* that "heedlessness" to which human beings are prone.

The new *jihād* is thus a consistent expression of historical Islamic tradition. Or so bin Ladin and his colleagues assert. In this essay, I shall question that assertion. I shall suggest that bin Ladin's *jihād* is new, not only in the sense that it is up to date, but in the sense that it is a departure from tradition — an example of *bid'a,* that is, an "innovation." To put it another way, I shall argue that there is a gap between the new *jihād* and Islamic tradition, and further that this gap "judges" the new *jihād,* so that the latter is to be weighed in the balance and found wanting.

It is true that many people argue this way. And it seems an easy matter for historically minded scholars of ethics to cite texts and display the gap between the new *jihād* and Islamic tradition. Similarly, it seems an easy matter for many Muslims to point to this gap. Indeed, most American Muslim groups followed the attacks of September 11, 2001, by issuing public statements disassociating Islam from the actions undertaken by certain of their co-religionists. In support of such disassociation, the usual citation was Qur'an 5:32, to the effect that the holy book of Islam so condemns anyone who takes a life without just cause, that it is as though that person had killed the entire world. Unfortunately, the verse was usually quoted without further content, and such statements left one with many unanswered questions. Qur'an 5:32 is a powerful verse, but it doesn't settle much in this case, not least because it leaves bin Ladin's arguments about when killing is justified and who should be killed — that is, arguments that attempt to specify a just cause — without a response.

In this essay, as in other publications, I've tried to take a more difficult road.[5] In matters of war and other issues, Islamic tradition may be construed as a long conversation about God's *Sharī'a* or path. One reads the Qur'an, studies the example of the Prophet, analyzes the judgments of great scholars with respect to the right and wrong of particular questions of practice, and then one *argues* about how each and all of these

---

5. Aside from the essays cited in n. 4 above, see my article on "War, Peace, and the Imperatives of Justice in Islamic Perspective: What Do the 11 September 2001 Attacks Tell Us About Islam and the Just War Tradition?" in Paul Robinson, ed., *Just War in Comparative Perspective.*

relate to current circumstances. In what follows, I want to display an argument among Muslims. In particular, I want to show how some who actually agree with bin Ladin on many things nevertheless find reason to criticize some aspects of the *jihād* he advocates as inconsistent with Islamic tradition. I begin by outlining some historic themes of Islamic political thought and then provide a brief account of the modern career of these themes. I follow with the material that is at the "heart" of this essay, namely, four "moments" in a conversation among Islamists regarding the new *jihād*. I end by offering some conclusions about the current state of the debate within contemporary Islam regarding the justification, use, and conduct of armed force and the nature of political responsibility.

The History of Islamic Political Thought

Classical Themes

Over the course of fourteen centuries, Islamic political thought has centered on two great themes. The first of these emphasizes the importance of establishing a just public order, while the second focuses on notions of honorable combat.

Historically speaking, Muslim scholars held that the establishment of a just public order is an obligation. Some said it was so by God's command; others said this was a dictate of reason. In either case, they usually thought of the phrase "just public order" in terms of a state defined by an Islamic establishment. We would put it this way: a just public order is one in which Islam is the established religion; where the ruler is a Muslim, and consults with recognized Islamic authorities on matters of policy; finally, where groups committed to other religions could live in safety, because they are "protected" by the Islamic establishment. This pattern held for many Muslim thinkers from the time of the early Islamic conquests (in the seventh century c.e.) through the demise of the Ottoman caliphate (in 1924).

Notions of honorable combat developed in connection with reflection on the duty to establish a just public order. The idea was that, under certain conditions, the establishment, maintenance, and defense of justice would require armed force. When such conditions occurred, armed force or combat was to be conducted in accord with norms of honor. For example, resort to combat needed authorization by publicly recognized authorities. Such authorities should make sure that fighting occurred in connection with a just cause, and with the intention of building, maintaining, or protecting public order. The same authorities should consider whether or not fighting would be a proportionate response to perceived injustice, whether Muslim forces were likely to succeed, and whether fighting would serve the end of building the kind of public order that serves peace. Finally, they were to consider whether combat is the most fitting way to pursue justice, considering the circumstances — in other words, are there alternative ways to seek justice that might be more appropriate in a given case?

In addition to these considerations, those fighting for justice were to be governed by the saying attributed to the Prophet Muhammad: "Do not cheat or commit treachery. Do not mutilate anyone, nor should you kill children." Other reports indicate that Muhammad further prohibited the direct and intentional killing of women, the very old, those physically or mentally handicapped, monks, and others. The idea was that honorable combat involved soldiers fighting soldiers and noncombatants are never to be the direct target of military action. Of course, there are times when combat involves taking aim at a military target, knowing that there is a strong likelihood of indirect harm to civilians (that is, "collateral damage"). In such cases, Muslim scholars debated many issues related to the use of particular weaponry: Should a fighting force make use of mangonels or hurling machines, for example? The concern in these cases was that certain weapons might cause disproportionate or excessive damage to civilians, even though the direct target of the weapon was military in nature.

Modern Tensions

For the last eighty years, the tradition of Islamic political thought has been under stress or under dispute. In itself, this is not unique. Traditions are always susceptible of dispute. That is, they are so for as long as they are *living* traditions. One generation bequeaths to the next a framework for discussion; the new generation tries to establish a "fit" between that which is handed down and its own set of circumstances. That is the nature of tradition. In Arabic, *al-turāth* or "tradition" is that which is handed down or bequeathed by one generation to the next. When people stop arguing about a tradition, this is a sign that it is no longer viable.

Thus, Muslim argument is nothing new. Nevertheless, one could say that the last eighty years mark a period of particular stress, in which the most contentious point has been the question, "What constitutes a just public order?" In 1924, the new Turkish Republic withdrew support for the Ottoman ruler. This effectively abolished the last remaining symbol of the great empires of the Middle Period, as well as of the older notions of a universal state governed by an Islamic establishment. In the years following, and indeed for much of the twentieth century, Muslim intellectuals argued about the shape a modern Islamic political order might take. One part of that argument focused (and still focuses) on the sort of legal regime such an order should have. Must a properly Islamic state be governed by divine law only, in the sense that its laws and policies are derived directly from the Qur'an, the example of the Prophet, and interpretive precedents established by the consensus of recognized scholars (the *'ulamā'* or "learned")? Or can such a state form its laws and policies based on a more diverse set of sources? For example, can an Islamic state borrow from the legal codes of European nations, or shape its policies based on contemporary international practice? Those holding that an Islamic state must be governed by divine law only are sometimes called "fundamentalists" or "radicals." Those arguing for a more diverse set of sources are sometimes called "moderates." Neither of these terms is adequate. In what follows, I shall employ the more cumbersome, but I believe more accurate, terminology of "advocates of divine law governance" and "pluralists."

The focus on the meaning of the phrase "Islamic state" means, in effect, that most modern Islamic political thought is concerned with how one might fulfill the obligation to establish a just public order. More recently, however, attention has turned to the historic notion of honorable combat. We are familiar by now with the "pluralist" side of this debate. Post-9/11, many Muslims argue that, even if the advocates of divine law governance are right, and that the current state of political order is unjust, there are nevertheless limits on what one may do to affect change. There are some tactics, people say, that violate the Muslim conscience. This is especially true of tactics that make noncombatants or civilians into direct targets of military or paramilitary attacks. The conduct of martyrdom operations in Palestinian resistance to Israel is of concern in this regard. Even more, the use of indiscriminate tactics by Al-Qaeda is of concern.

Pluralist Muslims have been very clear in condemning Al-Qaeda tactics as a violation of Islamic tradition. Less well covered in American or European media is the fact that some advocates of divine law governance have also been vigorous in this regard. That is, there are those who share with Al-Qaeda a sense that a just public order must be governed by divine law only, yet who think Al-Qaeda's tactics are problematic, on Islamic grounds. We can get a sense of this by attending to four moments in an extended conversation between Muslim advocates of divine law governance, beginning in June of 2002.

Recent Discussion of Al-Qaeda Tactics among Advocates of Divine Law Governance

A. First Moment

The date is June 7, 2002. An Al-Qaeda spokesperson named Sulayman abu Ghayth publishes an article entitled "In the Shadow of the Lances" on the Internet.[6] Abu Ghayth (who had become well known for several statements following 9/11 and the beginning of U.S.-led action in Afghanistan) begins by indicating his purpose, to address the Muslim community and make sure it understands Al-Qaeda's arguments:

> Perhaps the Islamic community is waiting for an Al-Qaeda man
> to come out and clear up the many questions that accompany any
> communiqué, message, or picture [concerning 9/11], to know the

---

6. Abu Ghayth's article was originally published at http://www.alneda.com, which at the time was a frequent location for Al-Qaeda-related postings. The Web site changes URLs frequently, however, so that it is difficult to locate. A convenient translation of portions of the article is available at the Web site of the Middle East Media Research Institute (MEMRI), http://www.memri.org, where it is entry No. 388 in the "Special Dispatch Series." I quote from MEMRI's translation, with very slight alterations.

truth, the motives, and the goals behind conflict with the Great Idol of our generation.

Abu Ghayth's article develops in accord with this purpose. It is a defense of Al-Qaeda's program of fighting against the United States and its allies. He lists a number of reasons that justify such fighting. For example:

America is the head of heresy in our modern world, and it leads an infidel democratic regime that is based upon separation of religion and state and on ruling the people by the people via legislating laws that contradict the way of God and permit that which God has prohibited. This compels the other countries to act in accordance with the same laws in the same ways . . . and punishes any country [that resists] by besieging it, and then by boycotting it. In so doing, [America] seeks to impose on the world a religion that is not God's.

The United States, then, is a prime example of an unjust state, since it is not governed by divine law. Its injustice is compounded by the fact that it seeks to export this form of government. And, as we come to understand, the injustice of the United States is expressed by its willingness to use or to support the use of military force against those who would choose another model for political order. Abu Ghayth lists various places in which this is so: Palestine, Iraq, Afghanistan, Somalia, Sudan, the Philippines, Indonesia, Kashmir, and others. In many of the cases, he cites a number indicating (as he takes it) the number of innocents killed. This is critical to the argument. For abu Ghayth wants ultimately to justify not only armed resistance to the United States and its allies, but the kind of armed resistance advocated by the leaders of Al-Qaeda and related groups in the 1998 *Declaration on armed struggle against Jews and Crusaders*. In that document, Usama bin Ladin and others argued that fighting against Americans and their allies, "civilians and soldiers" is a duty for each and every Muslim able to do so. In other words, Al-Qaeda's strategy involves deliberate attacks on civilian, as well as military, targets. Abu Ghayth wants to provide a justification for this.

God said, "one who attacks you, attack as he attacked you," and also, "The reward of evil is a similar evil," and also, "When you are punished, punish as you have been punished."

These Qur'anic citations, as interpreted by recognized religious scholars, establish a right of reciprocal justice. According to this notion, victims of injustice have the right to inflict damage on those responsible for their suffering, in a manner proportionate to the harm suffered. According to this line of thought, the numbers of innocents killed by the United States suggests that

> We [Muslims] have not reached parity with them. We have the right to kill 4 million Americans, 2 million of them children, and to exile twice as many and wound and cripple hundreds of thousands.

It is important to note that abu Ghayth stipulates that the damage inflicted by the United States and its allies is both "direct and indirect." For his purposes, the distinction does not matter. Those who suffer have the right to inflict damage proportionate to their losses. And this, he writes, is the only way to deal with the United States.

> America knows only the language of force. This is the only way to stop it and make it take its hands off the Muslims and their affairs. America does not know the language of dialogue or the language of peaceful coexistence! America is kept at bay by blood alone.

B. Second Moment

Abu Ghayth's article provides an important defense of Al-Qaeda tactics. Other Muslims are not persuaded, however. And thus I turn to a second moment in recent conversation about Islam and fighting. On July 10, 2002, Aljazeera interviewed a well-known Saudi religious scholar and dissident, Shaykh Muḥsin al-ʿAwajī.[7] Two other dissidents joined by telephone. All three served time in Saudi prisons for criticism of the royal family and its policies of cooperation with the United States during, and especially following, Operation Desert Shield and Desert Storm in

---

7. Again, a convenient translation of portions of the transcript may be found at http://www.memri.org, Special Dispatch Series, entry number 400. Quotes are from the MEMRI translation.

1990–91. None of the three is friendly to U.S. policies with respect to historically Muslim states. Indeed, they are in favor of armed resistance to U.S. aggression, and approve the use of martyrdom operations.

The conversation then turned to Usama bin Ladin. Since the three scholars agree with Al-Qaeda on the necessity of government by divine law, and further on the justice of resistance to the United States and its allies, it is most interesting that they indicated that, after initial approval of bin Ladin, they and many others have changed their opinion. Shaykh al-ʿAwajī says:

> In the past, when he was fighting the Russians in Afghanistan, bin Ladin was the greatest of jihād warriors, in the eyes of the Saudi people and in the eyes of the Saudi government. He and the others went to Afghanistan with official support, and the support of the learned [the *ʿulamā* or religious scholars].

In some ways, this positive assessment of bin Ladin still holds, Shaykh al-ʿAwajī says:

> What the Saudis like best about bin Ladin is his asceticism. When the Saudi compares bin Ladin to any child of wealthy parents, he sees that bin Ladin left behind the pleasures of the hotels for the foxholes of jihād, while others compete among themselves for the wealth and palaces of this world.

Nevertheless, this positive judgment must now be qualified, because of Al-Qaeda's tactics. Bin Ladin is guilty of spreading discord among Muslims. He labels people as heretics when he has no proof, and some Al-Qaeda operations bring harm to Muslims. Bin Ladin and his colleagues also violate Islamic norms of honorable combat, and this is an important reason for qualifying earlier, positive assessments, as Shaykh al-ʿAwajī writes:

> ...he and those with him target innocent people, and I refer to the innocents on the face of the entire earth, of every religion and color, and in every region.

Recalling Islamic tradition on these matters, one cannot help but think of the saying of the Prophet: "Do not cheat or commit treachery. Do not

mutilate anyone or kill children [or other noncombatants]." Shaykh al-
'Awajī is far from approving of abu Ghayth's (or Al-Qaeda's) notion of
reciprocal justice. For him (and for those joining him on the show, since
they indicate agreement with all of his points on this matter), Muslims
are to fight with honor. This means, among other things, that they are
not to engage in direct attacks on noncombatants.

C. Third Moment

We should not forget that Shaykh al-'Awajī and his colleagues agree with
much of Al-Qaeda's program. As I have said, they are not favorably
disposed to U.S. policies in the Middle East and elsewhere. The point is
that they want to see Muslims fight according to traditional norms.

A different kind of criticism was articulated a few months later
by Shaykh 'Umar Bakrī Muḥammad of al-Muhajiroun ("The Emi-
gres"), a fundamentalist group based in the United Kingdom. Shaykh
'Umar's tract, *Jihad: The Method for Khalifah?* appeared at the Web site
www.almuhajiroun.com in September 2002.[8] While hardly an elegant
piece of work, and thus difficult to read, this tract attempts to evaluate
the place of armed struggle in the attempt to found a state governed
by divine law. The author then discusses the nature and place of armed
resistance in contemporary contexts.

According to Shaykh 'Umar, *jihād,* in the sense of "armed struggle," is
a term reserved for fighting authorized by an established Islamic government. This is the sense of the reference to *khalīfa* in his title. Literally, the
term suggests "succession" to the Prophet Muhammad. Shaykh 'Umar
uses the term as a designation for Islamic government. His discussion
reiterates one of the great themes of Islamic political thought, that is,
the necessity that justice be embodied in a political order. And, as he
indicates, when this political order is in place, it should seek to extend its
influence by appropriate means. These can and should include honorable
combat.

---

8. Following the July 2005 bombings in London (and thus, subsequent to the writing
of this essay), Shaykh 'Umar was deported from the UK for fomenting violence. His statements about those attacks present a confusing picture, not least in relation to the tract under
discussion. I hope to deal with this matter in a future essay.

For the last eighty years, the kind of authority indicated by the term *khalīfa* has been absent from political life. This fact sets the context for the rest of Shaykh 'Umar's argument. Muslims are required to work to change this situation, and to establish *khalīfa*. To that end, may or should they engage in *jihād*? The answer is no, first of all because of the nature of the concept. *Jihād* designates fighting that occurs under the auspices of an established government. By definition, then, fighting that takes place apart from such a government's authorization cannot be *jihād*. To this definitional "no" Shaykh 'Umar adds a second reason: Islamic political thought requires that authority be legitimate, in the sense of being established through a process of consultation and assent. The submission of Muslims to an authority thus ought not be compelled. Islamic government should be established through persuasion.

Shaykh 'Umar indicates that the process of consultation and assent may be conducted in a number of ways. He then moves to a discussion of contemporary resistance among Muslims. In his view, the Muslim community is in a kind of political twilight zone. Without a duly constituted *khalīfa,* there can be no fighting worthy of the title *jihād*. Yet Muslims are in need of defense, in Chechnya, Kashmir, and other locations. What are they to do?

As Shaykh 'Umar has it, Islam recognizes a right of extended self-defense. Everyone has the right to defend his/her own life, liberty, and property. Everyone also has the right, and in some sense the duty, to defend the lives, liberties, and properties of others who are victims of aggression. This kind of fighting is called *qitāl,* a word that quite literally indicates "fighting" or "killing." Where Muslims are under attack, their co-religionists around the globe may and should come to their defense. When they do, however, they should understand that fighting is delimited, first in terms of its goals. *Qitāl* is not *jihād*. As such, it is not a proper means of establishing Islamic government. Second, *qitāl* is limited in its means. Interestingly, in this *qitāl* and *jihād* are similar, since both are governed by norms of honorable combat, or as Shaykh 'Umar puts it, by the "pro-life" values of the Prophet Muhammad: "not killing women and children, not killing the elderly or monks, not targeting the trees or animals ... foreign forces occupying Muslim lands are legitimate

targets and we are obliged to liberate Muslim land from such occupation and to co-operate with each other in the process, and can even target
their embassies and military bases." Tactics that involve direct attacks
on noncombatants are ruled out, however.

D. Fourth Moment

Shaykh 'Umar's argument challenges Al-Qaeda's approach at a number
of points. Most important for our purposes, however, is the stipulation
that even defensive fighting, which almost by definition involves coming
to the aid of Muslims in emergency or near-emergency conditions, should
be governed by norms of honorable combat. It's not surprising, given
arguments like this, that the leadership of Al-Qaeda would respond.
Thus, in November 2002, Usama bin Ladin, or someone writing in his
name, published a "Letter to America" responding to Muslim and non-
Muslim criticisms of Al-Qaeda.[9]

The first part of the "Letter" is a list of reasons for fighting against the
United States and its allies. The grievances are familiar. On this point, the
"Letter" restates and extends grievances outlined in earlier documents,
not least Sulayman abu Ghayth's Internet article (above).

The second part of the text moves to the question of tactics.

> You may then dispute that all the above does not justify aggression
> against civilians, for crimes they did not commit and offenses in
> which they did not partake.

The concern here is clearly with arguments that Al-Qaeda tactics violate norms of honorable combat. The author of "Letter" does not accept
these. Two counterarguments are cited in justification of a policy of
attacking civilians as well as soldiers. First, the United States claims to
be a democracy.

> Therefore, the American people are the ones who choose their gov-
> ernment by way of their own free will; a choice which stems from
> their agreement to its policies.... The American people have the

ability and choice to refuse the policies of their government and even to change it if they want.

Second (and in a way reminiscent of abu Ghayth's argument), the author cites the *lex talionis.*

> God, the Almighty, legislated the permission and the option to take revenge. Thus, if we are attacked, then we have the right to attack back. Whoever has destroyed our villages and towns, then we have the right to destroy their villages and towns. Whoever has stolen our wealth, then we have the right to destroy their economy. And whoever has killed our civilians, then we have the right to kill theirs.

Harm suffered may be avenged by the infliction of damage proportionate to the original harm. Muslims have the right to kill U.S. and other "enemy" civilians, because the United States and its allies engage in actions that kill civilians on the Muslim side.

Concluding Remarks

What are we to make of this exchange? Primarily, I think it is important to know that such conversations take place. The post-9/11 discussion of Islam and fighting has tended to swing between two assertions: Either Islam has nothing to do with fighting of this type, or it has everything to do with it. Neither of these assertions is accurate. Neither catches the sense of Islamic tradition as a living reality, in which human responsibility is construed as a process of discerning God's will in particular circumstances by reading agreed-upon texts and reasoning according to established rules. To put it bluntly: in the *Sharī'a* vision, human responsibility is constituted by participation in an ordered process involving the giving and taking of reasons. In that light, it is important to get a sense of the conversations Muslims have about political justice and honorable combat.

Having said that, who won this argument? In one sense, that question must remain open — that is, in the sense that arguments continue. The tactics advocated by Al-Qaeda clearly raise important questions regarding the contemporary purchase of traditional notions of honorable combat. In another sense, however, the answer is clear enough. There is ample evidence for the gap between Al-Qaeda's *jihād* and Islamic tradition noted at the outset of this paper. The arguments between advocates of divine law governance in contemporary Islam make clear that advocating indiscriminate fighting, at least as a matter of settled policy, is a problematic course of action. What must be left open, or so I feel constrained to say at present, is whether there might be certain "emergencies" or extreme circumstances in which conscientious Muslims might argue that temporary or selected exceptions to the general norms of honorable combat might be justified, or at least that those carrying them out might be excused. The issue needs further analysis, not least by way of sustained attention to the rhetoric of Al-Qaeda and its Muslim critics.

There is, of course, more to be said with respect to the crisis in contemporary Islam regarding armed force and political responsibility. Indeed, as noted in my opening comments, there is much to be said generally about the matter of justification and war in contemporary expressions of the Abrahamic traditions. In these remarks, I have tried to show that these include conversations between "allied" groups of advocates of divine law governance, as well as between pluralists and advocates of divine law governance. This fact seems important in itself. Among other things, the post-9/11 Muslim discussion of Al-Qaeda tactics suggests the power of certain ideas; for example, that there are limits on what one can do, even when one is fighting for justice. In this sense, the post-9/11 conversation among Muslims goes back to the Qur'an itself, which at 2:190 indicates to Muslims:

> Fight against those who are fighting you
> But do not violate the limits.
> God does not approve those who violate the limits.[10]

---

10. My translation.

Chapter 14

STANDING BEFORE GOD

Human Responsibilities and Human Rights

Seyyed Hossein Nasr

What I have to say in this essay pertains not only to the Abrahamic religions but to all religions, and in many ways to the human condition itself, but I shall, of course, concentrate mostly on the tradition that I know best — that is, the Islamic tradition — with the awareness that the comments I make will apply elsewhere. On the deepest metaphysical level, to be human is to stand before God. It is metaphysically impossible to be human without standing before God, whether we are aware of that standing before God or not. This statement about human existence is asserted in the famous verse of the Qur'an, where it is said, "But His command, when He intendeth a thing, is only that he saith unto it: Be! and it is" (Qur'an 36:82). That is, to the Divine Command to be, our response is to exist. Therefore, our existence itself is none other than our response to the Divine Command to be. Human existence itself is a response to God and not an original state of being independent of any other reality, and herein lies the origin and the most profound metaphysical root of human responsibility because we are ourselves a response to God. We are not only responsible to God; we are ourselves a response.

The Meaning of Human Being

I shall speak not from the divine perspective here but from the human one, about what it means to be human in relation to God. Now, in

Translations of Qur'an passages in this essay are the author's.

order to understand what the human state involves, what it means to stand before God, I refer to two further verses of the Qur'an of singular importance for this issue, in addition to the discussion that apparently was held here about the question of *khalīfa* (vicegerent), concerning the role assigned to human beings in the myth of the creation of Adam and Eve in the Hands of God.[1] The first of the two verses to which I wish to refer is the verse from chapter 7 of the Qur'an where God, before creating the cosmos, before creating the earth, before creating the world, asked of human beings, "Am I not your Lord? They said: Yea, verily. We testify" (7:172). What does this verse mean? Most Muslims just glide over it, rarely thinking deeply because the depth is only for those who have reached the inner depth of their own being. It is not so easy to get to the meaning of this remarkable verse.

First of all, it means that we have a preexistence "with" God before the creation of the world. Second, all of the verbs in this sentence are plural and not singular. God did not only address Adam, but he addressed all human beings. We must note first the verb in God's question, "Am I not your Lord?" and second, in the human reply, they said, "Yea [*balā*]." While the verb in the case of God is singular, it is plural in the case of human beings. The response, "Yea," therefore involves not only Adam but *all* human beings, that is, to be human is to have said yes to God. Now if you deny that affirmation and negate it, that itself is a possibility because God has given us freedom to do so. (I shall address that issue below.) Nevertheless, to be human is to have said yes, and we hear the mark of this affirmation deep within our beings. That is how the most profound anthropology of Islam understands the situation of human beings standing before God.

And, finally, the third verse that I want to call to your attention reveals the secret of being human from Islamic point of view: it concerns the bearing of that *amāna*, or trust, that God has placed upon our shoulders. This is expressed in the outwardly enigmatic verse of the Qur'an from chapter 33 that says, "We offered the trust [*amāna*, which is related to

---

1. Needless to say, the word *myth* should be taken here in its original sense, so I can use it in its authentic sense, of course, and not to mean "unreality." This needs to be mentioned because many Muslims, like ordinary Americans, think that the word *myth* means something unreal. I do not mean that at all but speak of the "myth of creation" in the deepest sense of the word *myth*.

the word for "faith" in Arabic] unto the heavens and the earth and the mountains, but they shrank from bearing it and were afraid of it. And man assumed it. Verily, he has proven to be an oppressor and a fool" (33:72). This is a momentous verse in the sense that it points to the awesome responsibility of being human. One might see that if we had a choice to become human we would be, in a sense, out of our minds to do so, because we would have to bear such great responsibilities. To be human means bearing the tremendous responsibility of free will and the state of the vicegerency of God, which brings with it, of course, the greatest of all gifts, the gift of being able to draw nigh to God. This *amāna* was such a heavy burden that the mountains and the sky could not bear it precisely because to be human implies the possibility of both the affirmation and the negation of the Divine Principle, and therefore the possibility of perdition in the deepest sense of the word, which other creatures do not face.

Now I could expand on this question of trust a great deal but will not do so here. What is important in the present discussion is that at the heart of the Islamic message of what it means to be human is the bearing of this trust and the fact that this is indeed a very heavy trust that we must bear. This in turn means that as human beings we are "condemned" to a life of meaning. We are "condemned," in a sense, to a life that needs to have spiritual and moral significance. Therefore, even immorality and the denial of meaning in our lives, which is a possibility because of our human free will, even these land us in a situation and state in which we are not happy. The yearning for meaning is inseparable from human life, and nihilism is always a dead end, which, as we know, leads sometimes to psychological problems and even to the physical self-destruction of the person. We are not happy in a world that does not make sense. To make sense is to have meaning. Therefore, in the deepest sense you might say that God is meaning. In the deepest religious sense, we are in quest of meaning because we cannot live without it and we are in quest, whether we like it or not, of a life whose actions have some significance beyond themselves — that is, of an ethical life, a moral life from the religious point of view.

To be fully human is to have an awareness of the central reality of who we are. When we do not have full awareness of this, we are only accidentally but not fully human. To be fully human is to have this full awareness of our identity and to realize that God has given us free will for an end. It is to realize that both responsibilities and human rights have no reality without free will, which originates in the freedom to say yes or no to God now, or, in other words, either to remember our original "yea" and the acceptance of the divine trust or to decide to forget it as if we have never made our eternal preeternal covenant (*mīthāq*) with God.

Now, certain great mystics and Sufis of Islam such as Farīd al-Dīn 'Aṭṭār and others have some very provocative poems in which they assert that we did not ourselves decide to be human; therefore, we are not free, and it was God who decided for us to be human. But having made us human, God has nevertheless given us free will. The divine poet of the Persian language, Hafiz, has an incredible *ghazal* with a verse that says, "The heavens could not bear the weight of this trust; but the lot fell in my poor name." That verse poses a theological question of the deepest significance: Were we free not to be human? That is the question that many great theologians have posed. And here we can answer from the Islamic point of view with a no. We were not free to be or not to be human, because God chose us to be human, to stand before God. Once we stood before God, however, we stood as free beings. Then God asked us the question to which we were free to say yes or no. At that moment, we could have responded negatively: To the question, "Am I not your Lord?" we could have said, "No, Thou art not." But we said, "Yes." So freedom comes with the very act of being created as human beings, but we had no say in the act of creation itself. It is true that on the external level it is difficult to understand human freedom. There have been negaters of human freedom all the way from the psychological behaviorists at Harvard to the Islamic theologians of the school of al-Ashʿarī, as well as within Christianity, Judaism, Hinduism, and in all the religions of the world. In every religious and philosophical context one can find those who have negated human free will on a certain level. Nevertheless, our immediate awareness and consciousness of being human points directly to the reality of free will, and without that freedom there are neither responsibilities nor human rights. They all issue from this basic reality of the human state.

Human Freedom

Human free will is related in the Islamic context to man[2] having been chosen as God's "vicegerent" (*khalīfa*) on earth. The introduction to this volume discussed the similarities and differences between the Islamic conception of man as God's vicegerent in man and the Western (that is, Christian and Jewish) idea of the image of God — man made in the image of God.[3] But in fact these two formulations are not antithetical; they are not really different from each other in their essential meaning, but only different ways of expressing the same truth at the deepest level. In the case of *khalīfa* (vicegerent), it means a being who *represents* and thus *has* the powers of another being, as in the case, for example, of the viceroy of Queen Victoria in India. So, in a sense, that person is the image of the other person inasmuch as that person has the powers of the other person whom he represents. Thus, the two terms (*khalīfa; imago Dei*) are not antithetical images or metaphors. Rather, they are similar to each other. It is true that the Old Testament and the New Testament do not speak of the word *khalīfa,* or vicegerent, and that the Qur'an does. But what this term really means is clearly related to the concept of the "image of God." To be God's vicegerent on earth is in a sense to be "God-like" without in any way denying God's transcendence — for, of course, theologically, there is nothing like unto God — and to be "God-like" means to possess some of God's powers. That is precisely why we have free will. Again, from a theological point of view, God is both infinite necessity and infinite freedom. This is so because God, from the point of view of traditional metaphysics, is both absolute and infinite. If God were not necessity, there would be no world, and if God were not the absolutely free, there would be no human freedom. Moreover, the grandeur of the human state, which involves precisely the possibility of error or deviation, of doing right or wrong, of going toward or rejecting God, would not be there. Therefore, the concept of *khalīfa* (vicegerent) implies itself the presence of free will in human beings as does the concept of the "image of God."

2. By man we mean of course "men and women" — "man" in the sense of *homo* and *vir* in Greek and Latin, and not simply the male.

3. In addition to the introduction to this volume, see also the discussion of the Islamic conception of "vicegerency" in the essay by Abdulaziz Sachedina also in this volume.

There are other places where original Islamic sources refer to ideas related to the "image of God." One is in the Qur'an where God says, "I breathed my Spirit into him [man]" (15:29). God has breathed God's Spirit into Adam and that is the foundation of why human life is sacred and why human beings must be moral if they are going to be human beings in the real sense of the term. I shall come back to this issue in a moment.

Also, the very term "image" also appears in a *ḥadīth,* that is, in one of the "sayings of the Prophet," which says, *Khalaqa'Llāh 'ādam 'alā ṣūratihi,* that is, "God has created man upon his *ṣūra,*" a term that can be translated as both "image" and "form" (but perhaps "form" is more appropriate here). In any case, *ṣūra* does not mean "image" in the sense of a painting, or pictorial image. Islam, like Judaism, is aniconic in its sacred art and does not find acceptable the making of an image of God. "Thou shalt not make a graven image," one of the commandments revealed to Moses, is also accepted in Islam. So "image" must not be understood here as painting, but rather this *ḥadīth* means "being the theophany of all of the Names and Qualities of God." That is why we can, in fact, play God-like roles in this world. That is the key reason why we have an environmental crisis. The essence of the environmental crisis comes to this: we have the capacity to try to play the role of God on earth and destroy other species. No other creature on earth can wreak such havoc on the earth and destroy other creatures as can humans. Only we can do that. So the very fact that we are able to destroy the environment on a global scale is indirect proof of the existence of God if we really understand the deeper claims of causality involved.

Freedom and Divine Law

This freedom of choice, which is also a moral choice and which God has given us, must, of course, manifest itself on the level of action. And here Islam, like Judaism (and especially Orthodox Judaism), emphasizes very much the law that is given by God. Because we are given this freedom of choice, being who we are, we need some guidance not to fall from the right path. If we had no freedom of choice, there would be no need for revelation or Divine Law. On a more mystical level you might say that God loves us, but love cannot be based on coercion. Love has to be based on attraction. Therefore, there must be something in the soul receptive to that which attracts. On the level of action, we have to do certain things in order to make the channeling of this attraction possible. In the case of Islam, this is grounded in Divine Law and its ethical content, although other elements are also involved, including especially sapiential knowledge, or *ma'rifah*. In this regard, Judaism and Islam are close together. Both religions assert the idea that there is a sacred law that is given by God and that God is the ultimate legislator. In the case of both religions, ethics is to a large extent related to this sacred law.

Now, you might say, in the case of Christianity, Christ came to break the "letter" (or the "form") in the name of the "spirit," in the name of the spiritual law of which he spoke. Legal matters pertaining to society and the individual in the matter of, for example, kosher or *ḥalāl* food, economic transactions, and so forth, are all abrogated in the name of the spiritual laws. But in Islam, as in Judaism, these matters are related to the sacred law and the actual level of action, which does not mean the giving up of our choice and responsibility because to follow the law requires our making a choice at the fundamental existential level discussed earlier. Many people feel that such obedience to the law turns the religious life into something automatic and mechanical but that is not at all the case. Our following the law is our response to God on the basis of our responsibility to God's demand upon us and is based on free choice and not automatic coercion.

From the Islamic point of view, and I believe, in a deeper sense, from all religious points of view, all human rights issue from human responsibilities. Responsibilities come before rights. The idea that we have inalienable rights which we talk about all the time today is only half the equation. The emphasis on rights, only without considering responsibilities, is a dangerous eclipse of the other half of the equation. Today we live in a world in which people believe that they have all kinds of rights without feeling the responsibilities that go with them. This one-sided viewpoint is one of the factors that is destroying the world and the civilization in which we live. Now, in the Islamic context, each of the human rights that we have issues, as I said, from the responsibilities that we hear before God and vis-à-vis God's creatures by virtue of our being human.

Let me then turn first to the responsibilities. We have, first of all, our responsibility toward God. Our responsibility toward God is an existential one since we are ourselves responses to God's command "to be." Therefore, to be responsible is to be sincere and true to our own primordial nature, to our own most profound nature, to our deepest level of existence and, of course, not our fallen nature, for we are ourselves in our very existence that response. To be fully human is to stand before God, as I said at the very beginning. This is the human condition. That is why, in fact, certain people in today's world sometimes say that we are "hardwired to God." I hate to use these modern technological terms, but indeed there is something in the human state and human nature that, no matter what condition it is in, sooner or later turns to these ultimate questions and to Ultimate Reality Itself. Whether we use the term *God* or something else, there is something beyond us that attracts us. We are never satisfied with what we are. There is always a search for that which is beyond, which is above us and transcends us, and this search for that beyond characterizes the human state. "Above all to thine own self be true." To be responsible before God is simply to realize that we are in our deepest selves responses to God. To be oneself is to realize one's responsibilities before God.

There is, however, an ontological lack of equality between the two sides. We keep saying "God and man" or "God and woman," as if the two were on the same ontological level. Think of the painting of the Sistine Chapel by Michelangelo in which Adam and God are depicted as being in practically the same proportions. I believe that this crass anthropomorphism marked a grave illness in the body of Christian piety and theology at that time. God and man are depicted in practically the same proportions except that the finger of one is bit higher up and the finger of the other is bit lower. That kind of portrayal betrays the true ontological relationship between God and humans. The true ontological relationship is not based on any equality. Many people say, "Oh, God is in the imagination of human beings," and consequently they relegate the reality of God to their egos and seek to take on the ontological status of the Divine themselves. But, metaphysically speaking, God is the Source of our being; we are the effect of that Source. God is the Being who gave the command; we are the effect of that command (to use the language of the Qur'an in the verse that I have cited above). So now I turn from the metaphysical basis of our responsibility before God, the responsibility of responding to God's call and submitting ourselves totally to God, from which issue all other responsibilities, to those responsibilities themselves.

What are our other responsibilities? First, there is the responsibility to human beings. And this starts with ourselves. We are responsible by virtue of standing before God for ourselves. We are responsible for our own salvation, as every Christian would bear witness. Our primary responsibility in this world is to save our own souls. We cannot save anybody else's soul before we save our own; that is, our primary goal is to *be* good. This recognition is very important because we live in a world in which many people want to do good without being good. It is usually much easier to do good than to be good. For example, a person contributes to some kind of fund for the dispossessed or joins some charitable organization or goes to Africa to feed the poor. These are all laudable acts, but it is more difficult to meditate and remember God for a half an hour in your own room. It is much more difficult to attain the state of goodness than to do a good act. This externalization of goodness in the world in which we live is totally opposed to the perspective according to which goodness must first of all be rooted in our being before we turn to the world of action. As such, goodness must start from ourselves and ultimately from God who is the source of all goodness. To have responsibility to the human state requires, first of all, to be good, to live the good life, to live a moral life.

This responsibility extends also to the corporeal level, to the care of one's physical health. For example, suicide is banned by Islamic Law. Compared to all the great civilizations of the world, statistically, the least number of suicides occur in the Islamic world, except for the wretched situation of the Palestinians in Israel and Palestine, which is itself a great anomaly due to an anomalous situation. Suicide bombings elsewhere are also due to exceptional political situations in which some carry out such actions that are opposed by Islamic Law if innocent people become victims. Cases of desperation are not in any case the norm. If you take the number of people who commit suicide in Sweden or Illinois and compare it to the number in Egypt or Iran you will understand about what I am talking. The Islamic view of human existence and our responsibilities to ourselves on all levels underlying the ban against suicide is the reason. There is a very strong anathema against taking one's life because, since one has not given life to oneself, it is not one's right to take away this life. Our lives are simply not ours to take, according to our wishes.

Then there is the extension of this care for oneself outward to the family, then to the immediate part of our town, next to our city, to our country, and finally, to the whole of humanity. Here arises the question regarding our responsibility to people who are not of our religion or, in fact, have no religion at all. I shall come to that question in a moment.

Then we have a responsibility toward the rest of God's creation. This is one of the aspects of responsibility that, although mentioned very clearly in the Qur'an and in the *ḥadīth* (as also in other religions), has come to the surface more recently, thanks to the massacre of the world of nature that we are performing today in the name of human welfare — the destruction ranging from that of the Amazon rainforest to the lakes in the United States, and everything in between. The question of responsibility to all of God's creation, which is the foundation of the new theology of ecology, or theology of the environment, in which all the religions of the world are now involved, has its roots very deeply in classical Islamic texts. But now this responsibility to all of God's creation is being emphasized and accepted more and more due to the realities of the current situation and because in the past the rest of God's creation did not really need our care as much as it does now. Take, for example, the animals in Africa. In the past, they really did not need our care to survive. The tigers were doing fine. Now we have to keep a few tigers in zoos; otherwise the species will die out. So, in a certain paradoxical sense, our responsibility has increased immensely by virtue of our having forgotten our responsibility toward the creation of God. Having turned all our attention to ourselves, having forgotten both God and God's creation, we now have forced upon ourselves this tremendous responsibility of taking care that the coral reefs in Australia do not die out, for example. When Captain Cook went to Australia he did not have to worry about the coral reefs — they were doing fine. So this responsibility is now left for us in the situation in which we live and which we have ourselves created as a result of a lack of responsibility toward the natural world in the modern period.

Finally, there is a new responsibility, which was at one time also "potential" (like our responsibility for the coral reefs of Australia), and this is responsibility toward followers of other religions and respect for other religions — responsibility in the real sense and not only as an ad hoc diplomatic or political polite nodding of the head. Now, the Qur'an is very explicit about the universality of revelation (which is an issue for another day), as spoken of in the verse, "To every people [We have sent] a messenger" (10:48), and in many other verses.[4] This potential responsibility did not have to become an actuality until now with the new situation of our world. Today the question is not only that of respect but also of responsibility. A person who understands what it means to stand before God must realize his or her responsibility for respecting other religions. This responsibility is there not only for diplomatic reasons, not simply for expediency. It is necessary to realize fully our responsibilities before God.

The Sacredness of Human Life

It is from these responsibilities that all the rights that we call human rights issue. If we can fulfill these responsibilities, then we have corresponding human rights. Now, these human rights are all deeply related to a reality that we consider to be obvious, namely, the sacredness of the human being. Yes, human beings are sacred, but within the context of the modern paradigm this assertion is very paradoxical. And why is it paradoxical? Throughout history this was taken to be an obvious fact — that human life is sacred. In fact, all of life was taken to be sacred and the whole world was sacred in a certain sense. Especially human life was considered to be sacred by followers of all authentic religions. But today we have to reassert the question, "Why is it that human life is sacred?" We must reassert this question because today we have two very contradictory views of what the human being is, held by people in the same

4. In the first chapter of my book *The Heart of Islam: Enduring Values for Humanity* (San Francisco: HarperSanFrancisco, 2002), I have cited many of these verses, and I do not need to repeat them here.

buildings of the same universities and the same cities in which we live. But we do not want to face this contradiction. On the one side is the idea that the human being is nothing but a "suited-up" monkey whose head has grown a little bit. And the monkey is nothing more than something else we can trace back ultimately to molecules banging against each other in the primordial cosmic soup after the Big Bang. Now, I cannot on the basis of any logic understand what is sacred about this concept of human origin. What is sacred about the bowl of soup of molecules? Nothing. The experience of the sacred is often explained as an emotional response to something that has no basis in modern science, which most consider to be the only legitimate way of knowing acceptable in our society. Of course, there are many scientists who do not believe in this limited and reductionist perspective, but that is, logically speaking, irrelevant. The modern scientific or, rather, scientistic point of view of what constitutes the human state is that it is an accident that has occurred on a third-rate planet of a tenth-rate sun, and all of these things that you read about. So, what is sacred about it? Nothing, unless you use the term *sacred* only "poetically" and emotionally.

The other view is that which has always been confirmed by the religions and which now has to be reconfirmed over and over again. And that is that human life is sacred because of the presence of the Spirit that God breathed into man, because of the centrality of human beings in creation demonstrated in the trust that God has put on our shoulders, because of the freedom God has given us which also makes us responsible for God's creation. There are many ways in which this idea has been expressed in various religions, all the way from the Spirit of God breathed into man in Abrahamic religions to the sacrifice of Prajapati in Hinduism. There are many different forms of this truth, but always present is the idea of the sacredness of the Divine Principle, the Sacred as such manifested directly in the human order. When people talk about this matter, somebody always asks a question about non-theistic religions. Let us remember, however, that in Buddhism it is only through the human state that one can attain Buddhahood! If you are a Buddhist, what makes human life sacred is the fact that you cannot attain Buddhahood through being a turtle. You have to be born into a central state, which in this world is the human state, so hard to attain, as the Buddhists say. So in all religions, theistic and nontheistic, the reason why human life is sacred is obvious. But today we have to reassert the obvious, which is also directly related to the very basis of the reality of human responsibilities and human rights.

One of the great challenges before modern theologians today is to be brave enough to show that the religious view and the scientistic view cannot both be correct in this matter and that they contradict each other. Either one or the other is correct, and it is important not to gloss over this truth. It happens that in all cultures, whether it be Western, Islamic, Indian, or Japanese, laws are based on the older idea of the sacredness of human life. This is also fully evident in the U.S. Constitution, according to the laws of this land, and indeed, any other functioning society, for when a person commits murder, he or she is punished. But if you, let us say, take a mollusk and eat it, nothing happens to you. That poor mollusk also was alive; it had life. If you buy a lobster in Boston and throw it in boiling water and it turns color, nobody will punish you. Why is this so? It is because of the traditional idea of the sacredness of human life. The laws in lands near and far are, in fact, still based on the earlier idea of the sacredness of human life for reasons that were obvious in days of old, but which are not at all obvious today.

When we speak of responsibilities and rights, it is very important to bring out the significance of what the religions say about the sacredness of human life. What they say is remarkably similar. The view of various authentic religions is almost unanimous but expressed in different languages: some speak of the divine spark, others of the Buddha nature, or the Spirit of God within us. Some emphasize the image of the Divinity in man; others the *nous* of Plato in the center of man's being, and so on. It is incredible how many different expressions there are for that reality which bestows sacredness upon human life, but in depth they all express the same thing. The human state is the central state in this world, and this central state reflects directly the multitudes of divine possibilities. It is the only means of access on earth to the Divine, and with this comes both tremendous power and tremendous responsibility. Therefore, to kill a human being is the most heinous act. It is also very bad to kill a cat, but the killing of a human being is especially something detestable because of the state of humans in the cosmic hierarchy. The Qur'an goes so far as to say that to kill a single innocent person is to kill the whole of humanity. Respect for human life remains a central responsibility for all men and women and derives from the very nature of being human. One of the great tragedies of our time, however, is that, while we talk about human rights, we are inventing more and more means of getting rid of human life all the time in a thousand ways and also debasing human life, destroying its sacred quality and even threatening the biological means of life upon which human life depends. We do so without some times even knowing it, not only militarily but in other ways as well, such as through so-called economic development, which can end up being as lethal in the long run as bombs thrown on people's heads today. But I will not get into that issue here.

Inclusivism and Exclusivism

There is a very important question that comes up, however, if you define the human state in this way. The followers of various religions, especially the Abrahamic family, agree that human life is sacred and that we have certain responsibilities and rights based on that sacred character of human nature. But what about people who do not believe in any religion? I am not referring here to Zulus or some other tribe in Africa, who are practitioners of some form of primal African religion, or Hopis in America, for such people have their own profound religious traditions even if some ordinary believers in the Abrahamic religions are not aware of them. I mean people who have no religion whatsoever, agnostics and atheists or, even, aggressive atheists. What about them? What are their rights and what are our responsibilities to them? This is an important question that each religion must seek to answer on the basis of its own teachings. I will give you an answer from the Islamic point of view (I do not give myself the right to speak as a Christian or a Jewish theologian) which holds that, in principle, even the life of a person who denies God cannot be taken because of the fact that he or she is no longer a believer. Historically, unfortunately, this principle has not always been observed, although in the traditional Islamic world many skeptics, including some poets, have been known without their having been imprisoned or killed.

And the rationale of that is that such a person has been created by God and potentially can always turn back to God.

Now there is an argument about the question of apostasy, which is something else. In the old days, when religion was identified with the state, apostasy was considered as treason to the state. Furthermore, this equation was not unique to Islam. If someone in France in the Middle Ages became a Muslim, most likely he would be hanged or beheaded. At the present moment we do not live in the same political situation, whether in East or West, and therefore our responsibilities must be extended to the other even if that one be an atheist or an apostate, and not only to our co-religionists or, at most, only believers in religions in general. Respect for the life of a human being, whether we are speaking of a person who follows our religion, another religion, or no religion whatsoever, should be the same from the point of view expressed above because the religious person believes that the divine spark is in everyone. It is not limited to those who belong to our religion or to another religion but even to a person who denies all religions. This responsibility does not, however, absolve us of our responsibility to the truth at all levels and in every situation in our lives. Of course, to make this big jump is not such an easy thing, even in the semi-secularized society of America. Even today we have people in this country who appear on television and say, "The God of Muslims is an idol," and "My God is the real God." What are these people talking about? One can ask if they really understand what it means to stand before God. Of course, we have this kind of exclusivism not only in the United States but also in the Islamic world as well as in the Jewish community, Hinduism, and elsewhere — in fact, all over the world. There is no doubt about this fact. That is why pointing to responsibilities beyond the confines of our own religion is precisely such a great challenge, a challenge that all religions face today.

One must have a certain amount of sympathy for those whose understanding and concerns are limited to themselves and their immediate neighbors. The sympathy ceases, however, when they try to influence the world and the lives of countless other human beings on the basis of that exclusivism. It is natural for many human beings to think that only themselves, their children, and their cousins will go to heaven — that nobody else will get there. We have this same attitude held by some within every religion concerning not only adherents of other religions but even members of that religion itself. I have Muslim, Jewish, and Christian friends, all of whom believe that only their religious understanding is correct. Many Christians have called other Christians "pagans," or even worse, the "Anti-Christ." Many Muslims have called other Muslims *kāfir*, or "infidel." There are many Jews in Israel who do not consider the liberal Jews to be Jews at all. Such attitudes are to be seen everywhere and are not confined to one religion or country, but whenever they manifest themselves, they are signs of a lack of understanding of our full responsibilities as creatures standing before God.

One of our great challenges today is to understand why this is so. It is too easy to be a universalist. I have always said that real inclusivism is an inclusivism that also includes exclusivism. This might seem paradoxical, but it is nevertheless true. We must understand why a simple peasant in Italy is not interested in Mahayana Buddhism, does not care what happens to the Buddhists in China, and is just living his own life as a Christian. The same holds for a traditional Muslim, a Jew, or anybody else who lives within a still-homogeneous religious universe where his or her responsibilities and rights are understood within the confines of that world. That is perfectly understandable. But many today are based in a great center of learning, like a university, where this exclusivism and the limiting of one's responsibilities are no longer tenable because one comes face to face with others who are not "our own" but who are also "standing before God." One of the great challenges to all religions today is to develop a view of standing before God in such a way that our responsibilities not only include those within our own religion as well as toward our religious teachings, its laws, and so forth, but also includes responsibilities toward other religions and those who claim to have no religion at all. I think that, to a large extent, the future of the globe and the future of human existence depend on this issue along with that of our responsibility toward the natural environment.

The Absolutization of the Human State

Now, the question of human rights and human responsibilities conjures up a very important matter that I take every opportunity to bring up and to discuss whenever the occasion arises. It is something that I have called the "absolutization of the human state." Before modern times in all religions, it was God who was considered to be the Absolute. (This statement could also be made in a modified form for nontheistic religions.) I know this term *absolute* is not fashionable in philosophy departments these days in America. That does not bother me at all. We all have a sense of what it means to be absolute: that which is completely itself and excludes all otherness, all that is other than itself, that which is totally itself and relies on nothing else. That is the Absolute. Traditionally, God was considered to be the Absolute and human beings and everything else in creation were considered to be relative. We are born at a certain time; we pass through a particular cycle of life and we die. In this world we live in the domain of becoming; we live in the world of change; we live in the world of relationality; all these are relativities in comparison with the absoluteness of God. That is how our state was envisaged vis-à-vis God in traditional societies.

Then, after the Middle Ages, something happened, which I think is one of the most tragic consequences of Renaissance Humanism. And that is what I have called the absolutization of the human state, of the terrestrial human state; of course, not of celestial man in the original sense, but of fallen man, to use a Christian theological term, of man who has participated in what Christianity calls "original sin" and the subsequent Fall. In the modern world that was born with the Renaissance everything that is human came to be finally absolutized by taking away the rights of two other realities, the rights of God and the rights of God's creation. First, we have taken away the rights of God and then given these rights to ourselves, starting with politics and proceeding to nearly everything else. Second, we have taken the rights of other creatures for ourselves and usurped their rights. This is a very important matter, which makes the emphasis solely on human rights without the corresponding responsibilities so dangerous. The fact that an American automobile manufacturer can make a vehicle the size of a room, which, each time a person drives it, contributes indirectly to the death of a number of creatures on the surface of the earth; the total lack of respect for other creatures and total lack of thought of what will happen to our own grandchildren as far as the natural environment is concerned; to live and aggrandize the present moment in forgetfulness of the past and the future; to consume ever more to satiate the never-ending pursuit of our egos — all this is possible because of this absolutization of the human state derived from the *false* humanism of the Renaissance. This could not have occurred either in the earlier periods of Christianity, in medieval Japan, in Sung China, in Mamluk Egypt, or anywhere else.

This monopolization of rights for human beings is a very serious matter. Standing before God means remembering once again that we are ourselves responses to God's creative act. It is God alone who is the Absolute and to take this absoluteness unto ourselves is, finally, to destroy ourselves. In fact, one of the deepest theological lessons to be learned from what we are doing today is precisely this truth. To absolutize the human being is, finally, to destroy it. This false absolutization comes, first of all, through absolutizing our tastes and so-called needs, most of which are, in fact, pseudo-needs. They are not absolute at all, but in a consumer society, we, as consumers, absolutize our needs and claim that "we have to have this or that." And we can only have "this or that" at the expense of destroying nature and also of attacking directly or indirectly other countries for their resources, carrying out all the kinds of aggression that are going on around the globe today (which all of you know very well) rather than tightening our own belts and realizing the relativity of the human state and the Absoluteness of God. Forgoing the gratification of the fulfillment of every want is something we do not want to do, because we presume such gratification and satisfaction to be our inalienable right. So the question of human rights — about which everybody speaks and which is laudable on a certain level — has also become dangerous, theologically as well as ecologically speaking, because we tend to absolutize our transient life and have forgotten who we are. We have forgotten that we are in this world only temporarily; that this is not our permanent home; that we come from somewhere else and we shall go somewhere else; and that we have responsibilities that precede our rights, all of which are given to us by God because ontologically we are responses to God's creative Act and stand before God.

The Religious Foundation of Ethics

Another important point with which I want to conclude my discussion is that to understand the relationship between human responsibility, human rights, and ethics, it is not sufficient to appeal to human reason and to human nature alone. Now I know there is a long period of three or four centuries during which certain Western philosophers have sought to create a philosophical ethics that seems to be rationalistic and self-sufficient and that everybody should follow. If you know of any society that follows one of those ethical systems, please let me know! There may be a few graduate students in philosophy departments who have discussed such systems in theory, but these theories have never worked in actual practice in any society. All ethical norms that we have in all societies (to the extent that these norms have survived) had their roots originally in religion, in something that people believed had come from God, whether it be Jewish ethics, Christian ethics, Islamic ethics, Hindu ethics, you name it. And it is true also that, even in the case of those people who have turned against the religious foundation of ethics and tried to base ethics on a purely philosophical foundation, the content of that ethics is still more or less the old religious ethics.

Let us take as example, the sacredness of human life. "Thou shall not kill!" — that is one of the Ten Commandments. We still have that injunction in present-day societies. Some try to give other reasons why "thou shall not kill." They say, "No, God did not speak to Moses. I think this is the rational thing to do." But why is it the rational thing to do? You can sit down here with completely rigorous logic and argue the case. You can tear away at all religious foundations of this ethical teaching but you finally end up with the conclusion that the actual content of this "rational ethics" is mostly something that this man or woman as philosopher has *inherited*. So deep down, even the so-called rational ethics is based upon religious ethics, even Marxist ethics. Let us recall that this ethics is based to a large extent on charity, on a just distribution of wealth (not that they actually applied it in Russia, but at least on paper this is true). Marxism's intent is to overcome injustice. It is to be just and charitable to the poor and so on. From whence did all these values come into the head of Karl Marx, if not from Judaism and Christianity? So even the most atheistic type of ethics finds its essential foundation in the religious inheritance of certain moral and ethical attitudes.

The trouble is that once the religious foundation is destroyed, it becomes very hard to get human beings to live simply by ideology. Now this was tried with communism. It was tried in one of the great civilizations of the world, that is, in Europe (and of course in the recent half of the twentieth century in China and some parts of southeast Asia). Nineteenth-century Europe is the age in which ideology, to large extent, took the place of religion. Especially the powerful ideology of Marxism came out of nineteenth-century Europe, as did the Western ideology of liberalism and many other kinds of ideology. There were also the horrible ideologies of the twentieth century, such as fascism, which murdered millions of innocent people. Nor was communism any better than fascism. It caused the death of tens of millions of people. It did monstrous immoral acts but all in the name of a greater morality, in the name of the freedom of the people, of overcoming injustice, and so forth and so on. But this stage of history has now come to an end. The age of ideology as a "religion" is more or less over.

Now what has come back into the arena of history is what ideology replaced, namely, religion. Before ideology became the source of action, religion was the foundation of ethics. Ideology itself is a word that is so European that you cannot even translate it easily into non-European languages. In Turkish, it is simply rendered as *idéologie,* and in Persian also; we just copied the French word. And in Arabic they say *uṣūl al-'aqā'id.* That is perhaps the most classical translation in Arabic, but that term means something completely different in premodern Arabic vocabulary. It means "the principle of doctrine" and has nothing to do with "ideology." The word and, hence, the concept of "ideology" itself is alien to all traditional languages and cultures and is a modern invention. They have to torture these languages to be able to invent a word for it, but it has now penetrated into more cultures as it did in the West. In any case, the great danger today is that certain people now want to make religion itself an ideology. Rather than religion acting as a source for authentic ethics, in certain quarters it has become an ideology. This transformation is one of the most dangerous events that has taken place in the world in the twentieth century. You see it in the Islamic world, in Zionism, and in certain contemporary Christian currents that are not yet strong enough politically to become dominant but could do so soon. But this idea of turning religion into an ideology is there and it is of great significance as far as the question of human responsibilities and rights in relating to our standing before God is concerned.

In order to preserve the dignity of the human state, to allow human beings to live a moral and ethical life, and to fulfill their responsibilities to God and other human beings and the natural world, everything must be done to prevent religion from becoming an ideology. Religion must remain what it has always been, religion, which is very different matter from ideology. One of the great dangers we now face is this distortion of religion into ideology, which then enables people to fight in the name of religion in a modern context, disrespect the rights of others, and even kill in ways that are much more efficient and pervasive and very different from what had taken place in the days of old. People say humans have always fought in the name of religion. This is not precisely true. In the old days religion was part of cultural and national identity, and when people fought "religious" wars, most often they really fought for tribal or national identity or economic interest with a "religious flag" also waving. Even the Crusaders displayed these traits.

Today, something very different is taking place. It involves the conversion of religion into ideology and this change concerns the relationship between the foundation of ethics and theology. I think that to which we have to go back and what conferences such as this have to emphasize is the metaphysical and theological foundation of what it means to be human — what it means to "stand before God." From standing before God come responsibilities that we have to fulfill, as you might say, as reflections of the Absolute, representatives of universal values that we then have to apply to our human life. And with that central position on the earth comes the freedom of choice, which is imposed upon us by virtue of our being human. That is why, whether we like it or not, all messages from Heaven emphasize that to be human is to lead a moral life. It is impossible to be fully human without leading a moral life, and what we are, one could say, is to be condemned to a life that is meaningful. We are condemned to a search for meaning in our lives, meaning which can only be realized by our being spiritual and moral. All our rights are related to this profound reality of human existence.

The time has come for all of those who consider themselves to have heard the voice of Heaven in different languages at different times to join in a chorus to explain that human life cannot survive without ethics and ethics cannot survive without a correct understanding of what it means to be human. And I believe that understanding what it means to be human cannot be really achieved by us unless we realize that we stand before God not only in our preeternal existence but even now. Everywhere we go, everywhere we are, in a sense we are standing before God, and that "yea," the yes that we uttered in preeternity still echoes within us very much here and now. The degree to which we respond to that yes, accepting God's lordship and our responsibilities as human beings as the basis of our human rights, will determine not only our happiness as individuals in this world but also the very survival of the societies in which we live.

INDEX OF
NAMES AND SUBJECTS

Index of
Scriptural References